Rockwell

O'Sullivan

NOSTALGIA FOR NAREMBURN

The Ancestors Of
Robert Archibald Rockwell &
Octavia Corelli O'Sullivan

**Nostalgia For Naremburn: The Ancestors of Robert Archibald Rockwell & Octavia Corelli O'Sullivan
by Dr. Tracy Rockwell (1955)**

Volume 8
of the Rockwell Genealogies

First Published in Australia in 2023
by Pegasus Publishing
PO Box 980, Edgecliff, NSW, 2027

Orders: pegasuspublishing@iinet.net.au
www.pegasuspublishing.square.site

Copyright © Pegasus Publishing
An Ashnong Pty Ltd Company

Text copyright © Pegasus Publishing

A CIP catalogue record for this book is available from the National Library of Australia.

ISBN: 978-1-925909-13-5

Printed and sold on Demand by:
Pegasus Publishing   www.pegasuspublishing.square.site
Ingram Lightning Source   www.ingramspark.com

Front Cover: Image of 'Long Gully Bridge, known as the Suspension Bridge, which links the suburb to Cammeray, has become a recognised symbol of Northbridge. The bridge was completed in January 1892 and purchased by the NSW government in 1912.

Opposite: The immense steel arches of the newly opened Sydney Harbour Bridge, about 1935.

NOSTALGIA FOR NAREMBURN

The Ancestors Of
Robert Archibald Rockwell &
Octavia Corelli O'Sullivan

Volume 8
of the Rockwell Genealogies

By
Dr Tracy Rockwell

Pegasus Publishing

CONTENTS & PLATES

CHAPTERS...

LIST OF MAPS...

LIST OF FAMILIES & DESCENDANTS...

LIST OF PEDIGREE CHARTS...

▲ 'A Family Tree', by Norman Rockwell (1959).

DEDICATION

This genealogy is dedicated to the memory of Robert Archibald Rockwell, his wife Octavia Corelli O'Sullivan, their parents and associated kin. They struggled their entire lives, but their stoicism in surviving the many difficulties that came their way, is a reflection of their character and moral fibre for... "it's the past that tells us who we are, without which we lose our identity."

Stephen Hawking,

PREFACE

The purpose of this publication is to explore the genealogy of Robert Archibald Rockwell (1904-1966) and his wife Octavia Corelli O'Sullivan (1902-1976), who were both born in the inner western suburbs of Sydney. The journey examines the hereditary and ancestral families of Rockwell, Bantin, O'Sullivan and Shoveller in detail, and probes the significant lives of their immediate forebears.

This volume is exciting in its own right, but the Rockwell Genealogies are essentially one long book, and it could have been longer still. For ease of reading, I have divided the manuscript into a number of separate volumes, otherwise it would be impossible to make one single volume light enough to read in bed. So expansive and illuminating has been the research that I have been able to publish where possible, one volume for each of the great-great grandparents; one volume for our great grandparents and grandparents; and one final volume for my parents, which I feel would be both a respectful and honourable tribute to their presence upon this earth.

In recording this genealogy the task was threefold: to reveal what could be found of the life stories of our illustrious and honoured ancestors; to reproduce the 'old life' without either sentimentality or caricature; and to preserve pedigrees, stories, verses and traditions that otherwise might be hopelessly lost. Within these pages I hope to have stored such flotsam and jetsam as could be rescued from the waters of oblivion.

While it is encouraging to read that even great historians have insights that resemble our own, a major persuasion in undertaking this detailed work was to preserve my genealogical research accumulated across some 40 years of investigations. The publication of the 'Rockwell Genealogies' in an organised and interesting fashion, rather than passing on an indecipherable and ragged assemblage of notes, diagrams, tables and images, is self-evident, particularly for those that come after. My greatest fear is in presenting too much material, as "a wealth of information creates a poverty of attention." However, genealogy is not a precise undertaking and while evidence for some branches and ancestors has been voluminous, little or no evidence whatsoever has been revealed for someof the branches.

The initial goal of my work was to discover 'how my family ancestors came to reside in Australia,' which was originally envisioned to encompass one or two volumes. With Australia being such a young country, the main goal of the research was to understand 'how, when and why our ancestors arrived in Australia?' Researching and documenting the various family members not only identified and revealed how and where they lived, it also recognised the sacrifices they experienced and the contributions they made, without which, none of us would be here today.

As the research evolved and expanded, more distant antecedents from the old countries were increasingly identified, and it became both worthwhile and necessary to also examine the lives of more distant direct and indirect relatives. To learn more, I have made recent efforts to visit as many of the towns, cities, regions and countries of my ancestors as possible. As such, it has to date been a thrill to connect with, and walk in the footsteps of these forebears as "they are now like little ghosts, forever ebbing very slowly away from us."

Tracy Rockwell

Dip. Teach; BSc; MSc; PhD

Austin Avenell Bantin Barrett Crouch Drewe Leighton March

Morgan

Rockwell

Quicke

Rundle

ROBERT ARCHIBALD ROCKWELL
(1904-1966)

It is with great honour that I find myself in this unique position, as custodian of the 'Rockwell Genealogies,' and historian of ancestors at their best and sometimes at their worst. They knew kindness as well as cruelty, understanding as well as brutality, often suffering profoundly, but all now gone and no longer able to speak. It is for posterity that their lives have been researched, and like a window through which to view the past, to publish what is known of their stories.

The first section of this book retells, amongst a good deal of mystery and uncertainty, what is known of Augustus Rockwell and his wife Frances Austen, the stated parents of William Henry Rockwell. With sufficient information, they would have been the subject of volume one of these 'Rockwell Genealogies.' However, they have not been identified anywhere else except on the marriage and death certificates of their supposed son, William Henry Rockwell, and therefore must remain unverified.

Section two details the life of William Henry Rockwell, who was born in London or Kent about 1859, but in an era of compulsory registration, his certificate of birth remains undiscovered. We know he was somewhat of a 'character' and lived an exciting life as a seaman and cab driver, but he eventually married Elizabeth Carpenter (nee Bantin) in 1901. Whilst William may have been truthful, he could equally have had reasons to hide his origins.

Elizabeth was the daughter of English emigrants (see Volume 2), a widow with four children from a previous marriage, but she produced with William another five sons and a daughter. Third of these Rockwell sons was Robert Archibald Rockwell, who was born in 1904, and grew up in Glebe and Forest Lodge in Sydney, before marrying in 1926 to Octavia Corelli O'Sullivan.

Bignell

Hann

Eastman

Heffernan

Frawley

MacCarthy

OCTAVIA CORELLI O'SULLIVAN
(1902-1976)

Corelli, as she was known, was born in Leichhardt, Sydney in 1902, the second child of Humphrey Joseph O'Sullivan and third child of Lenore Mackie (nee Shoveller). Corelli's father Humphrey, was around 31 years old at her birth, himself born at Fish River Creek near Bathurst from an Irish father (see Volume 3). Corelli's 35 year old mother was born in Grafton, NSW from an English emigrant and yet another pioneer mother (see Volume 4).

Section three details the life of Humphrey Joseph O'Sullivan, who moved with his gold prospecting family from Bathurst to Grafton, Dalmorton and later to Moonee Creek just north of Coffs Harbour, and was very close to his mother Ellen O'Sullivan (nee Frawley). He later courted and married Lenore Mackie (nee Shoveller), also a widow with a previous daughter. Sadly, Humphrey died at the tragic young age of 35, silencing for decades the legacy of his illustrious Irish and royal ancestry. Lenore did all she could to provide for her three surviving daughters.

Bob and Corelli Rockwell went on to produce fours sons and two daughters and are the subject of section four of this book.

My task in writing of these now deceased ancestors, is threefold: to record the life-stories of these honourable, hard-working forebears who toiled throughout their lives to provide for their families; to reproduce the older Australian way of life without sentimentality or caricature; and to preserve pedigrees, stories, verses and traditions that otherwise might have been lost. In these pages I attempt to rescue, from the waters of oblivion, as much family 'flotsam and jetsam' as possible.

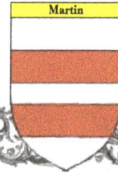

McGarry Mahony Martin O'Sullivan Sabine Saunders Shoveller Thompson

ACKNOWLEDGEMENTS

This book has been a pleasure to write, and I hope it is also a pleasure to read. A number of people and organisations have helped me write it, yet it would be impossible to acknowledge the assistance of each and every contributer fro this publication. Of notable mention however, are the the Society of Australian Genealogists in Sydney, the Mitchell and State Libraries of New South Wales, the Clarence River Historical Society, who pointed me in the right direction at the start of my research, especially in the early days from 1980. Of invaluable assistance also were a number of close relatives who provided their recollections for the preparation of this volume, most now deceased, but include interviews with Joy Corelli Hyde (nee Rockwell), Alice Maud Rockwell (nee Greenup), Lindsay Archibald Rockwell, Ronie Malcom Rockwell, Cheryl Joy Rockwell (nee Pooley), Janet Lenore Sippen (nee Rockwell) and Frank Hammond.

Online websites and resources have also been extraordinarily helpful in researching content for this publication and my sincere thanks goes to the NSW Govt Registry of Births, Deaths and Marriages and the State Archives of NSW. International websites were also consulted in this work, which include the International Genealogical Index (aka IGI or Family Search), Ancestry, as well as Wikitree and Wikipedia, which all have been invaluable sources of information, for which donations and fees have accordingly been made.

ABBREVIATIONS & SYMBOLS

The following abbreviations and symbols have been consistently used to summarise the historical information throughout the text. A legend is provided below to help make sense of the various systems and codes used in the production of this book.

One final note is that the following pages are interspersed with escutcheons that are a represention of the various ancestral families of Robert Archibald Rockwell and Octavia Corelli O'Sullivan. However, these are mostly included to delineate the family groups and as such do not, for the most part, represent any particular grant of arms or official blazon fro the branches of Rockwell, Bantin, O'Sullivan & Shoveller.

Legend of Abbreviations & Symbols

C&RE	Clarence & Richmond Examiner.	bc.	born circa.
CF	Copyright free image.	bp.	baptised.
GS	Government Servant (convict).	c.	circa [Latin], about.
IGI	International Genealogical Index.	d.	died.
MM	Maternal Maternal.	dc.	died circa.
MP	Maternal Paternal.	d.s.p.	decessit sine prole [Latin], died without issue.
NA	National Arch. of England & Wales.		
PM	Paternal Maternal.	dspm.	descessit sine prole mascula [Latin]; died without male issue.
PP	Paternal Paternal.		
PRO	Public Record Office, London.	dv.	divorced
SSD	Sands Sydney Directory.	d.v.p.	decessit vitae patre [Latin], died in father's lifetime.
SMH	Sydney Morning Herald.		
UV	Unverified.	fl.	flourished.
TES	Thomas Eastman Shoveller.	m.	married.
▲	Served in Australian Military Forces	mc.	married circa.
*	died before adulthood.	r.	reigned.
b.	born.	s.	succeeded

INTRODUCTION

As any family historian will tell you, genealogy is a very addictive pastime, with the ever-present thrill of discovering ones ancestors, or connecting to some great icon, aristocrat or even royalty. My passion for this amazing pastime developed into a keen interest from the early 1980s, when I was working with QANTAS as an international flight steward. During stays in London while flying the QF1 route, I would often spend my three layover days trawling through documents at Somerset House and the Public Record Office in search of long lost relatives.

Genealogy is an immensely rewarding and exacting pastime, but often frustrating, by nature of the fact that it is constantly evolving. I've often made the mistake of thinking that every possible facet has been uncovered about an ancestor, only to be surprised by some new piece of evidence, and so the research goes on, and on.

What makes genealogy difficult is investigating common names in places where there are lots of people eg. trying to find a Smith in New York would be next to impossible. Conversely, the task becomes easier when dealing with uncommon names, especially where there are fewer people, as possible linkages can be more readily presumed and proven. In researching our ancestors I was mostly fortunate in locating families that more often than not, had quite distinctive surnames, and resided for the most part in smaller towns and villages. The world wide web too, has brought about a revolution in genealogy, as we can today immediately research what years ago would have taken weeks and months.

In the former British colonies and America, few think it necessary to belong to a titled or landed family in order to have a pedigree worth recording. On the contrary, descent from anyone, esquire or artisan from colonial times is a source of pride; nor are these descendants diffident about their ancestors of any period, so long as they were honest people. Naturally, the knowledge or hope of distinguished ancestry is an additional stimulant in many cases.

By definition, the old right of succession belonging to a firstborn child was known as 'primogeniture', which benefitted families by preventing the subdivision of family estates. Primogeniture lessened the pressure today's families have to equally sub-divide property granted to beneficiaries. Historically however, younger sons of the nobility or the landed gentry across Europe had little or no prospect of inheriting property, and it was common for them to seek careers in the church, in military service by purchasing commissions, or in government.

But all of this was of no use without first being able to identify people. Surnames became necessary when governments introduced personal taxation. In England this was known as the 'Poll Tax.' Throughout the centuries, surnames in every country have continued to 'develop' often leading to astonishing variants of the original spellings. The early recording of births, deaths and marriages in England was voluntarily undertaken by the clergy of various local parish churches. Many of these original records have been copied into the International Genealogical Index (IGI aka 'Family Search') and are now directly accessible through the internet.

However, the increasingly poor state of English parish registration led to numerous attempts to shore up the system in the eighteenth and early nineteenth centuries. The Marriage Act of 1753 attempted to prevent 'clandestine' marriages by imposing a standard form of entry for marriages, which had to be signed by both parties and witnessed.

Additionally, except in the case of Jews, Quakers and Catholics, legal marriages had to be carried out according to the rites of the Church of England. Sir George Rose's Parochial Registers Act of 1812 laid down that all events had to be entered on standard entries in bound volumes. It also declared that the church registers of 'non-conformists' were not admissible in court as evidence of births, marriages and deaths. Only those maintained by the clergy of the Church of England could be presented in court as legal documents. This caused considerable hardship for non-conformists and Catholics. As a result, a number of proposals were presented to Parliament to set up a centralised registry for recording vital events in the 1820s, but none came to fruition.

Eventually, increasing concern that the poor registration of baptisms, marriages and burials undermined property rights, by making it difficult to establish lines of descent, coupled with the complaints of non-conformists, led to the establishment in 1833 of a parliamentary Select Committee on Parochial Registration. This committee took evidence on the state of the parochial system of registration, and made proposals that were eventually incorporated into the 1836 Registration and Marriage Acts. In addition, the government wanted to collect information on infant mortality, fertility and literacy to bring about improvements in health and social welfare. The medical establishment advocated these changes because there was a rapidly growing population in the northern towns, caused by the Industrial Revolution. Severe overcrowding resulted and links between poor living conditions and short life expectancy were then becoming known.

The answer was the establishment of a civil registration system. It was hoped that improved registration of vital events would protect property rights through the more accurate recording of lines of descent. Civil registration was also to remove the need for non-conformists to rely upon the Church of England for registration, and provide medical data for research. As a result, legislation was passed in 1836 that ordered the civil registration of births, marriages and deaths in England and Wales, which took effect from the 1st July 1837. An office was set up in London and the Department of Registrar Generals was established. Indeed, our ancestor John Shoveller LLD (1789-1847) with letters patent by the King William IV, was one of the commissioners that enquired into and made recommendations for the introduction of national registers for the recording of births, marriages and deaths across England and Wales.

England and Wales were subsequently divided into 619 registration districts (623 from 1851), each under the supervision of a Superintendent Registrar. The districts were based on the recently introduced poor law unions. The registration districts were further divided into sub-districts (possibly two or more), each under the charge of Registrars who were locally appointed. Compulsory registration of births, deaths and marriages was also introduced into Scotland (1854), Australia (1856) and Ireland (1864), and although not all events were rigorously registered, this same system continues today.

Where information has come to light, the 'Rockwell Genealogies' examines the ancestry of each of the great-great grandparents of the author. The information is presented sequentially from paternal to maternal ancestors, examining the known strands of information by relevant family root and branch. I would however, gladly welcome feedback and corrections that genealogists or family members may wish to contribute.

"Every wise man must remark on the instability of furtune, and those changes which very few escape, even in the prime of life and scarcely many who live to be old."

Geraldus Cambrensis, 12th Century

CIRCULAR QUAY, SYDNEY,
*Photo

Although less so today, in 1901 Circular Quay was alive with waterside activity.

THE ROCKWELL GENEALOGIES

Pedigree Chart 1 - The Ancestors & Descendants of Robert & Octavia Rockwell of Naremburn, NSW

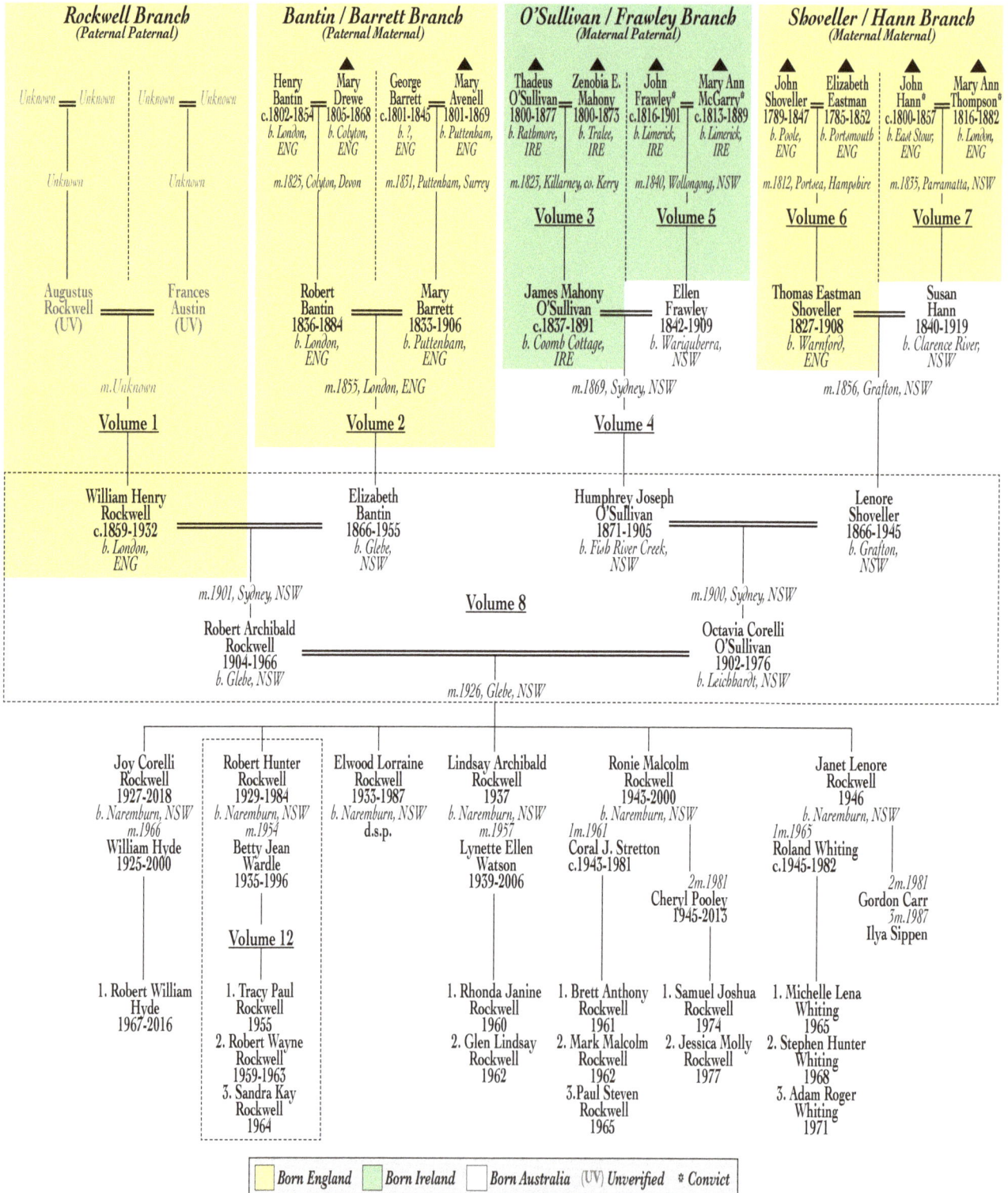

Rockwell Branch
(Paternal Paternal)

Unknown — Unknown   Unknown — Unknown

Unknown

Unknown

Augustus Rockwell (UV) — Frances Austin (UV)

m.Unknown

__Volume 1__

William Henry Rockwell
c.1859-1932
b. London, ENG

Bantin / Barrett Branch
(Paternal Maternal)

Henry Bantin
c.1802-1854
b. London, ENG
— Mary Drewe
1805-1868
b. Colyton, ENG

George Barrett
c.1801-1845
b. ?, ENG
— Mary Avenell
1801-1869
b. Puttenbam, ENG

m.1825, Colyton, Devon   m.1851, Puttenbam, Surrey

Robert Bantin
1836-1884
b. London, ENG
— Mary Barrett
1833-1906
b. Puttenbam, ENG

m.1855, London, ENG

__Volume 2__

Elizabeth Bantin
1866-1955
b. Glebe, NSW

m.1901, Sydney, NSW

O'Sullivan / Frawley Branch
(Maternal Paternal)

▲Thadeus O'Sullivan
1800-1877
b. Rathmore, IRE
— ▲Zenobia E. Mahony
1800-1873
b. Tralee, IRE

▲John Frawley*
c.1816-1901
b. Limerick, IRE
— ▲Mary Ann McGarry*
c.1813-1889
b. Limerick, IRE

m.1825, Killarney, co. Kerry   m.1840, Wollongong, NSW

__Volume 3__   __Volume 5__

James Mahony O'Sullivan
c.1837-1891
b. Coomb Cottage, IRE
— Ellen Frawley
1842-1909
b. Wariguberra, NSW

m.1869, Sydney, NSW

__Volume 4__

Humphrey Joseph O'Sullivan
1871-1905
b. Fish River Creek, NSW

m.1900, Sydney, NSW

Shoveller / Hann Branch
(Maternal Maternal)

▲John Shoveller
1789-1847
b. Poole, ENG
— ▲Elizabeth Eastman
1785-1852
b. Portsmouth, ENG

▲John Hann*
c.1800-1857
b. East Stour, ENG
— ▲Mary Ann Thompson*
1816-1882
b. London, ENG

m.1812, Portsea, Hampshire   m.1835, Parramatta, NSW

__Volume 6__   __Volume 7__

Thomas Eastman Shoveller
1827-1908
b. Warnford, ENG
— Susan Hann
1840-1919
b. Clarence River, NSW

m.1856, Grafton, NSW

Lenore Shoveller
1866-1945
b. Grafton, NSW

__Volume 8__

Robert Archibald Rockwell
1904-1966
b. Glebe, NSW
===
Octavia Corelli O'Sullivan
1902-1976
b. Leichhardt, NSW

m.1926, Glebe, NSW

Joy Corelli Rockwell
1927-2018
b. Naremburn, NSW
m.1966
William Hyde
1925-2000

Robert Hunter Rockwell
1929-1984
b. Naremburn, NSW
m.1954
Betty Jean Wardle
1935-1996

__Volume 12__

Elwood Lorraine Rockwell
1933-1987
b. Naremburn, NSW
d.s.p.

Lindsay Archibald Rockwell
1937
b. Naremburn, NSW
m.1957
Lynette Ellen Watson
1939-2006

Ronie Malcolm Rockwell
1943-2000
b. Naremburn, NSW
1m.1961
Coral J. Stretton
c.1943-1981

2m.1981
Cheryl Pooley
1945-2013

Janet Lenore Rockwell
1946
b. Naremburn, NSW
1m.1965
Roland Whiting
c.1945-1982

2m.1981
Gordon Carr
3m.1987
Ilya Sippen

1. Robert William Hyde
1967-2016

1. Tracy Paul Rockwell
1955
2. Robert Wayne Rockwell
1959-1963
3. Sandra Kay Rockwell
1964

1. Rhonda Janine Rockwell
1960
2. Glen Lindsay Rockwell
1962

1. Brett Anthony Rockwell
1961
2. Mark Malcolm Rockwell
1962
3. Paul Steven Rockwell
1965

1. Samuel Joshua Rockwell
1974
2. Jessica Molly Rockwell
1977

1. Michelle Lena Whiting
1965
2. Stephen Hunter Whiting
1968
3. Adam Roger Whiting
1971

| Born England | Born Ireland | Born Australia | (UV) Unverified | * Convict |

▲The Rockwell Genealogies spans 12 separate volumes and includes the ancestors and descendants of Robert Archibald Rockwell & Octavia Corelli O'Sullivan, featuring the 'Bantin/Barrett' branch (#2), the 'Mahony's of Dunloe' (#3), the 'O'Sullivan/Mahony' branch (#4), the 'Frawley/McGarry' branch (#5), the 'Shoveller/Eastman' branch (#6), the 'Hann/Thompson' branch (#7) and the 'Rockwell/O'Sullivan' great grandparents & grandparents (#8). NOTE: Volume 1 is reserved for the 'Rockwell' branch if evidence ever emerges. Volumes not listed above detail the ancestors and descendants of Betty Jean Wardle and include William Wallace Wardle & Mary Agnes Cummings, which feature the 'Cummins/Sheehan' branch (#9), the 'McDonald/Harvey' branch (#10) and the 'Wardle/Cummings' great grandparents & grandparents (#11). The final volume for 'Robert & Betty Rockwell' (#12), pays tribute to the presence of these ancestors upon this earth.

Chapter One

THE ROCKWELL ANCESTORS
(Possible paternal antecedents of Robert Archibald Rockwell)

Australia belongs in its culture, outlook and way of life with the European nations, and more particularly with the British Isles. Yet geographically, she is set between the Pacific and Indian Oceans and situated in the Asian and Pacific sphere. While the seas form a barrier against the world the country has no physical frontiers with other nations, but over time its isolation has transformed from a weakness to a strength. The mettle of its mainly European emancipists and immigrants were another strength for the young nation as its settlers formed the roads, built the bridges and towns, and fabricated the backbone of a new society. But as it was so much easier to emigrate to America, distance kept the Australians a small people.[1] Nevertheless, the country was gradually populated... and todays Australians find themselves here due principally to the efforts and deeds of their ancestors.

"Colonization had been thrust upon an acquiescent continent."

Marjorie Barnard, 1960 [2]

The Rockwell's In Australia

Unfortunately, all we know of the Rockwell ancestry in Australia begins with William Henry Rockwell (c.1860-1932) who was apparently born a twin in London about 1860, the son of Augustus Rockwell, an evangelist or missionary, and Frances (either Austin or

'Thruyac').[3,4] But problematically, no evidence has been found of William's parents, his twin brother or his date of birth. Therefore, without further documentation it is regrettably impossible at this stage to proceed beyond the 'brick wall', and write an ancestry for the Rockwell family in Australia. While a section of the Rockwell Genealogies has been reserved for this very story, it can only be written if and when evidence comes to light.

However, the present Volume does reveal what is known of William Henry Rockwell and his descendants including Robert Archibald Rockwell, his son and wife Octavia Corelli O'Sullivan as well as the families that contributed to their creation. The work methodically explores each of their hereditary branches, highlights significant individuals and describes what is known to date of their immediate forebears and descendants.

The process described in this book is a narrative history and it tells some of the great

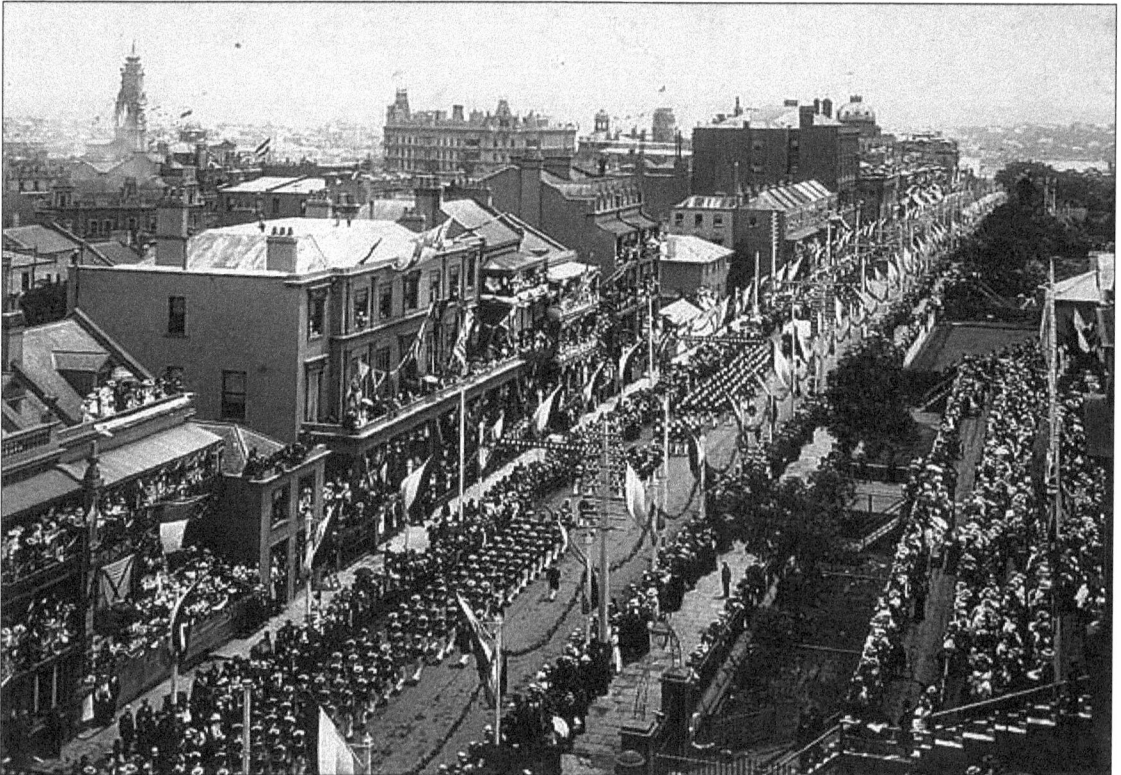

▲ Federation celebrations for a grateful nation in Sydney, 1 January 1901.

▲ 'Ferryboat, early morning in Sydney' by Harold Cazneaux, 1908.

stories of these families, which mostly commenced about 1860 and extended throughout the 1st and 2nd World Wars, and into the Cold War of the 1950s and 60s. But this is also a book written to entertain, and spans the Victorian and Edwardian periods and covers such momentous events as Federation, the Russian Revolution, the Great Depression, the rise of Fascism as well as the social movements of the 1960s. So... what better way to begin a genealogy of Rockwells than with an understanding of how, when and where the alluring surname of Rockwell was derived.

The Rockwell Surname

The surname 'Rockwell' is an English habitational name mostly drawn from locations in Buckinghamshire and Somerset. The former was earlier Rockholt, and was so named from Old English hroc 'rook,' which was perhaps a byname, plus holt 'wood'. The second element of the Somerset place is probably and more predictably, an Old English well, 'spring' or 'stream'. Variant forms of the name in local records are Rockewell, Rockall, Rokelle, Rockell, Rokewell and the original is possibly de la Rochelle, or de Rokella.

The distribution of families sharing the relatively uncommon name of Rockwell at the time of the 1891 England & Wales Census was quite small, ranging from just 22 to 47 family units. The main concentrations being in Lancashire and London, and surprisingly by then the Somerset branch had seemingly disappeared completely.

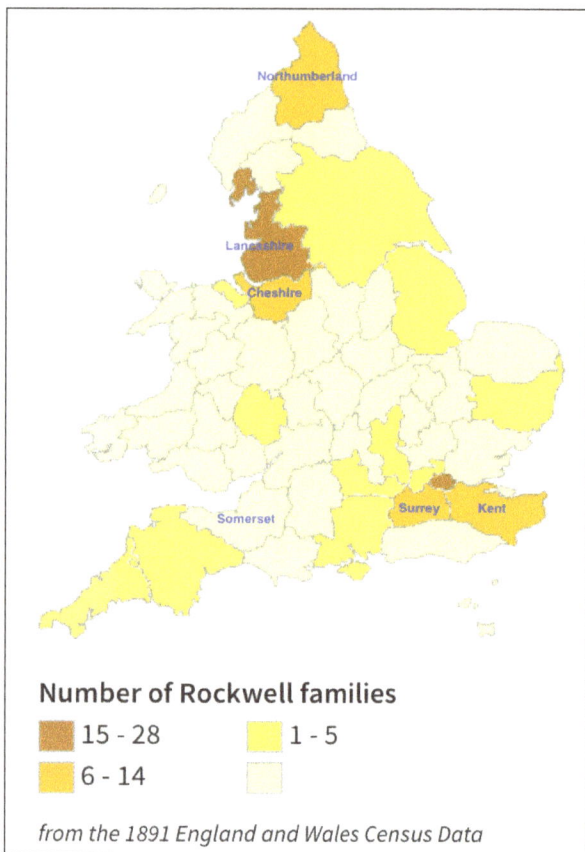

Number of Rockwell families

- 15 - 28
- 6 - 14
- 1 - 5

from the 1891 England and Wales Census Data

▲ *TOP (Left): Map of the distribution and density of Rockwell families across England and Wales in 1891 (Ancestry). (Right): 'Pedigree of Rockwell & Allied Families', from the records of the College of Arms, London, but likely not to be ancestors of William Henry Rockwell. ABOVE: George Lincoln Rockwell (center), head of the American Nazi Party, at a Black Muslim meeting in Washington, D.C. (from... National Galleries of Scotland).*

Famous & Notable Rockwells

Norman Rockwell (1894-1978)

Probably the most well known bearer of the Rockwell name was Norman Rockwell (1894-1978), a prolific American painter and illustrator. MORE INFO ON HIM? However, apart from sharing the name Rockwell, there is no known link to any Australian Rockwells that could prove a direct relationship at this point in time (no known relation).

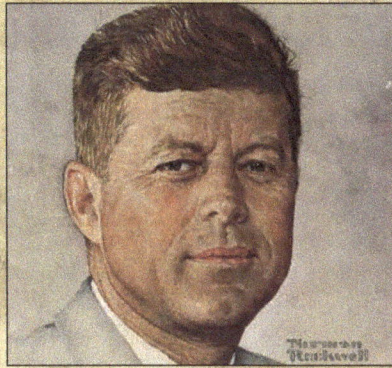

> "The secret to so many artists
> living so long is that every
> painting is a new adventure.
> So, you see, they're always
> looking ahead to something new
> and exciting. The secret
> is not to look back."
> — Norman Rockwell

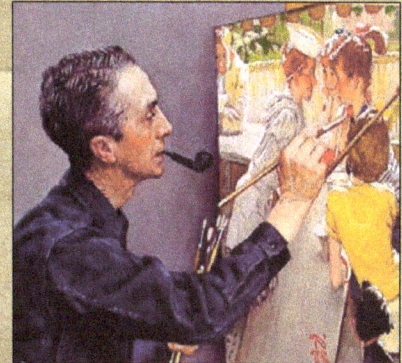

▲ LEFT: "The Runaway," by Norman Rockwell. Oil on canvas, 35 3/4" x 33 1/2"" Cover illustration for "The Saturday Evening Post," 20th September, 1958. RIGHT: Photographic portrait of Norman Perceval Rockwell (1894-1978).

Norman Rockwell

Norman Perceval Rockwell (February 3, 1894 – November 8, 1978) was a 20th-century American author, painter and illustrator. His works enjoyed broad popular appeal in the USA for their reflection of American culture. Rockwell is most famous for the cover illustrations of everyday life he created for 'The Saturday Evening Post' magazine over nearly five decades. Among the best-known of Rockwell's works are the Willie Gillis series, Rosie the Riveter, The Problem We All Live With, Saying Grace, and the Four Freedoms series. He is also noted for his 64-year relationship with the Boy Scouts of America (BSA), during which he produced covers for their publication Boys' Life, calendars and other illustrations. These works include popular images that reflect the Scout Oath and Scout Law such as The Scoutmaster, A Scout is Reverent and A Guiding Hand, among many others.

REMIS & VELISQUE

The Armorial Bearings of
· CHARLES · BRISTED · ROCKWELL ·
of Bristol, Rhode Island,
Gentleman.

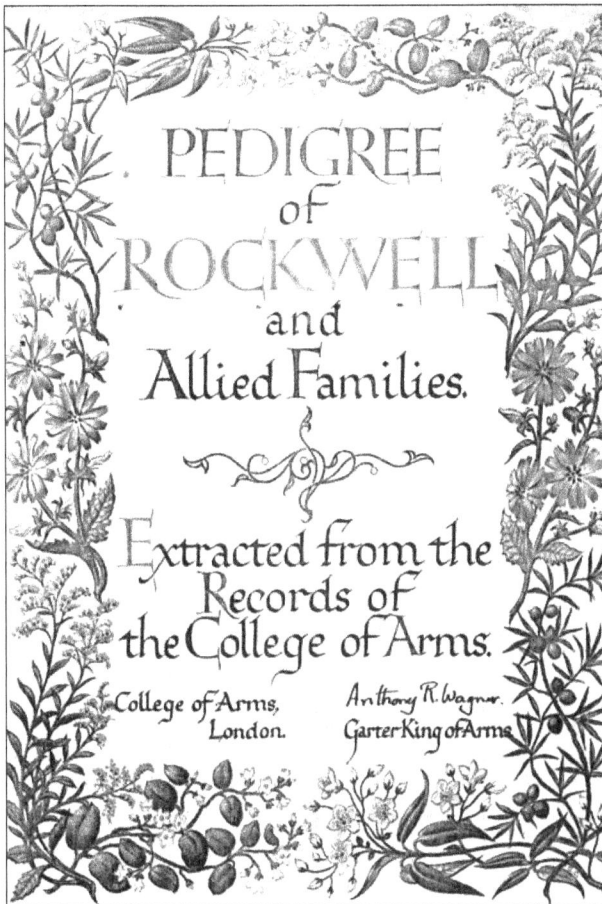

This Pedigree shows the descent of Henry Ensign Rockwell of Washington, District of Colum in the United States of America (1811-188 from John Rockwell of Fitzhead in the County of Somerset, England who was buried there 23 Feb ruary 1636/7. Through his ancestress Elizabet (born 2 November 1675) daughter of Job Drake and wife of Joseph Rockwell (1670~1733), Henr Ensign Rockwell is shown in a pedigree recorded in the College of Arms to have been descended fro King Edward the First, through the families of Bohun, Courtenay, Grenville, and Drake. This Pedigree further shows the descendants of the said Henry Ensign Rockwell, on both male and female lines, to the year 1966.

By Letters Patent under the hands and seals of Garter, Clarenceux and Norroy and Uls Kings of Arms dated 15 December 1966 the following honorary armorial bearings were grant to Charles Bristed Rockwell of Bristol, Rhode Island, Gentleman and his descendants and th other descendants of his grandfather the said Henry Ensign Rockwell late of Washington in the District of Columbia, Gentleman.

Arms: Argent seven Fountains three, thr and one on a Chief Sable three Boars he coupéd Or armed Gules. Crest: On a Wreath Argent and Azure A Boars head cou Or semy of fountains and armed Gules.

▲LEFT: Cover of 'Pedigree of Rockwell and Allied Families'; Crest for family of Rockwell (unrelated). RIGHT: Interior of 'Pedigree of Rockwell and Allied Families, awarded by Sir Anthony R. Wagner (Garter King of Arms) from Extracts from the Records of the College of Arms, 1967.

Charles Bristed Rockwell (1914-1995)

While flying to London as a Qantas Flight Steward in 1980, I spent some time researching ancestors at St. Catherine's House. Back then, I came across a rather interesting pedigree, and Grant of Arms in the name of a Charles Bristed Rockwell, and his ancestor named Henry Ensign Rockwell (1811-1882).

This family of Rockwell's descended from a William Rockwell (1591-1640), the son of John Rockwell (c.1560-1636/7) of Fitzhead in Somerset, who emigrated to America in 1630, aboard the "John and Mary", after which a dynasty of Rockwell's flourished in North America from the 17th century (no known relation).

George Lincoln Rockwell (1918-1967)

George Lincoln Rockwell (March 9, 1918 – August 25, 1967) was the founder of the American Nazi Party. Rockwell was born in Bloomington, Illinois, the first of three children of George Lovejoy "Doc" Rockwell and Claire (Schade) Rockwell.

Rockwell had a successful naval career, both on active duty and in the Naval Reserve. Called the "American Hitler" by the BBC, he became a source of inspiration for White Nationalists in the mid-1960s, and adopted a strategy to develop his Nazi political philosophy within the Christian Identity religious movement. However, on 25th August 1967, Rockwell was shot and killed while leaving a laundromat in Arlington, Virginia (no known relation).

▲LEFT: Willard Frederick Rockwell Sr. (1888-1978), was an American engineer businessman who helped shape and name what eventually became the Rockwell International Company. RIGHT: The Hollywood actor, Sam Rockwell at the 2012 Toronto International Film Festival.

Willard Frederick Rockwell, Sr. (1888-1978)

Willard Frederick Rockwell Sr. (March 31, 1888 – October 16, 1978) was an American engineer businessman who helped shape and name what eventually became the Rockwell International company. He created and directed a number of major corporations with a wide range of products for the automobile, aviation and related industries. By the 1970s he had become a leading figure in the American defense industry. "If it moves, we probably made something on it," was his boast (no known relation).

Samuel Rockwell (1968)

Samuel "Sam" Rockwell (born November 5, 1968) is an American actor known for a number of highly acclaimed independent and mainstream films (no known relation).

The Rockwell Arms, Colours and Motto

The origin of the Rockwell name is English and was first found in Essex, where they were seated from very early times. They were apparently granted lands by William the Conqueror, their liege Lord, for their distinguished assistance at the Battle of Hastings in 1066 A.D. Some of the first American settlers of this name and variants were William, Susannah, Ruth and John Rockwell, who settled in Nantasket in 1630. Thomas Rockwell settled in Virginia in 1637 along with Mary, while an Edward Rockwell arrived in San Francisco in 1850.

Over time, various Rockwell arms have been granted or developed that feature a number of different blazons.[5] Family motto's have also evolved and include: "Virtute probata" (Valor to judge), and "Totus pro meus deus quod rex regis" (All for my God and king), but these have usually been granted to individuals, rather than families. The Rockwell colours were established as sable (black) meaning constancy and grief; and argent (silver or white) meaning sincerity and peace. One theme does seem to be consistent across all families in the development of Rockwell arms, and that is the use of the boar's head as the beast or mascot to represent the family name.

The Rockwell Family Foundation

In the United States, the Rockwell Family Association (RFA), incorporated in 2018, is the legal successor to the Rockwell Family Foundation (RFF), which was established in 1992 by Francis W. Rockwell of East Bloomfield, Michigan.[6][2] After his untimely passing, his cousin Samuel F. Rockwell of Pittsburgh, Pennsylvania, maintained the association until his death in 2017. The RFF Board of Directors then decided to reorganize, with Ken Rockwell taking on the presidency, with Carolyn K. Rockwell as vice-president and editor of the newsletter. The reason for the name change was that another 'Rockwell Family Foundation', a charitable agency had created occasional confusion amongst members.

> "The purposes of this organization are to promote and celebrate the Rockwell family in the United States, Canada, and the world, by means of genealogical research and historical study of the various Rockwell lineages, the publication of findings thereof, the sponsorship of DNA testing, and the hosting and support of meetings and educational programs related thereto. As used here, the Rockwell family centers on, but is not limited to, the lineages of five colonial patriarchs: William and John of Windsor, Connecticut; John of Stamford, Connecticut; Josiah of New London and Norwich, Connecticut; and Robert (a.k.a. Robert Rockhold) of Virginia and Maryland."

The Rockwell Newsletter has been published continuously since 1992, and has included reports of genealogical research on the Rockwell family, features on individual Rockwells and businesses, landmarks, places featuring the Rockwell name, and announcements of special events. As stated in their by laws. A major project pursued by the RFF, which began in 2002 has been the DNA project, which RFA hopes to soon relaunch. But now to an examination of the Australian ancestors, who also bear the surname of Rockwell.

Where To From Here?

As mentioned previously, the ancestry of the Rockwell family in Australia remains undiscovered at this stage, the obstacle being an almost total lack of evidence to support

▲ The above crests are based on the coat of arms used by the Rockwell Family Foundation. LEFT: Per fess sable and argent, on chief three argent boar's heads, on base sable cross patee. Crest: Argent boar's head pierced by sword. RIGHT: Argent chevron sable with argent boar's head. Crest: None specified. Notably, all Rockwell 'arms' seem to feature boar's heads.

the existence of Augustus Rockwell and Frances Austin, the nominated parents of William Henry Rockwell. While William Henry Rockwell's ancestry has been reserved for Volume 1 of the Rockwell Genealogies entitled "A Genealogy of Augustus Rockwell & Frances Austin," it is yet to be written despite some theories having been proposed (*see Appendix A*). Therefore, the lineage of the Australian Rockwells begins with William Henry Rockwell, and all that is known of him begins in the year 1890 when at the age of 32 he was found working in Melbourne.

References

1. Barnard, M. (1962). "A History of Australia", Angus & Robertson, Sydney, p.3.

2. Barnard, M. (1962). "A History of Australia", Angus & Robertson, Sydney, p.479.

3. Victorian Dept of BDM. (1894). Marriage Certificate for William Henry Rockwell & Mary Bates (nee Brook) - #63/1894.

4. NSW Dept of BDM. (1901). Marriage Certificate for William Henry Rockwell & Elizabeth Carpenter (nee Bantin), #8525/1901.

5. Rockwell Coat of Arms [http://greatwhitefrost.net/kenmraz/arms/rockwell_coat_of_arms.htm]. Image - Copyright © 2004 - 2006, Ken Mraz.

6. The Rockwell Family Association. President: Ken Rockwell, Salt Lake City, Utah. Contact: kwrockwell@yahoo.com

Chapter Two

Rockwell

WILLIAM HENRY ROCKWELL

(Father of Robert Archibald Rockwell)

William Henry Rockwell was apparently born a twin brother, and was listed on his himself on both of his marriage registrations as being the son of Augustus Rockwell, an evangelist or missionary, and Frances (either Austin or 'Thruyac').[1,2] However, no evidence has been found of his parents, his twin brother or his date of birth.

Fortunately, William Henry Rockwell's year of birth can be inferred from his death in 1932, as he had attained the age of 72.[3] William was therefore born about the year 1860, which was a time in world history that saw the election of Republican Abraham Lincoln as President of the United States, which lead to the southern states seceding from the Union. During that year Great Britain was involved in the Opium Wars in China, and the Open Championship, also known as the British Open, was played for the first time at Prestwick Golf Club in Ayrshire, Scotland. Notable people born in 1860 included the Scottish novelist Sir Arthur Conan Doyle (22 May), the American Wild West show performer Annie Oakley (13 August), and World War I American General John J. Pershing (13 Sept).

William Henry Rockwell's ancestry has been reserved for Volume 1 of the Rockwell Genealogies entitled "A Genealogy of Augustus Rockwell & Frances Austin," but has not as yet been written despite some theories having been proposed (*see Appendix A*). The obstacle is an almost total lack of evidence to support the existence of Augustus Rockwell and Frances Austin, whom William nominated as his parents.

▲A bustling London during the late 1860's, the scene that young 14 year old William Henry Rockwell left behind about 1873.

Without any earlier evidence, the Rockwell ancestry at present begins with what is known of William Henry Rockwell, which in the year 1890 when at the age of 32 he was found to be working in Melbourne. Records reveal he was a sailor, and a hansom cab proprietor/driver in both Melbourne and Sydney. He was twice married, the father of six or perhaps seven children, and he was the patriarch of our branch of the Rockwell family in Australia. His second wife Elizabeth Carpenter (nee Bantin), was born in Glebe, Sydney of English parentage. Together, William and Elizabeth produced a large blended family of Carpenter and Rockwell children, with William fathering five sons and a daughter of his own.

William Henry Rockwell

What a wonderful experience it must have been to sail on the great clipper ships and comfortable steamers of the late 19th century. Having an ancestor relate tales of those adventurous days of sail would have been fascinating to hear. He was known to many as Bill Rockwell, and from all accounts he rounded 'Cape Horn' at the southern tip of South America some 13 times throughout his career as a seaman, aboard some truly magnificent vessels. Alas, if only we could go back in time.

Ancedotes from various family members state that William Henry Rockwell was apparently the son of an evangelist and missionary, and William himself reported his place of birth to have been in London or nearby Kent, England.[4] It has been known for some time that William Henry Rockwell declared his father to be Augustus Rockwell, and more recently, the discovery of William's first marriage also revealed the previously undecipherable maiden name of his mother to be Frances Austin.

But regrettably, research into William's ancestry has hit a brick wall, with no evidence of a marriage between his declared parents having been found. This supposed marriage is a conundrum as if these nuptials did actually occur, no evidence has been found to support it. It is therefore possible that William Henry may have adopted the surname 'Rockwell' as an alias, perhaps listing Augustus Rockwell as a fictitious father? But why, and for what purpose would have led him to do that?

Disappointingly, despite some 40 years of research, unravelling the birth and parentage of William Henry Rockwell remains elusive. Most recently, paternal DNA results from William's grandson, Lindsay Archibald Rockwell, as well as myself (a great grandson), have surprisingly revealed that the Rockwell antecedents originally arrived in England from Finland.[5] But this remarkable revelation may have occurred hundreds of years ago and raises more questions than it answers, so the search continues.

While all explanations remain possible, William did apparently have a twin brother, and reportedly a 'cruel' aunt who upset the harmony amongst the members of his family, which likely led to his unexpected departure from the family home at about 14 years of age.[6]

The Break With Britain

It could also have been possible that William developed into a rebellious lad, but whatever the cause, he departed from his home in England a couple of years either side of 1872-73. Independent of the events already mentioned, is a family anecdote that has been passed down for decades, recalling that:

> "William Henry may have had a twin brother, and possibly because their natural mother was alone, an aunt came to live with the family who was apparently quite cruel to the boys. The cruelty of their circumstances and upbringing must have taken their toll as their lives became very difficult, so William decided to leave his home and family at the very young age of just 14."
>
> *Alice Rockwell* [7]

Nothing more is known of William's twin brother except that he may have ventured to

▲ *The beautiful "Grace Harwar" clipper in full sail, c.1890, the type of ship William Henry Rockwell may have crewed on.*

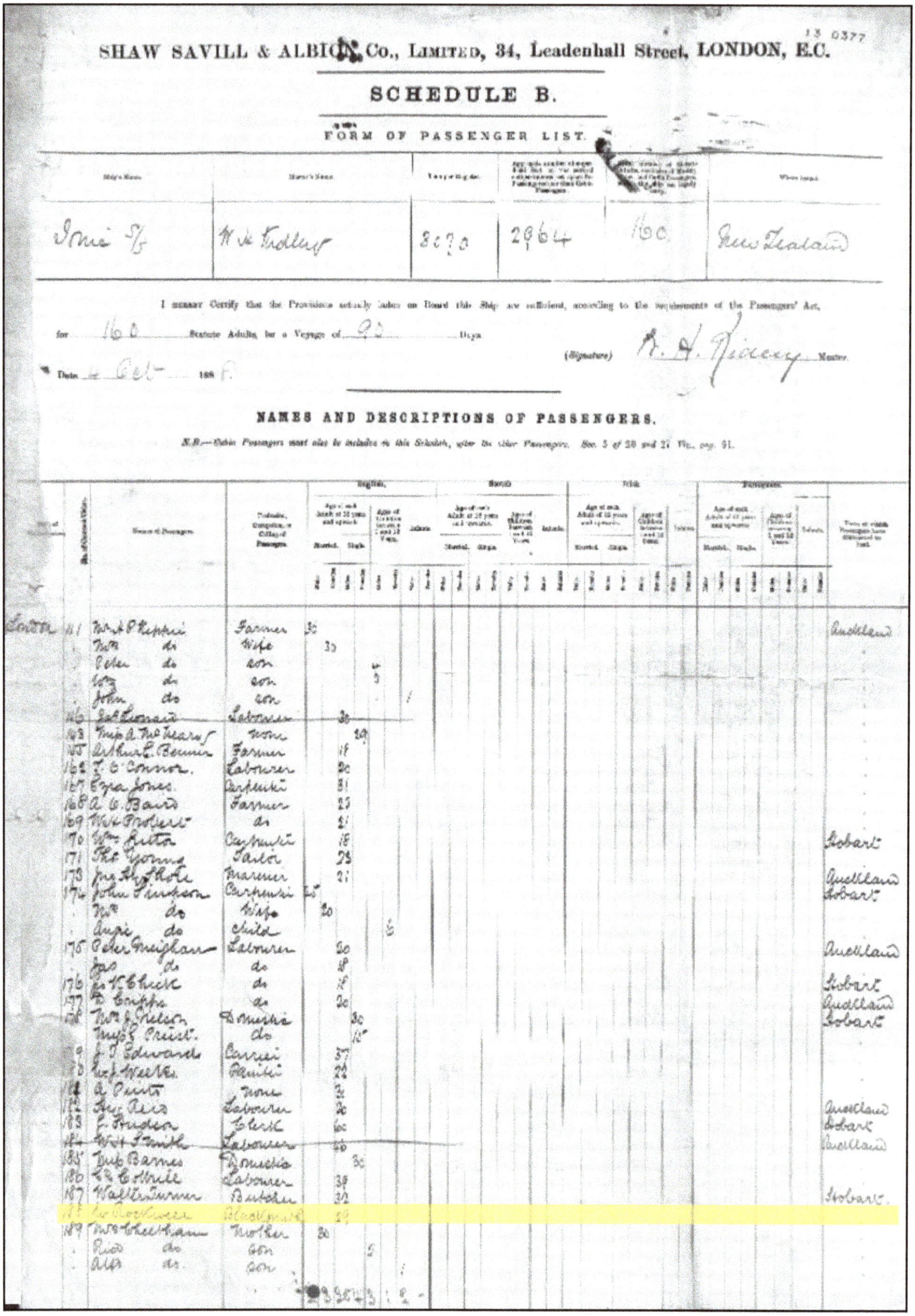

13 0377

SHAW SAVILL & ALBION Co., LIMITED, 34, Leadenhall Street, LONDON, E.C.

SCHEDULE B.

FORM OF PASSENGER LIST.

Ship's Name	Master's Name			Where bound
Ionic S/S	W. H. Fidley	3070	2964 160	New Zealand

I hereby Certify that the Provisions actually laden on Board this Ship are sufficient, according to the requirements of the Passengers' Act,

for 160 Statute Adults, for a Voyage of 90 Days.

(Signature) R. H. Fidley Master.

Date 4 Oct 188 .

NAMES AND DESCRIPTIONS OF PASSENGERS.

N.B.—Cabin Passengers must also be included in this Schedule, under the other Passengers. Sec. 5 of 26 and 27 Vic., cap. 51.

(handwritten passenger table — faded and partly illegible)

▲A possible identification for a W. Rockwell (passenger) - NZ Immigration Papers, into Auckland, 29 years, Single, English, Blacksmith, born 1859, perhaps worked for Shaw Savill & Albion Co Ltd.

▲ TOP: The "RMSS Ionic (I)" was built in 1883 by Harland & Wolff at Belfast of 4753 gross tons, a length of 440ft, a beam of 44ft 2in and a service speed of 14 knots. COLUMN 1 (Up): "SS Ionic" likely with WIlliam H. Rockwell on board arrives Hobart (Daily Telegraph [Launc.], 11 Feb 1888, p.2). (Down & COLUMN 2): Article about the arrival of the "RMSS Ionic" at Hobart (The Mercury, 11 Feb 1888, p.2). COLUMN 3 (Up): W. Rockwell - NZ Immigration, Passenger Lists, 1888 (Archives New Zealand, Passenger Lists, 1839-1973 [Citing Multiple Ships]). (Down): Advertisement for "RMSS Ionic" (Liverpool Mercury, 2nd Oct 1886, p.8).

North America, as there is a family recollection linking him to the United States.[8,9] As for the whereabouts of his alleged father Augustus Rockwell, nothing whatsoever is known, but he may have worked as a missionary in some far off land? The possibility of contacting missionary societies or researching church archives has not been explored to date, and these investigations could eventually unravel the paternal ancestry of William Henry Rockwell.

What William did and where he went between the ages of 14 and 32 are unknown, but from all accounts over the next 18 years he enlisted as ships crew and travelled the world

TOP (Left): William Henry Rockwell's impressive brass inlaid mahogany lap desk, and a view of its various contents and compartments, including a fuzzy wuzzy hair comb, sword fish beak & leather storage box. MID 1: The signature of William Henry Rockwell, c.1894; MID 2: Possessions held in the mahogany lap desk belonging to William Henry Rockwell. BELOW: The Melbourne docks crammed with clipper ships around 1890.

in the great clipper and steamships of the late 19th century.[10,11] In later life, he often stated to his family that he sailed for almost 20 years and rounded Cape Horn on 13 separate occasions, which was some feat in those days and one that would establish William as a thoroughly experienced seaman.[12]

The Clipper Ships

A clipper was a fast sailing ship of the middle to later third of the 19th century. They were yacht-like vessels, with three masts and a square rig. They could carry limited bulk freight, but were highly regarded, especially by old sea captains. "Clipper ships still hold their own for long sea voyages. There is a limit to the use of steam, and it is reached when the distance to be travelled makes the cost of coal and the space it occupies greater than the value of the cargo warrants."

Until some new motive power replaces steam, or it can be replaced by the use of petroleum or other concentrated fuel, the clipper still has an occupation, and the hearts of all old-time skippers will be gladdened by the sight of their white wings upon the seas." [13]

Where William ventured in those 'missing' years will hopefully someday be revealed. What we do know, is that after making visits to many places throughout the world, William Henry Rockwell was in the advantageous position of landing himself in the best possible situation, and he obviously developed a preference for the southern hemisphere over a cold and rainy England. Although clipper ships were faster than the early steamships, they depended on the vagaries of the wind, while steamers could keep to a schedule. Having started on sailing ships it is entirely possible that William may have changed over to crew aboard steam vessels at that time.

Although no listings conclusively identify William Henry Rockwell, research has revealed a number of seamen with the surname of Rockwell that worked aboard vessels in Australasian waters from the mid 1880s to 1900. By 1888, a William Rockwell was recorded with an occupation of 'blacksmith' aboard the "RMSS Ionic", which worked the New Zealand run.[14] This vessel left the Royal Albert Docks, London on the 29th December 1887, bound for Teneriffe, Cape of Good Hope, Hobart and New Zealand.

The Royal Mail Steam Ship, "RMSS Ionic" of 4753 gross tons, was built in 1883 by Harland and Wolff at Belfast at a length of 440ft, a beam of 44ft 2in and a service speed of 14 knots. A slightly larger version of the "SS Asiatic," she was launched on 10th January 1883 and was powered, for the first time, by a Harland and Wolff engine. A fast freighter with limited passenger accommodation, she was initially chartered along with the "SS

Whilst William Henry Rockwell may have acquired his brass inlaid wooden lap desk by any number of means including being forgotten, lost or stolen, an inscription inside the box reads: "April 26th 1851, died August 6th 1850(80?) at 12 Alphonsus Road, Drumcondra (Dublin), ELTA?; with perhaps a previous owner also inscribed in different handwriting... Elizabeth Bond, Nottingham Place, Dundalk (Louth, Ireland).

▲ TOP (Left): A record exists of an H. Rockwell (Henry?) as 2nd Mate aboard the "SS Warrego" from Cooktown, which arrived Sydney on the 6th January 1890 (James Usher, Master, Burthen 1550 tons). (Right): The "SS Arawatta", which William Henry Rockwell may have sailed in November 1898. ABOVE: More possessions from William Henry Rockwell's mahogany lap desk.

Doric" and the "SS Coptic" by the New Zealand Shipping Co.[15]

William Henry Rockwell may have been employed by the Shaw Savill Company for some time, and as a blacksmith he may have worked on a number of the Shaw Savill Company vessels.

By the 24th February 1888, the "RMSS Ionic" had docked in the Port of Wellington, New Zealand and the names and a description of the passengers and crew were handed to the New Zealand Immigration authorities. William Rockwell, blacksmith was listed on this

A SERIES OF ACCIDENTS.

William Rockwell, about 32 years of age, residing at 204 Napier-street, Fitzroy, was taken to the Melbourne Hospital yesterday and treated for abrasion to the face and hands. He was driving a hansom cab, and when turning round the corner of Spring and Collins streets he was thrown from his seat to the roadway. His injuries having been attended to he was removed to the watch house and locked up on a charge of drunkenness.

At the Carlton Police Court on Thursday, a man named William Rockwell was charged with unlawfully assaulting Henry Hoag, a machinist. The latter appeared with his head swathed in bandages. His statement was to the effect that on the 14th ult. he advertised for a machinist and housekeeper, and engaged a woman who subsequently proved to be Rockwell's wife. The woman had arranged to go to his place on the Saturday night following, but as she did not keep her agreement he (Hoag) went to the address she had furnished him at Canning-street to ascertain the cause. He there met the prisoner, who accused him of attempting to entice his wife away, and then brutally assaulted him, knocked him down, and whilst on the ground kicked him, the result being that his jaw was broken in three places. A constable then arrived on the scene and prevented Rockwell committing any further assault. He had remained an inmate of the hospital up till Saturday last, and was being treated as an outpatient. Constable Lawrence, who arrested Rockwell, stated to the bench that the medical officers at the hospital had informed him that Hoag was not yet out of danger, as symptoms of tetanus had appeared. In these circumstances the bench decided to remand the accused until Thursday next.

ENGAGING A HOUSEKEEPER.

ENCOUNTER WITH AN IRATE HUSBAND.

William Rockwell was called on at the Carlton bench yesterday to answer a charge of assaulting an elderly man named Henry Hoag. Particulars of the affair have been published. Briefly, complainant advertised for a housekeeper, and on 14th December the wife of defendant applied for the position, representing herself as a widow. It was arranged that she should call again two days later, but as she failed to keep the engagement, defendant went to the address she had given him. He found that she lived next door, and when he knocked the door was opened by defendant, who, without giving him an opportunity to speak accused him of trying to entice his wife away, and then knocked him down and kicked him, the result being that Hoag's jaw was broken in three places. In defence Rockwell denied that the assault had been committed as described. He stated that when Hoag called at the house he (defendant) ordered him away, but he declined to go, and a scuffle ensued. During this scuffle prosecutor fell, and he must have then received the injuries. He (defendant) was greatly excited, as complainant had made improper proposals to his wife when she called on him in reference to the situation, and had invited her to have some beer with him. Defendant's wife gave evidence substantiating the latter part of the evidence given by her husband. Dr. Lyons deposed that Hoag's injuries were of a permanent nature, and he would never be able to properly close his teeth. The bench took into consideration that defendant had received provocation, and had also been in gaol three weeks awaiting the hearing of the charge, and let him off with a fine of 20s. with £1 1s. costs; in default 14 days' imprisonment.

▲TOP: 1890 postcard of Collins St, Melbourne looking east toward Spring St. ABOVE (Left - Up): William Rockwell - Cab Accident (The Age, 19th Sep 1890, p.7). (Left - Down): William Rockwell Fitzroy Assault (Mt Alexander Mail, 6th January 1894, p.2). CENTRE: Standing outside of No. 204 Napier St, Fitzroy, in Melbourne, once the residence of William Henry Rockwell in 1890, is his great great grand-daughter, Olivia Hansen Rockwell (photo taken 2021). RIGHT: William Rockwell - Verdict of the Assault Charge on Henry Hoag (The Age, 12th January 1894, p.6).

▲ *Wagons, trams and hansom cabs service a very well dressed public on Collins St, Melbourne, c.1890.*

document as having passed through Hobart and was 29 years old, almost the exact age as William Henry Rockwell at the time.

Another possibility is that William Henry Rockwell emigrated to Australia at this time, as a record of a Mr. W. Rockwell (steerage passenger) was also found soonafter aboard the "SS Adelaide" (W. Lockyer, Master, Burthen-917 tons) from Melbourne to Sydney on the 22nd November 1888.

It may have been that William could even have lived in Sydney for a time as the Sands Sydney Directory has a record of a William Rockwell residing at 16 Norton St, Glebe in 1888, and then also at 64 Campbell St, Glebe in 1890.

More likely however, is that after basing himself in Melbourne, William transferred to work on what was known as 'coasters,' which were smaller vessels that linked the various maritime cities and towns around Australia. A record exists of a crewman named W. Rockwell (aged 38), as mate on the "SS Moreton" (H. Morrisby, Master, burthen 581 tons), which arrived in Sydney from Devonport, Tasmania on the 20th May 1890.

Although there is no certainty as to his exact movements, William's seafaring adventures must have been plentiful as the Rockwell family holds an impressive brass inlaid mahogany lap desk, which formerly belonged to him.[16] Apparently William's sons were under strict instructions to only open this box upon his death, and then it was to go to his first born son, William Henry Rockwell Jr., otherwise known as Bill Jr.

As William Henry Rockwell Sr. lived his last years and passed away at his son Bob Rockwell's house in Naremburn, it was understandable that the lap desk was kept in

1894 Marriage of William Henry Rockwell & Mary Bates

18	MARRIAGES solemnized in the District of	Bourke,			

No. in Register.	Where and when Married.	Name and Surname of the Parties.	Condition of the Parties. Bachelor or Spinster. If a Widower or Widow, Date of Decease of former Wife or Husband.	Children by each former Marriage. Living.	Dead.	Birthplace.
63	February 24th 1894 at 198 Johnston St. Fitzroy.	William Henry Rockwell, and Mary Bates,	Bachelor, Widow 1890	One	Three	Kent, England, San Francisco, America,

I, _____Peter Brown_____, being _____duly Registered_____,
do hereby certify that I have, this day, at _198 Johnston St. Fitzroy,_____ duly
celebrated Marriage between _William Henry Rockwell Sailor, of Queen's Parade, Clifton Hill_
and _Mary Bates Domestic, of Princes St. Carlton_____ after Notice
and Declaration duly made and published, as by law required (and with the written consent of_____
_____).

Dated this _Twentyfourth_ day of _February_ 18_94_

Signature of Minister, Registrar-General, or other Officer _Peter Brown Minister,_

in the Colony of Victoria.

Rank or Profession.	Ages.	Residence. Present.	Usual.	Parents. Names. (Mother's Maiden Name.)	Father's Rank or Profession.
Sailor,	33	Queen's Parade Clifton Hill,	Queen's Parade, Clifton Hill,	Augustus Rockwell, and Frances Rockwell (maiden name) Austin,	Evangelist
Domestic,	38	Princes St. Carlton,	Princes St. Carlton,	Robert Brook, and Louisa Brook, (maiden name) Butler	Sea Captain,

Marriage, according to the _Rites of the Church of Christ,_ was solemnized between us { _William Henry Rockwell_ _Mary Bates_

Witnesses { _Peter Brown_ _Johanna Speiss_

▲Marriage certificate for William Henry Rockwell and Mary Bates (nee Brook) on 24th February, 1894 (Victorian Births, Deaths and Marriages, #63/1894).

Robert's branch of the family. The last known family member in possession of William Henry Rockwell's mahogany lap desk was Samuel Joshua Rockwell (great grandson).[17] The contents of this box have been examined by the author, recorded, photographed and was returned to Sam in 2018.

The Melbourne Years

Being careful not to ignore possible clues, it is likely that William Henry Rockwell continued sailing for a period. However, by September 1890 he had probably cut back on his life at sea, and was found to be working as a hansom cab driver in Melbourne. William moved into a property at 24 Napier Street in the suburb of Fitzroy. Then on the 19th September 1890, the Age newspaper reported that 32 year old William Rockwell had been treated for abrasions to his face and hands after being thrown from his cab while turning a corner. He was locked up on this occasion as it was obvious that he was drunk at the time.[18]

But had William actually farewelled his sailing days altogether? His death certificate states that he arrived in the colony around the year 1892, although we now know that this was just a guess. He was still young, and it is possible that he might have continued his love of the sea by signing on to various crews as a casual employee, which provided him the flexibility to be a hansom cab driver during his shoreleave.

Documents show that William continued his work as a seaman. In 1893, a William Rockwell was listed as an unassisted passenger aboard the "SS Manapouri," which sailed from Wellington, New Zealand and arrived at the Port of Melbourne on the 19th January. However, by February of 1894 William Henry Rockwell had entered into his first marriage and recorded that he was working as a 'sailor', when he completed the marriage registration.[19]

The Marriage Of William Henry Rockwell & Mary Bates

Just how and when William Rockwell met his first wife, Mary Bates (nee Brook, c.1856-?) is unknown. Perhaps she once rode in William's hansom cab, they could have met in

▲LEFT (Top): William Henry Rockwell listed in 'Deserters of Wives & Children' (Victorian Police Gazette, 29 January 1896). (Mid): William Henry Rockwell listed in 'Deserters of Wives & Children' (NSW Police Gazette, 4 March 1896). (Above): William Henry Rockwell was listed in 'Deserters of Wives & Children' (Victorian Police Gazette, 1st December 1897, p.373). RIGHT: Portrait of William Henry Rockwell, likely taken for his first marriage in February 1894.

Melbourne, or they may even have met on one of William's voyages? Regardless of the circumstances, they had obviously entered into a domestic relationship before their marriage, as William was involved in another incident that made the Melbourne newspapers in early January of 1894.[20,21]

The episode involved a vicious assault by William upon a Mr Henry Hoag, who had seemingly called at the Rockwell residence about an employment offer for William's partner Mary. The altercation occurred after William accused Mr Hoag of trying to 'solicit his wife.' After being charged with breaking Mr Hoags jaw and spending three weeks in gaol, William was judged as having been provoked by Mr Hoag, who was attempting to entice his wife away, and he was let off with a fine of 20 shillings, with £1.1s. in costs.[22] This event demonstrates William's quick temper, but also he was obviously not afraid of defending himself, and is evidence of the survival instinct he had developed since leaving home as a young boy.

The newspaper articles incorrectly reported that William and Mary Bates were already married, however that didn't actually occur until some six weeks later. The wedding eventually took place at 198 Johnston St, Fitzroy according to the rites of the Church of Christ on the 24th February 1894 under Peter Brown (Minister). William Henry Rockwell declared himself as being 33, a bachelor who was working as a 'sailor' and residing at Queens Parade, Clifton Hill. William also recorded that his birthplace was Kent, England. Mary Bates (nee Brook) recorded her age as 38, an American born widow and a domestic of no occupation, who was residing at Princes St, Carlton. Mary also declared that, while she had a one year old child living with her, she had sadly lost three other children. The witnesses to the marriage were Laura Brown and Johanna Speiss.[23]

Neither William nor Mary Bates' parents could have been present at the wedding, although there is no reference to any of them being deceased. The newlyweds possibly moved into a residence either in Canning Street, or in Princes St, Carlton, along with Mary's child.

Mary's maiden name was Brook, but she had apparently either married or taken the name of Bates sometime before 1884. At the time of her marriage to William Henry Rockwell, Mary Bates declared that her three deceased children were Richard, Elsie and Charles Brook, for which none of the father's were known. But she apparently brought 10 year old Charles Henry Bates into the marriage.

BREACHES OF THE CITY BY-LAWS.—G. F. Marsh, for hanging up a horse to a fence, thus compelling foot passengers to leave the path and walk through the sand, was fined 2s. 6d., and costs. G. Thompson, charged with driving a cart along the footpath in Lincoln-street, was discharged. J. Greave was charged with tying his horse to a fence across a path, and was fined 5s., and costs. Wm. Rockwell, for driving along a footpath, was fined 5s., and costs. H. Gibbon, for tying up a horse across a path, was fined 5s., and costs.

▲LEFT: William Henry Rockwell - Driving Fine (West Australian, 14th February 1898, p.2). RIGHT: During his shore leave, William Henry Rockwell would pick up cab shifts in the various cities he visited, to earn additional income.

Marriages & Children of Mary Brook

Name	Born	Cert #	Mother	Father	Died	Cert #	Mother	Father
Brook, Richard	1875	#17469	Mary A. Brook	Unknown	1883	#867	Unknown	Unknown
?	?	?		?	1890	#11363	Unknown	Unknown
?	?	?		?	1893	#14932	Unknown	Unknown
Marriage to ? Bates	No Evidence in VIC?		-	-	-	-	-	-
Bates, Charles H.	1884	#1222	Mary Bates	Unknown	?	-	-	-
Brooks, Elsie Vics	1889	#32267	Mary (Davis)	Unknown	1890	#2540	Mary Brooks	Unknown
Brooks, Chas Ambrose	1892	#19882	Mary Brooks	Unknown	1892	#9126	Mary Brooks	Unknown
Marr. to Wm. Hy. Rockwell	1894	#1492	-	-	-	-	-	-
Thomas Peter Rockwell	1899	#10909	Agness Brooks	Unknown	?	-	-	-
Bridget Cath. Rockwell	1902	#13355	Mary Rockwell	Wm. H. Rockwell	?	-	-	-
Marr. to Thos. Sarsfield	1909	#1863	-	-	-	-	-	-

▲TOP: 1902 Birth certificate for Bridget Catherine Mary Rockwell (Victorian BDM #13055/1902). ABOVE: Data for the marriages and children of Mary Brook, the first wife of William Henry Rockwell.

Wife Deserter

By late 1895 the Rockwell's were residing at 20 Cromwell St, Collingwood, when it must have become obvious to William that things weren't going well in his marriage to Mary, and he decided to abscond. It was not long afterwards that Mary Rockwell filed a formal complaint with the Victorian Police and she had William branded as a 'wife deserter,' with notices published in the Victorian and NSW Police Gazettes from January 1896 to December 1897.[24,25,26] William was now a wanted man, albeit on the lower end of the scale.

William most likely returned to full-time work and perhaps took a long voyage to distance himself from the situation, unwilling at being forced to support a woman he no longer loved. There is evidence that William was indeed in Fremantle, WA in February 1898, as he received a fine there for reckless driving![27,28] Indeed, a family anecdote relates to William's visit to Western Australia, as when in Fremantle and being the gentleman that he was, he apparently once stepped in to protect a woman who was involved in a violent argument with another man. But events quickly turned against him as the woman picked up a knife and stabbed William's hand, demonstrating her disapproval of his interference. Although he was just acting to protect the woman, he wasn't to know that the couple were apparently married. William must have related this story to his boys, the lesson being to 'never interfere with a married couple having an argument.' This story was later conveyed to his daughter-in-law Alice Rockwell, perhaps in the form of some pre-marital advice, who passed it down accordingly.[29]

A 'William Rockwell' later showed up as a saloon passenger aboard the "SS Arawatta" (under Master Lee, 2000 tons), which departed from the Port of Melbourne and arrived in Sydney on the 21st November, 1898.

However, it seems that his estranged wife Mary Rockwell, wasn't finished with William just yet! It remains possible that William returned to Melbourne at some stage and a reconciliation of sorts might even have taken place. This is a possibility as Mary delivered two more children in Thomas Peter Rockwell, born 1899 and Bridget Catherine Mary Rockwell, born 27th March 1902, both at Richmond.[30,31] While the father of Thomas

ENVIRONS OF
MELBOURNE
Scale of English Miles

⬭ **RESIDENCES**
1. 204 Napier St, Fitzroy
2. Queens Pde, Clifton Hill
3. Princes St. Carlton
4. 20 Cromwell St, Collingwood

▲ Map of the 'Environs of Melbourne, c.1890' featuring the locations of Rockwell residences during the 1890s.

Ships Listing William Rockwell (1888-1902)

Dep Date	Dep Port	Ship Name	Name	Age	Page No.
Mar, 1898	Launceston	Pateena	Rockwell, Mr	37	1
Feb, 1899	Tasmania	Penguin	Rockwell, Mr	29	3
Jan, 1901	Burnie	Penguin	Rockwell, A C Mr	32	2

From Public Record Office Victoria, Outwards passenger lists, Record Series Number (VPRS): 948

1888, 22 Nov	Adl to Syd	Adelaide	Rockwell, William	?	?
1891, 27 Apr	Hob to Syd	Wendauru	Rockwell, William	?	?
1891, 5 May	Syd to Hob	Wendauru	Rockwell, William	?	?
1891, 8 Jun	Mel to Syd	Elgamite	Rockwell, William	?	?
1902, 9 Apr	Mel to Alb	Marloo *(1st Mate)*	Rockwell, William	?	?

Other possible sightings from Various Sources

▲ TOP (Left): A index of ships in Australian waters that listed a Mr, or William Rockwell as either a passenger or crew from 1888 to 1902. (Right): Whilst William Henry Rockwell may have acquired his brass inlaid wooden lap desk by any number of different means, an inscription inside the box reads: "April 26th 1851, Died August 6th 1850 (80?) At 12 Alphonsus Road, Drumcondra (Dublin), Elta (Eire?)"; with perhaps a previous owner also inscribed in different handwriting... "Elizabeth Bond, Nottingham Place, Dundalk (Louth, Ireland)". ABOVE: Looking south west across busy Darling Harbour from Dawes Point, with the original and Fort St School (middle left), c.1859. By the turn of the century, William Henry Rockwell had left Melbourne behind and settled in Glebe, which can be seen in the mid-background of this painting.

Rockwell was left blank, William Henry Rockwell was registered as the father of Bridget, albeit in William's absence.

While it is possible that William Henry Rockwell could indeed have fathered Mary's last two children, it is doubtful as they were estranged from about January 1896, and even if they rekindled the relationship, it seems to have ended by January 1898. Furthermore, William is not listed on Thomas Rockwell's birth certificate, and by the time Bridget Rockwell was born in March of 1902, William had already relocated, courted, married and moved in with his second wife in Sydney.

Mary Rockwell (nee Brook) seemingly had a track record of illegitimate offspring as she had previously given birth to four children all with unidentified fathers. It is possible that by naming William as the father of her latest two children, she hoped to retain her respectability, and perhaps gain some financial assistance. With William Henry Rockwell often being away as a sailor, naming him as the father of her children would have been a relatively easy thing to do. Investigations into what subsequently happened to Thomas Peter Rockwell, Bridget Catherine Mary Rockwell or their mother Mary have been unsuccessful. In any event, having relocated to Sydney, William now turned his attention to a 34 year old widow of four children, named Elizabeth.

After arriving in Sydney in 1900, and particularly after his second marriage in 1901, William Henry Rockwell's life became much easier to trace and seems never to have fallen foul of the law. From all reports he was a stern man and provided an admirable example of a hard working father to his boys. His five sons too, never fell in on the wrong side of the law and indeed, they were all involved with St Johns Church, Glebe, showing at the very least that William supported their religious development. If William Henry Rockwell did live a shadowy past, the evidence to support any transgressions has not been found.

Apart from snippets of information that have emerged during his time in Melbourne and Fremantle, questions abound about William's earlier days as a sailor, with his first 30 years being much less well known. This genealogy continues by researching William Henry Rockwell's second wife Elizabeth Carpenter (nee Bantin), as it is by her that the Rockwell family was formed, so it is her fascinating story that must next be told.

References

1. Victorian Dept of BDM. (1894). Marriage Certificate for William Henry Rockwell & Mary Bates (nee Brook) - #63/1894.
2. NSW Dept of BDM. (1901). Marriage Certificate for William Henry Rockwell & Elizabeth Carpenter (nee Bantin), #8525/1901.
3. NSW Dept of BDM. (1866). Birth for Elizabeth Bantin - #211/1866.
4. Victorian Dept of BDM. (1894). Marriage Certificate for William Henry Rockwell & Mary Bates (nee Brook) - #63/1894.
5. Family Tree DNA. (2019). Analysis for Tracy Rockwell (2019)... Y111 Paternal Haplogroup N-M231 (Finland).
6. Rockwell, Alice, 1911-1997 (Interviewee, 1980). 'Alice Rockwell (nee Greenup) interviewed by Tracy Rockwell on the 12th of June 1980, at Kyeemagh, Sydney'.
7. Ibid.
8. Ibid.
9. Hyde, Joy, 1927-2018 (Interviewee, 2001). 'Joy Hyde (nee Rockwell) interviewed by Tracy Rockwell on the 19th of August 2001, at Aspley, Brisbane'.
10. Ibid.
11. Rockwell, Alice, 1911-1997 (Interviewee, 1980). op.cit.
12. Hyde, Joy, 1927-2018 (Interviewee, 2001). op. cit.
13. Chadwick, F.E., Ocean steamships (1891) New York: C. Scribner's Sons, p. 225-226.
14. Wikipedia - "SS Ionic." [https://en.wikipedia.org/wiki/SS_Ionic_(1883)]. Retrieved 15 April 2021.
15. Ibid.
16. Rockwell, Cheryl, 1945-2013 (Interviewee, 2003). 'Cheryl Rockwell (nee Pooley) interviewed by Tracy Rockwell on the 23rd of April 2003, at St. Ives, Sydney'.
17. Ibid.
18. 'William H. Rockwell - Accident.' The Age, 19th Sep 1890, p.7.
19. Victorian Dept of BDM. (1894). Marriage Certificate for William Henry Rockwell & Mary Bates (nee Brook) - #63/1894.
20. William H. Rockwell - Assault on Henry Hoag.' The Age, 6th Jan. 1894, p.2.
21. 'William H. Rockwell - Assault on Henry Hoag.' The Age, 12th Jan. 1894, p.6.
22. Ibid.
23. Victorian Dept of BDM. (1894). Marriage Certificate for William Henry Rockwell & Mary Bates (nee Brook) - #63/1894.
24. 'William H. Rockwell - Deserters of Wives & Children.' Victorian Police Gazette, 29 January 1896.
25. 'William H. Rockwell - Deserters of Wives & Children.' NSW Police Gazette, 4 March 1896.
26. 'William H. Rockwell - Deserters of Wives & Children.' Victorian Police Gazette, 1 December 1897, p.373.
27. 'Wm. Rockwell - Fine.' West Australian, 14th February 1898, p.2.
28. 'W. Rockwell - Fine.' The Inquirer & Commercial News, WA, 18th February 1898, p.11.
29. Rockwell, Alice, 1911-1997 (Interviewee, 1980). op.cit.
30. Victorian Dept of BDM. (1899). Birth Certificate for Peter Thomas Rockwell, #10909/1899.
31. Victorian Dept of BDM. (1902). Birth Certificate for Bridget Catherine Mary Rockwell, #13355/1902.

Chapter Three

ELIZABETH BANTIN

(Mother of Robert Archibald Rockwell)

Elizabeth Bantin was the seventh child of Robert Bantin, a painter and paperhanger born in London, England in 1836, and Mary Barrett born 1834 from the tiny village of Puttenham, Surrey. They had married at St Pancras Church in London on the 1st December 1855 ahead of seizing an opportunity to emigrate to Sydney in 1857 aboard the "Admiral Lyons."[1]

Elizabeth was born on the 12th of October 1866,[2] a year in world history which saw the parliament of Canada meet for the first time in Ottawa, with the Dominion of Canada being created the next year. The Austro-Prussian War began when the Austrians and most of the medium German states declared war on Prussia, and it was the year that dynamite was invented by Alfred Nobel. In Australia, gold was discovered at Gympie in Queensland and the future Saint Mary MacKillop founded the Sisters of St Joseph of the Sacred Heart.

Notable people born in 1866 included the American outlaw Butch Cassidy (13 April), the prolific English writer Herbert George Wells (21 Sept), and the Scottish journalist, politician and future Prime Minister of the United Kingdom Ramsay MacDonald, who shared Elizabeths birthday. For a detailed account of Elizabeth Bantin's ancestry see Volume 2 of the Rockwell Genealogies - "To The Great South Land."

Elizabeth was preceded by no less than seven siblings, although only three had survived by the time Elizabeth arrived at Cowper St. in Glebe, Sydney, when she immediately became

▲ Birth certificate for Elizabeth Bantin, 12th October 1866 (NSW BDM #211/1866). ◀

the younger sister of Mary Robertia (8), Walter (4) and Lily (1). Although her parents were remarkably fertile, they had great difficulties with child mortality as no less than seven of their children were to die before the age of five. The first born had been Robert G. Bantin, who was born in London on the 13th November 1856. Elizabeth's parents then departed from Liverpool on the 13th June 1857, but sadly, the number '13' proved to be unlucky and their infant son Robert G. Bantin passed away on the voyage.

The purpose of the long journey south was to take charge over the paint and paperhanging business of Robert's maternal uncle, John Leighton Drewe, who had died the previous year. [Ref] Robert and Mary Bantin arrived in Sydney on the 15th September 1857, just three weeks after of the catastrophic loss of the "Dunbar" at Sydney Heads, one of the colonies worst ever maritime disasters.[3]

A Brief History of Glebe

The young couple soonafter settled into the developing suburb of Glebe,[Ref] which had already developed a fascinating history. In 1820 the Church and School Corporation had been given control of the Glebe lands with property auctions being held as early as 1828. Glebe Point Road was also created that year and the first 'Hereford House' was built in 1829, although it has since been demolished.

The elaborate 'Toxteth Park' property was completed in 1831, along with a number of other superb homes including Lyndhurst (1836), Margaretta Cottage (1836), Tranby (c.1840) and Rothwell Lodge (c.1840s). The future first prime minister of Australia, Edmund Barton was born in Glebe in 1849, which by that time had about 1,000 people residing there. The first mail arrived at Glebe about 1852, with the Glebe Island Abattoirs opening in 1857, the same year the Bantins arrived from England.

Glebe Public School opened in 1858, with gas lighting (1860) and town water (1862) following soonafter. By the time the Glebe Municipal Council had formed in 1859, the suburb's population had increased to over 3,700. At this time a number of notable buildings were erected including Rosebank House (c.1858), Bidura (1860), Hamilton (1860s), Briarbank (1862), the Australian Youth Hotel (before 1867), The Hermitage (1866) and Reussdale (c.1868). By 1861, the estimated population of Sydney and its suburbs climbed to approximately 95,000.

In 1870 the Blackwattle Bay swamp had been reclaimed and the number of inhabitants in Glebe was nudging 6,000. More notable structures were erected such as St. Johns Church (1870), the second Hereford House (1874), Benledi (1875), Kinrarra (1877) and the Mitchell St Terraces (Lorne, Park, Magnolia from 1875-9). Wentworth Park was proclaimed (1885), properties began to be sewered from 1885 and a steam tram service commenced to Glebe Point and Forest Lodge from the city.

Glebe Town Hall opened in 1880 and the terraced shops along Glebe Point Road began springing up. Other notable structures to be erected about this time were the Police Station (1883), Bellevue on Glebe Point (c.1883), Palmerston Terrace at 257-287 Glebe Point Rd (1882-4), Herberto Terrace at 2-18 Boyce St (1885), Cliff Terrace at 2-8 Crescent Lane (1888), the Glebe Courthouse (1889) and Kerribree (1889). However, by 1890 the colony's economy was stalled by a significant depression and much development came to a standstill.[4]

The Bantin Family

The first Australian born Bantin child was Mary Robertia Bantin, who arrived in 1858.[5] After her came Jane Bantin, who could have been born in 1860 (no birth found), but she died in 1861.[6] There was another male Walter H. [Bautin], born in 1862 and female Lilly V. [Bautin], born in 1865.[7,8] Rosa A. Bantin was also born in 1865, but she died in 1866.[9,10] It was in October of 1866 that Elizabeth was born, but sadly, both Walter and Lilly V. Bantin tragically died in 1867, aged just five and two respectively.[11,12] Elizabeth of course, never met her grandparents in England, and sadly her surviving grandmothers Mary Bantin (nee Drewe) and Mary Barrett (nee Avenell) both died in England, in 1868 and 1869 respectively.

By 1869 with Mary Robertia Bantin aged 11, Elizabeth at the fragile age of just 2½, and having already lost six of her siblings, the two surviving sisters were joined by another sister in Jane Matilda Bantin.[13] Jane was followed by Richard John Bantin in 1870[14] and a Francis Bantin, who sadly died in 1873.[15] The last child to arrive in the Bantin family was George Barrett Bantin, who was named after his maternal grandfather and was welcomed into the family in 1874.[16]

▲ LEFT: Glebe Public School (c.1870) was erected by 1858 and was likely the local school for the Bantin children from the 1860s. RIGHT: Elizabeth Bantin most likely worshiped at St. Johns Church, Glebe, which was built c.1870.

Like most folk of the time, the Bantins were parishioners of the Anglican faith, and most probably attended at St. Barnabas Church on Broadway, or perhaps occasionally at St. Johns Church on Glebe Point Road. The Bantins were residing in Glebe when the official opening of St. John's Church at Glebe occurred on the 21st of December 1870.[17] Robert Bantin was 35, Mary 37, Mary Robertia 12, Elizabeth 4 and Jane Matilda just an infant. Being a painter and paperhanger, perhaps Elizabeth's father even worked on the interior and exterior decoration of St. Johns Church?

The Sands Sydney Directories records the Bantin family as living in Glebe at a number of different addresses, from the time they arrived in 1857:

Robert & Mary Bantin in Sands Sydney Directory for 1860 to 1894 [18]

1861 - 5 Kensington St. (Parramatta & Botany Sts)	1879 - Parramatta Rd. Glebe (Business?)
1863 - Cowper St. Glebe	1884 - 8 Campbell Tce., Campbell St. Glebe
1873 - Broughton St. Glebe	1885 - 11 Talfourd St. Glebe
1875 - Cowper St. Glebe	

Little is known of Elizabeth's education except that she would have begun school around the year 1872. The Bantin children were most likely to have attended either St. Johns Church school, Glebe Public School (from 1880), or Forest Lodge Public School (from 1883).

Unfortunately, few anecdotes have survived of Elizabeth's teen or young adult years, however as a 17 year old she would no doubt have attended the wedding of her older sister Mary Robertia Bantin to Auguste Thuaux in 1883.[19] Tragically however, the very next year, and at the age of only 18, Elizabeth lost her father Robert Bantin on the 29th of May 1884, aged just 48.[20] This left her mother Mary Bantin to care for her younger siblings Jane (15), Richard (14) and George (10). Another five years would go by before Elizabeth was to meet and marry her first husband, an English born carpenter, who coincidentally went by the name of Arthur Carpenter.

▲ King St. Sydney c.1900. The bustling scene that Elizabeth Bantin would have confronted as a young lady in Sydney.

Chart 3.0 Descendants of Elizabeth Bantin & Arthur Carpenter

Arthur Carpenter 1861-1896 = Elizabeth Bantin 1866-1955

m.1889 at St Pauls Church, Redfern, NSW

| William H. Sampson 1897-1958 *Driver* | AileenVera Carpenter 1890-1985 | Arthur Clazebrook Carpenter 1891-1967 | Lillian T. Thomas 1901-1982 | Eric D'Arcy Carpenter 1893-1980 | Mabel Charlotte Jolly 1891-1964 | Leslie Harold Carpenter 1895-1971 | Hilda Elizabeth Porter 1900-1944 |

m.1925 Glebe, NSW — *m.1922 Sydney, NSW* — *m.1915 Woollahra, NSW* — *m.1919 Dudley, England*

Shirley Madge Sampson 1929-2001 m.1954 Stanley T. Warmeant 1929-1984 d.s.p.

Arthur Frederick Carpenter 1923-2000 m.1950 Edith V. Turner 1920-2012
1. Ken Carpenter
2. David Carpenter
3. Martin Carpenter
4. Karen Carpenter
5. Timothy Carpenter
6. Glen Carpenter
7. Troy Carpenter
8. Roebe He?
9. Niall?

Evelyn Muriel Carpenter 1925-2000 m.1964 Arthur J. Tetley 1933-1999
1. Brian Tetley
2. Kylie Tetley

Donald Carpenter 1933-1989 d.s.p.

Arthur Eric Carpenter 1916-2014 m.1948 Una Gladys Pitt 1923-2010
1. Eric W. Carpenter 1951
2. Female Carpenter

Gwendolyne Lavelle Carpenter 1920-2012 m.1950 Charles M. Henderson 1918-1983
1. Lyndal Henderson
2. Stephanie Henderson

1m.1939 Colin Ross Semple 1919-1998 d.s.p.

Aileen Phyllis Carpenter 1921-1992

2mc.1942 Roy Francis Drew 1920-1995 d.s.p.
1. Judith E. Drew 1945-2019
2. John Drew 1946-2018
3. Helen Drew
4. Sue Drew
5. Valerie Drew
6. Peter Drew
7. Geoffrey Drew

Leslie Darcy Carpenter 1925-1984 d.s.p.

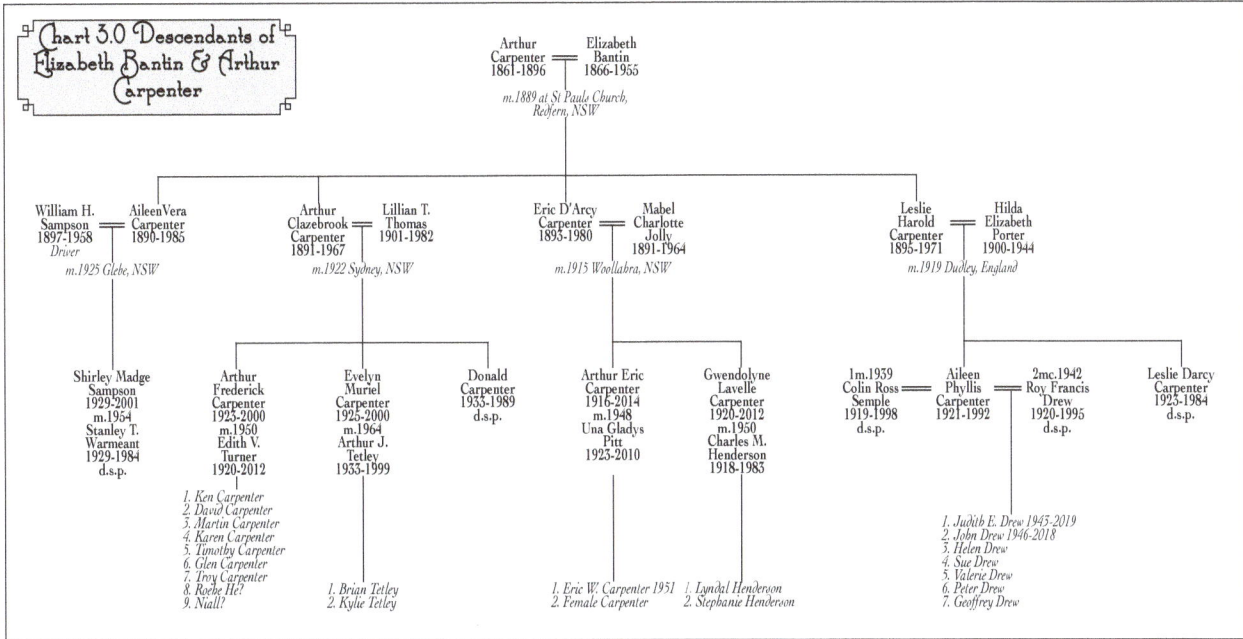

AileenVera Carpenter

Stanley Thomas Warmeant

Shirley Madge Sampson

Arthur Clazebrook Carpenter

Arthur Frederick Carpenter

Edith V. Turner

Eric D'Arcy Carpenter

Mabel Charlotte Jolly

Arthur Eric Carpenter

Una Gladys Pitt

Charles M. Henderson

Gwendolyne Lavelle Carpenter

While at the annual picnic of the St. John's Baptist Sunday School, Glebe, at Correy's Gardens, yesterday, a schoolboy named Leslie Carpenter, living at the Kiama College, Hereford-street, Forest Lodge, fell from a limb of a tree while searching for birds' nests. He sustained a compound fracture of each arm, and concussion of the brain. After being attended to by Dr. Blaxland, of Concord, he was taken by the Civil Ambulance to the Sydney Hospital, where Dr. Shellshear admitted him for treatment.

Arthur Eric CARPENTER, 11.8.1916 - 5.4.2014 At Culburra Retirement Village Formerly of Greenwell Point and Bronte. Much loved father, grandfather and great-grandfather Aged 97 years.

A long life well lived Privately cremated at Worrigee Cemetery,

Nowra Murphy Family Funerals (02) 4423 0722

Sydney Morning Herald, 12 April, 2014

Arthur Frederick CARPENTER (1923-2000) & Edith Veronica CARPENTER (nee Turner, 1920-2012). September 24, 2012. Peacefully at Garrawarra Nursing Home. EDITH'S relatives and friends are invited to her funeral service at Woronora Crematorium, West Chapel, on Tuesday (October 2, 2012) commencing 2.30 p.m.

Sincerity Funerals (02) 9540 9559

Sydney Morning Herald on 28 Sep 2012

▲ABOVE (Left): Les Carpenter's Injury (Newcastle Morning Herald, 2nd Dec 1907, p.5). (Centre): Arthur Eric Carpenter (grandson of Elizabeth Bantin & Arthur Carpenter) - Death Notice (SMH, 12 April 2014). (Right): Edith Veronica Carpenter (nee Turner) - Death notice (SMH, 28 Sept 2012).

Documents for Aileen Vera Carpenter (1890-1985) & Family

REGISTER BOOK for the use of Ministers authorized to celebrate Marriages under the Acts Nos. 15 and 17, 1899.

MARRIAGES Solemnized in the District of _____, in the State of New South Wales, by _____, at

REGISTER BOOK for the use of Ministers authorised to celebrate Marriages.

MARRIAGES Solemnized in the State of New South Wales, by _____

FOREST LODGE

WARMEANT, Shirley. — March 6, 2001, late of Waterfall, formerly of Jannali. Much loved wife of Stan (deceased).

Aged 72 years.

At Peace.

SHIRLEY'S family and friends are invited to attend her funeral service, to be held at Olsen's Chapel, corner Old Princes Highway and Toronto Parade, Sutherland, on Tuesday (March 13, 2001), at 2 p.m.

OLSENS
Australian Owned
Family Business Since 1944

A.F.D.A. Sutherland. 9545 3477

▲ *TOP: William H. Sampson & Aileen Vera Carpenter - Marriage Certificate (NSW Dept of BDM, #16577/1925). MID: Stanley Thomas Warmeant & Shirley Madge Sampson - Marriage Certificate (NSW Dept of BDM, #22613/1954). ABOVE (Left): Well dressed passengers board the tram to Forest Lodge, Sydney c.1897. (Right): Death & funeral notices for Shirley Warmeant (nee Sampson), granddaughter of Elizabeth Bantin (SMH, 8 March 2001).*

The Marriage of Elizabeth Bantin & Arthur Carpenter

Although we don't know the circumstances of how they met, Elizabeth Bantin aged 23, married for the first time on the 18th September 1889, at St. Pauls Church, Redfern to Arthur (1864-1896), the son of George Carpenter from Manchester, England.[21] The year 1889 saw the completion of the railway network between Adelaide, Brisbane, Melbourne and Sydney, and Sir Henry Parkes delivered the 'Tenterfield Oration,' which called for the Federation of the six Australian colonies. Arthur and Elizabeth subsequently brought a daughter and then three sons into their family.

Undoubtedly, Elizabeth and her young family likely attended the marriages of her younger siblings Jane Matilda Bantin to John William Jones in 1892,[22] and Richard John Bantin to Clarissa Bonfield in 1893.[23] Unfortunately, Elizabeth Bantin sadly lost her husband Arthur in 1896, apparently from consumption (tuberculosis).[24]

Descendents of Elizabeth & Arthur Carpenter

1. Aileen Vera Carpenter (1890-1985)

Aileen Vera Carpenter was first born of Elizabeth's ten children on the 12th March 1890.[25] She was only seven years old when her father died, but she was apparently a great help to her mother Elizabeth and assisted in rearing all the children that came after her, especially the Rockwell boys during her teen and young adult years. Aileen would most probably have attended school at Forest Lodge or Glebe Public School.

At 35 years of age, Aileen married in 1925 at Glebe to a younger man William (1897-1958), a transport driver and the son of William and Ethel Sampson.[26] Aileen delivered her only child, Shirley Madge Sampson (1929-2001) in 1929. Aunty Aileen, as she was known would occasionally invite her half-brother Bob Rockwell's family over for afternoon tea, but sternly frowned upon any misbehaviour by his more than playful Rockwell children.[27]

As the years rolled by Aileen Sampson took up residence at 892 King Georges Rd, South Hurstville and became increasingly protective of her mother, but never warmed to her step-father, William Henry Rockwell. She succeeded in pulling her mother away from William as he was not an easy man to live with, but they apparently reconciled more than once. However, after William Henry Rockwell suffered his stroke, Aileen took her mother in for good, and Elizabeth Rockwell remained with her only daughter for the rest of her days. Aileen was to live the longest of all Elizabeth's children, reaching the age of 95, with her sole descendant being her daughter Shirley (*see 3.1 Descendants of Elizabeth Bantin & Arthur Carpenter*).

2. Arthur Clazebrook Carpenter (1891-1967) ▲

Arthur Clazebrook Carpenter (1891-1967), was their second child born in October of 1891, and was just six when his father died.[28] He too would most probably have attended

#N467215 Arthur Frederick Carpenter (1923 - 1973)

▼The Volunteer Defence Corps (VDC) was an Australian part-time volunteer military force of World War II modelled on the British Home Guard.

CARPENTER, Arthur Frederick; Service Number - N467215; Date of Birth: 13/8/1923; Place of Birth - Leeton NSW; Place of Enlistment - Nth Gogeldrie NSW on 13/3/1942; Next of Kin - (Father) CARPENTER Arthur. He was a grandson of Elizabeth Carpenter (nee Bantin).

World War Two Service

LANCE CORPORAL
ARTHUR FREDERICK CARPENTER
N467215

SERVICE	AUSTRALIAN ARMY
DATE OF BIRTH	13 AUGUST 1923
PLACE OF BIRTH	LEETON, NSW
DATE OF ENLISTMENT	13 MARCH 1942
LOCALITY ON ENLISTMENT	NORTH GOGELDRIE, NSW
PLACE OF ENLISTMENT	LEETON, NSW
NEXT OF KIN	CARPENTER, ARTHUR
DATE OF DISCHARGE	30 SEPTEMBER 1945
POSTING AT DISCHARGE	17 BATTALION VOLUNTEER DEFENCE CORPS PART TIME DUTY

Australian Government
Department of Veterans' Affairs

Documents for Arthur Clazebrook Carpenter (1891-1967) & Family

Soldier Settlement Scheme

The New South Wales government introduced the Returned Soldiers Settlement Act in 1916. Soldiers were eligible to apply for Crown Lands if they had served overseas with the Australian Imperial Forces or with the British Defence Service. The soldiers also needed to have been honourably discharged to be eligible.

Crown land was used where possible, but much land was acquired. By 1924, just over 24 million acres (97,000 km²) had been acquired or allocated. Of this nearly 6.3 million acres (25,000 km²) was purchased and 18 million acres (73,000 km²) was crown land set aside and 23.2 million acres (93,900 km²) had been allotted through 23,367 farms across Australia.

The States wished to take an active role in recognising the contribution of soldiers. The land was available on affordable terms and they could also receive advances of money to make improvements to the land, which was often in poor condition. They could also use the money for equipment, plant, stock and seeds. However, soldiers who had received smaller blocks of land often experienced significant hardships.

SURRENDERS OF LEASES WITHIN AN IRRIGATION AREA.

Yanco Land District. Yanco No. 1 Irrigation Area.—Keith M. M'Mutrie. 57a., parish Yarangery; Winifred H. Williams, 50a., parish Yarangery; Arthur C. Carpenter, 204a. 1r. parish Tenningerie.

Arthur Claybrook Carpenter's premises, Farm 998, Leeton, were visited at 10.30 a.m. on the 18th, when the drains, walls and floors were very dirty and the yard appeared to have not been cleaned for weeks. Fined £2 and 8/- costs.

NOXIOUS WEED SUMMONSES.

Mr. W. A. Flynn, police magistrate, who relieved Mr. H. L. Adams, at the monthly sittings of the Leeton Petty Sessions Court, on Tuesday and Wednesday, was reminded he was back in Leeton, when the cases for failing to destroy Bathurst Burrs were listed by the W.C. and I.C. Arthur Clazebrook Carpenter, Richard Parker Crozier, Harold Lammas and Anton Marinus Foulsen were each fined £1 and 8/- costs for failing to keep down Bathurst Burrs.

NOXIOUS WEEDS

BLACK AND SAFFRON THISTLE GROWERS

CONTRIBUTE OVER £30 IN FINES

BURR GROWERS NEXT

The long list of cases set down for hearing before the police magistrate Mr. T. W. Cohen, at the Leeton petty sessions court on Tuesday afternoon, appeared on the face of it a late night, but 23 noxious weeds cases were dealt with practically the stroke of a pen. Each sent in a plea of guilty and a fine of £1 with 8/- costs was imposed against each of the following settlers:— Herbert David Anderson, James Stephen Aylett Michael James Broadhurst, Arthur Clazebrook Carpenter, Mary

Arthur Carpenter, according to the inspector's report had not cleaned up any weeds. It was a pretty dirty farm of 200 acres. This time last year he had a previous conviction. Defendant said that since the last week in March he had been busy getting his rice crop off. The P.M. said: "So far as I'm concerned you'll have to keep the weeds down, or find it very expensive." Fined £8, and 8/- costs.

INTERFERENCE

FARMER FINED

Fined £3 with costs and ordered to pay £15 compensation to the W.C. and I.C., Arthur Glazebrook Carpenter, of Farm 998, Gogeldrie, was charged before Mr. D. F. Parker P.M., in the Leeton Court of Petty Sessions, last week, with having interfered with a Commission structure. The defendant, it was stated, was taking a header from one place to another. He had to cross two bridges belonging to the Commission and pulled the sides off the bridges in doing so. The damage so caused amounted to £15.

Forfeiture of Holdings Within Yanco No. 1 Irrigation Area

Non-irrigable Lease No. 24, portion No. 485, parish of Willimbong; area, 297 acres 1 rood; holder, Walter Frederick Pinhorn.

Irrigation Farm Lease No. 1449, portion 3, parish of Hebden; area, 226 acres 2 roods; holder, William Thomas Edmondson.

Irrigation Farm Lease No. 1110, portions Nos. 198, 199, 200, parish of Tenningerie; area, 605 acres; holder, Arthur Clazebrook Carpenter.

FURTHER SHIRE RATE JUDGMENTS

Willimbong Shire obtained the following judgments at Leeton Small Debts Court on Wednesday. Mary Stevenson (executrix of the estate of the late Hugh Stevenson) £11/5/6, costs 8/-; Wilfred Thomas Henham, £22 6/1, costs £1/7/6; William Williams, £20/13/9; costs £1/3/0; Henry Hall Lehman, £21/12/8; costs £1/1/6; Arthur Carpenter, £26/9/6, costs 18/6; Sarah Alive McDowell, £29/3/1, costs £1/1/6.

In the Court of Petty Sessions before the P.M. yesterday, Arthur C. Carpenter was charged on summons with failing to return expired certificate of registration of a trailer. Defendant did not appear and the case was heard ex-parte. Sergeant Dunn gave formal evidence. A letter from defendant to the Transport Department, stating that the certificate had been sent in, but no acknowledgement received was put before the court, also letter from the Transport Office stating that the certificate had not been received. Defendant was convicted and a fine of 10/- with 8/- court costs, in default two days' imprisonment, was imposed.

Arthur Frederick CARPENTER (1923-2000) & Edith Veronica CARPENTER (nee Turner, 1920-2012), September 24, 2012. Peacefully at Garrawarra Nursing Home. EDITH'S relatives and friends are invited to her funeral service at Woronora Crematorium, West Chapel, on Tuesday October 2, 2012 commencing 2.30 p.m. Sincerity Funerals Serving Sydney's South Ph: 9540 9559

Sydney Morning Herald, 28 Sept. 2012

▲LEFT COLUMN: 1-Leases (The Albury Banner, 1st July, p.44); 2-Unclean Dairies (The M'bidgee Irrigator, 20th March, p.5); 3-Fine (The M'bidgee Irrigator, 24th May, p.2). CENTRE COLUMN: 1-Fine (The M'bidgee Irrigator, 25th Feb, p.2). 2-Fine (The M'bidgee Irrigator, 22nd June, p.2). 3-Farming Fine (The Murrumbidgee Irrigator, 30th July 1929, p.1). RIGHT COLUMN: 1-Forfeit Holding (The Albury Banner, 14th March, p.35); 2-Judgements (The M'bidgee Irrigator, 25th July, p.2); 3-Fine (The Riverine Grazier, 21st May, p.2). ▶Mrs Arthur Carpenter [Lillian T. Thomas - Workers for Soldiers Day (The Sun, 4th March, p.19).

WORKERS FOR SOLDIERS' DAY

Mrs. E. Croft with the friends who will assist her at her stall to-morrow. From left to right the picture shows:—Back row: Mrs. Arthur Carpenter, Mrs. H. C. McIntyre, Mrs. Norma Taylor, Mrs. F. Holdridge, Miss Mary Doberer. Middle row: Miss B. Howse, Mrs. C. H. Tindale, Mrs. E. Croft, Mrs. S. Standford, Mrs. C. Wood. Front: Mrs. Cecil Disher, Mrs. Colin Graham.

#2804 Arthur Clazebrook Carpenter

Arthur Clazebrook Carpenter (Reg. #2804) enlisted in the AIF on the 7th June 1915 at Victoria Barracks, Paddington, NSW. He listed himself as being 23yrs and 9 mths of age and was working as a 'Groom', but gave his mother's postal address as 11 Charles Street, Forest Lodge, Sydney. He was 5'5.25" tall, grey eyes, fair complexion with fair hair and was a C of E.

▶Arthur Clazebrook Carpenter was born in 1891, at Glebe, to Arthur Carpenter and Elizabeth Bantin.

He embarked from Australia on the 30th September 1915 aboard "HMAT Argyllshire." He was initially assigned to the 9th Reinforcements from 6th Jan. 1916 then transferred on the 13th Feb. to the 53rd Battalion in defence of the Suez Canal against the Turks. On the 8th March he was transferred to the 5th Division A.F.A. and from there was 'taken on strength' by the 25th Howitzer Brigade at Tel el Kebir and posted to the 114th Battery, and transferred again to the 115th Battery two months later.

On the 19th June 1916 his brigade proceeded from Alexandria aboard the "SS Canada" to France and disembarked in Marseilles on the 25th June. He was then transferred back to the 114th Battery and fought with the 14th Field Artillery Brigade for the remainder of the war as a Gunner and Saddler.

He returned to Australia aboard the "SS Kildonian Castle" on the 21st March 1919, disembarked on the 19th May 1919 and was discharged on the 2nd July 1919. On the 12th March 1920 he received the 1914/15 Star (#2147), the British War Medal (#19104) and the Victory Medal (#18885).

▲The "HMAT Argyllshire" that conveyed Arthur C. Carpenter to Egypt in Sept. 1915; The AIF encampment at Tel el Kebir, Egypt; Field Artillery Brigade at Instructional Camp, Swanage, England (18th Sept 1916) Arthur C. Carpenter fought alongside a similar brigade of AIF soldiers. ◀Bringing up the howitzer shells for another pounding of 'Fritz's' lines by the 54th Siege Battery in 1917. ▼The "SS Kildonian Castle" brought Arthur C. Carpenter safe home to Australia in May 1919.

#5662 Leslie Harold Carpenter

Leslie Harold Carpenter (Reg. #5662) followed his elder brother Arthur to war and enlisted in the AIF on the 10th Jan. 1916 at Victoria Barracks, Paddington, NSW. He listed himself as being 20yrs and 5mths of age and was working as a drover, but gave his mother's postal address as 11 Charles Street, Forest Lodge, Sydney. He was 5'7.75" tall, grey eyes, fair complexion with dark brown hair, and was a C of E.

He embarked from Australia on the 3rd June 1916 aboard "HMAT Kyarra" [A55]. He was assigned to the 3rd Battalion (12th to 23rd reinforcements) many of whom had only recently been withdrawn from the Gallipoli campaign. He disembarked in Plymouth on the 3rd August 1916. By 16th November 1916 the 3rd Australian Division arrived in France from England where it had been training since its arrival from Australia. The division was sent to the 'nursery' sector around Armentieres as part of II ANZAC Corps, but they returned to the trenches in the final phase of the Somme campaign, which ended in November and spent the terrible winter of 1916-1917 consolidating the forward positions near Bapaume, France. In 1917, the Australians were again heavily engaged at Bapaume in March, at Bullecourt and Messines in May and June and from September to November, in the great battle of the Ypres offensive – Menin Road, Polygon Wood, Broodseinde, Poelcapelle and Passchendaele. The casualties sustained made it difficult to maintain the strength of the Australian divisions and a partially formed 6th Australian Division was disbanded in order to provide reinforcements.

In March and April 1918, the Australian Corps played a prominent part in the defence of Amiens, Hazebrouck and Villiers-Bretonneux, during a massive German multi-pronged attack in France and Belgium known as the 'Kaiserschacht' or the Spring Offensive.

Leslie Carpenter was promoted to Lance Corporal on the 27th April 1918. He was wounded in action on the 21st June 1918 and invalided for the remainder of the war. While recovering from his wounds, he met and then married Hilda Elizabeth Porter on the 4th January 1919 and she returned to Australia with Les aboard the same troopship. They sailed aboard the "SS Canberra" on the 23rd July 1919, disembarked on the 14th September 1919 and Les Carpenter was discharged on the 30th October 1919. On the 12th March 1920 he received the 1914/15 Star, the British War Medal (#47389) and the Victory Medal (#46274).

▲ "HMAT Kyarra" A55 the ship that conveyed Leslie H. Carpenter to England; Wounded men of the 3rd Australian Division surrounded by the bodies of their dead comrades at the railway cutting on the Ypres-Roulers line during the battle of Passchendaele in October 12th, 1917. ▶The wartime marriage certificate of Leslie H. Carpenter and Hilda Elizabeth Porter. ▼AIF soldiers recovering from their injuries in a London Hospital in 1918; The French town of Bapaume in ruins 1917; Les Carpenter was decorated with an AIF Wound Stripe.

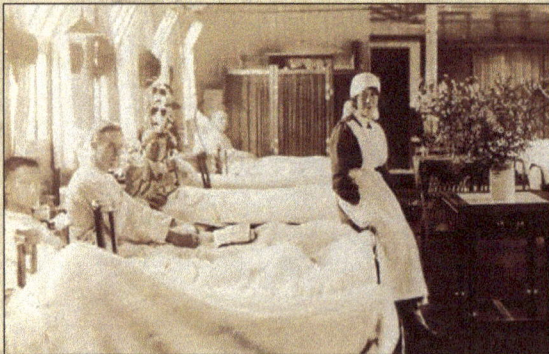

school at Forest Lodge Public School. Sadly, we know little of Arthur's early life except that he was evicted from the family home by his step-father William Henry Rockwell, probably about 1908.

Prior to the commencement of World War I, Arthur C. Carpenter may have married an Alice E. Brien sometime in 1914? However, Arthur enlisted in the AIF on the 7th June 1915. He fought as a gunner in the artillery brigades of the 5th Division in both the Suez and in France. After returning from the war he married in 1922 to Lillian Theresa Thomas (1901-1982), with whom he resided on his property at Leeton, NSW.[29]

Arthur was a beneficiary of the 'Soldier Settlement Scheme' and was allocated 'Farm 1110' at Whitton, later purchasing 'Farm 998' at North Gogeldrie, NSW. But he seemed to struggle with farming as he racked up a string of fines and summonses for various minor incursions of the farming code. Arthur died in Leeton, NSW in 1967 and produced three children (see 3.1 Descendants of Elizabeth Bantin & Arthur Carpenter).

3. Eric D'Arcy Carpenter (1893-1980)

Eric Carpenter was born in 1893 and was the third child of Elizabeth and Arthur

▲ TOP (Left): Lane in Redfern c.1911, by Harold Cazneaux. (Right): Aileen Sampson's residence at 892 King Georges Rd. South Hurstville. ABOVE: 1940 Hurstville South Public School - Class 6B 1940 with Shirley Madge Sampson (circled).

Carpenter.[30] He married twice... first on 25th September 1915 at All Saints Church, Woollahra to Mabel Charlotte Jolly (1891-1964) with whom he had at least two children.[31] And secondly some 50 years later to Rose Maud Chase in 1965.[32] Eric Carpenter worked as a chauffeur for the W.D. & H.O. Wills Tobacco Co. in Rosebery.[33] For his children by his first marriage (*see 3.1 Descendants of Elizabeth Bantin & Arthur Carpenter*).

4. Leslie Harold Carpenter (1895-1971) △

Leslie Harold Carpenter (1895-1971), was born in August of 1895.[34] Young Leslie experienced a terrible fall at the age of 12, but apparently made a full recovery.[35] Little is known of Les Carpenter prior to his joining the AIF, but he followed in the footsteps of his big brother Arthur, and enlisted in the AIF in January of 1916.

Les Carpenter was allocated to the infantry in the AIF 3rd Division in France. Unfortunately, he was wounded and invalided out of the war. Whilst recovering in an English hospital Les Carpenter met Hilda Elizabeth Porter (1901-1944), and they married on the 4th January 1919 at the Dudley & Stafford Registrar Office in London.[36] Les and 'Tis,' as she was known, returned to Australia together in 1919 aboard the troopship "SS Canberra."

3.1 Descendants of Elizabeth Bantin & Arthur Carpenter

Elizabeth Bantin (1866-1955), was born in Glebe, she married on the 18th September 1889 at St Pauls Church, Redfern to Arthur (1864-1896), son of George CARPENTER of Manchester, England, with issue:

1. Aileen Vera Carpenter (1890-1985), married in 1925 at Glebe to William H. S. SAMPSON (1897-1958), with issue:
1.1 Shirley Madge Sampson (1929-2001), married in 1954 to Stanley (1929-1984), son of Alfred & Minnie WARMEANT of Wales, no issue.

2. Arthur Clazebrook CARPENTER (1891-1967) △ (#2804) married in 1922 at Sydney to Lillian Theresa Thomas (1901-1982), with issue:
2.1 Arthur Frederick CARPENTER (1923-2000), △ (#N467215) was married in 1950 to Edith Veronica Turner (1920-2012) in Petersham (# 9672), with issue:
a. Ken CARPENTER
b. David CARPENTER
c. Martin CARPENTER
d. Karen Carpenter
e. Timothy CARPENTER
f. Glen CARPENTER
g. Troy CARPENTER
h. Roehe He ?
i. Niall Euan ?

2.2 Evelyn Muriel Carpenter (1925-2000) married in 1964 to Arthur J. TETLEY (1933-1999),with issue:
a. Brian TETLEY (?)
b. Kylie Tetley (?)
2.3 Donald CARPENTER (1933-1989), issue unknown.

3. Eric D'Arcy CARPENTER (1893-1980), married in 1915 at Woollahra to Mabel Charlotte Jolly (1891-1964), with issue:
3.1 Arthur Eric CARPENTER (1916-2014), △ (#NX114786) married in 1948 to Una Gladys Pitt

(1923-2010) in Sydney, with issue:
a. Eric Westhorpe CARPENTER (1951)
b. Female Carpenter (?)
3.2 Gwendolyne Lavelle Carpenter (1920-2012), married in 1950 to Charles M. HENDERSON (1918-1983), with issue:
a. Lyndal Lavelle Henderson (1951)
b. Stephanie Henderson (?)

4. Leslie Harold Carpenter (1895-1971), △ (#5662) married in 1919 in London to Hilda Elizabeth Porter (1901-1944), with issue:
4.1 Aileen Phyllis Carpenter (1921-1992), married firstly in 1939 to Colin Ross SEMPLE (1919-1998), no issue. Aileen married scondly in 1942 to Roy Francis DREW (1920-1995), with issue:
a. Judith E. Drew (1943-2019)
b. John DREW (1946-2018)
c. Helen Drew
d. Sue Drew
e. Valerie Drew
f. Peter DREW
g. Geoffrey DREW
4.2 Leslie Darcy CARPENTER (1923-1984), no issue.
* Died before adulthood - d.s.p.

▲TOP: Marriage certificate for Elizabeth Bantin and Arthur Carpenter, 18th Sept 1889 (NSW BDM #1321/1889). ABOVE: Funeral Notices for Arthur Carpenter (SMH, 11 March 1897, p.10).

▲LEFT: The Carpenter children grew up in the inner city neighbourhood of Glebe, where the kids gathered in gangs and played on the streets as photographed by Harold Casneaux in 'Surry Hills Street', 1911. RIGHT: Nos. 24, etc., Hunt-street from views taken during 'Cleansing Operations,' Quarantine Area, Sydney, photographed by John Degotardi Jr., 1900. ABOVE (From left): Eric D'Arcy Carpenter & Mabel Jolly, at the marriage of their daughter Gwendolyne Carpenter to Charles M. Henderson, with Mrs Henderson, c.1950.

Les and Tis may have lived around Willoughby for a time, but soonafter the couple bought a property at Lake Cargellico, NSW, also via the Soldier Settlement Scheme. Joy Corelli Rockwell remembers that they called Les's wife 'Aunty Tis' as she was always drinking cups of tea. They may have produced a daughter and a son, possibly also named Les, who was rumored to have joined the Army Commando's during World War II.[37] However, no evidence has been found of their existence to date. Hilda wife passed away in late May of 1944 at just 43 years of age, with Les Carpenter dying almost 30 years later, aged 75 at Seaford in Victoria in 1971, without children.[38]

Abandoned

Following the death of her husband Arthur Carpenter in 1896, Elizabeth was left in a perilous position as a widow of four young children, although her mother Mary Bantin, and her sisters would no doubt have stood by her when they could. After a respectful period, she began her search for a new partner. Apparently Elizabeth was a very stately lady and she placed an advertisement in the newspaper personals for a man of good charcter and honourable intentions, which was eventually replied to by an admirer, by mail some time in early 1901.

Fortunately, the initial meeting and circumstances surrounding how Elizabeth met her second husband have been passed down through the family, whereby after corresponding for a period, the couple arranged to meet on the corner of Glebe Post Office. They were to recognize each other by Elizabeth holding a white handkerchief, and the gentleman wearing a white flower in the button hole of his coat lapel.[39] There must have been some 'sparks' at the outset, as by the end of the year, they had married.

References

1. NSW State Archives & Records. Index to Assisted Immigration 1844-1859, 'Admiral Lyons', p.37. (Reels 2138, 2475).
2. NSW Dept of BDM. (1866). Birth for Elizabeth Bantin - #211/1866.
3. Wikipedia - "Dunbar", [https://en.wikipedia.org/wiki/Dunbar_(ship)] Retrieved 23 March 2023.
4. The Glebe Society. "Glebe History." [https://www.glebesociety.org.au/about-glebe/history-heritage/]. Retrieved 21st January 2020.
5. NSW Dept of BDM. (1858). Birth Certificate for Mary Robertia Bantin, #???/1366.
6. NSW Dept of BDM. (1861). Death Certificate for Jane Bantin, #01435/1861.
7. NSW Dept of BDM. (1862). Birth Certificate for Walter H. Bautin, #2769/1862.
8. NSW Dept of BDM. (1865). Birth Certificate for Lily V. Bautin, #2955/1865.
9. NSW Dept of BDM. (1865). Birth Certificate for Rosa A. Bantin, #2954/1865.
10. NSW Dept of BDM. (1866). Death Certificate for Rosa A. Bantin, #01798/1866.
11. NSW Dept of BDM. (1867). Death Certificate for Walter H. Bantin, #2454/1867.
12. NSW Dept of BDM. (1867). Death Certificate for Lilly Bantin, No. #2420/1867.
13. NSW Dept of BDM. (1869). Birth Certificate for Jane Matilda Bantin, #3405/1869.
14. NSW Dept of BDM. (1870). Birth Certificate for Richard Bantin, #3650/1870.
15. NSW Dept of BDM. (1873). Birth Certificate for Francis Bantin, #3603/1873.
16. NSW Dept of BDM. (1874). Birth Certificate for George Barrett Bantin, #3686/1874.
17. St. John's Church, Glebe, NSW - Parish Records.
18. Sands Sydney Directory (1860-1884). Robert Bantin, Painter & Paperhanger, Glebe.
19. NSW Dept of BDM. (1883). Marriage Certificate for Mary Robertia Bantin & Augusta Thuaux, #1497/1883.
20. NSW Dept of BDM. (1884). Death Certificate for Robert Bantin, #134/1884.
21. NSW Dept of BDM. (1889). Marriage Certificate for Elizabeth Bantin & Arthur Carpenter, #1321/1889.
22. NSW Dept of BDM. (1892). Marriage Certificate for Jane Matilda Bantin & John W. Jones, #2151/1892.
23. NSW Dept of BDM. (1893). Marriage Certificate for Richard John Bantin & Clarissa Bonfield, #519/1893.
24. NSW Dept of BDM. (1897). Death Certificate for Arthur Carpenter, #1172/1897.
25. NSW Dept of BDM. (1890). Birth Certificate for Aileen V. Carpenter, #13122/1890.
26. NSW Dept of BDM. (1925). Marriage Certificate for William H. Sampson & Aileen Vera Carpenter, #16577/1925.
27. Hyde, Joy, 1927-2018 (Interviewee, 2001). 'Joy Hyde (nee Rockwell) interviewed by Tracy Rockwell on the 19th of August 2001, at Aspley, Brisbane'.
28. NSW Dept of BDM. (1891). Birth Certificate for Arthur C. Carpenter, #13638/1891.
29. NSW Dept of BDM. (1922). Marriage Certificate for Arthur Clazebrook Carpenter & Lillian Theresa Thomas, #13263/1922.
30. NSW Dept of BDM. (1893). Birth Certificate for Eric D. Carpenter, #13871/1893.
31. NSW Dept of BDM. (1915). Marriage Certificate for Eric D'Arcy Carpenter & Mabel Charlotte Jolly, #16745/1915.
32. NSW Dept of BDM. (1965). Marriage Certificate for Eric D'Arcy Carpenter & Rose Maud Chase, #18766/1965.
33. Rockwell, Alice, 1911-1997 (Interviewee, 1980). 'Alice Rockwell (nee Greenup) interviewed by Tracy Rockwell on 12 June 1980, at Kyeemagh, Sydney'.
34. NSW Dept of BDM. (1895). Birth Certificate for Leslie H. Carpenter, #19850/1895.
35. 'Leslie Carpenter - Injuries.' Newcastle Morning Herald, 2nd Dec 1907, p.5.
36. UK Dept of BMD. (1919). Marriage Certificate for Leslie Harold Carpenter & Hilda E. Porter, #6b/1375 (Dudley).
37. Hyde, Joy, 1927-2018 (Interviewee, 2001). op. cit.
38. Victoria Dept of BDM (1971). Death certificate for Leslie Harold Carpenter #9359/1971.
39. Rockwell, Alice, 1911-1997 (Interviewee, 1980). op.cit.

Chapter Four

WILLIAM HENRY ROCKWELL & ELIZABETH BANTIN

(Parents of Robert Archibald Rockwell)

Australia came of age with Federation on the 1st of January 1901, with a number of firsts paving the way. That year saw the first parliament convened in Parliament House, Melbourne with the first flying of the Australian National Flag. Edmund Barton became the 1st Prime Minister of Australia, and John Hope, the 7th Earl of Hopetoun its first Governor-General.

However, problems continued elsewhere in the world with the Boxer Rebellion, an anti-foreign, anti-colonial, and anti-Christian movement occurring in China between 1899 and 1901. Marconi sent the first transatlantic radio message in 1901 and Queen Victoria died and was succeeded by King Edward VII. In Australia the Immigration Restriction Act was introduced forming the basis of the White Australia policy, and over 100 people were killed in Sydney with an outbreak of the Black Death.

The Marriage of William Henry Rockwell & Elizabeth Carpenter

But these events were secondary to William Henry Rockwell and Elizabeth Carpenter (nee Bantin), who following a brief courtship, were married by George Hay (Minister) in the Independent Presbyterian Church at 177 Liverpool St, Sydney on 16th December 1901, toward the end of Australia's momentous year of Federation.[1]

At this time William was working as a hansom cab driver, he was 39 years old and resided at Riley St, Surry Hills. But contemptedly, William had listed himself as being a bachelor, a claim that was of course false. Indeed, there is no evidence of a Rockwell divorce in the Victorian Divorce papers from 1895 to 1905, so William was actually a bigamist! Elizabeth

▲ TOP: The Glebe Post and Telegraph Office, where Elizabeth and William Henry Rockwell held their first meeting. ABOVE (Left): On his arrival in Sydney, William Henry Rockwell resumed driving a hansom cab. (Right): In 1901 William Henry Rockwell amongst many others would have been gob-smacked by this new invention being driven around the streets of Sydney. This particular car belonged to the late Mr. Mark Foy. The postcard reads in 'Mark Foy's hand' – "Car I bought from Massachusetts. French car about 1901, in Sydney. £150." (Photo owned by David Manson and sourced from Serpolette's Tricycle, The Early Motor in Australasia, Newsletter, No 6, December 2012 who state Mark Foy was a "pioneer NSW motorist").

on the other hand, was listed as a domestic residing with her mother Mary Bantin, at 11 Talfourd St, Glebe. The wedding was witnessed by H. Foley for William and Irene Barker for Elizabeth.[2]

William Henry Rockwell was a brave man to take on a 35 year old widow with four children in tow. Elizabeth's daughter Aileen, was around 13 years of age at the time, but while she probably didn't know it then, she grew to much dislike her new step-father. Like it or not, the four Carpenter children turned William's solo existence into a household of six hungry mouths. During this time William worked the cab ranks at Railway Square and Central Railway with his horse and stately hansom cab.[3] Sadly, we don't know the names of any of his horses, although they would no doubt also have been revered members of the Rockwell household.

An interesting issue in the age of horse drawn transport was the major problem it presented in the form of manure, which gave rise to the employment of what became known as the 'Block Boys,' who stood at intersections and were paid for scooping up the manure.

William and his new bride must have been an eager pair as it seems Elizabeth was already six weeks pregnant before their marriage, and soon after the wedding they had their first son in William Henry Rockwell Jr., who was born at 67 Hereford St. Forest Lodge on the 31st of July 1902.[4] William Henry Jr. was baptised at St. Johns Church, Glebe on the 24th August 1902 by S.S. Tovey (Minister).

Bill Rockwell Sr., mostly worked as a 'cabman' right from the time he was wed, as he listed that occupation on both his second marriage certificate and on the birth certificate of his first born son.

Next to arrive in the Rockwell household were the first of two sets of twins, with Norman John Rockwell (aka Jack) and Muriel Rockwell, being born on 7th July 1903 at the same address, and baptised at St. Johns Church, Glebe on the 9th August 1903 by Herbert Kithey (Minister).[5,6] The fourth Rockwell child was Robert Archibald Rockwell (aka Bob Rockwell), who arrived on the 1st November 1904 also at 67 Hereford St, Forest Lodge.[7] Robert was baptised at St. Johns Church, Glebe on the 30th November 1904 by S.S. Tovey (Minister).

Elizabeth remained close to her widowed mother during her birth years, who conveniently lived nearby at 85 Derwent St. Glebe. By 1905, Elizabeth and William Henry Rockwell and their growing family (Aileen 15, Arthur 14, Eric 12, Leslie 10, William 3, Jack and Muriel 2, and Robert 1), would have undoubtedly attended the wedding of Elizabeth's younger brother George Barrett Bantin, who married Florence Fortesque that year.[8] Unfortunately, in October the following year, Elizabeth who was pregnant again with her second set of twins, lost her mother and close confidant Mary Bantin, from senility and heart failure.[9]

The youngest and last of William and Elizabeth Rockwell's children arrived as a second

▲The marriage certificate of William Henry Rockwell and Elizabeth Carpenter (nee Bantin), 16th December 1901 (NSW BDM #8525/1901).

▲ *William Henry Rockwell in his Hansom Cab No. 353, c. 1905.*

set of twins in Alfred Barrett Rockwell (aka Mick) and Ernest Barrett Rockwell (aka Ernie), who arrived on the 2nd of January 1907, Alf being born some four hours before Ernie.[10]

By this stage the family had moved up the street to 99 Hereford St, Forest Lodge. Like their older siblings, the twins were also baptised at St. Johns Church, Glebe, the ceremony being conducted on the 6th March 1907, by S.S. Tovey (Minister).[11,12]

Tragically, just a year later, their only daughter Muriel passed away aged only four, on the 4th of February 1908, and was buried by Kinsela and Sons, Funeral Directors at Rookwood Cemetery.[13] Elizabeth apparently had another stillborn girl between Bob Rockwell and the twin boys, but could never understand why she wasn't able to bear a Rockwell daughter.[14]

The early 1900's were a tough time in Sydney, so with a large family of his own growing up around him, William made the unpopular decision to send the teenage Carpenter boys out to fend for themselves. Muriel's death in an overcrowded house was very probably the motivation for William's decision. Just as William had been forced out of home some 33 years previously, Arthur and Eric Carpenter were both apparently sent from the house, aged 17 and 15 respectively. Young Les Carpenter may have also been evicted about 1907, as he was residing at Kiama College in Glebe in that year, aged just 12.[15]

Being a Carpenter and the only girl in the family, this event was never forgotten by Aileen who remained in the home and close to her mother. Despite the fact that she couldn't take to her step-father, Aileen always helped Elizabeth in rearing the young Rockwell boys. But she always defended the Carpenters, who were never formally adopted by William.[16]

William Henry Rockwell made the newspapers in the spring of 1909 when his horse with its cab in tow, bolted down York Street and collided into a cart. The accident was reported in the Sydney newspapers under the banner 'Exciting Lunch-Hour Bolt.'[17]

All of the Rockwells were baptized at St. Johns Church in Glebe, so the family had a strong connection with that church over many years. Apparently all five Rockwell boys had good singing voices, particularly Bill Jr., and photographs of the boys in their church choir robes reveal that St. Johns Church in Glebe played an important part in the lives of the Rockwell family.

The Rockwell boys would also have been welcomed by the teaching staff at Forest Lodge Public School where they attended in turn, one after the other from 1906 to 1920. Whether the Rockwell boys attended school elsewhere after Forest Lodge, is unknown.

None of the Rockwell boys were old enough to enlist in the Australian Imperial Forces sent to the Middle East and Europe in 1915, and although Bill Jr. turned 17 in July of 1918, he just missed the call up when the war ended on the 11th November 1918. However, their two half-brothers in Arthur and Les Carpenter, would have been their heroes along with their first cousin Henry Ingelson Jones, who all enlisted. While all of Elizabeth's eight sons survived the war, the tragic death of her nephew Henry Ingelson Jones, brought the loss of her sister's only son, which occurred just two months prior to the termination of hostilities!

Sadly, Elizabeth's younger brother George Barrett Bantin, died in 1919 from the influenza epidemic.[18] As the young Rockwell boys grew into men they began to go their separate ways. Bob Rockwell followed in his father's footsteps for a while and worked as a cabman. Ernie who had the fighting spirit, took to boxing and was apparently NSW amateur champion in 1926/27.[19]

The Hansom Cab

The hansom cab was a horse-drawn carriage designed and patented in 1834 by Joseph Hansom, an architect from York. The vehicle was developed and tested by Hansom in Hinckley, Leicestershire, England. Originally called the Hansom safety cab, it was designed to combine speed with safety, with a low centre of gravity for safe cornering. Hansom's original design was modified by John Chapman and several others to improve its practicability, but retained Hansom's name.

Cab is a shortening of cabriolet, reflecting the design of the carriage. It replaced the hackney carriage as a vehicle for hire, with the introduction of clockwork mechanical taximeters to measure fares, and the name transformed over time to become a taxicab.

Hansom cabs enjoyed immense popularity as they were fast, light enough to be pulled by a single horse (making the journey cheaper than travelling in a larger four-wheel coach) and were agile enough to steer around horse-drawn vehicles in the notorious traffic jams of 19th century London. There were up to 7500 hansom cabs in use at the height of their popularity and they quickly spread to other cities, such as Dublin in the United Kingdom, as well as continental European cities, particularly Paris, Berlin, and St Petersburg. The cab was introduced to other British Empire cities and to the United States during the late 19th century, being commonly used in Sydney, Melbourne and New York City.

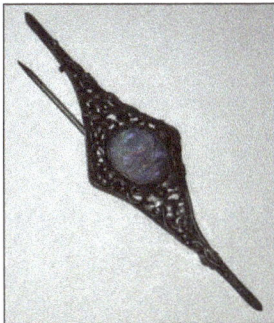

▲LEFT: A selection of brooches in William Henry Rockwell's lapdesk. RIGHT: Portrait of William Henry Rockwell, taken on his wedding day to Elizabeth Bantin, 16th December 1901. He was a brave man to take on a widow and care for four young children.

GIBBS SHALLARD & Co's MAP OF THE CITY OF SYDNEY AND SUBURBS

Scale 20 Chains to 1 Inch

City of Sydney Ward Boundaries shewn thus
Municipality
Water Reserve
Tramway Lines

RESIDENCES
1. Talfourd St, Glebe (Bantin)
2. Riley St, Surry Hills
3. 67 Hereford St, Glebe
4. 230 St Johns Rd, Glebe
5. 11 Charles St, Forest Lodge

Map of Sydney City & Suburbs, c.1900.

NOTE.— The radius of each circle represents a distance of one mile...

PARRAMATTA RIVER

NORTH SHORE
ST LEONARDS

NORTH HYTHE
SOUTH HYTHE
FIVEDOCK
BOURKE TOWN
BIRKENHEAD

BALMAIN
GLEBE
THE GLEBE
FOREST LODGE
LYNDHURST
PYRMONT

CALLAN PARK
BARRY OWEN
BROUGHTON
DOBROYD

LEICHHARDT
LEICHHARDT
MARYVILLE
HAY HILL
ELSWICK
SYDENHAM WEST

ASHFIELD
PETERSHAM STATION
STANMORE PLATFORM
NORTH KINGSTON
SOUTH KINGSTON
NEWTOWN
MACDONALDTOWN PLATFORM
MACDONALDTOWN

CAMPERDOWN
University
CHIPPENDALE
REDFERN
SURRY
SYDNEY TERMINUS

CHARLESVILLE
LEWISHAM
NORWOOD
STANMORE
ENMORE
PETERSVILLE
VIRGINIA WATER

MARRICKVILLE
FRANKFORD PARK
BELLE RETIRO

ALEXANDRIA
WATERLOO ESTATE
WAT...

CREMORNE

Robertson's Pt.

D

PORT

Fort Denison

Garden Island

Potts Pt.

Elizabeth Bay

OF

ROY

ard

DARLINGHURST

PADDINGTON

Military Barracks

P

PARK

RIFLE RANGE

Asoat Cricket Ground

MOORE

PARK

Agricultural Society's Ground

Water Reserve, 768 acres

V

RANDWICK

Randwick

Grand Stand

Race Course

LACHLAN MILLS ESTATE

JACKSON

Bradley's Head

Shark Island

Clarke Island

Darling Pt.

Double Bay

THOMSON ST

DOUBLE BAY

PIPER ESTATE

WOOLLAHRA

SMITHERS

WAVERLEY

VICTORIA

ORANGE

STEPHEN

STANLEY ST

RANDWICK

COOGEE

Bishops Court

Bottle & Glass Mooring

Sharker Steel Pt.

Fort

Hermit Bay

Point Piper

Blackburn Cove

Rose Bay

South Bay

E

K

BELLEVUE ESTATE

Bellevue

HEAD ROAD

O

W

NELSON

HOOPER

ORANGE ST

YARRA

DOUGLAS ST

W

VAUCLUSE

RETREAT

Diamond Bay

E

L

BONDI ESTATE

R

Bondi Bay

Ben Buckler

Dixon's Bay

Nelson Bay

Waverley Gen. Cem.

X

Shark Pt.

Little Coogee Bay

Gordon's Bay

PACIFIC OCEAN

PRINTED & PUBLISHED BY GIBBS, SHALLARD & Cº PITT ST

▲ Sydney 'cabbies' waiting at the hansom cab rank in Bridge St, Sydney, which was a favourite rank for William Henry Rockwell, c.1900. ◄ The 'Block Boys' in action, cleaning up the manure on a Sydney street corner about 1898.

Horse Transport & The Block Boys[27]

Until the advent of the motor vehicle, the principal means of transportation, whether of people or goods, was by horse. Up until the early 1900's cabs, buses, carts and drays were all horse drawn, with horse manure becoming a real problem for growing cities.

Local Councils needed to clear the manure not only for health reasons, but also to keep the traffic moving. Sydney's streets were washed down daily with water and disinfectant, which also assisted in keeping down the dust.

In the 1870's, Sydney City Council made a profit on the disposal of manure, selling it for 10 shillings ($1) per load. In contrast, a labourer could be hired for seven shillings (70 cents) per day. By the 1890's, the Council's employment of adult males for such purposes had given way to the independent employment of young boys who darted in and out of the traffic shovelling up the manure and depositing it into containers.

Officially the boys were called 'block boys', but unofficially they were also known as 'sparrow starvers'. Block boys were mostly lads just out of school. Later equipped with uniforms, scoops on wheels with long handles and brooms, they shovelled horse manure from the streets and placed it in recessed receptacles in the footpath. From there it was removed to a Council depot and sold to the public as fertiliser.

Being older, Elizabeth's children from Arthur Carpenter were first to the altar with Eric (1915), Leslie (1919), Arthur (1922) and then Aileen (1925) all marrying before any of the Rockwell boys. Elizabeth applied for a 'Separation Allowance' to the Finance Secretary on account of her two sons Arthur and Leslie, having fought in World War I, but the claim 'could not be considered' and was denied. Separation allowances compensated members for the time they spent away from their dependants for Service reasons. It recognised the effects on the member of

▲ Bustling traffic on the Pyrmont Bridge looking toward Sydney, showing the absolute dependance on horse power. ▶ Transcription of the birth certificate of William Henry Rockwell Jr. on 31st July 1902 (NSW BDM #21886/1902).

separation from home and the additional costs that could be incurred due to that separation.

Around 1925, youngest member of the family Ernie Rockwell, experienced a bad fall off a building that was a showroom for new cars, somewhere in William St, East Sydney. Apparently the plunge was in the order of 30 feet, but he was lucky enough to grab hold of a water pipe on his way down, which apparently broke his fall. Although we don't know what Ernie was doing on the building, his father soon afterwards inspected the spot and commented to Elizabeth...

BIRTH TRANSCRIPTION from
NSW Registry of Births, Deaths and Marriages

Transcription requested by	TRACY	ROCKWELL	18-Oct-01

Registration Number	21886
Date of Birth	31 JUL 1902
Birth Place	67 HEREFORD STREET, FOREST LODGE, GLEBE
Name	WILLIAM HENRY
Sex	Male
Father	WILLIAM HENRY ROCKWELL
Occupation	CAB MAN
Father's Age	40
Father's Birthplace	LONDON, ENGLAND
Date of Marriage	19 DEC 1901
Place	SYDNEY, NSW
Previous Issue	NOT LISTED
Mother Maiden Name	ELIZABETH FORMERLY BANTON LATE CARPENTER *
Mother's Age	35
Mother's Birthplace	GLEBE, SYDNEY, NSW
Informant	ELIZABETH ROCKWELL, MOTHER, 67 HEREFORD ST
Accoucheur	DR. MULLER
Nurse and/or Witness	MISS LEVER, MRS JONES
Registered	20 SEP 1902, GLEBE
Comments	* NOW ROCKWELL

▲ TOP (Left, Top Line): Jasperware Cameo; Snuff Box (brass); Decorated Locket (4 x silver stamps); 5 petalled cloth flower; Large winding key. (2nd Line): Thistle decorative plate; watch wristband; Buddha in orange & green; cast iron toy rifle; stainless steel recessed blade; 4 x chains. TOP (Right, Top Line): Two chain stops; Chain hasp; Small winding key; Chain end; Australia & Sthn Cross charm (stg sil); Shield with 'WW' initials (stg sil); Gold heart charm. (2nd Line): Engraved rose gold bar 'Joy'; Double headed serpent hook; Miniature happy face; Round gold button with chain & 'GM' initials (proud 106); Turqoise & white diamond cufflinks (stg sil); (3rd Line): Gold stamped oval with 'RR' initials [1st Nov, 1928]; Sharks tooth; Opal; Small gold chain; AIF Memorial Charm [2nd Aug, 1918]; brass button; Gold tooth cap. (Bottom Line): Black & white stone; 2 x rough emeralds; Small clear crystal. ABOVE (Top Line): Three dice (two ivory); Sydney Wharf Labourers Union Badge, #3045 [1902, Wm H.]; 2 x Victory Medals - The Triumph of Liberty and Justice - The Peace of 1919 (Amor Ltd); Horseshoe 'Good Luck' medal. (Bottom Line): Cabmens Union Badge, Sydney (Miller & Morris); Pen Nib; Ship Badge 'God Speed Green???' (sterling silver); 2 x AIF Badges.

"I don't know how that boy survived!"[20]

It wasn't long after this incident that William Henry suffered a stroke in his home at 11 Charles St. Forest Lodge, which could even have been brought about by the shock of Ernie's fall. He was thereafter affected in speech and possessed a shaky gait and hands, but apparently still managed to walk down to the local hotel with the assistance of his cane for a 'schooner' or two.[21]

Except for Alf, the Rockwell boys all married in a rash of weddings, and moved away from home between the years 1926 and 1928. Bob Rockwell wedded first to Octavia Corelli O'Sullivan in 1926, followed by Ernie to Alice Maud Greenup, and Norman (Jack) to Stella Rosamond Edgerton both in 1927, then Bill Jr. married Rose May Menier in 1928. Alf followed 11 years later when he married Olive Ruth Loader in 1939.

Following his stroke, William remained a sick man and apparently needed much looking after, and as Elizabeth couldn't care for him well enough, she placed him in an old man's home. Aileen was married by this stage and may have had something to do with this decision. Nevertheless, Elizabeth obviously didn't want to live alone and so she went to reside with Aileen, her husband William and her granddaughter Shirley in Hurstville, as she thought she could be of more help that way than being by herself.[22]

The arrival of grandchildren in quick succession accompanied the four weddings with Joy Corelli Rockwell (1927), Ronald Ernest Rockwell (1927), Richard Adrian Rockwell (1928), Norman Alfred Rockwell (1928), Robert Hunter Rockwell (1929) and Elaine Faye Rockwell (1930) all arriving in quick succession over a three year span.

Later Bob and Ernie Rockwell visited their father William at the nursing home and were apparently shocked at the conditions. Bob commented to Ernie that... "no way is the old man going to die in that home, he can come and live with me!" So Bob and Octavia Corelli Rockwell took in their invalided father William Henry, to live with them at their new rented residence at 48 Slade St, Naremburn, and apparently Elizabeth even returned to her husband for a time. Before William Henry died however, they split for the final time as he must have been difficult to care for, and Elizabeth returned once again to reside with her daughter Aileen, at Hurstville.[23]

The Masonic Lodge

During their formative years and into middle and old age, the Rockwell brothers and cousins became very involved with the Masonic movement. The comraderie and brotherhood enticed most of the Rockwell men into their ranks, and at one stage there

Residences of William Henry Rockwell & Elizabeth Bantin

NSW National & Sands Sydney Directorie's	Electoral Rolls
1898 — 102 Bay St, Glebe?	1906, West Sydney (Forest Lodge Polling Place), #2192, Elizabeth Rockwell (F), 67 Hereford St, Domestic Duties & #2193, William H. Rockwell (M), 67 Hereford St, Cab Driver.
1903 — 67 Hereford St, Forest Lodge	1908, West Sydney (Forest Lodge Polling Place), #864, Elizabeth Rockwell (F), 99 Hereford St, Domestic Duties & #865, William H. Rockwell (M), 99 Hereford St, Cab Driver.
1908 — 99 Hereford St, Forest Lodge	1909, West Sydney (Forest Lodge Polling Place), #947, Elizabeth Rockwell (F), 99 Hereford St, Home Duties & #948, William H. Rockwell (M), 99 Hereford St, Cab Driver.
1913 — 230 St Johns Rd, Glebe	1913, West Sydney, #1110, Elizabeth Rockwell (F), 99 Hereford St, Glebe, Home Duties & #1111, William H. Rockwell (M), 99 Hereford St, Cab Driver.
1915 — 11 Charles St, Forest Lodge	1915, Dalley (Subdivision of Forest Lodge), #1067, Elizabeth Rockwell (F), 11 Charles St, Home Duties & #1068, William H. Rockwell (M), 11 Charles St, Cab Driver.

◄The Rockwell residence from 1908-1913 was at 99 Hereford St. in Forest Lodge. ►The Rockwell residence at 230 St Johns Road, Glebe (1913-15). ▲The Rockwell family resided at 11 Charles St. in Forest Lodge throughout the years from 1915 to 1926, with his stables always nearby.

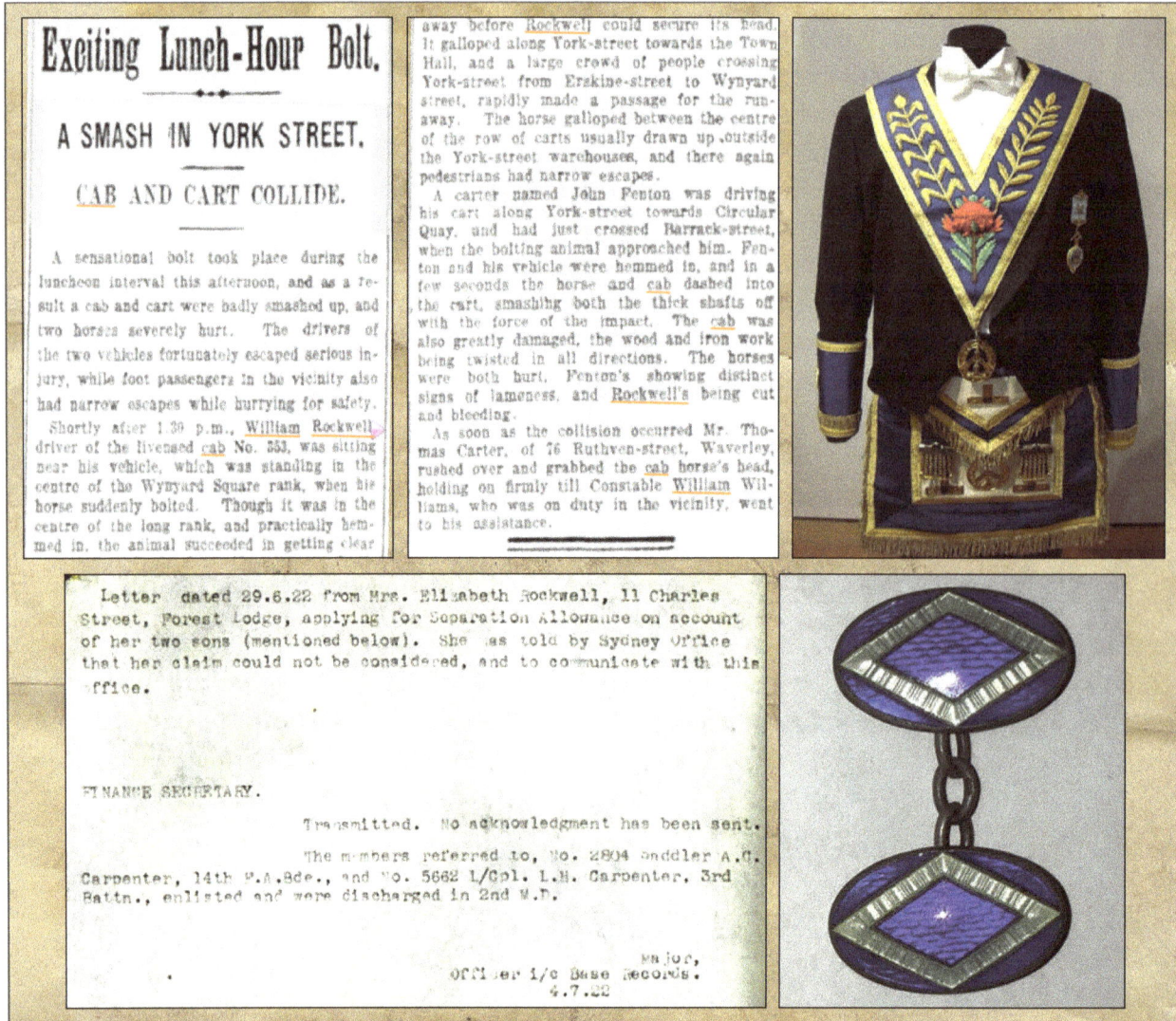

Exciting Lunch-Hour Bolt.

A SMASH IN YORK STREET.

CAB AND CART COLLIDE.

A sensational bolt took place during the luncheon interval this afternoon, and as a result a cab and cart were badly smashed up, and two horses severely hurt. The drivers of the two vehicles fortunately escaped serious injury, while foot passengers in the vicinity also had narrow escapes while hurrying for safety.

Shortly after 1.30 p.m., William Rockwell, driver of the licensed cab No. 353, was sitting near his vehicle, which was standing in the centre of the Wynyard Square rank, when his horse suddenly bolted. Though it was in the centre of the long rank, and practically hemmed in, the animal succeeded in getting clear

away before Rockwell could secure its head. It galloped along York-street towards the Town Hall, and a large crowd of people crossing York-street from Erskine-street to Wynyard street, rapidly made a passage for the runaway. The horse galloped between the centre of the row of carts usually drawn up outside the York-street warehouses, and there again pedestrians had narrow escapes.

A carter named John Fenton was driving his cart along York-street towards Circular Quay, and had just crossed Barrack-street, when the bolting animal approached him. Fenton and his vehicle were hemmed in, and in a few seconds the horse and cab dashed into the cart, smashing both the thick shafts off with the force of the impact. The cab was also greatly damaged, the wood and iron work being twisted in all directions. The horses were both hurt, Fenton's showing distinct signs of lameness, and Rockwell's being cut and bleeding.

As soon as the collision occurred Mr. Thomas Carter, of 76 Ruthven-street, Waverley, rushed over and grabbed the cab horse's head, holding on firmly till Constable William Williams, who was on duty in the vicinity, went to his assistance.

Letter dated 29.6.22 from Mrs. Elizabeth Rockwell, 11 Charles Street, Forest Lodge, applying for Separation Allowance on account of her two sons (mentioned below). She was told by Sydney Office that her claim could not be considered, and to communicate with this office.

FINANCE SECRETARY.

Transmitted. No acknowledgment has been sent.

The members referred to, No. 2804 Saddler A.G. Carpenter, 14th F.A.Bde., and No. 5662 L/Cpl. L.H. Carpenter, 3rd Battn., enlisted and were discharged in 2nd M.D.

Major,
Officer i/c Base Records.
4.7.22

▲TOP (Left): The newspaper report of William Henry Rockwell's runaway hansom cab (Evening News, 1st Sept 1909, p.5). (Right): Masonic regalia as worn by William Henry Rockwell's sons and grandsons. ABOVE (Left): Elizabeth Rockwell's application for a Separation Allowance, 1922. (Right): Cufflinks from William Henry Rockwell's lap desk.

were possibly eight Rockwell's up on the dais of Lodge Fidelity Lewis. The Grand Master in attendance apparently commented that he... "had never seen such a phenomenon in all the years of his masonry." This was around the year 1955 and probably included Bill Jr., Richard (Bill's Jr's son), Jack (Norman), Bob, Mick (Alfred), Graham (Alfred's son), Ernie and Norman (Ernie's son)!

William Henry himself apparently never joined the Masons, so how and why did his sons and grandsons become so involved in masonry? Although none of Bob Rockwell's four sons ever joined the Masons, he himself became a staunch member and was in both the Red and Blue Lodges, and also in the Cryptic Lodge. He was apparently a very good ritualist and possessed a lot of regalia in the form of Masonic collars and jewels. Ernie's daughter Elaine Faye Banks (nee Rockwell), apparently kept Jack Rockwell's masonic jewel, from when he was in Lodge Acacia.[24]

The Deaths of William Henry & Elizabeth Rockwell

William Henry Rockwell passed away aged 74, at his son Bob Rockwell's residence at 48 Slade St, Naremburn, on the 1st of July 1932 of arteriosclerosis and myocarditis. The informant at the death was his son Bob Rockwell of the same address. The death certificate stated that William's father was Augustus Rockwell, an evangelist and that his mother was Frances Thruyac, and his occupation was listed as a cab proprietor. The Church of England minister who conducted the burial service was Alfred Smith and the witnesses were Joseph K. Manning and J. Latts (*Rookwood Cemetery, Zone C, Section 10, Plot-#4493*).

William Henry's birthplace was listed as London, England and he was reported to have

ROCKWELL.—July 1, 1932, at his son Robert's residence, 48 Slade-street, Naremburn, William Henry, beloved husband of Elizabeth Rockwell and father of William, Jack, Robert, Alfred, and Ernest, in his 74th year. At rest. Late of Forest Lodge.

ROCKWELL.—The Relatives and Friends of the late WILLIAM ROCKWELL are advised that his Funeral will leave Wood Coffill's Mortuary Chapel, 810 George-street, Sydney, THIS AFTERNOON, at 2.30 o'clock, for Church of England Cemetery, Rookwood. By road.
WOOD COFFILL LIMITED,
Motor Funeral Directors.

CERTIFIED COPY FURNISHED UNDER PART V OF THE REGISTRATION OF BIRTHS, DEATHS AND MARRIAGES ACT, 1973.

DEATH REGISTERED IN NEW SOUTH WALES, AUSTRALIA.

I, JOHN BRETTELL HOLLIDAY, HEREBY CERTIFY THAT THE ABOVE IS A TRUE COPY OF PARTICULARS RECORDED IN A REGISTER KEPT BY ME.

ISSUED AT SYDNEY. 28TH AUGUST, 1979.

PRINCIPAL REGISTRAR.

▶TOP (Left): William Henry Rockwell (c.1926) at the wedding of one of his sons, who, except for Alf, were all married between 1926 and 1928. (Right Column): 1-Death & funeral notices for William Henry Rockwell (SMH, 2nd July 1932, p.12). 2-The unmarked gravesite of William Henry Rockwell at Rookwood Cemetery is indentified by the author (c.1980). ABOVE: Death certificate of William Henry Rockwell, 2nd July 1932 (NSW BDM #13545/1932).

been in the colony of NSW for some 40 years. The death certificate further stated that he was married in Sydney to Elizabeth Carpenter formerly Bantin, and was 33 years old at the time (which should have read 43). The five Rockwell boys were listed together with their ages at the time as 'living', while one female Muriel Rockwell, was noted as being deceased.[25]

By this stage, all of the Rockwell boys were young married men rearing families of their own and they regrettably couldn't afford a memorial for their fathers grave, so he was buried on the 2nd July 1932 by Wood Coffill Ltd in the General Zone at Rookwood Cemetery in an unmarked grave. Perhaps at some stage his descendents might pool resources to erect a suitable memorial?

After her husbands death, Elizabeth Rockwell spent her 23 remaining years residing with her daughter Aileen Sampson and granddaughter Shirley at 892 King Georges Rd, South Hurstville. Although she had been twice widowed, she expressed wishes to be buried

NSW DEATH REGISTRATION TRANSCRIPTION		REF NO 1955/9914
NAME	ELIZABETH ROCKWELL	
DATE OF DEATH	4 JUN 1955	
PLACE	892 KING GEORGES ROAD, SOUTH HURSTVILLE	
OCCUPATION		
SEX	FEMALE	
AGE	88	
CONJUGAL STATUS	WIDOW	
PLACE OF BIRTH	GLEBE POINT NSW	
TIME IN AUST COLONIES		
FATHER	ROBERT BANTIN	
OCCUPATION	PAINTER	
MOTHER	MARY BARRETT	
PLACE OF MARRIAGE	1. REDFERN NSW	2. SYDNEY NSW
AGE AT MARRIAGE	1. 23	2. 35
NAME OF SPOUSE	1. ARTHUR CARPENTER	2. WILLIAM HENRY ROCKWELL
CHILDREN OF MARRIAGE	1. AILEEN V 65, ARTHUR C 63, ERIC D 60, LESLIE H 58, LIVING; NONE DECEASED	2. WILLIAM H 53, NORMAN J 52, ROBERT A 50, ERNEST 48, ALFRED 48 (TWINS), LIVING; 1 FEMALE DECEASED
INFORMANT	S WARMEANT, GRAND-SON, 892 KING GEORGES ROAD, SOUTH HURSTVILLE	
CAUSE OF DEATH	1. CARDIO VASCULAR DEGENERATION	2. SENILITY
LENGTH OF ILLNESS	1. YEARS	2. -
MEDICAL ATTENDANT	F J HOWELL	
DATE LAST SEEN		
DATE OF BURIAL		
PLACE OF BURIAL		
MINISTER & RELIGION		
UNDERTAKER		
WITNESSES		
CREMATION DATE	6 JUN 1955	
CREMATION PLACE	WORONORA CREMATORIUM	
CREMATION INFORMANT	C T SMITH, SUPERINTENDENT	
CREMATION RELIGION	NOEL DELBRIDGE, CHURCH OF ENGLAND	
CREMATION WITNESSES	J BROCK	
REGISTERED	6 JUN 1955 - HURSTVILLE	

ROCKWELL, Elizabeth.—June 4, 1955, at her daughter's residence, 892 King George's Road, South Hurstville (after a long illness), widow of the late W. H. Rockwell and beloved mother of Aileen (Mrs. Sampson), Arthur Carpenter, Eric Carpenter, Les Carpenter, William, Jack, Robert, Ernest, and Alfred Rockwell, aged 88 years. At rest.

ROCKWELL. The relatives and friends of the late Mrs Elizabeth Rockwell are kindly invited to attend her funeral, to leave our private chapel, 2 Carrington Avenue, Hurstville. This afternoon after service commencing at 3 o'clock, for the crematorium, Woronora. Labor Motor Funerals, 2 Carrington Avenue, Hurstville. Burial place, Wall of Memories, Panel '22.

Sydney Morning Herald, June 4th, 1955

IN LOVING MEMORY OF
OUR DEAR MOTHER
ELIZABETH ROCKWELL
DIED 4th JUNE 1955
AGED 88 YEARS.

▲ TOP (Left): Photograph of Elizabeth Rockwell formerly Carpenter (nee Bantin) taken about 1950. (Right): Transcription of the death certificate of Elizabeth Rockwell, 4th June 1955 (NSW BDM #9914/1955). ABOVE (Left): Death notice for Elizabeth Rockwell on the 4th June 1955 (SMH, 4th June 1955). (Mid): Funeral notice for Elizabeth Rockwell (1955). (Right): Memorial wall plaque at Woronora Crematorium for Elizabeth Rockwell.

▲ *Castlereagh Street, Sydney looking south from Market Street, around th time of Elizabeth Rockwell's death in the mid 1950s.*

alongside her second husband William Henry Rockwell.

When Elizabeth Rockwell eventually died of cardio-vascular degeneration, and senility on the 4th of June 1955, the Rockwell boys wanted their mother to be buried alongside their father as per her wishes, but Aileen Sampson wouldn't hear of it! Aileen reasoned that as her mother had lived with her for the past 23 years, she could take matters into her own hands and bury Elizabeth as she saw fit![26] Accordingly, Elizabeth was cremated and now rests alone with a memorial at Woronora Crematorium, Sutherland *(Wall of Memories' Row-22HH, Plot-#0104)*.

Where To From Here?

The union between William Henry Rockwell and Elizabeth Carpenter (nee Bantin) produced six children, 14 grandchildren and close to 40 great grandchildren. The following chapter reveals is all that is currently known about their descendants with their respective families.

References

1. NSW Dept of BDM. (1901). Marriage Certificate for William Henry Rockwell & Elizabeth Carpenter (nee Bantin), #8525/1901.

2. Ibid.

3. Rockwell, Alice, 1911-1997 (Interviewee, 1980). 'Alice Rockwell (nee Greenup) interviewed by Tracy Rockwell on the 12th of June 1980, at Kyeemagh, Sydney'.

4. NSW Dept of BDM. (1902). Birth Certificate for William Henry Rockwell Jr., #21886/1902.

5. NSW Dept of BDM. (1903). Birth Certificate for Muriel Rockwell, #20948/1903.

6. NSW Dept of BDM. (1903). Birth Certificate for Norman John Rockwell, #20949/1903.

7. NSW Dept of BDM. (1904). Birth Certificate for Robert Archibald Rockwell, #32224/1904.

8. NSW Dept of BDM. (1905). Marriage Certificate for George Barrett Bantin & Florence Fortesque, #5763/1905.

9. NSW Dept of BDM. (1906). Death Certificate for Mary Bantin, #12426/1906.

10. Rockwell, Alice, 1911-1997 (Interviewee, 1980). op. cit.

11. St. John's Church Glebe (1907). Baptismal Record for Alfred Barrett Rockwell, 6th March 1907 (Baptism, Burial, Confirmation, Marriage and composite registers in the Anglican Church Diocese of Sydney Archives).

12. St. John's Church Glebe (1907). Baptismal Record for Ernest Barrett Rockwell, 6th March 1907 (Baptism, Burial, Confirmation, Marriage and composite registers in the Anglican Church Diocese of Sydney Archives).

13. NSW Dept of BDM. (1908). Death Certificate for Muriel Rockwell, #994/1908.

14. Rockwell, Alice, 1911-1997 (Interviewee, 1980). op. cit.

15. Rockwell, Alice, 1911-1997 (Interviewee, 1980). op. cit.

16. Rockwell, Alice, 1911-1997 (Interviewee, 1980). op. cit.

17. 'William H. Rockwell - Exciting Lunch-Hour Bolt.' Evening News, 1st September 1909, p.5.

18. NSW Dept of BDM. (1919). Death Certificate for George Barrett Bantin, #22265/1919.

19. Rockwell, Alice, 1911-1997 (Interviewee, 1980). op. cit.

20. Rockwell, Alice, 1911-1997 (Interviewee, 1980). op. cit.

21. Rockwell, Alice, 1911-1997 (Interviewee, 1980). op. cit.

22. Rockwell, Alice, 1911-1997 (Interviewee, 1980). op. cit.

23. Rockwell, Alice, 1911-1997 (Interviewee, 1980). op. cit.

24. Rockwell, Alice, 1911-1997 (Interviewee, 1980). op. cit.

25. NSW Dept of BDM. (1932). Death Certificate for William Henry Rockwell, #13545/1932.

26. Rockwell, Alice, 1911-1997 (Interviewee, 1980). op. cit.

27. Bytes Daily (9 Jul 2011). Blockboys/Sparrowstarvers [http://bytesdaily.blogspot.com.au/2011/07/blockboyssparrowstarvers.html].

Chapter Five

THE DESCENDANTS OF WILLIAM HENRY
ROCKWELL & ELIZABETH BANTIN

The union between William Henry Rockwell and Elizabeth Carpenter (nee Bantin) produced six children, 14 grandchildren and close to 40 great grandchildren to date. The following information is all that is currently known about these descendants and their respective families.

1. William Henry Rockwell Jr. (1902-1970)

William Henry Rockwell Jr. was born on the 31st July 1902, just 7½ months after the wedding of his parents. He was baptised at St. Johns Church, Glebe on the 24th August 1902. Being the first son, his certificate of birth, the details of which were provided by his mother Elizabeth, revealed interesting information about the young Rockwell family at the time.

Bill Jr. attended Forest Lodge School and at the age of 26 he married in 1928 to Rose May (3 July 1902-1963), the daughter of Frederick Menier and Florence Weigall.[1] Bill Jr. worked at the Eveleigh St. Railway workshops, and they produced a son in 1935, who they named Richard Adrian Rockwell. They resided at 9 Heath St, Five Dock from 1934 until the death of Rose in 1963. Their only son Richard, who was born in 1935 tragically died

William Henry Rockwell Jr. & Family

			Parents' Names.				
When Baptized.	When Born.	Child's Christian Name.	Christian.	Surname.	Abode.	Quality or Profession.	By whom the Ceremony was performed.
1902 August 24	31st July	William Henry	William Henry Elizabeth	Rockwell	67 Morford St	[illegible]	[illegible]

Death Notices

ROCKWELL, Richard Adrian. March 16th 1956, at Royal Prince Alfred Hospital, dearly loved son of William and Rose Rockwell of 9 Heath St. Five Dock.

Funeral Notices

ROCKWELL, Richard Adrian. The relatives and friends of Mr. & Mrs. W.H. Rockwell of 9 Heath St. Five Dock are invited to attend the funeral of their dearly loved son Richard Adrian to leave St. Albans Church of England, Five Dock, this day after service commencing at 9.30am for Rookwood Cemetery. Geo. Andrews UA2808-9, 237-9 Liverpool Rd. Ashfield

ROCKWELL. Lodge Edward Hungerford No. 839 U.G.L. of N.S.W. The officers and brethren of the above lodge are invited to attend the funeral of their late esteemed Bro. Dick Rockwell. For particulars see family notice. Regalia. W. R. Buchanan, Worshipful Master, J.V. Roach, Sec.

Sydney Morning Herald, 19th March 1956

TOP: Baptism for William Henry Rockwell Jr. held on the 31st July 1902 at St Johns Church, Glebe (Baptism, Burial, Confirmation, Marriage and composite registers in the Anglican Church Diocese of Sydney Archives). ABOVE (Left): Death and funeral notices for Richard Adrian Rockwell (Sydney Morning Herald, 19th March 1956). (Right): Memorial for Richard Adrian Rockwell at Rookwood Cemetery.

aged just 22 on the 16th March 1956 at Royal Prince Alfred Hospital (cause unknown), and was buried at Rookwood Cemetery (*Anglican, Sect-13, Row-20, #868*).[2,3] Bill Jr.'s wife Rose May Rockwell, passed away in 1963 at Five Dock,[4] after which Bill purchased a property at Mullumbimby and moved north for a few years, but he developed pneumonia and his heart wasn't strong enough to see it through. Bill Jr. himself passed away in 1970 at Mullumbimby (cause unknown), at the age of 69 (*memorial location unknown*).[5]

2. Muriel Rockwell (1903-1908)

Muriel Rockwell was born as a twin along with her brother Norman John Rockwell on the 7th July 1903 and was baptised at St Johns Church, Glebe on the 9th August.[6,7] Tragically she died on the 4th February 1908 at Camperdown Children's Hospital, at the tender age of just 4½, cause unknown.[8] Muriel was buried on the 5th February 1908 at Rookwood Cemetery (*General Section (Anglican), Zone C, Plot RRRR, Grave No. 218*).

2. Norman John Rockwell (1903-1973)

Norman John Rockwell was also born as a twin with his sister Muriel Rockwell on the 7th July 1903 and was baptised at St Johns Church, Glebe on the 9th August.[9] Norman, or Jack as he was better known, attended Forest Lodge School, and later married on the 5th November 1927 to Stella Rosamond (1903-1939), the daughter of William Edgerton and Alberta MacDonald who were orginally from Albert Park, Victoria.[10] Jack worked at a box factory in Five Dock amongst other callings.[11] His wife Stella Rockwell passed away just 12 years after their marriage in 1939 (*Rookwood Cemetery, Zone C, Section 12, Grave 4632*).[12] They never had children and little else of Jack's life is known. Years later, Jack followed his brother Bill Jr. to Mullumbimby where he ramained for some time, but when the property was sold he returned to Sydney and moved in with Ernie and Alice, before winding up at Glenfield Masonic Homes which became the founding site of The Frank Whiddon Masonic Homes of NSW.[13] Jack likely passed away on the 6th of October 1973, likely of heart disease at the age of 69 (*memorial location unknown*).[14]

4. Robert Archibald Rockwell (1904-1966)

Robert Archibald Rockwell was the fourth Rockwell child born to the family in just three years and arrived on the 1st November 1904 at the family home at 67 Hereford St, Forest Lodge.[15] Like his brothers, Robert (aka 'Bob') attended Forest Lodge School and was a diligent student in school, always played by the rules and as a young man he would assist his father in caring for the horses in the family cab business.

St. Johns Church, Glebe

Within three years of establishing the first settlement in Australia at Sydney Cove, Governor Arthur Phillip gave over 400 acres to the Rev. Richard Johnson, the first chaplain of the settlement to clear and farm. The area was called the 'glebe' or church lands. However, Johnson was caustic of the quality of the land saying "400 acres for which I would not give 400 pence."

In the 1830's a portion of the glebe lands was given to support the Bishop of Australia, Bishop Broughton. Being the Bishop's place or village, the allocation was called 'Bishopthorpe' but in fact the bishop never lived on them.

The parish of St. Johns Bishopthorpe was created in 1856 from the original parish of Christ Church, when it was decided that the Bishopthorpe estates should be subdivided and sold on leasehold. The Rev. William Macquarie Cowper was chosen as the incumbent of the new parish, the first Australian born clergyman.

The first services were taken in the Rector's home until a permanent church and school hall (also used as a day school and Sunday school) was built in 1857 in St. John's Road opposite the present church. Before long it was clear that the building was unable to cope with the needs of the growing community.

The erection of a permanent church commenced in 1868. The foundation stone was laid by the Earl of Belmore (Governor of New South Wales) in place of H.R.H. the Duke of Edinburgh who had been wounded in an assassination attempt at Clontarf just days earlier. The church was officially opened on the 21st of December, 1870, inspired by the vision of the famous colonial architect Edmund Blackett and completed by his sons. The Church building and its Courtyard are listed in the NSW Heritage Register.

▲St. Johns Church, Glebe, formed a substantial part of the upbringing for the young Rockwell boys.

Muriel Rockwell & Norman John (Jack) Rockwell & Family

PAGE

BAPTISMS Administered in the Parish of _____ in the County of _____ in the Year 18__ .

When Baptized.	When Born.	Child's Christian Name.	Parents' Names. Christian.	Surname.	Abode.	Quality or Profession.	By whom the Ceremony was performed.
Aug. 9th	July 4th	Muriel	William & Elizabeth	Rockwell	64 Hereford St. Forest Lodge	Cabman	Herbert Kitley
Aug. 9th	July 7th	Norman John	William & Elizabeth	Rockwell	67 Hereford St. Forest Lodge	Cabman	Herbert Kitley

REGISTER BOOK for the use of Ministers authorized to celebrate Marriages under the Acts Nos. 16 and 17, 1899.

MARRIAGES Solemnized in the District of _____ , in the State of New South Wales, by _____ , at

No.	When and Where Married	Names and Surnames of the Parties	Designation or Employment	Usual Place of Residence	Condition of the Parties	Birthplace	Age	Father's Christian Name and Surname / Mother's Christian Name and Maiden Surname	Father's Rank or Profession
299	5th November 1927	Norman John Rockwell / Stella Rosamond Egerton	Machinist / Domestic duties	Forest Lodge / Erskineville	Bachelor / Spinster	Forest Lodge / Albert Park Victoria	30 / 24	William Henry Rockwell / Elizabeth ... — William Egerton / Elizabeth Macdonald	...

The Consent of _____ the _____ of the Bridegroom, was given in writing to the Marriage.
The Consent of _____ the _____ of the Bride, was given in writing to the Marriage.
This Marriage was solemnized between us N.J. Rockwell / Stella Egerton   In the presence of us _____
By me _____ Officiating Minister
According to the rites of the _____

In Affectionate Remembrance of

Muriel Rockwell

who departed this life

On 4th Day of February 1908

Age 4½ Years

" Suffer little Children to come unto Me."

C. Kinsela & Sons, Funeral Directors, 116 Oxford Street, City.

ROCKWELL.—February 25, at Royal Prince Alfred Hospital, Stella Rosamond, beloved wife of Norman J. Rockwell, Abbotsford, also beloved youngest daughter of Mrs. A. G. Egerton, Annandale, also dearly loved sister of George, Herbert, Evelyn, Violet. Peace, perfect peace.

ROCKWELL.—The Relatives and Friends of Mr NORMAN J. ROCKWELL, of Great North Road, Abbotsford, are invited to attend the Funeral of his beloved WIFE, Stella Rosamond; to leave the private chapel of Motor Funerals Limited, 30 City Road, City, THIS AFTERNOON, at 2.30 o'clock.

ROCKWELL.—The Relatives and Friends of Mrs. A. G. EGERTON, of Annandale, and HERBERT, GEORGE, EVELYN, and VIOLET EGERTON, and HARRY, are invited to attend the Funeral of her beloved DAUGHTER, their youngest SISTER, and his AUNT, Stella Rosamond Rockwell. For particulars, see previous notice.
MOTOR FUNERALS LIMITED, A.F.D.A.

ROCKWELL. — The relatives and friends of the late Mr NORMAN JOHN ROCKWELL, late of Glenfield, are invited to attend his funeral, to leave the Metropolitan Funeral Home, Railway Parade, Burwood, this day, after service commencing at 10.40 a.m. for the Rookwood Crematorium. Parking at rear of Funeral Home, off Railway Parade.
METROPOLITAN BURIAL AND CREMATION SOCIETY, A.F.D.A. ROCKDALE. 59 6066, 59 0439.

ROCKWELL. — Members of Lodge Acacia No. 329 are requested to attend the funeral of their late Wor. Brother, NORMAN ROCKWELL. For details see family notice.
J. CHRISTIE, W.M. J. W. BONE, Secretary.

RE the estate of NORMAN JOHN ROCKWELL, late of Glenfield, in the State of New South Wales, retired boxmaker, deceased.—Probate of the will dated 16th March, 1960, granted by the Supreme Court of New South Wales on the 13th day of November, 1973.—Pursuant to the Wills, Probate and Administration Act, 1898-1954; Testator's Family Maintenance and Guardianship of Infants Act, 1916-1954; and Trustee Act, 1925-1942: the Public Trustee, the executor of the will of the said Norman John Rockwell, who died on the 6th day of October, 1973, hereby gives notice that creditors and others having any claim against or to the estate of the said deceased, are required to send particulars of their claims to the said Public Trustee, at his branch office hereunder mentioned, on or before the 1st day of February, 1974, at the expiration of which time the said Public Trustee will distribute the assets of the said deceased to the persons entitled, having regard only to the claims of which he then has notice. D. LEWIS, Branch Manager, Public Trust Office, cnr Moore and Northumberland Streets, Liverpool 2170.   8551—$4

▲TOP: Baptism for the twins Muriel Rockwell & Norman John Rockwell, held on the 7th July 1903 at St Johns Church, Glebe (Baptism, Burial, Confirmation, Marriage and composite registers in the Anglican Church Diocese of Sydney Archives). MID 1: The marriage certificate of Norman John Rockwell and Stella Rosamond Edgerton, held on the 5th November 1927 at St Johns Church, Glebe (NSW BDM #17407/1927). MID 2: Tiny stamped silver spoon found in William Henry Rockwell's brass inlaid lap desk; Photo of Norman John Rockwell. (Right): Memorial card for Muriel Rockwell, who died on the 4th February 1908. ABOVE (Left): 1,2 &3-Stella Rockwell - Death & funeral notices on the 25th Feb 1939 (SMH, 27th Feb 1939, p.10). (Centre): 1&2-Norman John Rockwell - Funeral announcements (SMH, 9 Oct 1973); (Right): Probate notice for Norman John Rockwell (Govt Gazette of the State of NSW, 30 Nov 1973, p.5191).

▲ TOP (Left): Robert, William & Norman Rockwell as choirboys at St. Johns Church, Glebe about 1914. (Right): The twins Ernest and Alfred Rockwell also joined St. Johns Church, Glebe as choirboys, c.1918.

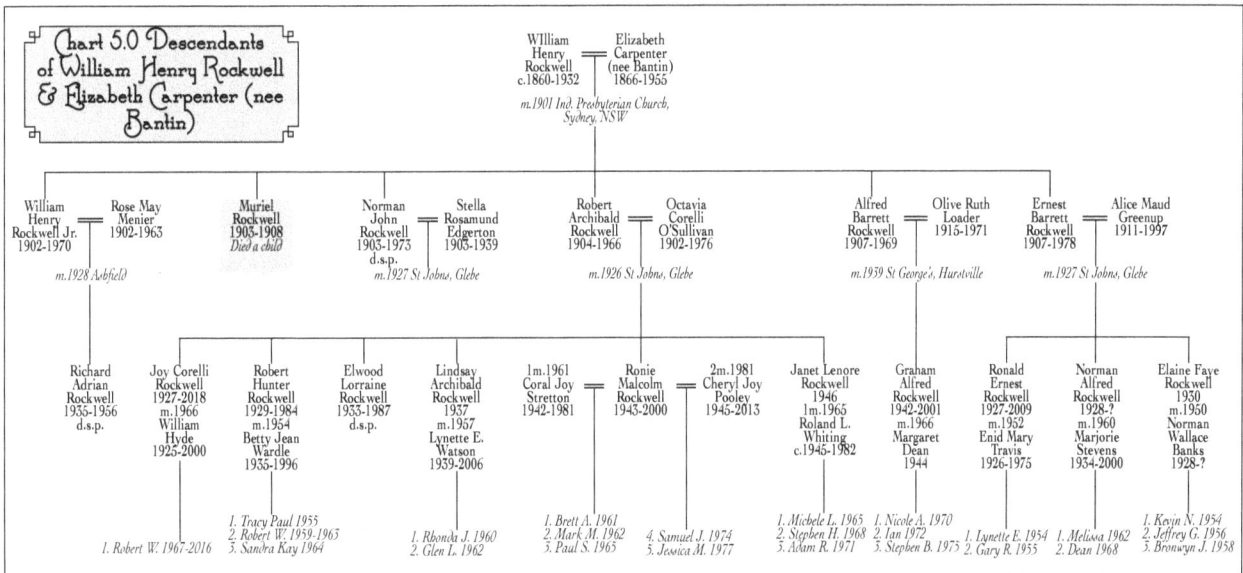

Chart 5.0 Descendants of William Henry Rockwell & Elizabeth Carpenter (nee Bantin)

William Henry Rockwell c.1860-1932 = Elizabeth Carpenter (nee Bantin) 1866-1955
m.1901 Ind. Presbyterian Church, Sydney, NSW

- William Henry Rockwell Jr. 1902-1970 = Rose May Menier 1902-1963 — m.1928 Ashfield
- Muriel Rockwell 1903-1908 Died a child
- Norman John Rockwell 1903-1973 d.s.p. = Stella Rosamund Edgerton 1903-1939 — m.1927 St Johns, Glebe
- Robert Archibald Rockwell 1904-1966 = Octavia Corelli O'Sullivan 1902-1976 — m.1926 St Johns, Glebe
- Alfred Barrett Rockwell 1907-1969 = Olive Ruth Loader 1915-1971 — m.1939 St George's, Hurstville
- Ernest Barrett Rockwell 1907-1978 = Alice Maud Greenup 1911-1997 — m.1927 St Johns, Glebe

Children:
- Richard Adrian Rockwell 1935-1956 d.s.p.
- Joy Corelli Rockwell 1927-2018 m.1966 William Hyde 1925-2000
  - 1. Robert W. 1967-2016
- Robert Hunter Rockwell 1929-1984 m.1954 Betty Jean Wardle 1935-1996
  - 1. Tracy Paul 1955
  - 2. Robert W. 1959-1965
  - 3. Sandra Kay 1964
- Elwood Lorraine Rockwell 1933-1987 d.s.p.
- Lindsay Archibald Rockwell 1937 m.1957 Lynette E. Watson 1939-2006
  - 1. Rhonda J. 1960
  - 2. Glen L. 1962
- 1m.1961 Coral Joy Stretton 1942-1981
  - 1. Brett A. 1961
  - 2. Mark M. 1962
  - 3. Paul S. 1965
- Ronie Malcolm Rockwell 1943-2000 = 2m.1981 Cheryl Joy Pooley 1945-2013
  - 4. Samuel J. 1974
  - 5. Jessica M. 1977
- Janet Lenore Rockwell 1946 1m.1965 Roland L. Whiting c.1945-1982
  - 1. Michele L. 1965
  - 2. Stephen H. 1968
  - 3. Adam R. 1971
- Graham Alfred Rockwell 1942-2001 m.1966 Margaret Dean 1944
  - 1. Nicole A. 1970
  - 2. Ian 1972
  - 3. Stephen B. 1975
- Ronald Ernest Rockwell 1927-2009 m.1952 Enid Mary Travis 1926-1975
  - 1. Lynette E. 1954
  - 2. Gary R. 1955
- Norman Alfred Rockwell 1928-? m.1960 Marjorie Stevens 1934-2000
  - 1. Melissa 1962
  - 2. Dean 1968
- Elaine Faye Rockwell 1930 m.1950 Norman Wallace Banks 1928-?
  - 1. Kevin N. 1954
  - 2. Jeffrey G. 1956
  - 3. Bronwyn J. 1958

Bob Rockwell was first amongst his brothers to the altar when he married Octavia Corelli (1902-1976), the daughter of Humphrey and Lenore O'Sullivan, at St. John's Church in Glebe on the 21st of September 1926, with the Rev. F. W. Tugwell officiating. At this time Bob was residing with his parents at 11 Charles St. Forest Lodge, and working as a cabman. Corelli was listed as a 'domestic' and was residing at 4 Upper Bayview St, North Sydney with her twice widowed mother Lenore O'Sullivan.[16] Although neither of them would have known it, Corelli brought into the marriage a unique Irish ancestry as a direct descendant of the O'Sullivan's of Rathmore, and the Mahony's of County Kerry, in Ireland (see Volume 3). She was also a descendant of two Australian pioneering families. Her paternal grandmother Ellen Frawley, was a daughter of the Frawley pioneers of the Monaro and Pambula region of south coast New South Wales (see Volume 5), while her maternal grandmother Susan Hann, was a daughter of the Hann pioneers of the Clarence River and Grafton region of northern New South Wales (see Volume 7).

Robert Archibald Rockwell worked as a stevedore and postal clerk, but died on the 17th September 1966, of a heart attack at Royal North Shore Hospital.[17] He was the

▲ Unlike America, horse transport was still a necessary part of life in Australia, even well after the end of World War I.

When Baptized.	When Born.	Child's Christian Name.	Parents' Names.		Abode.	Quality or Profession.	By whom the Ceremony was performed.
			Christian.	Surname.			
1904	10	Robert	William Henry	Rockwell	67	Cabman	S. S. Terry
November 30	November	Archibald	Elizabeth		Hughes St		

LEFT & CENTRE: Bob and Corelli Rockwell on their wedding day, 21st of Sept 1926. RIGHT: Bob Rockwell at Bradley's Head taken about 1963.

shortest lived of his brothers at just 62 years of age. His wife Corelli outlived him by ten years, but developed dementia and died at the Laurels Nursing Home, Meadowbank on the 4th July 1976, aged 75.[18] They are remembered at the Northern Suburbs Crematorium with memorial plaques (*Location-25VV*). Bob and Corelli Rockwell produced six children, and their family and descendants are discussed in much greater detail in Chapters 12 to 16. (*see 6.1 Descendants of Robert Archibald Rockwell & Octavia Corelli O'Sullivan*).

5. Alfred Barrett Rockwell (1907-1969)

Alfred Barrett Rockwell was first born of the second set of Rockwell twins, with his brother Ernest Barrett Rockwell and attended Forest Lodge School. By 1930 with all his brothers married and his parents separated by ill health, Alf Rockwell (aka Mick) was living alone at 8 Gottenham St in Glebe.[19] He married at St George's Church, Hurstville on

5.1 Descendants of Robert Archibald Rockwell & Octavia Corelli O'Sullivan

Robert Archibald Rockwell (1904-1966), born at his home in Glebe. He married on the 21st Sep 1926 at StJohn's Church, Glebe to Octavia Corelli (1902-1976), dau of Humphrey & Lenore O'Sullivan, with issue:

1. Joy Corelli Rockwell (1927-2018), born 13th Apr 1927 at Naremburn. She married on the 9th Apr 1966 at St Cuthbert's Church, Naremburn to William HYDE (1925-2000), with issue:
1.1 Robert William HYDE (1967-2016) ◭

2. Robert Hunter ROCKWELL (1929-1984), born 25th Jun 1929 at Naremburn. He married on the 15th Jan 1954 at Sydney to Betty Jean (1935-1996), daughter of William W. Wardle & Mary A. Cummings, with issue:
2.1 Tracy Paul ROCKWELL (1955)
2.2 Robert Wayne ROCKWELL (1959–1963)*
2.3. Sandra Kay Rockwell (1964)

3. Elwood Lorraine ROCKWELL (1933-1987), born 9th Dec 1933 in Naremburn. He had partners, but never married, with no issue.

4. Lindsay Archibald ROCKWELL (1937), ◭ born 2nd Nov 1937 in Naremburn. He married on the 14th Sep 1957 at St Cuthbert's Church, Naremburn to Lynette Ellen (1939-2006), daughter of Hugh & Alice Watson, with issue:
4.1 Rhonda Janine Rockwell (1960)
4.2 Glen Lindsay ROCKWELL (1962)

5. Ronie Malcolm ROCKWELL (1943-2000), born 26th Feb 1943 at Naremburn. He married firstly in 1961 to Coral Joy Stretton (1942-1981), with issue:
5.1 Brett Anthony ROCKWELL (1961)
5.2 Mark Malcolm ROCKWELL (1962)
5.3 Paul Steven ROCKWELL (1965)

Ronie married secondly in 1981 to Cheryl Joy Pooley (1945-2013), with issue:
5.4 Samuel Joshua ROCKWELL (1974)
5.5 Jessica Molly Rockwell (1977)

6. Janet Lenore Rockwell (1946), born 22nd Feb 1946 at Naremburn. She married firstly on the 19th Jun 1965 at St Cuthbert's Church, Naremburn to Roland Lawrence WHITING (c.1945-1982), with issue:
6.1 Michelle Lena Whiting (1965)
6.2 Stephen Hunter WHITING (1968)
6.3. Adam Roger WHITING (1971),

* Died before adulthood - d.s.p.

NB. The family of Robert and Octavia Corelli Rockwell are the subject of chapters 12 to 16.

▲Aerial view of Sydney and Circular Quay on the day of the official opening of the Sydney Harbour Bridge, 19th March 1932.

the 11th November 1939 to Olive Ruth (1915-1971), the daughter of William and Lucy Loader.[20] Mick and Olive sadly lost a pair of twins at birth, although its unsure whether that was before of after their only other child Graham arrived in 1942. There were lots of twins in the Rockwell family line! Mick apparently worked as a barman at 'Shanny's Hotel' in Hurstville for many years.[21] In 1942 they produced a son in Graham Alfred Rockwell (*see 6.2 Descendants of Alfred Barrett Rockwell & Olive Ruth Loader*).

By all reports, Mick died in his backyard of a heart attack on the 30th August 1969. However, perhaps due to an estrangement, his wife Olive refused to tell Ernie any information about the funeral. Ernie apparently had to get the details from Metropolitan Funeral Parlours. Undaunted, Ernie told his wife Alice that he was determined to attend the service and commented... "there is no way I'm going to miss the funeral, as that man's blood flows through my veins!"[22]

Alfred Barrett Rockwell is remembered with a memorial at the Woronora Cemetery (*Portion-FF, Row-Rose Garden 1, Plot 0046*). His wife Olive lies next to him (*Plot-0048*).

In a freakish turn of events in early May 2001, I was asked by one of my physical education students at Sydney University, if I knew of a young physical education teacher by the name of Ian Rockwell? I was unsure, but being a Rockwell I was intrigued to look up the family tree, quickly realising that Ian was the son of Graham Alfred Rockwell. I immediately picked up the phone and called Graham. We had a great conversation in which I informed him of the work I'd done on the family history, and before closing I pledged to send him details and catch up soon.

Tragically and very unfortunately only three weeks later, Graham Rockwell unexpectedly

When Baptized.	When Born.	Child's Christian Name.	Parents' Names.		Abode.	Quality or Profession.	By whom the Ceremony was performed.
			Christian.	Surname.			
1907 March. 6	1907 2nd January	Alfred Barrett	William Henry & Elizabeth	Rockwell	99 Harford Shire	Pub Proprietor	S. J. Terry
1907 March 6.	1907 2nd January	Ernest Barrett.	William Henry & Elizabeth	Rockwell	99 Harford Shore	Pub Proprietor	S. J. Terry

BAPTISMS Administered in the Parish of ... in the ... County of ... in the Year 18 .

▲ABOVE: Baptism for the twins Alfred and Ernest Barrett Rockwell, held on the 2nd January 1907 at St Johns Church, Glebe (Baptism, Burial, Confirmation, Marriage and composite registers in the Anglican Church Diocese of Sydney Archives).

5.2 Descendants of Alfred Barrett Rockwell & Olive Ruth Loader

Alfred Barrett Rockwell (1907-1969), was born in Glebe, and later married on the 11th November 1939 at St George's Church, Hurstville to Olive (1915-1971), dau. of William & Lucy Loader, with issue:

1. Graham Alfred ROCKWELL (1942-2001), married 18th May 1966 to Margaret Dean (1944). Graham died on the 27th May 2001 and is buried at Macquarie Park Cemetery, with issue:

1.1 Nicole Margaret Rockwell (1970), married on the 7th July 1990 to Ian Geoffrey THONG (1959) with issue:
a. Daniel Ian THONG (1993)
b. Joshua Graham Francis THONG (1997), now known as Theresa Joshua Thong.
c. Rebecca Nicola Thong (1999)

1.2 Ian Graham Dean ROCKWELL (1972), aka 'Rocky' married Lisa ? He completed a Bachelor of

Rockwell | *Loader*

Social Science in Physical Education and Outdoor Recreation, and then a Graduate Diploma of Education. After teaching PD/H/PE and working as a sportsmaster for 11 years, he realised his passion was in the outdoors and became the owner and director of Boomerang Adventures. Taking students out of the classroom and teaching them in a different environment brought him great satisfaction. His issue is as follows:
a. Amber Rockwell (?)
b. Jacob ROCKWELL (?)
c. Mitchell ROCKWELL (?)
d. Zara Rockwell (?)

1.3 Stephen Barrett ROCKWELL (1975), married in 2002 to Susan Clare Merewether. (1977), with issue:
a. Matthew Stephen ROCKWELL (2007)
b. Luke Andrew ROCKWELL (2009)
c. Michael P.eter ROCKWELL (2012)
d. Jonathan Richard ROCKWELL (2014)

* Died before adulthood - d.s.p.

Alfred Barrett Rockwell & Family

ROCKWELL, Graham Alfred. — May 27, 2001, late of St Ives, dearly loved husband of Margaret, much loved father of Nicola, Ian and Stephen, special son-in-law of June and Eric, father-in-law of Ian and Lisa, grandfather of Daniel, Joshua, Rebecca, Amber and Jacob.

Aged 58 years.
In God's presence forever.

A funeral service to celebrate the life of GRAHAM will be held at Christ Church (Anglican), Cowan Road, St Ives, on Friday (June 1, 2001), at 10.30 a.m. Following the service the cortege will then proceed to Macquarie Park Cemetery.

ANN WILSON FUNERALS
AUSTRALIAN OWNED
FDA of NSW
9971 4224

MEREWETHER — ROCKWELL. — Rick and Beverly Ann Merewether, of Killara, have much pleasure in announcing the engagement of their younger daughter, Susan Clare, to Stephen Barrett, the youngest son of Margaret and the late Graham Rockwell, of St. Ives.

▲TOP: The marriage certificate of Alfred Barrett Rockwell and Olive Ruth Loader, held on the 11th November 1939 at St Georges Church, Hurstville (NSW BDM #21737/1939). MID (Left): Photo of Alfred Barrett Rockwell (1907-1969), c.1957. (Centre): Photo of Dr. Graham Alfred Rockwell (1942-2001), the son. (Right): Photo of Ian 'Rocky' Rockwell, son of Graham, grandson of Alf and great grandson of William Henry Rockwell. ABOVE (Left & Centre): Death and funeral notices for Graham Alfred Rockwell (1942-2001). (Right): Engagement announcement for Stephen Barrett Rockwell (SMH, 7th April 2002).

died on the 27th of May 2001, aged just 58, and sadly before we had an opportunity to organise a meeting. Graham Alfred Rockwell is remembered with a memorial at the Macquarie Park Cemetery (*Portion-AJ, Hare Lawn, Row-31, Plot 013A*).[23]

6. Ernest Barrett Rockwell (1907-1978) ⚠

Ernest Barrett Rockwell was the second born of the second set of Rockwell twins, and he arrived on the 2nd January 1907 and was baptised on 6th March at St Johns Church, Glebe.[24] Ernie was probably exposed to all the antics of his four older brothers as he was growing up, and apparently grew into a street-wise young man.

Albert 'Tibby' Cotter (1883-1917)

KILLED IN ACTION.

ALBERT COTTER, CRICKETER.

Mr. J. H. Cotter, of Monteith, Glebe-road, Glebe, has been notified that his youngest son, Trooper Albert ("Tibby") Cotter, was killed in action in Egypt on October 30. He left Australia on active service in August, 1915.

Albert Cotter was one of the most consistent of the State's leading cricketers. He was born in Phillip-street, Sydney, December 3, 1884, and was therefore 32 years of age. He received his education at the Forest Lodge Public School and the Sydney Grammar School.

THE LATE TROOPER COTTER.

His career in first-class cricket began with the Glebe Club, in 1900, and very quickly he established himself as a brilliant bowler—one of the fastest, in fact, that the State has ever had. He was, as well, a batsman of considerable merit. His highest scores made with the bat for his club were 156 and 127. The former included sixteen 6's, and was made against Waverley, on Waverley Oval.

He made his first appearance in international cricket in 1903, when he was included in the New South Wales team against Warner's English Eleven, and in that match took five wickets for 44, and three for 56. This was followed by participation in the fourth and fifth test matches of that season, and thence forward he was firmly established in international ranks.

He visited England twice with Australian Elevens—in 1905 and 1909. His career in big cricket lasted nine years—until the famous split with the Board of Control in 1911.

▲Albert Cotter, an ex-student of Forest Lodge School, killed in action (SMH, 20 Nov 1917, p.8). Identity disc taken from the body of trooper Cotter prior to his burial, and Cotter's test cricket ball was turned into a memorial souvenir by his family for the ANZAC Memorial Collection [National Museum of Australia].

Albert "Tibby" Cotter (3 December 1883 – 31 October 1917) was an ex-student of Forest Lodge Public School and Sydney Grammar School. He was also an Australian cricketer who played in 21 Tests between 1904 and 1912 (89 wickets, average 28.64), and 115 first-class matches between 1901 and 1914 (including 123 wickets, average 23.45 for New South Wales).

On 31 October 1917 the 4th Light Horse Brigade, of which the 12th Regiment was part, captured Beersheba by a brilliant cavalry-style charge. Although Cotter was there as a stretcher-bearer, he actually took part in the charge itself, and "was shot from the saddle during a mounted charge on a Turkish position." His brother John had been killed in Belgium serving with the 4th Battalion just three weeks earlier.

"Cotter was killed in a mounted charge on Beersheba at dusk on the 31st October 1917. Early next morning, together with Trooper O'Rourke of our troop, I was detailed to collect saddlery and personal effects. We were surprised to find Cotter amongst our casualties, knowing he had been detailed for that day as a stretcher bearer. It seems he had changed places with another Light Horseman because he wanted to be in the mounted charge." (The Crookwell Gazette, 1 March 1933).

Dr. Graham Alfred Rockwell

Graham Alfred Rockwell (1942-2001) grew up in Hurstville as an only child and lived there all his childhood life, except for the year he stayed at the Margaret Reid Orthopaedic Hospital for Crippled Children at St Ives after contracting polio during the mid 1950's Sydney pandemic peak. Graham was placed in an iron lung and would finally overcome the paralysis in every area of his body except his left leg. Graham did not let his withered leg and a calliper define his life, which would have been the impression of the mechanics who got tasked with making modifications to his black convertible car to allow for his disabled access hand clutch.

Being a Hurstville boy, he was an avid supporter of The St George Dragons well before their 11 consecutive premierships from 1956-1966, but somewhat attributes their demise to the fact that 1967 was the first year he took his new bride from the Manly-Warringah district to their first match of live football.

Graham fell in love with Margaret Dean when they met working in the Pharmacology Department at the University of Sydney. He went on to complete his PhD in Biochemistry and after finishing commenced with CSIRO as a research scientist. Margaret was also an only child and became a very long serving high school Science teacher.

After they were married, Graham and Margaret lived their early days together in a variety of Northern Beaches suburbs including North Manly, Mona Vale and Dee Why before building their family home in Forestville where they moved in 1976.

Graham developed a keen sense of adventure which expanded into travel. His work with the Bible Society would see him undertake many trips to America before embracing the opportunity to learn a new scientific method would see him spend live with his young family in San Diego California from 1978-1979. Graham was also an early adopter. The first home computer was bought in 1980 and Graham and Margaret would visit China in the mid 1980s at a time when tourism was not at all common.

After doing research for over 30 years, Graham became the Occupational Health and Safety Officer for CSIRO in the late 1980s and then was appointed at the National Occupational Health and Safety Officer for the Commonwealth Bank in 1996. He also acted as the Officer in Charge of Polling Stations for many years and was appointed a Lay Preacher by the Anglican Diocese of Sydney.

Graham would meet five of his ten grandchildren before he died. He was always very committed to and loving of his precious family.

By Nicole Thong (nee Rockwell), dau, 27th April 2022

EMPIRE DAY AT THE GLEBE

Preparations are being made in the Glebe district to make Empire Day a memorable occasion, at least for the children in attendance at the various schools there. Recently a representative meeting of parents and teachers was held at the Glebe Town Hall, and it was decided to arrange for a monster picnic for the youngsters, at Epping Recreation Ground. The Empire League has presented to the Forest Lodge School a flag which will be unfurled on Empire Day, Of. 25. Last year the Glebe School received a flag from the league.

▲TOP: Ernie Rockwell (circled) at Forest Lodge Primary School (c.1918). ABOVE (Left): Empire Day at Glebe (The Australian Star, 5th May 1908, p.2). (Right): The very idea of a day that would …"remind children that they formed part of the British Empire, and that they might think with others in lands across the sea, what it meant to be sons and daughters of such a glorious Empire", and that "the strength of the Empire depended upon them, and they must never forget it."

Ernie Rockwell also attended Forest Lodge School, and apparently first met Alice at ten years of age whilst she was living in Glebe, and Ernie was residing in Forest Lodge.[25] Consequently, he became the youngest amongst his brothers to wed, when he married Alice Maud (1911-1997), the daughter of Albert and Maud Greenup on the 16th July 1927 in Sydney.[26] Although Ernie and Alice married while she was pregnant, they went on to produce three children in quick succession with their marriage lasting for over 51 years.

Joy Rockwell remembers being told that Ernie was very strict with his children and they apparently sat at a different dinner table from their parents, with their father having a far-reaching cane or strap for any misbehaviour.[27]

Ernie was an electrician by trade and they first resided in Earlwood, then moved to Banksia.[28] Between the wars, Ernie joined the AIF on the 18th November 1930 and was a sergeant in the radar unit at Townsville, and perhaps also worked as a cook. However, by 1935 he had left the army and on the 22nd August 1935 joined G.J. Coles Pty. Ltd. Ernie worked for Coles continuously for the next 36 years, being most well known as the elevator operator at the King St. City store, where he retired on the 8th January 1972.[29] As a small boy I still remember meeting Ernie, with my father Bob Rockwell Jr (his nephew), when we once entered the elevator at Coles in the city, and he was so surprised, but pleased to see us.

Ernie was the longest lived of the five Rockwell brothers, but passed away on the 12th June 1978, aged 71, and was buried at Woronora Cemetery.[30] Following Ernie's death, his wife Alice moved to Moat Avenue, Brighton Le Sands where I interviewed her in company with her daughter Elaine in June 1980, which provided much of the anecdotal information for this chapter.

During the interview Alice recollected that the last time she remembered seeing my father, Robert Hunter Rockwell was at Alf and Olive's wedding at Hurstville in 1940.

▲ TOP: Forest Lodge Superior Public School, 1st XI, 1912 with the headmaster, William Bardsley and scorer Tom Brown (with score book), and William Henry Rockwell Jr. (circled). ABOVE: The future Sir Robert Askin, Premier of NSW is somewhere in this photograph of 6th Class at Forest Lodge Public School in 1920 (Ernie & Alf Rockwell are circled).

Forest Lodge School[33]

Forest Lodge was named after a house built in the area in 1836 by Ambrose Foss (1803-1862). Foss was a prosperous chemist, grocer and dentist in colonial Sydney who became an alderman and church deacon, also co-founding the Congregational Church in New South Wales. The Forest Lodge estate originally comprised a grant made to Foss of "thirty-one acres, two roods and fifteen perches" under the hand of Sir George Gipps and dated March 8, 1840. He gave his new home the name of Forest Lodge because it was "surrounded by great trees." A real estate advertisement in 1848 described the house as "that delightful residence at the Glebe... consisting of seven rooms, pantry, storeroom, kitchen, coach-house, stable and other detached offices." The word 'glebe' means land owned by the church and the suburb was referred to as 'the Glebe' until the early 20th century. In 1846, Forest Lodge passed into the hands of naturalist and surgeon Dr George Bennett who owned it until 1865 when it became the home of department store founder David Jones. Sadly, the house was demolished in 1912 and today apartments stand on the site, which is opposite the school at 208-210 Bridge Road.

The imposing gate on Bridge Road, retained for its architectural and historic interest, serves as a reminder of when Forest Lodge Public School operated as three distinctly separate departments: Boys, Girls and Infants. The school originally opened in 1883 as just a Boys' and Infants' school, but by 1885 the attendance rose to over 400, entitling the school to a separate girls' department. In 1886 a large schoolroom, 19.5m x 7.5m, was added to the existing building with seating for 200 girls and the 'Girls' School' gate was built. The Boys' and Infants' entrance was via the Ross Street gate, and boys could also enter by the Charles Street gate, where the male WC was then located. With the addition of the Girls' School enrolments at this time numbered about 1000 (there are 315 students today) and it remained around this figure for the next 25 or so years. Even with the high rate of truancy, classrooms were bursting at the seams; lessons were held in hatrooms, weathersheds, corridors and outdoors, and classroom lessons rotated. Further extensions in 1913 gave the school 19 classrooms, allowing an average class size of a more 'manageable' 50 pupils. Boys' and girls' education remained separated at NSW public schools until co-education was introduced in the early 1960s.

MR. BARDSLEY ON HOLIDAY.—Mr. Bardsley, head master of the Forest Lodge Public School, and father of Warren Bardsley, the famous cricketer, spent his Easter vacation on the Macleay, a considerable portion of the time being spent at Crescent Head, where the worthy pedagogue thoroughly enjoyed himself.

▲ Two photographs of Forest Lodge Public School from Ross Street.

Apparently Joy (13), Robert (11), Elwood (7) and Lindsay (4) were with Bob Rockwell and Corelli at the time. During the wedding reception Corelli must have said to Bob "Oh, I do love babies" and Alice overhearing this, commented to Ernie... "fancy her saying that, just look at those four little ones pulling her all about!" The last time Alice and Ernie saw Corelli Rockwell, they were told of Ronie Rockwell having flown to Germany after separating from his first wife.[31]

While obviously fond of one another, these anecdotes demonstrate that the five Rockwell brothers sadly weren't very close, with the brothers rarely getting together and most of the cousins having never met! I wonder whether this distant behaviour was a Rockwell trait or whether the estrangement between the brothers had another explanation. It seems quite possible that whereas sisters tend to maintain close relationships, over time brothers allow themselves to become distant, often pulled apart by vindictive and jealous wives, an unfortunate consequence of marriage.

All the Rockwell brothers shared a firm sense of discipline, which was probably passed down from their father. Sadly, they all died of heart failure with Ernie Rockwell having four separate attacks, the last being the one that killed him. On the positive side, Ernie was apparently both prudent and frugal, leaving his family quite comfortable. Alice passed away on the 28th February 1997, aged 86 (*see 6.3 Descendants of Ernest Barrett Rockwell & Alice Maud Greenup*).[32] Ernest Barrett Rockwell is remembered with a memorial at the

Ernest Barrett Rockwell & Family

Ernest Barrett Rockwell (Reg. #155459) enlisted in the AIF on the 18th November 1930 at Forest Lodge, NSW. He recorded himself as being 23yrs & 11mths of age, was working as an 'Electrician', and gave his address as 18 Gottenham Street, Glebe. He was 5' 8" tall, 8st 9lbs (55kgs) and initially signed up for a period of 3 years in the Militia Forces.

He was appointed to the 55th Battalion, 2nd Division Signals, but being peacetime his official record states nothing other than that he resigned from the army sometime in 1936, then recalled on the outbreak of war from 1939 to 1946.

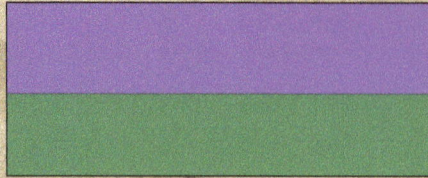

Will exchange No. 2 Brownie box camera for a set of 8 or 12oz. boxing gloves. Ernest Rockwell, 11 Charles St., Forest Lodge, N.S.W.

Death Notice

ROCKWELL, Marjorie (Marj.) February 24th, 2000, at Karinya Palliative Care Unit, Berry, aged 65, late of Ulladulla, formerly of Engadine, beloved wife of Norm, loved mother and mother-in-law of Melissa and John, Dean and Heather, loved grandma of Kelsey.

Funeral Notice

The relatives and friends of the late Marj. Rockwell are invited to attend her funeral service to be held in Milton, Ulladulla. Funeral Services, Chapel 2, Camden Street, Ulladulla, on Monday (February 28, 2000), at 10.00am. At the conclusion of the service there will be a private cremation.
MILTON ULLADULLA FUNERAL SERVICES
2 Camden St. Ulladulla
Ph: (02) 4454 0722 AFDA

Sydney Morning Herald, 24th February 2000

▲ TOP (Left): Photo of Alice Maud Greenup. (Centre): Ernie's regimental colour patch & an advertisement for boxing gloves in the 'The World News', 2nd Feb. 1924, p.34; (Right): Ernest Barrett Rockwell, youngest son of William Henry and Elizabeth Rockwell, c.1930 in his military uniform, having enlisted in the AIF between the wars from 1930 to 1936. MID (Left): Ernie and Alice Rockwell at their wedding in 1927, with Norman 'Jack' Rockwell behind. (Right): The twins Ernie and Alf Rockwell at Graham Rockwell's wedding in 1966. ABOVE (Left): Photo of Ernie Rockwell's second son Norman Alfred Rockwell, wife Marjorie (nee Stephens) with children Dean and Melissa, and Marjorie's mother, c.1974. (Right): Death and funeral notices for Marjorie Rockwell (nee Burke), daughter-in-law of Ernie and Alice Rockwell (SMH, 24th February 2000).

5.3 Descendants of Ernest Barrett Rockwell & Alice Maud Greenup

Ernest Barrett Rockwell (1907-1978), was born in Glebe, and later married on the 16th July 1927 at St Pauls Church, Redfern to Alice Maud (1911-1997), dau. of Albert & Maud Greeup, with issue:

1. Ronald Ernest ROCKWELL (1927-2009), *mechanic, married in 1952 to Enid Mary Travis (1926-1975). Ron died on the 12th June 2009 and is buried at Wollongong Memorial Gardens. With issue:*

1.1 Lynette Enid Rockwell (1954), married in 1975 to Ian Douglas HEELEY (1954), with issue:
a. Karyn Michelle Heeley (1980) married Mr. Harmston, with issue:

1.2 Gary Ronald ROCKWELL (1955), mechanic, issue unknown

Rockwell

Greenup

2. Norman Alfred ROCKWELL (1928), *married in 1960 to Marjorie Burke (1934-2000), with issue:*

2.1 Melissa Rockwell (1962), married to John ?, with issue:
a. Kelsey (?)

2.2 Dean ROCKWELL (1968), married to Heather ?

3. Elaine Faye Rockwell (1930), *married in 1950 to Norman Wallace BANKS (b.1928), with issue:*

3.1 Kevin Norman BANKS (1954)

3.2 Jeffrey Gordon BANKS (1956)

3.3 Bronwyn Joan Banks (1958)

* Died before adulthood - d.s.p.

▲ *The inner city streets of Sydney during the mid 1960's.*

Woronora Cemetery (*Portion-HH, Row-Evergreen Shrub Garden 16, Plot 0112*), with his wife Alice alongside(*Plot-0114*).

This genealogy continues through Robert Archibald Rockwell, the third son of William Henry Rockwell and Elizabeth Bantin, who married Octavia Corelli O'Sullivan. Therefore this genealogy next examines Corelli's parents, Humphrey Joseph O'Sullivan and his wife Lenore Mackie (nee Shoveller), who both originated from Grafton and the Clarence River District of northern New South Wales.

References

1. NSW Dept of BDM. (1927). Marriage Certificate for Norman John Rockwell & Stella R. Edgerton, #1740/1927.

2. Richard Adrian Rockwell - Death notice (Sydney Morning Herald, 19th March 1956).

3. NSW Dept of BDM. (1956). Death Certificate for Richard Adrian Rockwell, #938/1956.

4. NSW Dept of BDM. (1963). Death Certificate for Rose May Rockwell, # 20736/1963.

5. NSW Dept of BDM. (1970). Death Certificate for William Henry Rockwell Jr., #42096/1970.

6. NSW Dept of BDM. (1903). Birth Certificate for Muriel Rockwell, #20948/1903.

7. St Johns Church, Glebe - Baptismal Record for Muriel Rockwell held on the 7th July 1903 at (Baptism, Burial, Confirmation, Marriage and composite registers in the Anglican Church Diocese of Sydney Archives).

8. NSW Dept of BDM. (1908). Death Certificate for Muriel Rockwell, #994/1908.

9. St Johns Church, Glebe - Baptismal Record for Norman John Rockwell, held on the 7th July 1903 at (Baptism, Burial, Confirmation, Marriage and composite registers in the Anglican Church Diocese of Sydney Archives).

10. NSW Dept of BDM. (1927). Marriage Certificate for Norman John Rockwell & Stella R. Edgerton, #17407/1927.

11. Rockwell, Alice, 1911-1997 (Interviewee, 1980). 'Alice Rockwell (nee Greenup) interviewed by Tracy Rockwell on the 12th of June 1980, at Kyeemagh, Sydney'.

12. NSW Dept of BDM. (1939). Death Certificate for Stella Rosamond Rockwell, #5767/1939.

13. Rockwell, Alice, 1911-1997 (Interviewee, 1980). op. cit.

14. NSW Dept of BDM. (1973). Death Certificate for Norman John Rockwell, #65959/1973.

15. NSW Dept of BDM. (1904). Birth Certificate for Robert Archibald Rockwell, #32224/1904.

16. NSW Dept of BDM. (1926). Marriage Certificate for Robert Archibald Rockwell & Octavia Corelli O'Sullivan, #15695/1926.

17. NSW Dept of BDM. (1966). Death Certificate for Robert Archibald Rockwell, #27190/1966.

18. NSW Dept of BDM. (1976). Death Certificate for Octavia Corelli Rockwell (nee O'Sullivan), #15733/1976.

19. Alfred Barrett Rockwell (#7221) - Resident at 8 Gottenham St, Glebe (West Sydney, NSW, Australia, Electoral Rolls, 1903-1980).

20. NSW Dept of BDM. (1939). Marriage Certificate for Alfred Barrett Rockwell & Olive Ruth Loader, #21737/1939.

21. Rockwell, Alice, 1911-1997 (Interviewee, 1980). op. cit.

22. Rockwell, Alice, 1911-1997 (Interviewee, 1980). op. cit.

23. Death Notice for Graham Alfred Rockwell (Sydney Morning Herald, 31st May 2001).

24. St Johns Church, Glebe - Baptismal Record for Ernest Barrett Rockwell, held on the 6th March 1907 at (Baptism, Burial, Confirmation, Marriage and composite registers in the Anglican Church Diocese of Sydney Archives).

25. Rockwell, Alice, 1911-1997 (Interviewee, 1980). op. cit.

26. NSW Dept of BDM. (1927). Marriage Certificate for Ernest Barrett Rockwell & Alice Maud Greenup, #10459/1927.

27. Hyde, Joy, 1927-2018 (Interviewee, 2001). 'Joy Hyde (nee Rockwell) interviewed by Tracy Rockwell on the 19th of August 2001, at Aspley, Brisbane'.

28. Rockwell, Alice, 1911-1997 (Interviewee, 1980). op. cit.

29. G.J. Coles Personnel Dept. (1980). Ernest Barrett Rockwell - Retired 8th January 1972. Personnel Records.

30. NSW Dept of BDM. (1978). Death Certificate for Ernest Barrett Rockwell, #13359/1978.

31. Rockwell, Alice, 1911-1997 (Interviewee, 1980). op. cit.

32. Death Notice for Alice Maud Rockwell (Sydney Morning Herald, 2 March 1997).

33. Forest Lodge Public School (2016). School History [https://forestlodg-p.schools.nsw.gov.au/about-our-school/history.html].

Chapter Six

O'Sullivan

HUMPHREY JOSEPH O'SULLIVAN

(Father of Octavia Corelli O'Sullivan)

Humphrey Joseph Vincent O'Sullivan was the eldest child of James Mahony O'Sullivan, born about 1837, a gold miner who had emigrated in 1859 from Ireland, and Ellen Frawley the first white child born 1842 in the Monaro District on the far south coast of New South Wales. They had married at St Mary's Cathedral in Sydney on the 3rd August 1869 ahead of going bush to prospect for gold.[1]

Humphrey's birth occurred on the 5th May 1871,[2] a year in world history which saw the continuance of the Franco-Prussian War, caused primarily by France's determination to reassert its dominant position in continental Europe. This brought on the proclamation that year of the German Empire with Otto von Bismarck becoming its first Chancellor. In Australia, the telegraph cable from London was brought ashore at Darwin. Notable people born in 1871 include the future president of Germany, Friedrich Ebert (19 August), the American pioneer aviator and co-inventor of the airplane, Orville Wright (19 August), and New Zealand physicist, and recipient of the Nobel Prize in Chemistry Ernest Rutherford, (30 August).

Humphrey O'Sullivan was born at Fish River Creek, near Bathurst in New South Wales, better known today as the town of Oberon.[3] His 33 year old father James Mahony O'Sullivan, was an Irish emigrant from Coomb Cottage, Rathmore, co. Kerry who listed himself as a miner on the birth certificate. His 28 year old mother Ellen Frawley, listed

▲ *Gold was first discovered in Australia on 15 February 1823, by assistant surveyor James McBrien, at the Fish River, near Bathurst, but the finds were suppressed by the colonial government to avoid a disruption of the infant colony. But 50 years later, this backwater became the birthplace of Humphrey Joseph O'Sullivan on the 5th May 1871.*

her birthplace as Twofold Bay, as that was presumably more recognisable than her actual birthplace, the homestead of "Warragubera" near today's town of Bega.

Unfortunately, Humphrey O'Sullivan's life was tragically cut short by pnuemonia, which also placed in peril all knowledge of his ancient and illustrious ancestry. It was only through the devotion of his determined and resourceful future wife and mother of his daughters, Lenore Shoveller, that Humphrey's extraordinary legacy eventually resurfaced through his descendants, as they would later become the parents of Octavia Corelli O'Sullivan.

The Ancestry of Humphrey Joseph Vincent O'Sullivan

Although a little shorn of its splendour over the years, Humphrey received from his father a noble ancestry, which can be traced back through the ancient Irish families of O'Sullivan, Mahony, MacCarthy, and through the dynastic and aristocratic houses of FitzGerald and Butler to draw blood from not just one, but most of the illustrious royal houses of England, Ireland, France, Scotland and Wales.

"If it be lawful to claim a share in the merits of by-gone generations, his name is adorned by the virtues and the greatness of a glorious array of ancestors..."

From 'Sermons of Abbe MacCarthy" by Nicolas Tuite de MacCarthy & C. Mahony [4]

For a detailed account of Humphrey Joseph O'Sullivan's fascinating paternal ancestry see Volumes 3 and 4 of the Rockwell Genealogies - "The Mahonys of Dunloe,"[Ref] and "The Path That Few Tread: A Genealogy of James Mahony O'Sullivan."[Ref] Humphrey's

28 year old mother descended from the opposite end of the social spectrum, as both her parents were transported convicts. However, even she could make a proud assertion, as in 1842 she became one of the very first white pioneer children born in the Monaro District on the far south coast of New South Wales. For a detailed account of Humphrey Joseph O'Sullivan's fascinating maternal ancestry see Volume 5 of the Rockwell Genealogies - "Prisoners & Pioneers: A Genealogy of John Frawley & Mary Ann McGarry."[Ref]

As his father was prospecting for gold at the time, Humphrey's birth wasn't registered until nine weeks later on the 11th of July, when his parents were able to journey into Bathurst for his baptism. But Humphrey's father had no luck at the Fish River, so they packed up and returned to Sydney, before heading north to the developing Clarence River District and the town of Grafton.

It was in Grafton that Humphrey was soonafter joined by a brother in James Alexander O'Sullivan who arrived in 1872.[5] The family increased again with another brother and

▲ TOP (Left): Gold diggers arriving at Bathurst on their way to Ophir in 1851. (Right): Howick St, Bathurst outside the Duke's Hotel, c.1871. ABOVE: The 1871 Birth certificate of Humphrey O'Sullivan (NSW BDM #6704/1871).

sister, but they unfortunately died as infants, before John Washington O'Sullivan joined the family in 1877.[6]

James Mahony O'Sullivan had moved his family north, but not to the township of Grafton, but to the shanty village of Dalmorton, that had sprung up in response to the thousands of prospectors that flocked there in the mid 1870s.

Little is known of the daily movements of the O'Sullivan family and where they lived and worked, but it must have been disruptive given the demands of goldmining. However, one thing was certain, being Catholics of Irish stock, their family was bound to increase, and it did.

A sister for Humphrey arrived in the person of Mary Zenobia O'Sullivan in 1879, but she unfortunately died in the same year.[7] Then in 1880, Ellen Theresa O'Sullivan was born,[8] and was quickly followed by Blanche Zenobia O'Sullivan whose birth was registered at Glenn Innes in 1882.[9] Two more boys arrived being named William O'Sullivan at Moonee Creek in 1884, and Rupert Clarence O'Sullivan in Grafton in 1886, but they sadly died as infants both in the same year as their birth.[10,11] Then another daughter was born in 1888 who also died as an infant.[12] Humphrey's last sibling, another sister arrived in 1891 and was named in honour of her paternal Irish grandmother, Zenobia O'Sullivan, but she too succumbed to the rigours of pioneering life in the Australian bush.[13]

The rugged mining lifestyle was overwhelmingly responsible for the high infant mortality in this family, but the exact causes of death have not been identified. Under such trying circumstances, life was extraordinarily difficult for a family with five children in tow, and the inconveniences they endured is a testament to their strength and resilience.

▲ Prospecting for gold required bush camping skills in the 1870's, and Humphrey Joseph O'Sullivan was born into such an environment.

▲ *TOP (Left): Prince Street, Grafton, c.1874. (Right): The "SS Australian" was a well-known 'coaster' on the Sydney-Clarence River route. ABOVE: The bark slab hut was home to many pioneers in the country regions.*

Despite the many hardships, letters written by Humphrey reveal that he must have had the benefit of a decent schooling as his writing exhibits a fine style, and demonstrates an excellent use of vocabulary and language. After 1872, the O'Sullivans resided for the most part in the Clarence River District and north of Coffs Harbour, so Humphrey probably attended small schools at Dalmorton and Moonee Creek.

Dalmorton was one of those many towns in Australia, whose rise and fall was traceable to the discovery and depletion of gold. At one stage it had 3000 inhabitants, five hotels, three stores, a post office (opened 1872), a school (from Jan.1879 to Nov.1883) and its own annual races. However, with most of the ore removed by 1895, it declined quickly as the miners moved on to more productive goldfields.

Although James Mahony O'Sullivan remained at Dalmorton to work his claims, he took on a conditional purchase of land at Moonee Creek in 1883, and moved the family there after erecting a bush home on the property.

At this time most of the white population lived in simple slab or bark dwellings, but schooling was an important public service required by the early settlers. In early 1885, George Shephard made a hurried trip to Grafton, where the Schools Inspector agreed to supply a teacher "when the residents had built a school."[14] Shephard wasted no time in

▲ TOP (Left): The old schoolhouse at Dalmorton. (Right): The Dalmorton Tunnel. ABOVE: Dalmorton was one of those many towns in Australia, whose rise and fall was traceable to the discovery and depletion of gold.

complying, and organised the cutting of slabs for the flooring and walls, the splitting of shingles for the roof... and the building was completed "within a week" at a cost to the settlers of £20.[15]

By March 1885, the 'slab hut' opened as a 'Provisional School' under Miss Ida A. Archibald, who became the very first teacher.[16] Miss Archibald was succeeded by Mr. David J. Stuart, and by the second half of 1886 it was downgraded to a half-time school to be shared with Bonville. By 1889, a Mr. Henry T. Schaefer was appointed teacher.

A State school was already operating with all available children attending at Woolgoolga by 1886, with other small schools coming into existence. As Moonee Creek lies almost equidistant between Woolgoolga in the north and Coffs Harbour in the south, the O'Sullivan boys could have attended either school, with perhaps the first to open being their choice. By 1885, Humphrey was 14, James 13 and young John was 8 years old, but it wasn't long before Moonee Creek had a school of its own.

Most of the children travelled to their schools on horse-back or in a sulky, which is a type of buggy drawn by a horse, as did the teacher. The 'school paddock' usually meant the acres put aside for the pupil's ponies to graze during school hours.[17]

Being the eldest, Humphrey bore witness to each of the seven deaths of his siblings, which would have given him a thankful prespective on his own life.

Moonee Creek School

It seems that following the funeral of Henry Cook, a local fisherman who had fallen from the rocks at the end of April 1886, "the selectors came to a mutual understanding to erect a school at Moonee Creek. They will contribute their own labor, put their hands in their pockets to the extent of about 20s each, and add the State subsidy of £10, and hope to have a school up in about a fortnight."[18]

Moonee School was situated near 'White Bluff' headland on the western side of the Pacific Highway, with eight acres being set aside for school purposes on the 28th January 1887. Although Mr. Arthur W. Apsey was the first teacher at Moonee Creek school from

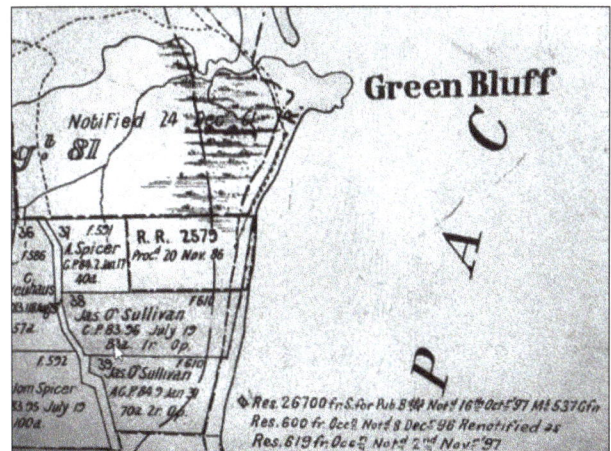

TOP: Neighbours of the O'Sullivans were John Carrall and his family outside their first home in Coffs Harbour (CH & District Hist Soc.). ABOVE (Left): 'A Bush Burial', painted by Frederick McCubbin (1890). (Right): Conditional Purchases for James O'Sullivan just south of Moonee Creek, which today is some of the most prime beachside land in the country (NSW Dept of Lands Office Map).

April 1886, his appointment was officially ratified on the 3rd March 1887 in the Sydney Morning Herald.[19] When the school first opened, the enrolment was eleven and remained about this figure until 1896, with the O'Sullivan children amongst them.

Mr. Apsey shared the appointment half-time with the small school hut erected at Bucca. Both schools measured just 14 feet by 12 feet and were constructed of slabs and bark, with shingle roofing.[20] The teachers would travel by horseback spending three days at Moonee and two days at Bucca one week, then vice versa the next, and boarded with local families, like the Skinners at Moonee Creek. In explaining why he was late returning to school after the Easter holiday in 1887, Mr. Apsey wrote:

> "Although I left Grafton before one o'clock I was benighted before I got to Mr. Sweenie's (30 miles from Grafton) owing to the bad state of the roads, and was compelled to camp with some roadmen. It was half past nine at night when I reached there, as I was compelled to walk on foot from the bridge to the cutting owing to the frequent bog holes. I opened at the usual hour next morning although I had to ride 20 miles before opening."

Arthur W. Apsey (Teacher), 11th April 1887 [21]

Other teachers followed at Moonee Creek including Mr John Fraser (appt. April 1889), Mr. John McPherson (appt. May 1892) and Mr. John Algie (appt. June 1894).[22]

Unfortunately, Humphrey's father passed away on the 10th of June 1891 at the age of

▲TOP: Humphrey and his mother Ellen O'Sullivan on the 1891 Census, with others living at Moonee Creek (1891 NSW Census). ABOVE (Left): Depiction of the O'Sullivans around the campfire en route to Moonee Creek in 1883. (Right): School children from either Coffs Harbour Provisional School, built 1885, or Korora School, which began in 1893 (Coffs Harbour & District Historical Society).

The Pacific Highway [24]

Initially, the primary mode of transport for the coastal regions was by boat. However, from the small roads that began to radiate out from the various towns, the intervening hills were eventually crossed to create a continuous route from town to town, but due to the large rivers, this did not occur along the entire coast until the first decade of the 20th century. By contrast a continuous inland route from Newcastle to Brisbane via the tablelands had been in existence since about the 1840s. A direct coastal route between Sydney and Newcastle was not completed until 1930, and completion of the sealing of the Pacific Highway did not occur until 1958 (at Koorainghat, south of Taree). The last of the many ferries across the northern coastal rivers was not superseded by a bridge until 1966 when the Harwood Bridge across the south channel of the Clarence River was completed, although the north channel had been bridged in 1931.

The Pacific Highway has a chequered history, as the general location of the original route travels from the junction with the Bradfield Highway on the Sydney Harbour Bridge in Milson's Point, through to the NSW-QLD Border. The route in the 21st century is in some cases unnumbered, but other sections include Metroad 1, Metroad 10, State Route 83, and State Route 111. The Pacific Highway (SR83) from Somersby to Doyalson was renamed Central Coast Highway, back in August 2006. The highway traces its origins back to an early settler, George Peat, who owned the land between the Hawkesbury River and Moonee Creek. To provide access to his property, Peat began a ferry service across the Hawkesbury River in 1844 and surveyed, then constructed a road between Hornsby and Kariong in 1854. After his death in 1870, the ferry service was abandoned and the road fell into disrepair, finally closing to all traffic in 1899, following the completion of the Sydney-Newcastle railway.

However, demand for a land route between Sydney and Newcastle dated back to the early 20th century, while the only access was via the sea or via a long route through the town of Wiseman's Ferry. In the 1920s, the then Main Roads Board undertook a series of surveys to form an easier and more reliable route north from Sydney. In 1928 construction began on upgrading the old road and converting it to modern standards, plus creating a new route north, utilising some of the abandoned Peat's Ferry Rd, while improving the horizontal and vertical alignments. In May 1930 the ferry service across the Hawkesbury River was re-established to service the new road until such times that a bridge became necessary, and June 1930 marked the completion of the concrete surfacing.

Prior to 1925, highway construction for motor vehicles on the north coast of NSW was almost non existant. During the time of the Hornsby to Gosford contruction, improvements were made to roads between Gosford and Newcastle as part of the link. On May 17th 1929, the route was named the 'Great Northern Highway'. The work from Hornsby to Gosford cost almost £1 million, however it was money well spent, cutting the trip time from Sydney to Newcastle from 9 to just 4½ hours. The route of the original Pacific Highway, which is still more or less the case now, generally parallels the NSW coast, touching the coast when difficult terrain meant the road had nowhere else to go. The following key dates show the gradual upgrading of the Pacific Highway:

- 1931: In May, after pressure from the Queensland Govt, the coastal highway linking Sydney and Brisbane was named the Pacific Highway.
- 1931: the Main Roads Board (MRB) built a bridge over the Nambucca River at Macksville, which replaced a vehicular ferry.
- 1934-36: building of a bridge over north arm of Bellinger River constructed at Raleigh, bridge over Terranorra Inlet of the Tweed River at Tweed Heads, bridge over the Clarence River at Mororo and the Tweed River at Barney's Point.
- 1935: first ever Australian construction of bow-string arch bridge over Shark Creek at Maclean.
- 1936: Burringbar Range deviation and O'Sullivan's Gap upgrade at Bulahdelah.
- 1936: Timber suspension bridge opened to traffic over the Hastings River near Port Macquarie.
- 1938: the highway between Murwillumbah and Mullumbimby was realigned and raised above flood level.
- 1938: construction of Peats Ferry Bridge at Brooklyn commenced with completion in May 1945 due to the war. A plaque on the southern end of the bridge serves as a monument to the energy and skill of the workmen.
- 1940s: construction of the bridge over the Hunter River at Hexham (completed 1952), bridge over Karuah River Booral, bridge over Coffs Creek near Coffs Harbour, bridge over Burringbar Creek at Burringbar, subway under the North Coast Railway Line at Crabbes Creek.
- 1948: proposal for the opening span bridge at Swansea, south of Newcastle.
- 1950s: bridges constructed at these locations: Karuah River in Karuah, Wollomba River at Nabiac, and Macleay River in Kempsey.
- 1960: in May, NSW's first ever gazetting of a motorway took place, a section of the highway just under a mile in length at Mount White.
- 1961: Port Macquarie bypassed
- 1966: August 20 saw the opening of the bridge over the Clarence River at Harwood. Also opening of a 4.6 mile deviation in the same area.

A dusty link road in what later became part of the Pacific Highway, on the north coast of New South Wales.

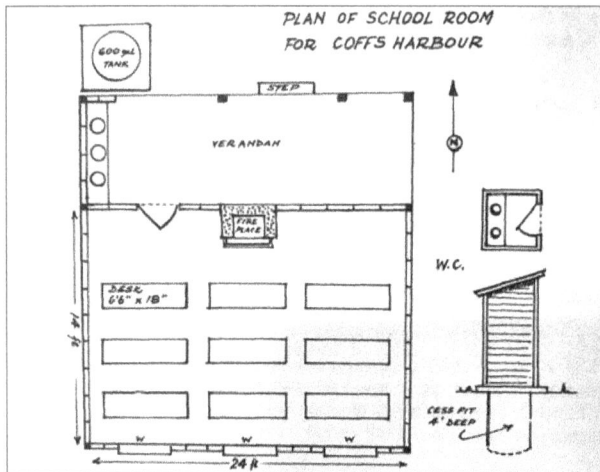

▲ TOP (Left): Plan for building Coffs Harbour Public School for £65, in the closing months of 1896. (State Archives of NSW [Ref: 5/15430 A]). (Right): 1886 The Public Schools Act provided for the appointment of Itinerant teachers for 'Half-time' schools (NSW Dept of Ed. (1980) Sydney and the Bush - A Pictorial History of Education in NSW). ABOVE: Early one-teacher school and pupils in the Coffs Harbour District. (CH & District Hist Soc.).

53 and 11 months, leaving to fend for themselves his 49 year old wife and five children.[23] The death certificate stated that James Mahony O'Sullivan died of bronchitis at South Grafton, and that his family were residing at Moonee Creek, just to the north of Coffs Harbour, on a 60 acre 'selection' taken up by their father in 1883.

In the next few years Humphrey gained employment as a labourer, most probably in and around Grafton, or perhaps even at Dalmorton. However, living and working in close proximity to Grafton inevitably brought Humphrey into contact with a young mother by the name of Lenore Mackie (nee Shoveller). We know from Humphrey's letters that they first met during one of the Clarence River floods. It was on this occasion that Lenore confided in him regarding her marital troubles, which related to her scoundrel of a husband, John Henry Mackie.

In early January of 1894, which was perhaps prior to the death of Lenore's estranged husband, Humphrey O'Sullivan had expressed his love and affection for her. Humphrey must certainly have fallen heavily for Lenore as he began writing the most eloquent of letters. Being the perfect gentleman and most respectful, he made sure to also write Lenore's mother Susan Shoveller, about the situation and his future intentions.

Travel During The 1890's

Looking back, it is fascinating to note that at this time, travelling between the coastal towns and cities of Australia was mostly undertaken by 'coasters', in the form of small to medium sized paddle and steam ships. The road network hadn't as yet been developed as motor cars weren't seen prior to the early 1900s. There were virtually no bridges and the mostly horse drawn carts and caravans used a network of independently operated punts to cross the many lakes and rivers that intersected the landscape, from where the dusty roads

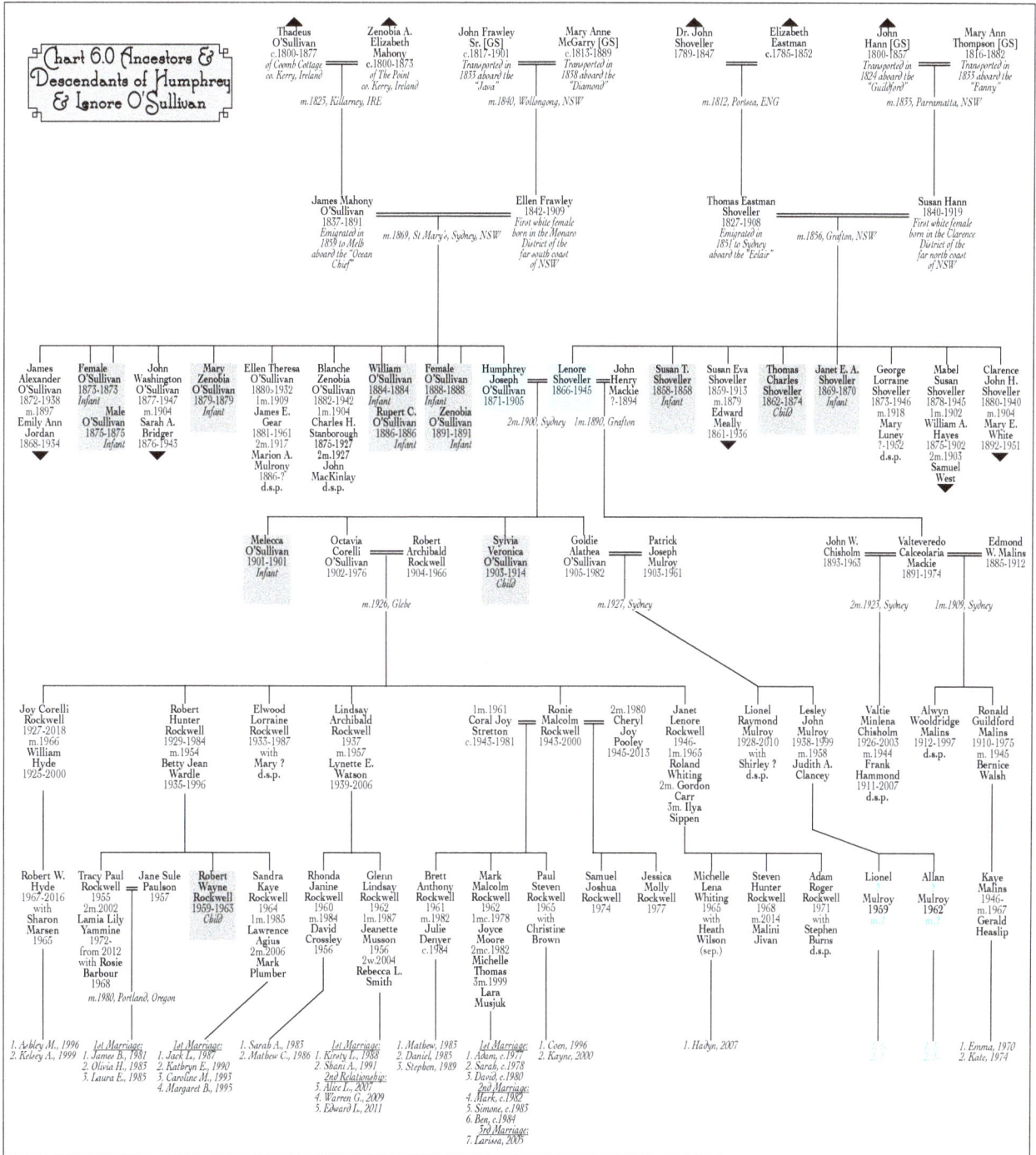

Chart 6.0 Ancestors & Descendants of Humphrey & Lenore O'Sullivan

Thadeus O'Sullivan c.1800-1877 of Coomb Cottage co. Kerry, Ireland
Zenobia A. Elizabeth Mahony c.1800-1873 of The Point co. Kerry, Ireland
m.1825, Killarney, IRE

John Frawley Sr. [GS] c.1817-1901 Transported in 1833 aboard the "Java"
Mary Anne McGarry [GS] c.1813-1889 Transported in 1838 aboard the "Diamond"
m.1840, Wollongong, NSW

Dr. John Shoveller 1789-1847
Elizabeth Eastman c.1785-1852
m.1812, Portsea, ENG

John Hann [GS] 1800-1857 Transported in 1824 aboard the "Guildford"
Mary Ann Thompson [GS] 1816-1882 Transported in 1833 aboard the "Fanny"
m.1835, Parramatta, NSW

James Mahony O'Sullivan 1837-1891 Emigrated in 1859 to Melb aboard the "Ocean Chief"
m.1869, St Mary's, Sydney, NSW
Ellen Frawley 1842-1909 First white female born in the Monaro District of the far south coast of NSW

Thomas Eastman Shoveller 1827-1908 Emigrated in 1851 to Sydney aboard the "Eclair"
m.1856, Grafton, NSW
Susan Hann 1840-1919 First white female born in the Clarence District of the far north coast of NSW

James Alexander O'Sullivan 1872-1938 m.1897 Emily Ann Jordan 1868-1934

Female O'Sullivan 1873-1873 Infant
Male O'Sullivan 1875-1875 Infant

John Washington O'Sullivan 1877-1947 m.1904 Sarah A. Bridger 1876-1943

Mary Zenobia O'Sullivan 1879-1879 Infant

Ellen Theresa O'Sullivan 1880-1932 1m.1909 James E. Gear 1881-1961 2m.1917 Marion A. Mulrony 1886-? d.s.p.

Blanche Zenobia O'Sullivan 1882-1942 1m.1904 Charles H. Stanborough 1875-1927 2m.1927 John MacKinlay d.s.p.

William O'Sullivan 1884-1884 Infant
Rupert C. O'Sullivan 1886-1886 Infant

Female O'Sullivan 1888-1888 Infant
Zenobia O'Sullivan 1891-1891 Infant

Humphrey Joseph O'Sullivan 1871-1905

Lenore Shoveller 1866-1945
John Henry Mackie ?-1894
2m.1900, Sydney 1m.1890, Grafton

Susan T. Shoveller 1858-1858 Infant

Susan Eva Shoveller 1859-1913 m.1879 Edward Meally 1861-1936

Thomas Charles Shoveller 1862-1874 Child

Janet E. A. Shoveller 1869-1870 Infant

George Lorraine Shoveller 1873-1946 m.1918 Mary Luney ?-1952 d.s.p.

Mabel Susan Shoveller 1878-1945 1m.1902 William A. Hayes 1875-1902 2m.1903 Samuel West

Clarence John H. Shoveller 1880-1940 m.1904 Mary E. White 1892-1951

Melecca O'Sullivan 1901-1901 Infant

Octavia Corelli O'Sullivan 1902-1976
Robert Archibald Rockwell 1904-1966
m.1926, Glebe

Sylvia Veronica O'Sullivan 1903-1914 Child

Goldie Alathea O'Sullivan 1905-1982
Patrick Joseph Mulroy 1903-1961
m.1927, Sydney

John W. Chisholm 1893-1963
Valteveredo Calceolaria Mackie 1891-1974
2m.1925, Sydney 1m.1909, Sydney

Edmond W. Malins 1885-1912

Joy Corelli Rockwell 1927-2018 m.1966 William Hyde 1925-2000

Robert Hunter Rockwell 1929-1984 m.1954 Betty Jean Wardle 1935-1996

Elwood Lorraine Rockwell 1933-1987 with Mary ? d.s.p.

Lindsay Archibald Rockwell 1937 m.1957 Lynette E. Watson 1939-2006

Coral Joy Stretton c.1943-1981 1m.1961
Ronie Rockwell 1943-2000
Cheryl Joy Pooley 1945-2013 2m.1980

Janet Lenore Rockwell 1946- 1m.1965 Roland Whiting 2m. Gordon Carr 3m. Ilya Sippen

Lionel Raymond Mulroy 1928-2010 with Shirley ? d.s.p.

Lesley John Mulroy 1938-1999 m.1958 Judith A. Clancey

Valtie Minlena Chisholm 1926-2003 m.1944 Frank Hammond 1911-2007 d.s.p.

Alwyn Wooldridge Malins 1912-1997 d.s.p.

Ronald Guildford Malins 1910-1975 m.1945 Bernice Walsh

Robert W. Hyde 1967-2016 with Sharon Marsen 1965

Tracy Paul Rockwell 1955 2m.2002 Lamia Lily Yammine 1972- from 2012 with Rosie Barbour 1968 m.1980, Portland, Oregon
Jane Sule Paulson 1957

Robert Wayne Rockwell 1959-1963 Child

Sandra Kaye Rockwell 1960 1m.1985 Lawrence Agius 2m.2006 Mark Plumber

Rhonda Janine Rockwell 1964 m.1984 David Crossley 1956

Glenn Lindsay Rockwell 1962 1m.1987 Jeanette Musson 1956 2w.2004 Rebecca L. Smith

Brett Anthony Rockwell 1961 m.1982 Julie Denyer c.1984

Mark Malcolm Rockwell 1962 1mc.1978 Joyce Moore 2mc.1982 Michelle Thomas 3m.1999 Lara Musjuk

Paul Steven Rockwell 1965 with Christine Brown

Samuel Joshua Rockwell 1974

Jessica Molly Rockwell 1977

Michelle Lena Whiting 1965 with Heath Wilson (sep.)

Steven Hunter Rockwell 1968 m.2014 Malini Jivan

Adam Roger Rockwell 1971 with Stephen Burns d.s.p.

Lionel Mulroy 1959 m.?

Allan Mulroy 1962 m.?

Kaye Malins 1946- m.1967 Gerald Heaslip

1. Ashley M., 1996
2. Kelsey A., 1999

1st Marriage:
1. James B., 1981
2. Olivia H., 1985
3. Laura E., 1985

1st Marriage:
1. Jack L., 1987
2. Kathryn E., 1990
3. Caroline M., 1993
4. Margaret B., 1995

1. Sarah A., 1985
2. Mathew C., 1986

1st Marriage:
1. Kirsty L., 1988
2. Shani A., 1991
3. Alice L., 2007
2nd Relationship:
4. Warren G., 2009
5. Edward L., 2011

1. Mathew, 1983
2. Daniel, 1985
3. Stephen, 1989

1st Marriage:
1. Adam, c.1977
2. Sarah, c.1978
3. David, c.1980
2nd Marriage:
4. Mark, c.1982
5. Simone, c.1983
6. Ben, c.1984
3rd Marriage:
7. Larissa, 2005

1. Coen, 1996
2. Kayne, 2000

1. Hadyn, 2007

1. Emma, 1970
2. Kate, 1974

▲ The ancestors and descendants of Humphrey & Lenore O'Sullivan.

gradually began to stretch out like a spiders web.

Where To From Here?

With his life cut short at just 35 years of age, the legacy of Humphrey Joseph O'Sullivan passed to his daughters through his wife Lenore Mackie (nee Shoveller), and it is her two marriages and unfortunate yet fascinating story of survival that must next be told.

References

1. NSW State Archives & Records. Index to Assisted Immigration 1844-1859, 'Admiral Lyons', p.37. (Reels 2138, 2475).

2. NSW Dept of BDM. (1866). Birth for Elizabeth Bantin - #211/1866.

3. NSW Dept of BDM. (1871). Birth Certificate for Humphrey Joseph O'Sullivan, #6704/1871.

4. MacCarthy, Nicolas Tuite de [1769-1833] & Mahony, C. (1848). 'Sermons of Abbe MacCarthy,' James Duffy, Dublin, p.xiii.

5. NSW Dept of BDM. (1872). Birth Certificate for James Alexander O'Sullivan, #10684/1872.

6. NSW Dept of BDM. (1877). Birth Certificate for John Washington O'Sullivan, #12652/1877.

7. NSW Dept of BDM. (1879). Birth Certificate for Mary Zenobia O'Sullivan, #14077/1879.

8. NSW Dept of BDM. (1880). Birth Certificate for Ellen Theresa O'Sullivan, #15152/1880.

9. NSW Dept of BDM. (1882). Birth Certificate for Blanche Zenobia O'Sullivan, #16046/1882.

10. NSW Dept of BDM. (1884). Birth Certificate for William O'Sullivan, #238151884.

11. NSW Dept of BDM. (1886). Birth Certificate for Rupert C. O'Sullivan, #21301/1886.

12. NSW Dept of BDM. (1888). Birth Certificate for female O'Sullivan, #?????/1888.

13. NSW Dept of BDM. (1891). Birth Certificate for Zenobia O'Sullivan, #?????/1891.

14. England, G.E. (1978). 'The Coffs Harbour Story - Centennial.' Nth Coast Newspaper Co. Ltd.

15. Hemmings, C.T. (ed.) (1988). 'Coffs Harbour High School: The First Fifty Years 1938-1988.' Coffs Harbour.

16. Fletcher, J. & Burnswood, J. (1983). 'Government Schools of NSW, 1848-1983.' NSW Dept of Education, Sydney.

17. Holder, B.J. (1984). 'The History Of The Coastal Strip Known As 'Look-At-Me-Now': Moonee Creek Settlement (100 Years). The Skinner Family and Descendants. Coffs Harbour, p.72.

18. 'A Farming District In the North,' Australian Town & Country Journal, 22nd May 1886, p.21.

19. Teaching Appointments (Sydney Morning Herald, 9 March 1887, p.5).

20. Holder, B.J. (1984). op.cit.

21. Local School Histories - 11th April 1887 (Held at Coffs Harbour Historical Society).

22. Ibid.

23. NSW Dept of BDM. (1891). Death Certificate for James Mahony O'Sullivan, #6676/1891.

24. Wikipedia - The Pacific Highway (Australia), [https://en.wikipedia.org/wiki/Pacific_Highway_(Australia)].

Chapter Seven

Shoveler

LENORE SHOVELLER
(Mother of Octavia Corelli O'Sullivan)

Lenore Shoveller was the fourth child of Thomas Eastman Shoveller, an adventurer turned storekeeper and later accountant who was born at Warnford, Hampshire in 1827, and Susan Hann the first white child born 1840 in the Clarence River District on the far north coast of New South Wales. Theirs was the first marriage to be celebrated at the new Anglican Church in Grafton on the 6th March 1856.

Leonora (aka Lenore) was born on the 13th of November 1866,[1] a year in world history which saw the parliament of Canada meet for the first time in Ottawa, with the Dominion of Canada being created the next year. The Austro-Prussian War began when the Austrians and most of the medium German states declared war on Prussia, and it was the year that dynamite was invented by Alfred Nobel. In Australia, gold was discovered at Gympie in Queensland and the future Saint Mary MacKillop founded the Sisters of St Joseph of the Sacred Heart.

Notable people born in 1866 included the American outlaw Butch Cassidy (13 April), the prolific English writer Herbert George Wells (21 Sept), and the Scottish journalist, politician and future Prime Minister of the United Kingdom Ramsay MacDonald. For a detailed account of Lenore Shoveller's paternal ancestry see Volume 6 of the Rockwell

▲ Birth certificate for Lenore Shoveller at Alice Street, Grafton on the 13th November 1866 (NSW BDM #9029/1866).

Genealogies - "The Long Road to Grafton,"[Ref] and Volume 7 for her maternal ancestry - "To The Big River: A Genealogy of John Hann & Mary Ann Thompson."[Ref]

Lenore Shoveller was born at Alice Street, Grafton and baptised on the 3rd of February 1867 (incorrectly registered as Leonora Shweller).[2] Her 39 year old father had emigrated from England in 1848 and was listed as a 'storekeeper' on her birth certificate. Lenore's father was also a well respected member of the growing community, and had in fact been the first Lord Mayor of Grafton in 1859, albeit temporarily. In an uncanny twist of fate, her 26 year old mother was widely acknowledged as the first white female born in the Clarence River District in 1840. Lenore's birth was reported in the local paper:

SHOVELLER—On the 13th instant, at her residence Grafton, Mrs. Thomas Shoveller, of a daughter.

The Clarence & Richmond Examiner, 20th November, 1866

Lenore was preceded by three siblings in Susan T. Shoveller, who was born on 15th May 1858, but died in the same year.[3] Susan Eva Shoveller, who arrived on the 24th August 1859, and Thomas Charles Shoveller, born 6th October 1862, the latter two being baptised on the 21st of December 1862.[4,5] Life in the newly established northern New South Wales town of Grafton was an exciting place to be in 1866. Her maternal grandparents John Hann and Mary Ann Thompson had been convicts, but also pioneers of that region and had contributed much to the formation and development of the growing township.

Although just a year old, her father Thomas Eastman Shoveller was quick to select land in Leonora's name on the 18th April 1867. Forty acres were taken up at the junction of the Lawrence Road and the Richmond Road in the County of Lawrence. It adjoined her uncle William Olive's 40 acres, and the property was two miles south of the Travellers Rest Inn.

On the 6th December 1869 another sister arrived in Janet Shoveller, to Thomas and Susan although unfortunately, she also died as an infant the very next year.[6]

As a six year old, Lenore looked up to her 13 year old sister Susan Eva and 10 year old brother Thomas Charles, and likely attended at the public school in Grafton. The NSW government school system began in 1848, but it wasn't until 1880 that attendance was mandatory, when children between six and 14 years were required to attend no less than 70 days per half year. In the Clarence River District, children made their way to school often over long distances on foot or by horseback, and they hardly ever wore shoes.

Then in 1873 another brother arrived in the person of George Lorraine Shoveller.[7] Unfortunately, tragedy befell the Shoveller family on the 30th November 1874, which occurred just after Lenore's 8th birthday, when their beloved son and brother Thomas Charles Shoveller, was drowned in the Clarence River, aged only 11.[8]

Lenore never knew her paternal grandparents John and Elizabeth Shoveller, who had died in England. Her maternal grandfather John Hann, had also met a gruesome end south of Grafton in 1857, but her sole surviving grandma Mary Matilda Hann, was still going strong and resided in Grafton.

By 1875 the electoral roll reveals that the Shovellers had moved and were residing at South Grafton. Lenore and family would also have attended Church regularly as was the custom of the day, with visits into Grafton now having to be made by taking the ferry. This was most likely undertaken at Christ Church Grafton, where the Shoveller and Hann families were parishioners.

Two more younger siblings for Lenore were born into the family when Mabel Shoveller arrived on the 3rd June 1878 (bapt. 24th August 1878), and Clarence John Hann Shoveller was born on 19th August 1880 (bapt. 14th November 1880).[9,10]

▲TOP (Left): 1860's Semi Detached Home at 58-60 Queen St, Grafton. (Right): Thomas Fisher's 'Grafton Stores' followed on from Thomas Shoveller's 'Clarence River Stores'. ABOVE: The eastern side of Prince Street, Grafton looking south-east from Pound St, with Pott's Beehive Store in the foreground, and the School of Arts in the background, about 1872, as Lenore Shoveller would have known it.

Relatives of Lenore Shoveller on her 15th Birthday (13th Nov 1881)

Hamlet DALBY & Mary Ann Hann & Family		
Ethel Mary	b.1873	8
Horatio G.	b.1875	6
Evaline L.	b.1877	4
Norma L.	b.1879	2
Morvere O.	b.1883	Unborn
Alethea Goldie	b.1886	Unborn

Percival GREAVES and Lucy Hann & Family		
Eleanor Mary	b.1865	16
Charles Frederick W.	b.1866	15
Christabella Lucy	b.1871	10
Georgina Annie	b.1873	8
Percival Charles	b.1879	2
Barbara Clementina	b.1880	deceased
Frederick W. B.	b.1886	Unborn

George HANN & Jeanette Baird & Family		
Henry J.	b.1869	12
Julianna	b.1871	10
Mary Matilda	b.1873	8
George Josef	b.1876	5
Jeanette C.	b.1878	3
Ida Jane	b.1880	1
William J.	b.1883	Unborn
Hamlet Clarence	b.1885	Unborn
G. Plummer	(adopted)	

John HANN & Rebecca Priestley & Family		
Male	b.1863	deceased
Ellen E.	b.1864	deceased

Joseph HANN & Margaretta Strauss & Family		
John George	b.1860	21

Joseph	b.1862	19
Jane	b.1864	17
Emily Georgina	b.1866	15
Annah Catherina	b.1868	13
Henry Oswald	b.1870	11
Osbert Clinton	b.1872	9
Aubrey	b.1874	7
Mary Matilda	b.1875	6
Oliver Hogburn	b.1877	5
Hamilton Hampton	b.1878	3
Ivy Pearl	b.1880	1
Clara Marlen	b.1883	Unborn

William HANN & Matilda Page & Family		
Mary Adelaide	b.1874	7
Hamlet Horace	b.1876	5
Percival William	b.1878	3
William Harold	b.1880	1
Lurline Matilda	b.1882	Unborn
Ernest Walnoth	b.1884	Unborn
Winifred Sarah	b.1886	Unborn
Eustace George	b.1889	Unborn
Rockleigh Elwyn	b.1890	Unborn
Charles Ralph	b.1891	Unborn

William OLIVE & Jane Hann & Family		
Sarah Jane	b.1855	26 & marr.
Edwin William	b.1856	25
Elizabeth Mary	b.1858	23 & marr.
Louisa Grace	b.1859	22 & marr.
Joseph John	b.1861	20
Emma Elizabeth	b.1862	19
Fanny	b.1864	17
Susan Ada	b.1865	16

Charles George	b.1867	14
Lucy Matilda	b.1869	12
Janet Maria	b.1871	10
Frederick Jordan	b.1873	8
David John	b.1874	7
Archibald Clarence	b.1877	4
Thomas Griffin	b.1880	1

James RODGERS & Sarah Hann & Family		
Mary Jane	b.1860	21
Sarah Ann	b.1861	20
John William	b.1863	18
George Alexander	b.1864	17
James Morven	b.1865	16
Charles Joseph	b.1867	14
Emily Rebecca	b.1868	13
Lucy Ellen	b.1870	11
Arthur Henry	b.1872	deceased
Arthur Henry	b.1874	7
Andrew Herst	b.1875	6
Alice Eveline	b.1879	deceased

Thomas SHOVELLER & Susan Hann & Family		
Susan T.	b.1858	deceased
Susan Eva	b.1859	22 & marr.
Thomas Charles	b.1862	deceased
Leonora	b.1866	15
Janet Eva	b.1869	deceased
George Lorraine	b.1873	8
Mabel	b.1878	3
Clarence John	b.1880	1

William STARLING & Emily Hann		
No Issue		

pTOP (Left): Lenore's extended family living in and around Grafton was enormous. Here a large family enjoys a picnic on the Clarence River, during the 1880's. (Right): Significant family gatherings would have brought out most of Lenore's close relatives. ABOVE: Full list of Lenore's 80+ Aunts, Uncles and cousins from her maternal Hann side of the family, with their age at 13th Nov 1881.

By this time, in addition to her brothers and sisters, Lenore was no doubt close to many of her numerous maternal relatives, totalling an incredible 18 aunts and uncles as well as no less than 74 first cousins on her maternal side alone! This came about as Lenore's mother, Susan had nine brothers and sisters, who all married and produced large families. On her fathers side, Lenore also had a further seven aunts and uncles and 15 cousins, although with all of these residing in England, she likely never met any of them.

Being the 25th grandchild on the Hann side of the family, Lenore would have had to fight for her grandmothers attention. In fact, by Lenore's 15th birthday on the 13th November 1881, she had over 58 siblings and first cousins from the various related families, with another 12 yet to be born, in addition to eight that had already died. A list on the previous page contains the names of the various siblings and cousins of Lenore Shoveller as at that day, with their respective years of birth.

These families mostly all resided in Grafton, and assuming they gathered together for special occasions, one can just imagine what the picnics, birthdays, Christmas's and other special family gathering's would have been like, with all those children and family running around. Where would they have put them and how could they have fed them all? And how could Grannie Hann ever remember the names of all those kids?

Lenore was naturally closer to those in her own age bracket, which were Fanny, Susan and Charles Olive; Jane and Emily Hann; George, James and Charles Rodgers; and Eleanor and Charles Greaves. More than 30 of these children attended school at the same time as Lenore and many of her cousins were likely in the same class!

Lenore was affectionately known as 'Luddie,' but the entire extended family were thrown into mourning in June 1882 when their matriarch, Mary Ann Hann passed away in Grafton,

LOST to-day (Monday). a PET KANGAROO The finder will be rewarded upon returning it to LENORE SHOVELLER.

LOST, on Friday afternoon, a MAGPIE. Finder rewarded. LENORE SHOVELLER, Prince-street.

LOST, on Sunday, a LADIES' RIDING WHIP. Finder rewarded by LENORE SHOVELLER.

Free Selections.

THE following portions were selected on Thursday at the Grafton Land office :—
Leonora Shoveller. Grafton. 40 acres, county Clarence, parish of Lanitza, being measured portion No. 59. Deposit paid, £8. A non-residential application.

▲ TOP (Left): 1-Lenore loved her pets and placed advertisements for her - 'Lost Kangaroo' (Clarence & Richmond Examiner, 27th April 1886, p3); 2-'Lost Magpie' (Clarence & Richmond Examiner, 7th Feb 1888, p3); 3-Lenore's town of Grafton was situated in the middle of the Clarence River wilderness; 4-Selections in the name of Lenore Shoveller (Clarence & Richmond Examiner, 12th Jan 1889, p8). (Right): Lenore could have been the archetype for Ethel C. Pedley's book 'Dot and the Kangaroo' (1899). ABOVE: A pioneering family establishes a bush home at Washpool Creek, Solferino.

where hundreds of family and friends gathered for her funeral.[11]

Genealogy is a pastime where dates and records are important, but it is more difficult to unravel an ancestors's character and personality. Fortunately, Lenore Shoveller left a venere that provides a glimpse into her temperament. As a young woman she was obviously besotted by animals, and living in a rural environment provided plenty of opportunities to foster pets. We know she was fond of Australian animals as at the age of 19 she advertised a reward for the return of her lost 'pet kangaroo.' Then 20 months later she posted another reward notice, this time for the return of her lost 'pet magpie!' These sound like curious pets, but they weren't unusual for a country girl and characterise Lenore as a kind and nurturing individual. Lenore could even have been the archetype for Ethel Pedley's 'Dot And The Kangaroo', an

▲ LEFT: Portrait of Henry Ernest Searle, who was of the same age and a classmate of Lenore. MID: 'Searle's Monument' off Gladesville Point in Sydney Harbour. RIGHT: "Professional Champion Sculler of the World" - Searle as caricatured by Spy (Leslie Ward) in Vanity Fair, September 1889.

Henry Ernest Searle [18]

Henry Ernest Searle (1866-1889), was a professional Australian sculler, who became the World Sculling Champion from 1888 until his premature death from typhoid in 1889.

Born on the 14th July 1866 at Grafton, New South Wales to Henry Samuel Searle, bootmaker, and his wife Mary Ann, née Brooks. The family later moved to Esk Island, lower Clarence River, where they farmed at a subsistence level.

Searle soon learnt to scull and rowed his brother and sisters three miles (4.8km) to and from school every day. At 18 Searle first competed in a skiff race and for three years raced with some success at local regattas. His first important victory was the defeat of a Sydney professional in an out-rigger handicap at Grafton in January 1888.

Moving to Sydney, Searle was coached by an established sculler Neil Matterson, and with the financial backing of John and Thomas Spencer (Sydney brothers who a decade earlier had backed Edward Trickett), he began a strenuous training programme and won four contests between June and October.

After failing to obtain a match-up with the former World Champion Ned Hanlan, Searle challenged the then champion Peter Kemp. The match took place on the 27th October 1888 on the Parramatta River. The usual £500 was at stake as well as the title. At the start, Searle took the lead and although Kemp made great efforts he could never overtake the leader who won by about twenty lengths in a time of 22m.44s. Thus Searle became World Champion.

Searle, Matterson and other 'cracks', including Bill Beach, next competed in the 'Grand Aquatic Carnival', which was rowed in Brisbane between the 5th and 11th December.

In one heat Searle and Matterson continually and deliberately fouled Beach, for which they were disqualified from the heat but not, to the public's annoyance, from the carnival. Consequently, they finished first and third in the final after Beach refused to row.

In 1889 with his stocks low Searle, accompanied by Matterson, travelled to England to race the Canadian champion William Joseph O'Connor for a £500 prize. This race was held on the Thames River over the Championship Course. It was reported that 100,000 people were on hand to watch the race. O'Connor was first away and rowing at a high stroke rate, he soon had an advantage of half a length. However at the 'Crabtree', Searle had drawn up level and shortly afterwards was a length ahead. A little later O'Connor was showing signs of distress and after this, the remainder of the race was a procession. Searle won by about ten lengths in the fast time of 22m and 42s.

While returning to Australia in the "SS Austral", Searle contracted typhoid fever and left the ship at Melbourne. He tragically died three weeks later on the 10th December 1889 at the Williamstown Sanatorium, after a very public illness. The colonies plunged into mourning with editorials, poems and sermons bewailing the loss of the young hero. Thousands lined Melbourne streets to see his body pass, and in Sydney an estimated crowd of 170,000 packed the city for his memorial service. Approximately 2500 attended in stifling heat to see him buried in the Maclean cemetery.

Marriage of Lenore Shoveller & John Henry Mackie

SCHEDULE E.
(19 Victoria No. 30.)

(COPY OF) CERTIFICATE OF MARRIAGE.

I, *Charles Capel Greenway* being

a Clergyman, the Minister of

do hereby Certify, that I have this day, at

duly solemnized Marriage between

John Henry Mackie

residing at *Grafton*

Widower

Laura Shoveller

residing at *Grafton*

Spinster

after Declaration duly made as by law required.

DATED this *Third* day of *March* 1890

C Greenway (Signature of Minister or Registrar)

John H Mackie

Lenore Shoveller

George Shoveller

(Signature of Witnesses)

MARRIAGE.
MACKIE—SHOVELLER.—On the 3rd March inst., by the Ven. the Archdeacon, in Christ Church Cathedral, Grafton JOHN HENRY MACKIE, of Auckland New Zealand, to LEONORA, daughter of Thomas Shoveller, of Grafton

GRAFTON POLICE COURT.
ON Tuesday, before the P.M. and Mr. E. M. Ryan, J P.
James Murray, on remand, was charged with disobedience of a summons from the Hillgrove Bench, issued for non-payment of rent to one Woodhouse. A telegram was read from Hillgrove to the effect that the amount owing had been paid, and the warrant was therefore cancelled. Mr. Norrie appeared for defendant, having generously conducted the defence.
Leonora Mackie v John Henry Mackie.—Proceedings taken for an order for maintenance. Complainant deposed that her husband contributed scarcely anything to her support since she married him about two years ago. For the past eight months she received nothing from him. She has one child.

John Henry Mackie was summoned for disobeying an order of the Court enjoining him to pay towards the maintenance of his wife, Leonore Mackie. An order was given for the arrest of defendant.

M U S I C.
MRS. MACKIE is prepared to receive PUPILS for the Piano. References to present pupils and their parents. REDUCED TERMS. LENORE MACKIE, Fitzroy-street, Grafton, opposite the Church of England Schoolroom.

◀ABOVE: The marriage certificate for John Henry Mackie and Lenore Shoveller, 3rd March 1890. ▲TOP: 1-John Henry Mackie and Lenore Shoveller Marriage notice (Clarence & Richmond Examiner, March 22nd, 1890, p4); 2-Court proceedings against John Henry Mackie (Clarence & Richmond Examiner, 18th June 1892, p3); 3-Summons for John Henry Mackie (Clarence & Richmond Examiner, 16th Aug 1892, p3); 4-Lenore Mackie was an accomplished pianist and advertised for music pupils (Clarence & Richmond Examiner, 8th July 1893, p5). ▼(Left): and written notice of the birth of Valtie in 1891, perhaps written by Thomas Eastman Shoveller. (Right): Arrest warrant for John Henry Mackie (NSW Police Gazette, 1892).

Lenore baby born 25th March Wednesday 11
Got a wire from Mackie on 21st March 18

NEW SOUTH WALES POLICE GAZETTE.
·1892¶
Grafton.—A warrant has been issued by the Grafton Bench for the arrest of John Henry Mackie, charged with disobeying a Magisterial order for the support of his wife. He is about 28 years of age, 5 feet 9 inches high, rather slight build, sallow complexion, fair hair mixed slightly with gray, clean shaved except small incipient moustache, large ears which stand out wards, rather thin lips, thin features, decayed upper front tooth, glaring look, walks as if something wrong with left leg; dressed in long paget coat; a tailor; drinks heavily. Last heard of in Tenterfield.

1899 Australian children's book about a little girl named Dot who gets lost in the Australian outback and is eventually befriended by a kangaroo and several other marsupials.[12,13]

Lenore was also an accomplished horsewoman from her earliest years and was apparently well equipped with all the necessary horseriding gear, as evidenced by an advertisement for her 'lost riding whip' in August of 1889.

Interestingly, Lenore shared her birthyear and birthplace with a boy named Henry Ernest Searle, who later became rowing champion of the world. Having grown up together and attended the same school in Grafton, they surely knew one another. When in his early 20's Henry Searle, became the pride of Grafton and a national hero, by winning the world rowing championship!

▲The March 1890 Grafton flood still holds the record of 8.13m above average river level. ▶TOP: Images of Grafton during the record Grafton floods of 1890.

The Marriage of... Lenore Shoveller & John Henry Mackie

As Lenore was nearing 23 years old, she met a young Tasmanian born man who had recently arrived from Auckland, by the name of John Henry Mackie. The year was 1890 and was marked by the massacre at Wounded Knee in South Dakota, and also brought the death of the great Dutch painter Vincent van Gogh (29 July). However, a clutch of notable people were born in 1890 including the president of North Vietnam Ho Chi Minh (19 May), the English born actor Stan Laurel (16 June), the American comedian Groucho Marx (2 Oct), U.S. general and 34th President of the United States Dwight D. Eisenhower (14 Oct), and the future President of France Charles de Gaulle (22 Nov).

Lenore and John mackie decided to marry on the 3rd of March 1890 at the Anglican Cathedral Church at Grafton, with the ceremony being conducted by Charles Capel Greenway (Minister).[14] On the marriage certificate John Mackie was recorded as a bachelor residing at Grafton, and gave his occupation as a 'tailor's cutter.' Lenore Shoveller was listed as a spinster, also residing at Grafton. The marriage was witnessed by Lenore's younger brother George Shoveller and the mother of the bride Susan Shoveller, with the event being reported in the local newspaper.[15]

The Flood of 1890

But just over a week later came torrential rain and massive destruction in Grafton from the largest known flood ever to inundate the region. The incredible height of 8.13m (26.5') above normal river level was measured on the 11th March 1890, and still stands today as the record flood level on the Clarence.

> "Water, water everywhere and not a drop to drink!"
> from "The Rime of the Ancient Mariner," by Samuel Taylor Coleridge.

However, along with the rest of the towns folk, the young couple overcame the disaster as just over a year later they celebrated the birth of their unusually named child, Valteveredo Calceolaria Mackie, which occurred on the 25th of March 1891.[16]

▲ Following the catastrophic floods of 1893 and the death of her husband John Mackie the next year, Lenore Mackie (nee Shoveller) left the beautiful Clarence River District behind to take up ownership of Bowden's Hotel, in Sydney in early 1895.

Their good fortune began to unravel after that when it became evident that John Henry Mackie was not really interested in providing for his young wife and child. Lenore most probably consulted her father for litigational assistance and subsequently filed an order in the Grafton Police Court for maintenance against her estranged husband. By mid 1892 the relationship had irretrievably broken down, when Mackie was issued with a 'maintenance order' by the local court. After further legal action, Lenore was confronted by the prospect of supporting herself and her baby girl unassisted. John Henry Mackie either didn't agree with the findings or he couldn't make the payments and the Court susequently issued an order for his arrest.

With Mackie having deserted the marriage, Lenore sought ways to support herself and her daughter, and being an accomplished painist she turned to music, revealing yet another talent that she had acquired. She placed an advertisement in the local newspaper offering piano lessons at her father's home in Fitzroy Street, Grafton, which was conveniently just opposite the Church schoolroom. Lenore must have been quite an accomplished pianist.

Death of John Henry Mackie

Apparently, John Henry Mackie was a problem drinker and somewhat of a ladies man. His untimely end came in 1894 while apparently chasing a young lady around a kitchen table, when he was stricken by a massive heart attack.[17] There had likely been no contact with her husband's family in the first place, but now separated by death there was contact at all with the Mackies.

Although, Lenore likely received support from her own family following the death of John Henry Mackie, she was nevertheless alone with a three year old daughter to care for, and the 1890's were a difficult period for a young widowed mother to survive. Finding herself at loose ends, Lenore found some comfort in the attentions of a young man who descended from Irish roots, and it is their struggles and their story that this genealogy addresses next.

References

1. NSW Dept of BDM. (1866). Birth for Elizabeth Bantin - #211/1866.
2. NSW Dept of BDM. (1866). Birth Certificate for Leonora Shweller [sic. Shoveller], #9029/1866.
3. NSW Dept of BDM. (1858). Birth Certificate for Susan T. Shoveller, #7416/1858.
4. NSW Dept of BDM. (1859). Birth Certificate for Susan Eva Shoveller, #7801/1859.
5. NSW Dept of BDM. (1862). Birth Certificate for Thomas Charles Shoveller, #8141/1862.
6. NSW Dept of BDM. (1869). Birth Certificate for Janet E. A. Shoveller, #10165/1869.
7. NSW Dept of BDM. (1873). Birth Certificate for George Lorraine Shoveller, #11288/1873.
8. NSW Dept of BDM. (1874). Death Certificate for Thomas Charles Shoveller, #5065/1874.
9. NSW Dept of BDM. (1878). Birth Certificate for Mabel Shoveller, #13336/1878.
10. NSW Dept of BDM. (1880). Birth Certificate for Clarence John Hann Shoveller, #15169/1880.
11. NSW Dept of BDM. (1882). Death Certificate for Mary Matilda Hann, #8344/1882.
12. Wikipedia - 'Dot and the Kangaroo' [https://en.wikipedia.org/wiki/Dot_and_the_Kangaroo].
13. Pedley, Ethel C. (1920). 'Dot And The Kangaroo', Angus & Robertson, Sydney.
14. NSW Dept of BDM. (1890). Marriage Certificate for John Henry Mackie & Lenore Shoveller, #3797/1890.
15. Ibid.
16. NSW Dept of BDM. (1891). Birth Certificate for Valteveredo Calceolaria Mackie #14676/1891.
17. NSW Dept of BDM. (1894). Death Certificate for John Henry Mackie, #3418/1894.
18. Wikipedia - Henry Ernest Searle [https://en.wikipedia.org/wiki/Henry_Ernest_Searle].

Chapter Eight

HUMPHREY JOSEPH O'SULLIVAN & LENORE SHOVELLER

(Parents of Octavia Corelli O'Sullivan)

In 1894 the president of France Marie François Sadi Carnot, was assassinated. The iconic Tower Bridge opened for traffic in London. At the initiative of Baron Pierre de Coubertin, the International Olympic Committee was founded at the Sorbonne, in Paris. And South Australia became the first Australian colony, and the second place in the world to grant women the right to vote, as was the first Parliament in the world to allow women to stand for office with the Constitutional Amendment (Adult Suffrage) Act.

Proposal by Humphrey Joseph O'Sullivan

By early 1894, Lenore had become acquainted with a man, some five years younger than herself, who quickly became infatuated with her. They first met in Grafton during the catastrophic 1894 floods, but their relationship swiftly reached the point where the subject of marriage was broached. His name was Humphrey Joseph O'Sullivan, and being a gentleman he penned a letter to his beloved Mrs Lenore Mackie on the 13th January 1894.[1] Six months later Humphrey wrote another letter to Lenore's mother Mrs Susan Shoveller, expressing his love for her daughter and his honourable intentions.[2] Fortunately, both these letters have survived. In the midst of her troubles, Lenore probably wasn't thinking of her immediate future and whether she was keen to enter into a second marriage at this point is unknown, but later events were to eventually force her hand.

Proprietor of Bowden's Hotel, Sydney

Taking 'the bull by the horns,' Lenore next travelled to Sydney and most likely with financial advice and support from her father Thomas Eastman Shoveller, she decided to purchase a hotel in the heart of the city. Taking an incredible leap forward, Lenore bought

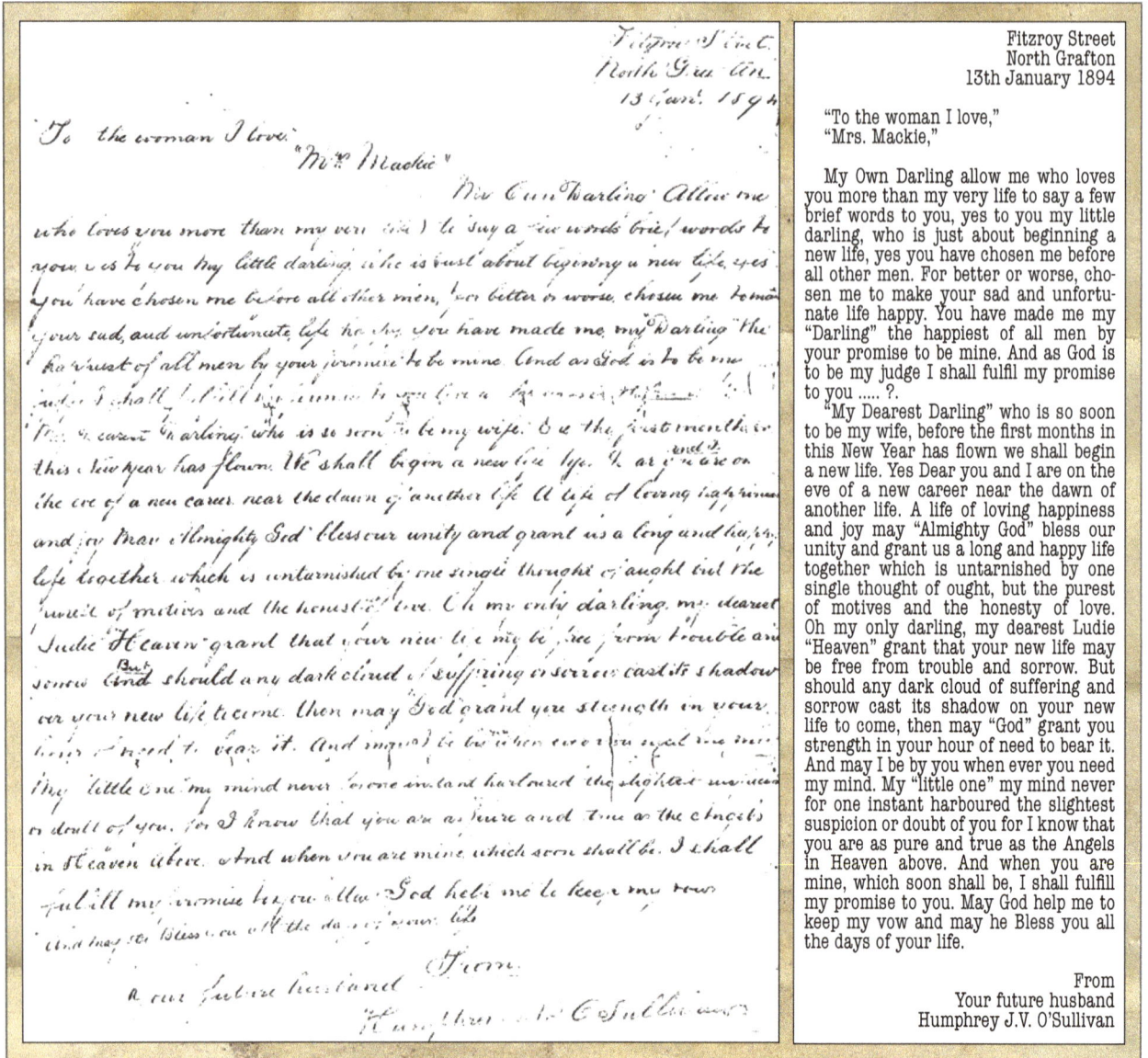

Fitzroy Street
North Grafton
13th January 1894

"To the woman I love,"
"Mrs. Mackie,"

My Own Darling allow me who loves you more than my very life to say a few brief words to you, yes to you my little darling, who is just about beginning a new life, yes you have chosen me before all other men. For better or worse, chosen me to make your sad and unfortunate life happy. You have made me my "Darling" the happiest of all men by your promise to be mine. And as God is to be my judge I shall fulfil my promise to you ..... ?.

"My Dearest Darling" who is so soon to be my wife, before the first months in this New Year has flown we shall begin a new life. Yes Dear you and I are on the eve of a new career near the dawn of another life. A life of loving happiness and joy may "Almighty God" bless our unity and grant us a long and happy life together which is untarnished by one single thought of ought, but the purest of motives and the honesty of love. Oh my only darling, my dearest Ludie "Heaven" grant that your new life may be free from trouble and sorrow. But should any dark cloud of suffering and sorrow cast its shadow on your new life to come, then may "God" grant you strength in your hour of need to bear it. And may I be by you when ever you need my mind. My "little one" my mind never for one instant harboured the slightest suspicion or doubt of you for I know that you are as pure and true as the Angels in Heaven above. And when you are mine, which soon shall be, I shall fulfill my promise to you. May God help me to keep my vow and may he Bless you all the days of your life.

From
Your future husband
Humphrey J.V. O'Sullivan

▲ LEFT: Humphrey Joseph O'Sullivan's letter to Lenore in January 1894. RIGHT: Transcription of Humphrey Joseph O'Sullivan's letter of January 1894. (NB: Two of his letters have survived, but there were likely more).

the lease on 'Bowden's Hotel' in Elizabeth St. Sydney from a Mr. Edward S. Ebsworth.[3,4,5]

Bowden's Hotel first came about when Thomas Kite from Bathurst built a city residence on this site in the 1840s, which later became a pub run by a Mrs Bowden. The small corner building became a Sydney landmark because a large Norfolk Pine that grew through the middle of it, which was often used as a coat rack by the hotel patrons. The building and tree were demolished in 1909.[6]

Anecdotal evidence from family sources claim that Lenore may have won the £500 she needed to make the acquisition, but how exactly she did this is unclear. The transaction occurred on the 23rd May 1895 and cost Lenore £400 cash and she took £100 on loan, which was full payment of the purchase money for the lease, license, furniture, goodwill and effects of Bowden's Hotel.[7]

Where Lenore was able to lay her hands on such a sum and why a simple country girl would even contemplate purchasing a hotel says something about Lenore's drive and ambition. Given the male dominated, late 19th century society in which she lived, it is hard to understand how a single mother, with a four year old daughter in tow, could make such

Fitzroy Street
North Grafton
4th July 1894

Mrs. [Susan] Shoveller,
Dear Friend,

It is with feelings of pleasure that I remember my short stay at your place. And allow me to thank you for your kindness, and also for your kind and motherly advice that you gave me which shall not be forgotten. But "Dear Friend" although all those are appreciated by me they are small compared with that which I am going to write about, and for which I can never sufficiently repay you for. But that God may repay you with eternal happiness I humbly pray. Dear Friend, by granting to me my request you have made me feel a happy man and you at least have done your part to promote my own and your 'darling daughter's' future happiness. And may "Heaven" reward you for it. And I smartly hope that you shall never have cause to regret confiding to my keeping your "dear daughters" future happiness and honour. "God" grant that I may live to fulfil my word for on my part "Death" alone can prevent me, while dear "Luddie" continues true. To her I gave my first love and my only love, and if anything so bitter were ever to happen, as that should part us two, then as "God above" is my witness, I swear, that I shall never love another as long as I shall live.

Dear Friend, I shall tell you how I first became acquainted with "Luddie". It was a few weeks ago one Sunday night when the flood was rising I helped her to put some of her furniture out of flood reach, and she being unable to sleep on account of the close proximity of the flood, stayed up and I gladly stayed up with her. Well we sat together familiarially chatting away the long weary hours by the fireside. And it was then that she told me all about her unfortunate life, and confided to my keeping all her unhappy secrets, and she seemed to tell me so truthfully and simply all, and appeared to conceal nothing, and for trusting me so faithfully almost a perfect stranger to her, my whole heart went out to her in her loneliness, and I loved her better than if she were the happiest and richest woman in the whole world. I would now willingly give cancel five years of my life to see her real happy and for her to forget her past sad life for ever. Well Mrs. Shoveller before I parted from her that night I asked her to be mine and half falteringly she said yes and a few nights after she gave me her answer she promised me. Considering all she has gone through I think she has borne her part nobly. She has contrived to earn an honest and independant living and above all she has preserved her name and honour from the slightest stain or reproach. And now that has placed those treasures in my keeping, they shall ever remain unblemished and pure, as far as my manhood, and my health, and strength, shall last.

Dear Friend, they say that self praise is no recommendation and neither I think it is, but I do not as you may think, say it to praise myself but because I am a stranger to you and under the circumstances I think that it is quite right to let you know. But I frankly tell you this that I can honestly and truthfully say and look the world in the face, and defy any living soul to truthfully lay any wrong at my door, there is not the slightest stain upon the name I bear. The only disgrace is poverty and luck has been against me, and that, no man can avoid. But thank God he has blessed me with uncommon good health and strength, and those gifts shall be used in the interest of the woman I love, and the fatherless little child that she loves so well. Thanking you for all your kindness and good advice.

And wishing you a long and happy life with "God's Blessing". I wish you good-bye and good luck.

I remain your affectionate friend.
Humphrey Joseph Vincent O'Sullivan

▲TOP: Humphrey Joseph O'Sullivan's letter to Lenore's mother, Susan Shoveller, in July 1894. ABOVE: Transcription of Humphrey Joseph O'Sullivan's letter to Lenore's mother, Susan Shoveller, in July 1894.

a financial leap. But the decision speaks volumes for Lenore's determination and what she thought she was capable of achieving.

The move was obviously a great opportunity to make a better life for herself and young Valtie, as she undoubtedly knew that both accommodation and spirits were a lucrative

Lenore Mackie & 'Bowden's Hotel'

Water Licensing Court.

The usual weekly meeting of the Water Licensing Court was held at noon to-day, before Mr. Addison, S.M. (presiding), and Mr. Penny, L.M.

The following transfers of publicans' licences were granted: Edward E. Ebsworth to Lenore Mackie, Bowden's Hotel, Elizabeth-street, Sydney; Erskine S. Smith to James Burge, Oxford Hotel, Erskine-street; Emily Fletcher, widow and administratrix in the estate of John Fletcher (deceased), to herself, Prince of Wales Hotel, Waverley-road, Woollahra; Eilen Kelly to W. E. Keetley, Athletic Hotel, Arthur street, Surry Hills.

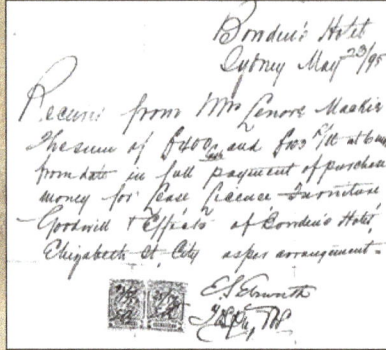

▲ Lenore Mackie - Transfer of Publican's License from the Licensing Court (SMH, 12 Sept 1895, p3). ▶CENTRE: 1-Receipt for Bowden's Hotel, 23rd May 1895. 2-Advertisement for Lenore Mackie's 'Bowden's Hotel' (Clarence & Richmond Examiner, 21st September 1895, p8). RIGHT: 1-Publican's License (Evening News, 22nd May 1893, p5); 2-Lenore Mackie v Dyson Injunction (Newcastle Morning Herald, 31st October 1895, p4); 3-Bankruptcy (Clarence & Richmond Examiner, 24th December 1895, p5); 4-Land Selection forfeited (Clarence & Richmond Examiner, 25th August 1896, p4). ▼Photograph of the rear of Lenore Mackie's 'Bowden's Hotel', corner of Hunter and Castlereagh Streets, Sydney, c.1907.

Bowden's Hotel
Sydney May 23/95

Received from Mr Lenore Mackie The sum of £400 and fees 5/- at bank from date in full payment of purchase money for lease licence furniture goodwill & effects of Bowden's Hotel Elizabeth St City as per arrangement.

E. Ebsworth

BOWDEN'S FAMILY HOTEL.

ELIZABETH-STREET (one door from Hunter-st.)
SYDNEY.

Affords country visitors the best accommodation in Sydney

For COMFORT, RESPECTABILITY,

ITS CENTRAL POSITION, AND

MODERATE CHARGES

Hot and cold water baths.
Telephone for the use of visitors.

LENORE MACKIE, Proprietress.

LICENSING COURT.

The weekly meeting of the Water Police Division of the Licensing Court was held at noon yesterday. Transfers of publicans' licenses were granted from Lenore Mackie, of Bowden's Hotel, Elizabeth-street, to Frank Dyson; and from Henry J. Ackland, of Ackland's Family Hotel, Queen-street, Woollahra, to Henry J. Ackland, jun. A renewal of the publican's license held by Samuel E. Van, of Van's Hotel, Waverley-road, Waverley, was granted.

The matter of Frank Dyson against Lenore Mackie was again before the Chief Judge in Equity yesterday on an application to continue an injunction which had been granted restraining the defendant from selling certain goods and chattels at Bowden's Hotel, Sydney, comprised in a bill of sale in connection with a suit for specific performance of an agreement made by the defendant with the plaintiff for the purchase of her interest in the bill of sale and certain promissory notes. After hearing affidavits, his Honor thought it would be better if the parties came to a settlement. He would allow the matter to stand over until Monday, the injunction to continue in the meantime.

In the Sydney Bankruptcy Court, re Henfrey and Co. and others v. Lenore Mackie, an order sequestrating the estate was made. The act of bankruptcy was fixed as the 7th December.

The provisional reversal of forfeiture of Leonora Mackie's c.p. of 40a., Lanitza, has been revoked, and the selection now stands forfeited.

An Injunction Motion.

The matter of Frank Dyson against Lenore Mackie was again before the Chief Judge in Equity to-day on an application to continue an injunction which had been granted restraining the defendant from selling certain goods and chattels at Bowden's Hotel comprised in a bill of sale in connection with a suit for specific performance of an agreement made by the defendant with the plaintiff for the purchase of her interest in the bill of sale and certain promissory notes. Mr. W. A. Walker, instructed by Mr. F. Burcher, appeared for the plaintiff, and Mr. Rolin, instructed by Mr. Quinlan, for the defendant. After hearing affidavits, his Honor thought it would be better if, instead of wasting time, the parties came to a settlement. It was clear the case ought to be settled, and if the parties only met in a friendly way and exercised a little common sense they could settle it in five minutes. It was just as well to remind litigants occasionally that at the end of litigation there was such a thing as a bill of costs. He would allow the matter to stand over until Monday, the injunction to continue in the meantime. If the parties came to terms the court should be at once informed in order that the injunction might be removed.

In Bankruptcy.

CREDITORS' PETITIONS.
...Henfrey and Company, ...gh-street, Sydney; Tucker ..., of George-street, Syd... ...e Rutty, of Margaret-st... v. Lenore Mackie, of Cro... ...ydney, recently of Bowd... ...izabeth-street, Sydney, wid... ...to be heard on December...

HEARING OF CREDITORS' PETITIONS.
Re Elliott Brothers v. William Leman Thomas. The matter stood over until the 27th instant, as a settlement was pending.
Re Henfrey and Co. and others v. Lenore Mackie. The order sequestrating the estate was made. The act of bankruptcy was fixed as the 7th December, and Mr. N. F. Giblin was appointed official assignee.
Re Fisher and Macansh v. James Fugler Montgomery. The order sequestrating the estate was made. The date of the act of bankruptcy was fixed as 6th December. Mr. Palmer was appointed official assignee.

▲TOP: The rear balcony of Bowden's Hotel at the corner of Hunter and Castlereagh Streets, Sydney, c.1900. (artist unknown). ABOVE (Left): Lenore Mackie - Injunction Motion (Evening News, 30 Oct 1895, p.6). (Right): 1-Lenore Mackie - Bankrupt y(Evening News, 11 Dec 1895, p.6); 2-Lenore Mackie - Creditors Petitions (SMH, 21st Dec 1895, p7).

business. The receipt, which has been held in the family for over 120 years, bears witness to the transaction for Bowden's Hotel from Mr Ebsworth.

Bowden's Hotel was located at 1-3 Elizabeth Street, Sydney, just one door from Hunter Street and was situated close enough to Circular Quay to provide lodging for travellers and visitors who used the various coastal and foreign ships that arrived daily.

Unfortunately, Lenore soon ran into difficulties and wasn't bringing in enough income

[2361]

Department of Lands,
Sydney, 10th September, 1898.

APPROVAL OF AFTER-AUCTION PURCHASES.

IT is hereby notified that the following applications under section 56 of the Crown Lands Act of 1895 have been approved. The balance of purchase money must be paid subject to the same terms and conditions as were notified in the Gazette in connection with the offering at auction on the dates specified hereunder.

J. H. CARRUTHERS.

No. of Papers.	Name of Applicant.	Date of Application.	Land District.	Portion.	Parish.	County	Allotment.	Section.	Town or Village.	Date.	Place.	Area. a. r. p.	Price. £ s. d.	Period for Payment of Balance.
Aln. 98-10969	Humphrey Joseph O'Sullivan.	1896. 2 Aug.	Bellingen	...	Coff	Fitzroy	4	6	Coff's Harbour	21 June, 1898	Coff's Harbour	0 1 0	5 0 0	12 months.
10971	Michael Regan	10 ,,	do	215 & 221.	South Bellingen	Raleigh	...	...	Raleigh	6 Sept.				
10846	Henry Green	16 ,,	Bourke	...	Bourke	Cowper	21	92	Bourke	8 June				
11208	Margaret Shakespear	22 ,,	Condobolin	211	Condobolin	Cunningham	...	...	Condobolin	6 Jan.				
10801	Thomas John Oldham	13 June	Deniliquin	...	Mara	Cadell	7	12	Womboota	23 July.				
10891	William Turner	26 July	Murwillumbah	180	Terranora	Rous	...	...	Chinderah	7 Dec.				
11174	John Davis	6 Aug.	Picton	...	Couridjah	Camden	27	2	Thirlmere	13 Feb.				
11096	Thomas Clarke	13 ,,	Walgett North	...	Cumborah	Finch	6	14	Cumborah	22 ,,				

Grafton District Court.

UNDEFENDED CASES.

Verdicts were given for plaintiffs in the following cases:—

W. Zietsch v. Humphrey O'Sullivan, £4

▲TOP: Humphrey Joseph O'Sullivan purchased land in Coffs Harbour, Sept 1898 (NSW Govt Gazette, 10th Sep 1898, p. 7253). INSET: Humphrey Joseph O'Sullivan in Grafton Court (The Clarence River Advocate, 8 March 1898, p.2). ABOVE: Circular Quay about 1895.

to pay her debts. Making her situation all the more difficult, a family rumour has it that some of her employees had been taking monies out of the business without her knowing. Just four months after opening, she was forced to transfer the publican's license to a Mr. Frank Dyson, who then proceeded to take out an injunction to prevent her from recovering any of her investment. Sadly, Lenore lost Bowden's Hotel, and just folded the whole thing up. In a repeat of misfortunes encountered by her father, the creditors pushed Lenore into bankruptcy, which was formally declared on the 7th December 1895. She was able to walk away from the whole fiasco, but lost all the time and effort she had put into the failed venture, plus her £500 investment.

Young Valtie would have been oblivious to these events, and commenced school around 1896, attending either at Crown Street or Fort Street School on Observatory Hill. Although she was now living in Crown Street Sydney, Lenore often travelled back to Grafton by coastal steamer, to visit her parents and relatives, and always took Valtie along with her.

As the year 1896 began, it was clear that Lenore had failed in her attempt to carve out an independent future for herself and little Valtie. As a bankrupt, Lenore now had few options left to secure her future, and falling pregnant in early 1900, she consented to a second marriage with Humphrey Joseph O'Sullivan.

The Marriage of Humphrey O'Sullivan & Lenore Mackie

The last year of the 19th century was 1900, which saw the continuation of the Boer War in South Africa. That year also brought about the establishment of the British Labour Party with Ramsay MacDonald as its first secretary; the Exposition Universelle, the second Olympic Games and the first line of the Paris Métro all opened in Paris; and the first electric bus became operational in New York City. Queen Victoria gave her royal assent to the Commonwealth of Australia Constitution Act, but in Sydney over 1,000 tonnes of waste

▲ TOP: St. Mary's Cathedral, Sydney in 1900, without the main knave extension or the twin spires, the wedding venue for Humphrey and Lenore O'Sullivan. ABOVE: Marriage Certificate for Humphrey Joseph O'Sullivan and Lenore Mackie (nee Shoveller), 11 July 1900 (NSW BDM #5186/1900).

▲ TOP: Macquarie St, Sydney, festooned for the Federation celebrations of 1901. ABOVE (Left): 1-The 1901 NSW Census return by Humphrey Joseph O'Sullivan; 2-Lenore O'Sullivan's 1903-04 Electoral registration for Glebe, NSW. (Right): The O'Sullivans resided at 83 Burfitt St. Leichhardt from 1901 to 1903.

was removed from demolished buildings, in areas affected by an outbreak of the bubonic plague.

While the Irish writer Oscar Wilde passed into history (30 Nov), notable persons born in 1900 included the American actor Spencer Tracy (5 April), English naval officer and last Viceroy of India Lord Louis Mountbatten, 1st Earl Mountbatten of Burma (25 June), and American entrertainer Sammy Davis Sr. (12 Dec).

Although they had met six years earlier, the pledge Humphrey made to marry Lenore in his letter of January 1894, took a long time to come about. Was Lenore unsure of her feelings for Humphrey, or was Humphrey the cause of the delay? Was Lenore, a Protestant, unsure of marrying for a second time, and to a Catholic? Did she question marrying a man that was five years younger than her? We shall never know, but being pregnant obviously helped sway her decision. Regardless of the reasons for the lengthy delay, the wedding eventually took place in Sydney under the auspcies of Rev. Patrick Charles Cregan at St. Mary's Cathedral, Sydney on the 11th July 1900, according to the rights of the Church of Rome.[8]

Humphrey Joseph O'Sullivan was 29, a bachelor, was working as a labourer and was residing at Waitara. Lenore Mackie (nee Shoveller) also recorded her age as 29 (but was actually 33), a widow, of no occupation and living at 90 Princes St. Sydney (probably St Peters).

Although Humphrey's father James Mahony O'Sullivan was deceased, his mother Ellen O'Sullivan almost certainly travelled from Newcastle to attend the wedding. It is possible that Lenore's parents were also there, with both her younger brother George and sister Mabel definitely attending. Lenore's nine year old daughter Valtie Mackie, may even have been a flower girl at the wedding. The ceremony was witnessed by Arthur Edward Nagle for Humphrey and Lenore's younger sister Mabel Shoveller. This union brought together two otherwise distinct families from Catholic and Protestant backgrounds, blending centuries of religious legacy in a mix of socio-cultural heritage.

The newlyweds moved into a residence at Leichhardt. At this time Lenore was 34, Humphrey 29 and young Valtie was nine years of age. It was a favourable time as the 1st of January 1901 saw the Federation of Australia celebrations take place around the nation. Sydney was festooned with decorations and the newly designed Australian flag was

▲ The scene at 'Paddy's Market', by Harold Cazneaux, 1906.

▲ Death Certificate for Humphrey Joseph O'Sullivan, 30th June 1905 (NSW BDM #9853/1905).

paraded everywhere.

By the second week of January 1901, the motivation for the marriage became clear for all to see when Lenore gave birth to her second daughter in Melecca O'Sullivan.[9] Unfortunately, Melecca must not have been a healthy child and she died just four weeks later, on the 12th of February 1901, burial site unknown.

At this time the young family was living at 83 Burfitt St. Leichhardt, when just under a year later, Lenore gave birth to her third daughter in Octavia Corelli O'Sullivan, on the 1st of February 1902.[10] Humphrey was listed on Octavia's birth certificate as being a general labourer, and the witnesses included a Mrs. McCarthy, and Lenore's mother Mrs. Susan Shoveller.

Another happy event occurred in 1902 when Lenore's sister Mabel Shoveller married William Hayes,[11] but this didn't last long as William Hayes applied for and was granted a divorce on the grounds of adultery.[12] Mabel re-married one year later to Samuel West, who was of half-cast aboriginal descent.[13] Both of Mabel's weddings occurred in Sydney.

Without much of a break and perhaps under the influence of the Catholic background of her husband, Lenore gave birth to her third child in three years, another daughter. Sylvia Veronica O'Sullivan arrived in 1903, but by now the family had moved to 99 Ferry Road, in Glebe.[14]

Sometime in 1904 Lenore's younger brother Clarence John Hann Shoveller married Mary E. White in Sydney, and no doubt the O'Sullivans would have been in attendance.[15] Around this time also, Valtie began high school, which was at Fort Street School in The Rocks.

Despite only five of his 11 siblings surviving into adulthood, Humphrey's Irish roots made him determined to build a good sized family of his own. Perhaps hoping for a son, Lenore was soon bearing their fourth child in four years. But the child proved to be yet another daughter in Goldie Alathea O'Sullivan, who arrived on the 22nd February 1905, while the family were residing at 99 Ferry Road in Glebe.[16]

It is easy to imagine Humphrey and Lenore being happy at this stage in their lives, surrounded by a clutch of young daughters, but they were by no means secure. Humphrey presumably toiled as a general labourer on meagre wages, if indeed he could find work. On the other hand Lenore, a woman of aspirations, was kept at home caring for her newborn, her one year old and three year old girls. So it was a blessing when her 14 year old daughter Valtie developed into an important and necessary helper for Lenore. One thing we do know is that with a piano present, much music and singing came out of that home. Then tragically, the young family was riven by the untimely death of their breadwinner and protector.

The Death of Humphrey Joseph O'Sullivan

All the hopes and dreams of both Humphrey and Lenore came crashing to a halt when just four months after the birth of Goldie, tragedy again cast a shadow across Lenore's path and took Humphrey O'Sullivan from her. He apparently caught influenza, which progressed to bronchitis and he soon died at Royal Prince Alfred Hospital, on the 30th June 1905... at just 34 years of age.[17] The death certificate incorrectly stated that he was 32, but he died of 'acute lobar pneumonia', which he had apparently battled with for 13 days. The informant for Humphrey's death was his younger brother, John Washington O'Sullivan, who was residing at 7 Elizabeth St. in Paddington, at the time. The O'Sullivans, but particularly his mother Ellen were devastated by the loss. Humphrey was buried at the Roman Catholic section at Rookwood Cemetery on the 1st of July 1905 (*Section-D, Row-12, Plot-1159*). The inscription on the headstone was placed and paid for by his mother, Ellen O'Sullivan (nee Frawley).

Humphrey was obviously close to both his mother Ellen O'Sullivan, and his brothers and

▲*TOP (Left): 1-Humphrey Joseph O'Sullivan - Death notice (Clarence & Richmond Examiner, 1 July 1905, p5); 2-Humphrey Joseph O'Sullivan - Funeral notice (SMH, 1 July 1905, p26). (Right): Humphrey Joseph O'Sullivan - 'in Memorium' notices (placed in SMH, 30 June 1908, p.6). ABOVE (Left): In 1903 the O'Sullivans had moved to 99 Ferry Rd. Glebe. (Centre & Right): The grave and memorial headstone of Humphrey Joseph O'Sullivan at Rookwood Cemetery.*

sisters, as they all rallied around at his death. Lenore was obviously too distraught to even complete the required formal death papers, which was why John Washington O'Sullivan, stepped in. Furthermore, as Lenore probably couldn't afford a monument, Humphrey's mother paid for the burial and erected the memorial headstone.

Lenore had now lost two husbands, a daughter and a hotel, and was faced with the daunting prospect of singlehandedly providing for four young girls. Valtie was not listed on Humphrey O'Sullivan's death certificate as she was a Mackie, but she had just turned 14 and became a real strength for Lenore. Lenore's mother Susan, and her siblings George, Clarence and Mabel Shoveller were all supportive throughout this difficult period.

How close Humphrey's mother Ellen O'Sullivan, was to Lenore is unclear, but she passed away herself just four years later in Newcastle. An interesting question at this juncture, is whether Lenore kept contact with Humphrey's family, or if they communicated with her from this point on? We don't know, but it is quite possible that if contact between the two families was lost, it may have occurred around this time.

Where To From Here?

Without a son the untimely death of Humphrey Joseph O'Sullivan brought an end to the proud and unique O'Sullivan and Mahony lineage, which from this point forward could only be continued in the female line through his daughters. But before that became a possibility, his wife Lenore had to struggle for survival in caring for her four baby daughters, and it is her trials and tribulations that are the subject of the next chapter.

References

1. Humphrey Joseph O'Sullivan's letter to Mrs Lenore Mackie, 13th January 1894.
2. Humphrey Joseph O'Sullivan's letter to Lenore's mother, Mrs Susan Shoveller, on 4th July 1894.
3. Lenore Mackie - Transfer of Publican's License from the Licensing Court (SMH, 12 Sept 1895, p3)
4. Lenore Mackie - Advertisement for Lenore Mackie's 'Bowden's Hotel' (Clarence & Richmond Examiner, 21st September 1895, p8).
5. Lenore Mackie - Publican's License (Evening News, 22nd May 1893, p5).
6. 'Old Sydney Disappearing' (The Daily Telegraph, 26 November 1908, p.7).
7. Mrs Lenore Mackie - Receipt for £400 for Lease, License, Furniture & Goodwill for Bowden's Hotel, on 23rd May 1895.
8. NSW Dept of BDM. (1900). Marriage Certificate for Humphrey Joseph O'Sullivan & Lenore Mackie (Shoveller,) #5186/1900.
9. NSW Dept of BDM. (1901). Birth Certificate for Melecca O'Sullivan #7223/1901.
10. NSW Dept of BDM. (1902). Birth Certificate for Octavia Corelli Susan O'Sullivan #4112/1902.
11. NSW Dept of BDM. (1902). Marriage Certificate for Mabel Shoveller and William Hayes #8434/1902.
12. William Albert Hayes v Mable Hayes - Divorce Petition (The Australian Star, 17 March 1904, p.7).
13. NSW Dept of BDM. (1903). Marriage Certificate for Mabel Shoveller and Samuel West #7665/1903.
14. NSW Dept of BDM. (1903). Birth Certificate for Sylvia Veronica O'Sullivan #11867/1903.
15. NSW Dept of BDM. (1904). Marriage Certificate for Clarence John Hann Shoveller and Mary E. White #40/1904.
16. NSW Dept of BDM. (1905). Birth Certificate for Goldie Alathea O'Sullivan #12992/1905.
17. NSW Dept of BDM. (1905). Death Certificate for Humphrey Joseph O'Sullivan, #9853/1905.

Chapter Nine

O'Sullivan

Shoveller

LENORE O'SULLIVAN & HER GIRLS

The sad plight of a widow left on her own in destitute circumstances with four small girls in Sydney was a tragic outcome, and while Lenore would have received expressions of sympathy, there was no State sponsored welfare support in 1905. The best she could hope for would have been private subscriptions, but these never eventuated.

Twice Widowed With Children

Lenore was now in a perilous position, having been twice widowed with no alternative other than to secure the welfare of her four young girls. The Sands Sydney Directory reveals that Lenore relocated a number of times over the next 20 years, beginning with a move to 27 Broughton St. Glebe in 1906, and from there to 108, then 110 Cumberland St. in 'The Rocks', where they remained until 1912. The move proved not to be the best time to be residing in The Rocks as Bubonic Plague had broken out in that exact location in 1900 and persisted on and off until 1925. The rat population was known to be the carriers of the disease and so the city employed an army of 'rat catchers' to deal with the problem, and Sydney embarked upon a systematic cleansing of the inner city.

On the 22nd May 1908, following a period of senility, Lenore's father Thomas Eastman Shoveller passed away from valvular disease of the heart, at his home in Milton St. Grafton at the age of 81.[1] The informant was his son, George Shoveller and he was buried in the Church of England section at Grafton Cemetery, on the very same day with no known headstone. Thomas apparently had a poor heart for sometime, but his family were around him at his death, although whether Lenore and her young family journeyed to Grafton for his funeral, is unknown?

This was also the year that Lenore's daughter Valtie met and fell in love with Edmond W. Malins, and they were married in 1909, at Sydney.[2] With Valtie moving out, Lenore was

The Rocks

Residences for Lenore O'Sullivan (1906-1929) from Sands Sydney Directory

1906 - 27 Broughton St, Glebe	1915 - 192 York St, Nth, Mrs Lenore O'Sullivan	1924 - " "
1907 - " "	1916 - " "	1925 - 4 Upper Bayview St. Nth Sydney, Mr's Lenore
1908 - 108 Cumberland St, Mrs. L. O'Sullivan	1917 - " "	1926 - 99 Union St. Nth Sydney, w/George Langford
1909 - 110 Cumberland St, Mrs. L. O'Sullivan	1918 - " "	1927 - " "
1910 - " "	1919 - " "	1928 - 206 Walker St. Nth Sydney, Mrs. L. O'Sullivan
1911 - " "	1920 - 192 Cumberland St, Mrs Lenore O'Sullivan	1929 - 260 Penshurst St. Willoughby
1912 - 197 Gloucester St, Mrs Lenore O'Sullivan	1921 - 192 York St Nth, Mrs Lenore O'Sullivan	w/Mrs R. Rockwell & Mr. Horace Vicars
1913 - " "	1922 - " "	
1914 - " "	1923 - " "	

▲TOP (Left): Rat catchers in 'the Rocks' to thwart the spread of Bubonic Plague, c.1900. (Right): Children playing in the 'Argyle Cut' in 'the Rocks', Sydney, c.1912. MID: Residences for Lenore O'Sullivan in the 'Sands Sydney Directory.' ABOVE: The local street kids gather at Cumberland Place, the residence of Lenore O'Sullivan and her daughters from 1908 to 1924. The Rocks at this time was hardly a positive environment for four growing young ladies.

left alone to care for her three very young girls in Corelli (7), Sylvia (6), and Goldie (4).

Living in 'The Rocks', the O'Sullivan girls attended the Fort Street Model School, established in 1849, which was the first government model school in the colony of New South Wales, also making it one of the oldest public schools in Australia.

Young Goldie joined her sisters Corelli and Sylvie at school in 1910, and they apparently often overheard the other children making jokes and commenting about their names, as they walked together into the playground... "Here comes Goldie, Sylvie and Bronzie!"[3]

On the 17th June 1910, Lenore's now married daughter Valtie Malins delivered her first child in Sydney, a son and first grandchild for Lenore, whom she named Ronald Guildford

Malins.[4] Valtie followed up soonafter with another son, Alwyn Wooldridge Malins, who was born on the 12th March 1912, also in Sydney.[5] At this time, Lenore had moved around the corner and was now residing at 197 Gloucester Street.

Unfortunately, the marriage of Lenore's daughter Valtie didn't last long as Edmond W. Malins died in 1912 of a brain tumor, at the frightfully young age of just 27.[6] The dreadful event left Valtie in a similar situation that her mother had been in years before, except she now had to care for two infant boys.

In 1913, Lenore's older sister, Susan Eva (now Meally) passed away in Grafton, aged 54.[7] Then yet another calamity must have paralyzed Lenore in 1914, when her young 11 year old daughter Sylvia Veronica O'Sullivan, passed away on the 2nd September.[8] This distressing event also co-incided with the outbreak of World War I.

Sylvia's devastating death left Lenore with only Corelli (12) and Goldie (9) at home. If she continued on, Corelli would have commenced high school around this time, as she turned 13 on the 1st of February 1915.

World War I

Although World War I had broken out across Europe in August of 1914, the shockwaves weren't really felt in Australia until the ANZAC campaign at Gallipoli in April of 1915. Neither of Lenore's brothers enlisted, but many of her relatives joined the Australian Infantry Force and were sent to the Middle East, the Dardanelles and Europe. Indeed, quite

Fort St Public School[18]

The oldest building at the original Fort Street site is the two storey former 1815 military hospital, now facing the expressway. This later became the famous Fort Street School, the first school to provide for teacher training in the colony. This building is now occupied by The National Trust Centre, and includes the S.H. Ervin Gallery, café and shop.

The history of public education in Australia began when the Governor of New South Wales, Charles Augustus FitzRoy, established a Board of National Education on the 8th January 1848 to implement a national system of education throughout the colony. The board decided to create two model schools, one for boys and one for girls. The site of the school was chosen as the old Military Hospital at Fort Phillip, on Sydney's Observatory Hill. This school was not only intended to educate boys and girls, but also to serve as a model for other schools in the colony.

The school's name was derived from the name of a street which ran into the grounds of the hospital and became part of the playground during its reconstruction. The street name is perpetuated in the small street in Petersham that leads to the present school. The school was officially established on 1 September 1849, when the conversion of the building was approved by the government.

The original school building is visible today beside the southern approaches to the Sydney Harbour Bridge. The establishment of Fort Street School marked the beginning of a non-denominational system of schooling, where the government undertook the education of its people, separate from religion.

In 1911, the school was split into one primary and two secondary schools: Fort Street Public School, Fort Street Boys' High School and Fort Street Girls' High School. Due to space limitations at Observatory Hill, in 1916 the Boy's school was moved to its present site at Taverner's Hill, Petersham. The Girls' school remained at Observatory Hill until 1975, when the two schools were amalgamated to form the current co-educational school at Petersham. During that time, its grounds continued to be consumed by the growing city; for example, the Sydney Harbour Bridge, which opened in 1932, took most of the playground. Fort Street Public School remains at Observatory Hill.

The school celebrated its sesqui-centenary in 1999. Its student population is now a diverse one coming from over 100 suburbs in Sydney, and over 600 of the 930 students speak over fourty different languages as their native tongue. Students past and present are called 'Fortians', leading to the expression, "Once a Fortian, always a Fortian."

▲ LEFT: Fort Street Public School - Needlework Class, c.1910. RIGHT: Girls in the playground at Fort Street School, c.1912.

Relatives of Lenore O'Sullivan (nee Shoveller) in WWI

From Jane & William OLIVE:			
Arthur Ernest James	1st C, 1R	at Home	
Charles Griffin James	1st C, 1R	at Home	
Clarence Edw. Murphy	1st C, 1R	at Home	
Reginald Roy Murphy	1st C, 1R	Returned	
James Henry Murphy	1st C, 1R	Returned	

From Joseph & Margharetta HANN:		
Joseph Hann Jr.	1st Cousin	Returned
Thomas James Hann	1st C, 1R	Died
Arthur Oswald Hann	1st C, 1R	at Home
Douglas Paul Hann	1st C, 1R	Returned
Percy Ernest Barnier	1st C, 1R	Returned

From Sarah & James RODGERS:		
Gilbert Every	1st C, 1R	Returned
Norman Ainsley Rodgers	1st C, 1R	Amputee
Herbert Leslie Rodgers	1st C, 1R	Died

From George & Jeanette HANN:		
Albert Edward Hann	1st C, 1R	Returned

From William & Matilda HANN:		
Rockleigh Elwyn Hann	1st Cousin	Returned
Harold William Hann	1st C, 1R	Returned

NB: C = cousin, R = generations removed

▲ TOP (Left): Martin Place, outside the GPO, c.1911. (Right): Early colour photograph of the Town Hall with the QVB in the background, c.1917. MID: War recruitment meetings opposite teh Queen Victoria Building (left), and outside David Jones, George Street, Sydney, c.1915. ABOVE (Left): List of Lenore O'Sullivan's cousins that enlisted in the AIF during WWI. (Right): WWI ANZAC Recruitment Poster. 1915

a number of Lenore's first cousins enlisted in the AIF, with some never to return.

Humphrey Joseph O'Sullivan's brothers were mostly too old, and their sons generally too young to enlist, but Humphrey's brother James Alexander O'Sullivan, even with a young family, courageously enlisted at the age of 42.

Lenore's first cousin Rockleigh Hann, enlisted in Brisbane on the 23rd of August 1915. Before leaving for Enoggera Barracks, he and Oswald Page were given a farewell party at the Imperial Hotel, and each was presented with a wristlet watch. Rockleigh sailed from Sydney aboard "HMAT Caledonia" on 30th November 1915 as a private in the 4th Pioneer Battalion, but he returned to Australia safely on the 5th of September 1919.

In 1915 Lenore moved her family to 192 York St. North in 'The Rocks', where they resided until 1924, while Goldie began her high school in 1917.

Following the death of her father in 1908, and her older sister Susan in 1913, Lenore's mother Susan Shoveller, saw no reason to remain in Grafton and she relocated to be closer to her children and grandchildren in Sydney, moving in with her son George Shoveller at Glebe. She was a regular visitor to the residence of Lenore and her girls, and would also have been the focus of many family occasions. Unfortunately, it was at her sons home that she passed away aged 79, on the 23rd of February 1919 and, was buried in an unmarked grave at Waverley Cemetery.[9]

Not long afterwards, Lenore O'Sullivan's daughter Valtie Malins married for a second time to Jack Chisholm and the happy event occurred in 1923 at Sydney.[10] Lenore attended her eldest daughters second wedding along with her half-sisters Corelli (21), and Goldie (18).

By 1925 Lenore and her daughters had moved across the harbour into a lovely terrace house at 4 Upper Bayview St., North Sydney. They had a wonderful view of Sydney Harbour

▲ TOP: Aerial view of the Sydney Harbour Bridge c.1932. ABOVE (Left): 1-Commemorative stamp for the opening of Parliament House, Canberra, 1927; 2-Commemorative stamp for the opening of the Sydney Harbour Bridge, 1932. (Right): The Overseas Shipping Terminal at Circular Quay, c.1931.

STATE LOTTERY

£5000 to Homebush

Main Prizes to Sydney

Sydney Monday.

State Lottery No. 331 was drawn to-day.

The first prize went to "In Anticipation" syndicate, c o L. G. Paddock, Barnes Bacon Co. Ltd., Homebush, and the second to "Star of Hope" syndicate, c o Lenore O'Sullivan, 24 Market street, Naremburn.

The third was won by "Stella and Irene" syndicate, c o C. Rosten, "Lucky Mart," 564 Willoughby Road Willoughby, and the fourth by "Will It Ever Come?" syndicate, c o Mr. William James, of the Beresford Hotel, Bourke-street, Darlinghurst.

Lottery No. 332 will be drawn on Friday.

FIRST PRIZE £5000
82454

SECOND PRIZE £1000
52851

▲TOP (Left): The winning Lottery notice for Lenore O'Sullivan (Armidale Express & New England Gen, Adv., 30 March 1936, p.4). (Right): Lenore O'Sullivan pictured in the front garden of her daughter Corelli's house at 24 Market St, Naremburn, around 1940.

as construction of the pylons for the new Sydney Harbour Bridge, were underway at that stage.

The very next year, Lenore's eldest daughter Valtie, gave birth by her second husband to a daughter, whom she also named Valtie. She arrived on the 15th June 1926, and became Lenore's third grandchild with the name of Valtie Minlena Chisholm.[11]

Meanwhile, Lenore's second daughter Corelli had also met an eligible young man and just a couple of months later, they married on the 21st of September 1926.[12] Robert Archibald Rockwell and Octavia Corelli O'Sullivan were wed according to the rights of the Anglican Church by the rector, Rev. F. W. Tugwell at St. Johns Church, Glebe, the tower of which had been deemed unsafe and completely rebuilt just two years earlier. The marriage was witnessed by Bob Rockwell's brother Norman and by Corelli's mother Lenore.

At that time Bob Rockwell was working as a cab driver and living at 11 Charles St. in Forest Lodge. Corelli was listed on the marriage certificate as residing at 4 Upper Bayview St, North Sydney and was involved in 'household duties.'

Following the death of her second husband Humphrey Joseph O'Sullivan in 1905, Lenore didn't become involved in any meaningful relationships, except that by 1926 she had moved into 99 Union St, North Sydney, where it appears that at the age of 60, she was co-habiting with a man by the name of George Langford (?-1938). However, it is likely that this relationship was relatively short-lived, or he may also have been a boarder?

In 1927, Canberra became the national capital of Australia, and this year also produced a fourth grandchild for Lenore, when Corelli gave birth to Joy Corelli Rockwell on the 13th April 1927.[13] Just three months later, Lenore's youngest daughter Goldie, married Patrick Joseph Mulroy on the 9th of July.[14] One might imagine that Lenore's family were all at this wedding including her eldest daughter Valtie Chisholm, with her husband Jack Chisholm, and teenage sons Ron (17) and Alwyn (15), along with her infant daughter Valtie. There would also have been Lenore's second daughter, and Goldie's sister Corelli, with her new husband Bob Rockwell and their infant daughter Joy. But another presense, unknown to most at the time, was the unborn child that Goldie was carrying!

Following Goldie's wedding Lenore was now on her own, but she continued to move from place to place and in 1928 was listed as residing at 206 Walker St., North Sydney.

Then in the following year she relocated to 260 Penshurst St. Willoughby, but later moved in with her daughter Corelli and the Rockwell family, and a person by the name of Mr. Horace Vicars, who was perhaps another boarder.

Lottery Winner

Little is known of Lenore O'Sullivan's life during the 'depression' years of the 1930's except that she continued to struggle. But Lenore always maintained links with her siblings George Shoveller, Mabel Shoveller (now West) and Clarence John Hann Shoveller, who were all in Sydney.

Then after years of struggle and loss, a stroke of good fortune finally came Lenore's way when on the 30th March 1936, with ticket #52851, she won second prize in the State Lottery, with a syndicate she called the 'Star of Hope.' Lenore collected an astounding £1000 in prize money, which was the equivalent of an average years salary, or around $100,000 in 2020 values. The win obviously helped her financial situation, enabling her to create a more comfortable life.[15]

From this point on, it is probable that Lenore lived on and off with her daughters for varying periods, welcoming more grandchildren into the world. Valtie and Jack Chisholm didn't have any further children, but Corelli and Bob Rockwell produced Robert Hunter Rockwell (1929), Elwood Lorraine Rockwell (1933), Lindsay Archibald Rockwell (1936), Ronie Malcolm Rockwell (1943) and Janet Lenore Rockwell (1946), the latter being named

▲TOP (Left): Australian soldiers on the Kokoda Track, in New Guinea, c.1943. (Right): Royal Marines marching in a victory parade in Sydney in 1945.
ABOVE: Ern Hill, aka 'the Dancing Man', in Elizabeth Street, Sydney during victory celebrations on VJ Day at the end of World War II, August 15, 1945.

▶ The last Will and Testament of Lenore O'Sullivan, 1945.

in honour of her grandmother. Goldie and Patrick Joseph Mulroy too, produced Lionel Raymond Mulroy (1928) and 11 years later, Lesley John Mulroy (1939).

World War 2

It was not long after the birth of Les Mulroy when the destiny of many peoples lives was cast by world events when Germany invaded Poland on 1st September 1939. Britain and France retaliated by declaring war on Germany, which immediately brought all of Britain's allies and former colonies into the war, including Australia. Most of Lenore's family missed the call to arms, however her two grandsons Ron and Alwyn Malins were both involved. Shortly afterwards, Lenore lost her younger brother

Clarence John Hann Shoveller in July 1940, aged 60 years.[16] Another blow to the family occurred when Lenore's grandson Alwyn, was captured by the Japanese as a result of the fall of Singapore, and unbeknown to everyone, became a prisoner of war.

After a long five year struggle, the war in Europe finally concluded on the 8th May 1945, to great celebrations around the world, including Australia. Life began to take a turn for the better with the harsh restrictions of the second world war gradually being wound down. The war against the Japanese in the Pacific continued for a few more months, but concluded in August 1945, when Japan was forced into unconditional surrender by the dropping of the atomic bomb on Nagasaki, and the hydrogen bomb on Hiroshima.

Death of Lenore O'Sullivan

Just as the world emerged from the darkness of the European war to celebrate their victory, Lenore O'Sullivan unfortunately slipped away from friends and family while residing at Eden St, North Sydney on the 21st of July 1945, at 78 years of age.[17] She wasn't able to greet her grandson Alwyn, on his release from Changi Prisoner of War Camp. Having been widowed twice and witnessing the loss of two daughters, Lenore had endured a great deal of hardship throughout her life. Her funeral announcement was brief and to the point, and she was cremated at Northern Suburbs Crematorium on the 23rd July 1945, with a simple memorial erected to honour her life (*Niche Wall, Location: CG101*).

306076 O'SULLIVAN LENORE late of Crow's Nest in the State of New South Wales—Widow. THIS is the last will and testament of me, Lenore O'Sullivan of No. 7 Eden Street Crows Nest Nth Sydney N.S.W. in the County of----- I HEREBY REVOKE all wills by me at any time heretofore made, and declare this to be my last will and testament. I appoint Robert Archibald Rockwell of 24 Market Street Naremburn Nth Sydney N.S.W. to be Executor of this my will, and direct that all my just debts and funeral and testamentary Expenses shall be paid as soon as conveniently may be after my decease. I GIVE AND BEQUEATH To my Eldest daughter Valtie Varida Calelerada Chisholm one book case and books (the works of Cowper) one shark's tooth brooch To my second eldest daughter Octavia Corelli Rockwell one dinning Table, and chairs, and one Glory box, and one dresser, one set of cannisters, one Rocking chair one keeper ring, 2 hearth rugs, one carpet one runner, white safe. To my youngest daughter Goldie Alathea Mulroy 1 bed and bedding, one wedding ring (gold) one Gramophone and records, and one big sideboard, one kitchen cabinet, and one ice chest, one Rocking chair 2 hearth rugs one settee, Velvet Curtains and hall runner. To my Granddaughter Joy Corelli Rockwell One Thalberg Piano The small polished box One coffee set, Crockery, ornaments. To my sister- Mabel West I leave the sum of One pound (£1:0:0) To my Brother - George Lorriane Shoveller, one sideboard Dated this twentyeighth day of June in the year of our Lord One Thousand Nine Hundred and forty five.   Signed   LENORE O'SULLIVAN.

SIGNED and declared by the said Lenore O'Sullivan the Testator as and for her last will in the presence of us, present at the same time, who, at her request, in her presence, and in the presence of each other, have subscribed our names as witnesses: R.G. WARREN R.H. SIMMONS.

9th October, 1945. On this date Probate of the last will of the abovenamed deceased was granted to ROBERT ARCHIBALD ROCKWELL the executor named in the said will. TESTATRIX DIED on the 21st day of July, 1945. ESTATE SWORN at the sum of £169:0:0 nett.

O'SULLIVAN.— July 21 1945 at hospital Lenore, late of Eden Street, North Sydney, aged 70 years.

◀The Last Will & Testament of Lenore O'Sullivan (Mackie nee Shoveller), 28th July 1945. BELOW: Death notice for Lenore O'Sullivan (SMH, 23 July 1945, p.12).

Funeral Notice

O'Sullivan – The Funeral of the late Lenore O'Sullivan will leave our Funeral Parlours This Day (Monday), at 1.45pm for the Northern Suburbs Crematorium. Whelan and Glacken, A.F.D.A., 263 Miller St. North Sydney, XB1510

Sydney Morning Herald, Monday, July 23, 1945

Although, only three of her five daughters had survived into adulthood, their legacy to their mother was 11 grandchildren and 17 great grandchildren, who today are direct descendants of, and owe their existence to Lenore O'Sullivan. Lenore left a simple hand written will bequesting her personal possessions to various family members. The following information is all that is known of the descendants of Lenore O'Sullivan (Mackie, nee Shoveller) from her two marriages.

Where To From Here?

Humphrey and Lenore O'Sullivan produced a family of four daughters, and following their fathers premature death the sisters had to negotiate growing up in Sydney's infamous Rocks district with only two surviving into adulthood. Their engaging stories are the subject of the next chapter.

References

1. NSW Dept of BDM. (1908). Death Certificate for Thomas Eastman Shoveller, #5484/1908.
2. NSW Dept of BDM. (1909). Marriage Certificate for Valtiveredo Calceolaria Mackie and Edmond W. Malins #10186/1909.
3. Hyde, Joy, 1927-2018 (Interviewee, 2001). 'Joy Hyde (nee Rockwell) interviewed by Tracy Rockwell on the 19th of August 2001, at Aspley, Brisbane'.
4. NSW Dept of BDM. (1910). Birth Certificate for Ronald Guildford Malins, #22382/1910.
5. NSW Dept of BDM. (1912). Birth Certificate for Alwyn Wooldridge Malins, #643/1912.
6. NSW Dept of BDM. (1912). Death Certificate for Edmond W. Malins, #13979/1912.
7. NSW Dept of BDM. (1913). Death Certificate for Susan Eva Meally, #12979/1913.
8. NSW Dept of BDM. (1914). Death Certificate for Sylvia Veronica O'Sullivan, #9782/1914.
9. NSW Dept of BDM. (1919). Death Certificate for Susan Shoveller, #1344/1919.
10. NSW Dept of BDM. (1923). Marriage Certificate for Valtiveredo Calceolaria Malins (Mackie) and John William Chisholm, #4905/1923.
11. NSW Dept of BDM. (1926). Birth Certificate for Valtie Minlena Chisholm, #?????/1926.
12. NSW Dept of BDM. (1926). Marriage Certificate for Octavia Corelli O'Sullivan and Robert Archibald Rockwell, #15695/1926.
13. NSW Dept of BDM. (1927). Birth Certificate for Joy Corelli Rockwell, #?????/1927.
14. NSW Dept of BDM. (1927). Marriage Certificate for Goldie Alathea O'Sullivan and Patrick Joseph Mulroy, #10303/1927.
15. Winning lottery notice for Lenore O'Sullivan (Armidale Express & New England Gen, Adv., 30 March 1936, p.4).
16. NSW Dept of BDM. (1940). Death Certificate for Clarence John Shoveller, #18255/1940.
17. NSW Dept of BDM. (1945). Death Certificate for Lenore O'Sullivan (Mackie, nee Shoveller) #13731/1945.
18. By John, Published July 11th, 2012 [http://blog.fortiansunion.org/2012/07/11/the-early-history-of-the-original-fort-street-school/].

NEW SOUTH WALES

REGISTRATION NUMBER
13731/1945

BIRTHS, DEATHS AND MARRIAGES REGISTRATION ACT 1995

DEATH CERTIFICATE

Date and place of death	Name and occupation	Sex and age	Cause of Death Duration of last illness; medical attendant; when he last saw deceased	Name and occupation of father. Name and maiden surname of mother	Informant
21st July 1945 Sacred Heart Hospice Darlinghurst late of 7 Eden Street North Sydney	Lenore O'Sullivan	female 78 years	Myocarditis some years senility E. G. Carroll registered 19th July 1945	Thomas Eastman Schavelles solicitor Susan Hann	R B Bicknell son-in-law 24 Market Street Naremburn

Particulars of Registration	When and where buried; name of undertaker	Name and religion of Minister and names of witnesses of burial	Where born and how long in the Australasian Colonies or States	Place of marriage, age, and to whom	Children of marriage
J Wells 23rd July 1945 SYDNEY.	23rd July 1945 delivered to the Northern Suburbs Crematorium Samuel Whelan of the firm of Whelan and Glacken 23rd July 1945 cremated at the northern suburbs crematorium Bruce St John Works superintendent	J H B Dillon Church of England A J Glacken & smith Harry Fraser	Grafton, N.S.W.	First Marriage Grafton, N.S.W. unknown years. Unknown. Mackie. Second Marriage Grafton, N.S.W. about 32 years Humphrey Vincent O'Sullivan (widowed)	Valtie b. 48 years living none deceased Octavia b. 42 years Goldie A. 39 living two females deceased

Before accepting copies, sight unaltered original. The original has a coloured background.

REGISTRY OF BIRTHS
DEATHS AND MARRIAGES

SYDNEY   20 March 2020

I hereby certify that this is a true copy of particulars recorded in a Register in the State of New South Wales, in the Commonwealth of Australia

Registrar

▲ Lenore O'Sullivan's Death Certificate (NSW BDM #13731/1945), showing parents and both husbands.

Chapter Ten

DESCENDANTS OF LENORE SHOVELLER, JOHN MACKIE & HUMPHREY O'SULLIVAN

The two marriages of Lenore Shoveller produced five daughters. The eldest was by John Henry Mackie in Valteveredo (b.1891), with the younger four born to Humphrey O'Sullivan being Melecca (b.1901), Octavia (b.1902), Sylvia (b.1904) and Goldie (b.1905). While two of the daughters died young, the surviving three managed to produce 11 grandchildren and 17 great grandchildren. The following information is all that is currently known about these descendants and their respective families.

Descendants Of Lenore Shoveller & John Henry Mackie

1. Valteveredo Calceolaria Mackie (1891-1974)

The sole descendant of Lenore Shoveller from her first marriage held at Grafton on the 3rd March 1890, to John Henry Mackie, was Valteveredo Calceolaria Mackie, who arrived on the 25th March 1891 at Grafton.[1] Her slightly unusual middle name was actually a flower called a lady's purse, also known as a pocketbook or slipperwort flower, which was from a genus of flowering plant in the 'Calceolariaceae' family.

The Daily Telegraph.

SYDNEY, FRIDAY, DECEMBER 13, 1912.

Funerals.

MALINS.—The Friends of Mrs. E. MALINS are kindly invited to attend the Funeral of her late beloved Husband, Edmund; to leave 19 Wilson-street, Woolloomooloo, THIS FRIDAY, at 2.30, for Waverley.

MALINS.—The Friends of Mrs. S. MALINS and FAMILY are kindly invited to attend the Funeral of her late beloved son and their Brother, Edmund; to leave their residence, 19 Wilson-street, Woolloomooloo, THIS DAY, at 2.30, for Waverley.

▲TOP (Left): Portrait of Valtie Mackie, c.1908. (Centre): The 'calceolaria' flower was the inspiration for Valtie Mackie's middle name. (Right): Portrait of Valtie Mackie, c.1908. ABOVE (Left): 1-Edmund Malins - Funeral notices (Daily Telegraph, 13 Dec 1912). 2-1923 wedding photo of Valtie Malins and her second husband, Jack Chisholm. (Right): Marriage Certificate for Valtevereda Calceolaria Malins (nee Mackie) and John William Chisholm, 7 June 1923 at St. Stephens Church, Sydney (NSW BDM #4905/1923).

Valtie Mackie & Edmund Malins

In 1908, at just 18 years of age, Valtie met and fell in love with Edmund W. Malins (1885-1912), and they were married in 1909 in Sydney.[2] Valtie and Edmund soon thereafter presented Lenore with a grandson in Ronald Guildford Malins at Sydney, on the 17th June 1910.[3] Valtie and Edmond's second son Alwyn Wooldridge Malins arrived soonafter on the 12th March 1912 at Sydney.[4]

Valtie turned 21 just two weeks later on the 25th of March 1912. Exactly one month after Alwyn's birth, an event that became world news occurred when the "R.M.S. Titanic" which had departed from Queenstown, Ireland, struck an iceberg and sank in the North Atlantic Ocean, with the loss of over 1500 lives on the 15th April, 1912.[5]

Unfortunately Valtie's first marriage didn't last long as Edmund W. Malins died of a brain tumor in 1912 at the very young age of just 27, leaving Valtie with two infant boys to care for.[6] It seemed as though Valtie was destined to repeat the tragic events of her mother's unfortunate life. The young boys likely attended Crows Nest Public School and St Cuthbert's Church at Naremburn with their widowed mother.

Eleven years after the death of Edmund W. Malins, Valtie married for a second time in 1923 at Sydney, to John William Chisholm (1893-1963).[7] John (aka Jack) Chisholm was born in London, England in 1893 and had worked as a seaman in the maritime services. Having been without a father since 1912, from all accounts, the boys apparently liked Jack and quickly warmed to their new step-father. Valtie's young sons Ron (13) and Alwyn (11) would no doubt have attended the ceremony.

The Chisholm Clan

The Chisholm surname descends from a Scottish clan that began in the Borders area, where they were known from as far back as 1249, but they are also a highland clan, whose chief is called 'The Chisholm.' In the 14th century Robert de Chisholme succeeded

▲ TOP (Left): Ron and Alwyn Malins at home at Willoughby, c.1930. (Right): Ron Malins (x) enjoying a cricket match, c.1935. ABOVE (Left): Valtie Calceolaria Chisholm (Malins, nee Mackie), c.1956. (Right): Valtie's son Alwyn Wooldridge Malins, in London, c.1970.

Alwyn. Malins. 13th oct. 1937.

from a drawing by Malins   Alwyn. Malins.

to his grandfather's title and lands as Constable of Urquhart Castle on Loch Ness. His son married a local heiress, and their son founded the line of Chisholm of Comer and Strathglass. Descendants of Robert's younger son returned to Roxburghshire, and members of that family later settled in Cromlix, Perthshire, producing a remarkable episcopal succession of William Chisholms. William I (d.1564) was Bishop of Dunblane; his nephew William II (d.1593) was Bishop of Dunblane and later of Vaison, near Avignon; and William III (d.1629), nephew of II, was also Bishop of Vaison.

The Chisholm clan fought for Bonnie Prince Charlie at the 'Battle of Culloden' under the chief's youngest son Roderick, who was killed by cannon fire before the final charge. After the battle, his body was found and protected by his two elder brothers, officers of the Royal Scots, who fought on the English side. Jacobite honour was more than satisfied afterwards however, for three of the eight legendary men of Glenmoriston, who sheltered the Prince and guided his escape in July and August 1746, were Chisholms. Whether Jack Chisholm was aware of his celebrated scottish ancestry and traditions is unknown.

On the 15th June 1926, Valtie and her husband Jack brought a new daughter into the world in Valtie Minlena Chisholm, a first grandaughter for Lenore.[8] At the time, her half-brother Ron was two days off turning 16 and Alwyn was 14. Of course young Valtie grew up thinking the boys were her natural brothers and they adored her. By 1931, Valtie and Jack Chisholm were residing at 344 Willoughby Road, Naremburn, and so the young Valtie Minlena commenced kindergarten in that year at Naremburn Public School. Being first cousins of the same age and, attending the same school and living so close to one another, young Valtie and Joy Rockwell developed a special relationship and remained close over the years.

Before World War II, Ron Malins had worked for the 'Dictaphone Company' in Bligh Street, Sydney. Once hostilities broke out, Ron joined the R.A.A.F. as ground staff and served in New Guinea.

With the rank of 2nd Lieutenant, Alwyn joined the British Admiralty as a clerk working for Naval Base Singapore, well before the Japanese captured the island on the 15th February 1942. Following the Japanese invasion, nearly 15,000 Australians and 35,000 British prisoners, including Alwyn were ordered to march to the eastern end of Singapore island, where they were interned as prisoners of war at the infamous Changi Prisoner of War Camp. Both Valties, mother and daughter tried repeatedly to keep in contact with Alwyn throughout the war, and fortunately he survived the ordeal.

Over two years passed before the D-Day invasion of Europe, which occurred on the 6th of June 1944 and just over a week later, Valtie's daughter, the young Valtie Minlena Chisholm married Frank Hammond on her 18th birthday, the 15th of June 1944 in Sydney.[9]

From a drawing by J.R. Flanagan.

Alwyn Malins

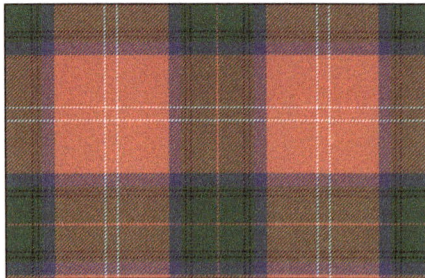

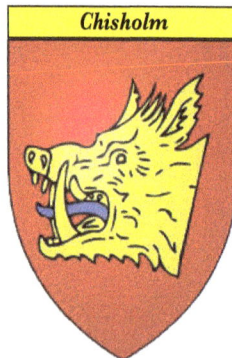

Chisholm

10.1 Descendants of Valtie C. Mackie, Edmund Malins & Jack Chisholm

Valtie Calceolaria Mackie (1891-1974), was born in Grafton, and married firstly in 1909 at Sydney to Edmund (1885-1912), son of William G.& Sarah MALINS, with issue:

1. Ronald Guildford MALINS (17 June 1910 - 1975), married in 1945 to Bernice Walsh (?-?), with issue:
1.1 Kaye Malins (b.1946) married 1967 to Gerald HEASLIP (?).
   1.1.1 Emma Heaslip (b.1970) married ??
   1.1.2 Kate Heaslip (b.1974)

2. Alwyn Wooldridge MALINS (12 Mar 1912 - 1997), unmarried, d.s.p.

Malins

Mackie

Chisholm

Valtie married secondly in 1923 at Sydney to John William CHISHOLM (1893-1963), with issue:

3.Valtie Minlena Chisholm (1926-2002), was born at Willoughby, and married in 1944 at Woollahra to Frank HAMMOND (1911-2007), no issue. (see Chapter 12).

▲TOP (Left): Baby photo of Valtie Minlena Chisholm, c.1927. (Right): Valtie Minlena Chisholm, c.1934. ABOVE (left): 1-Birth announcement of Valtie Minlena Chisholm, 15th June 1926. 2-The Chisholm Tartan. (Centre): The ancient scottish blazon of Chisholm. (Right): Valtie Minlena Chisholm and her half-brother Ron Malins on leave from the RAAF in Sydney, 1944. ▶OPPOSITE (Clockwise from top left): Valtie Chisholm & Valtie Minlena Chisholm in Sydney, 1945; Valtie Chisholm, c.1969; Valtie Chisholm and Valtie Minlena Chisholm at granddaughter Kaye Malin's wedding to Gerald Heaslip, 1967; Kate Heaslip (granddaughter of Ron Malins); Wedding photo of Emma, Gerald and Kaye Heaslip & husband; Emma Heaslip (granddaughter of Ron Malins); Valtie Chisholm and Valtie Minlena Chisholm in Sydney, 1944.

Jack Chisholm died on the 3rd August 1963 at Burwood,[10] and Valtie Sr., supported greatly by her daughter, survived her husband Jack by ten years before she too passed away on the 28th December 1973 at the respectable age of 83.[11]

After the war, Ron Malins married Bernice Walsh in 1945 and moved to Melbourne, where they went on to produce a daughter in Kaye Malins, who arrived on the 11th of February 1946. Kaye in turn, grew up and married Gerald Heaslip on the 9th of April 1967 in Melbourne. They in turn had two daughters in Emma Heaslip, who was born on the 5th of March 1970, and Kate Heaslip born on the 26th of August 1974, both in Melbourne. Ron Malins passed away in 1975 in Melbourne.[12]

On the other hand, after surviving being a Japanese prisoner of war, Alwyn headed straight for London and reputedly led quite an interesting life, preferring the company of his male friends. Around 1990 he returned to Australia and reconnected with his half-sister Valtie, half-cousin Joy and other extended relatives, but passed away in 1997. Alwyn was a very talented artist and left a few small, intricately detailed pen and ink line sketchings. The sole descendant of Valtie and Jack Chisholm was Valtie Minlena Chisholm (*see 10.1 Descendants of Valteveredo Calceolaria Mackie, Edmund Malins & Jack Chisholm*).

#60834 Ronald Guildford Malins (1910 - 1975)

▼ *Ronald Malins enlisted in the RAAF in September of 1941 at the Naremburn Enlistment Office.*

MALINS, Ronald Guildford; Service Number - 60834; Date of Birth: 17/6/1910; Place of Birth - Sydney NSW; Place of Enlistment - Naremburn NSW on 9/9/1941; Next of Kin - (Father) CHISHOLM F. He was a grandson of Lenore Mackie (nee Shoveller).

World War Two Service

CORPORAL
RONALD GUILDFORD MALINS
60834

SERVICE	ROYAL AUSTRALIAN AIR FORCE
DATE OF BIRTH	17 JUNE 1910
PLACE OF BIRTH	SYDNEY, NSW
DATE OF ENLISTMENT	9 SEPTEMBER 1941
LOCALITY ON ENLISTMENT	NAREMBURN, NSW
PLACE OF ENLISTMENT	SYDNEY, NSW
NEXT OF KIN	CHISHOLM, F
DATE OF DISCHARGE	21 JANUARY 1946
POSTING AT DISCHARGE	RD&TU

Australian Government
Department of Veterans' Affairs

#N235394 Alwyn Wooldridge Malins (1912 - 1997)

▼AIF Recruits in company drill. John Harold Shoveller enrolled too late and never left Australia or saw action.

SHOVELLER John Harold; Service Number - 96101; Year of Birth: 1899; Place of Birth - Manly NSW; Place of Enlistment - Manly NSW on 30 Sep 1918; Next of Kin - (Father) SHOVELLER Alfred Russell. He was a great grandson of John Shoveller LLD and Elizabeth Eastman.

World War Two Service

PRIVATE
ALWYN WOOLDRIDGE MALINS
N235394

SERVICE	AUSTRALIAN ARMY
DATE OF BIRTH	12 MARCH 1912
PLACE OF BIRTH	SYDNEY, NSW
DATE OF ENLISTMENT	4 JULY 1941
LOCALITY ON ENLISTMENT	NAREMBURN, NSW
PLACE OF ENLISTMENT	NORTH SYDNEY, NSW
NEXT OF KIN	CHISHOLM, V
DATE OF DISCHARGE	13 OCTOBER 1941
POSTING AT DISCHARGE	2 O S

Australian Government
Department of Veterans' Affairs

Caption ?????

L.P.—No. 8.

Any further communication should be addressed to—

The Secretary of the Admiralty, Bath.

Admiralty. BATH.

14th October, 19 43.

quoting " L.5333/43 " on the outside of the envelope as well as in the text.

Sir,

With reference to your letter of the 1st March, 1943, concerning your brother, Mr. Alwyn Malins, I am commanded by My Lords Commissioners of the Admiralty to inform you that no information has been received in the Admiralty as to his whereabouts.

2. A note has been made of your enquiry so that in the event of any information being received it will be sent on to you immediately.

3. I am to add that My Lords wish to express their sympathy with you in your present anxiety.

I am, Sir,
Your obedient Servant,

Nigel F. Abercrombie.

Mr. R.C. Malins,
"Coloo",
52, Bowen Terrace,
Brisbane, Queensland, AUSTRALIA.

THE LORD MAYOR'S PATRIOTIC AND WAR FUND OF N.S.W.
(N.S.W. Division of the Australian Comforts Fund)

P.S.
22ND Dec. 1941

Dear Ivo.

bought Neat to Singapore yesterday and a silk Kimono

Georgette Colored Handrchif and a monkey skin Bag with designs all over it. I posted them straight away but it may be a month before they arrive there, if there is any duty let me know and you can take it out of the money I send over to Bank. I think Dickie will like the bag as it is about 10 inches long with designs colored on it and made out of the skin of monkeys. You can let me know what you think of the silk as it is supposed to be about the best you can get. If things straighten out

IN YOUR LETTER DO NOT REFER TO
The name of your ship or other ships in the convoy or its escorts; the dates of sailing, ports of call, or probable destination; the description of troops aboard, any other information which, if intercepted would be of value to the enemy.

Over.

and the war finishes quickly I will be able to send Dickie some Jackets and bracelets etc from Siam with engraving etc on them and also things from Bali.

Hope you all have had a good Xmas

収容所 Camp	馬来泰	番號 No.	馬来
姓名 Name	Malins, Alwyn Wooldridge	生年月日 Date of Birth	12th March, 1912
國籍 Nationality	AUSTRALIAN	所屬部隊 Unit	No. Naval Base Police.
階級身分 Rank	Admiralty Police Officer. 2/Lt		
捕獲場所 Place of Capture	SINGAPORE 昭南	捕獲年月日 Date of Capture	昭和 17年 2月 15日 15 d 昭
父ノ名 Father's Name		母ノ名 Mother's Name	Valtie Calceolaria.
本籍地 Place of Origin	Sydney, Australia.	職業 Occupation	CLERK 馬記
通報先 Destination of Report	Mrs V C Chisholm, 544 Willoughby Road, North Sydney, Australia.	特記事項 Remarks	MIA

▲LEFT: War record for Alwyn Malins. RIGHT: Alwyn Wooldridge Malins, c.1935. ◀HM Naval Base at Singapore. ▼(Below): Letter from The Admiralty, 14th Oct 1943, re wherabouts of Alwyn Malins. (Bottom): Prisoners of war at the infamous Changi Prisoner of War Camp in Singapore.

L.P.—No. 8.

Any further communication should be addressed to—

The Secretary of the Admiralty, Bath.

Admiralty. BATH.

quoting " L.9333/43 "

14th October, 1943.

on the outside of the envelope as well as in the text.

Sir,

With reference to your letter of the 1st March, 1943, concerning your brother, Mr. Alwyn Malins, I am commanded by My Lords Commissioners of the Admiralty to inform you that no information has been received in the Admiralty as to his whereabouts.

2. A note has been made of your enquiry so that in the event of any information being received it will be sent on to you immediately.

3. I am to add that My Lords wish to express their sympathy with you in your present anxiety.

I am, Sir,
Your obedient Servant,

Nigel J. Abercromb

Mr. H.S. Malins,
"Coloo",
52, Bowen Terrace,
Brisbane, Queensland, AUSTRALIA.

His Majesty's Naval Base, Singapore

HM Naval Base, Singapore was completed in 1938, at a staggering cost of £60 million. The base covered 21 square miles (54 km2) and had what was then the largest dry dock in the world, the third-largest floating dock, and enough fuel tanks to support the entire British Navy for six months.

It was defended by heavy 15-inch naval guns stationed at the Johore battery, Changi, and at Buona Vista Battery. Other important batteries of smaller calibre were located at Fort Siloso, Fort Canning, and Labrador. Air defence relied on the Royal Air Force airfields at RAF Tengah and RAF Sembawang. Winston Churchill touted it as the "Gibraltar of the East."

After the fall of Malaya on 31 January 1942, Singapore came within range of the artillery guns of Imperial Japanese 25th Army positioned within sight of the base in Johore, which was poised to capture Singapore within two weeks. The base was subsequently captured, largely intact, by units of the advancing Japanese Army and remained in Japanese control through the end of World War II. The Japanese military detained about 3,000 civilians in Changi Prison, which was built to house only one-fifth of that number, but they also used the British Army's Selarang Barracks, near the prison, as a prisoner of war camp, holding some 50,000 Allied soldiers, predominantly British and Australian.

TOP: Prisoners of war in residence, and being released from the Changi Prisoner of War Camp in Singapore. ABOVE (Left): Australian and British prisoners of war were crowded into huts.

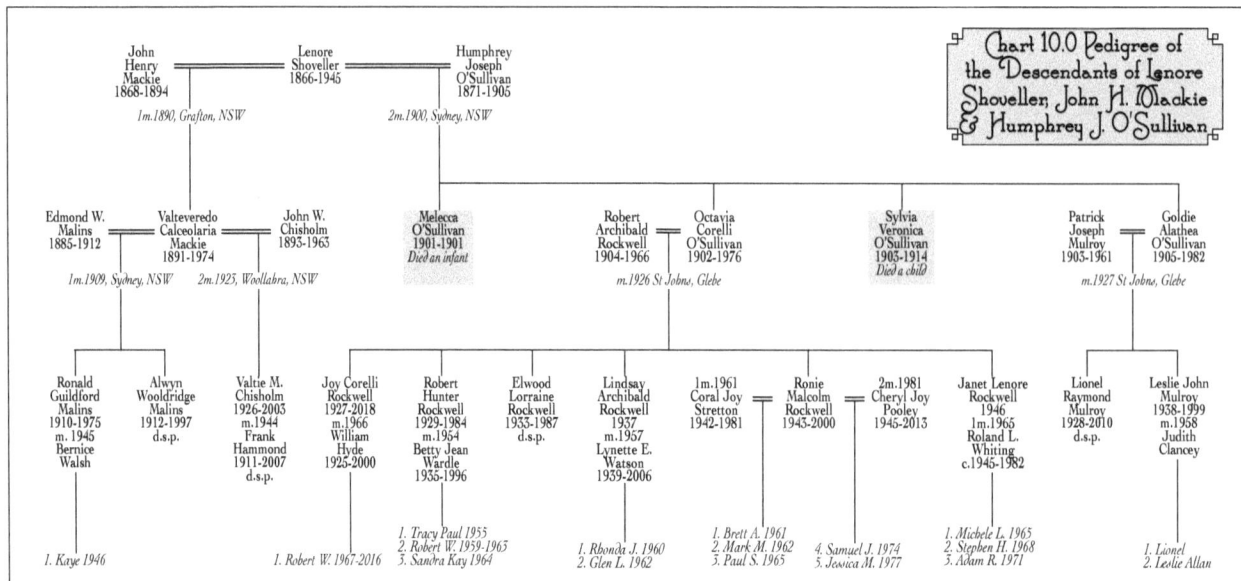

Chart 10.0 Pedigree of the Descendants of Lenore Shoveller, John H. Mackie & Humphrey J. O'Sullivan

John Henry Mackie 1868-1894 — Lenore Shoveller 1866-1945 — Humphrey Joseph O'Sullivan 1871-1905

1m.1890, Grafton, NSW   2m.1900, Sydney, NSW

Edmond W. Malins 1885-1912 — Valteveredo Calceolaria Mackie 1891-1974 — John W. Chisholm 1893-1963

1m.1909, Sydney, NSW   2m.1925, Woollahra, NSW

Melecca O'Sullivan 1901-1901 Died an infant

Robert Archibald Rockwell 1904-1966 — Octavia Corelli O'Sullivan 1902-1976

m.1926 St Johns, Glebe

Sylvia Veronica O'Sullivan 1903-1914 Died a child

Patrick Joseph Mulroy 1903-1961 — Goldie Alathea O'Sullivan 1905-1982

m.1927 St Johns, Glebe

Ronald Guildford Malins 1910-1975 m.1945 Bernice Walsh

Alwyn Wooldridge Malins 1912-1997 d.s.p.

Valtie M. Chisholm 1926-2003 m.1944 Frank Hammond 1911-2007 d.s.p.

Joy Corelli Rockwell 1927-2018 m.1966 William Hyde 1925-2000

Robert Hunter Rockwell 1929-1984 m.1954 Betty Jean Wardle 1935-1996

Elwood Lorraine Rockwell 1933-1987 d.s.p.

Lindsay Archibald Rockwell 1937 m.1957 Lynette E. Watson 1939-2006

1m.1961 Coral Joy Stretton 1942-1981

Ronie Malcolm Rockwell 1943-2000

2m.1981 Cheryl Joy Pooley 1945-2013

Janet Lenore Rockwell 1946 1m.1965 Roland L. Whiting c.1945-1982

Lionel Raymond Mulroy 1928-2010 d.s.p.

Leslie John Mulroy 1938-1999 m.1958 Judith Clancey

1. Kaye 1946

1. Robert W. 1967-2016

1. Tracy Paul 1955
2. Robert W. 1959-1965
3. Sandra Kay 1964

1. Rhonda J. 1960
2. Glen L. 1962

1. Brett A. 1961
2. Mark M. 1962
3. Paul S. 1965

4. Samuel J. 1974
5. Jessica M. 1977

1. Michele L. 1965
2. Stephen H. 1968
3. Adam R. 1971

1. Lionel
2. Leslie Allan

▲Memorial card for the first born daughter of Humphrey & Lenore O'Sullivan, Melecca O'Sullivan, died 12th February 1901.

Descendants Of Lenore Mackie (nee Shoveller) & Humphrey Joseph O'Sullivan

In the short five year period of their marriage Humphrey and Lenore O'Sullivan produced four daughters, although only two lived to adulthood and went on to produce families of their own, all likely none the wiser that their older sister Valtie had a different father. Humphrey and Lenore O'Sullivan produced the following issue:

2. Melecca O'Sullivan

Melecca O'Sullivan (1901-1901) was born at 83 Burfitt St, Leichhardt in mid January, 1901, but died just four weeks later on the 12th February 1901.[13]

3. Octavia Corelli Susan O'Sullivan

Octavia Corelli O'Sullivan (1902-1976) was also born at 83 Burfitt St, Leichhardt on the 1st February 1902,[14] 12 months following the death of her older sister Melecca. She was named for 'Octavia the Younger' (69 BC–11 BC), also known as 'Octavia Minor' or simply Octavia, who was the elder sister of the first Roman Emperor, Augustus, known also as Octavian.

Octavia Corelli O'Sullivan was better known by her middle name Corelli, which was given her after 'Arcangelo Corelli' (1653-1713), the famous Italian violinist and baroque composer. Her third name 'Susan' was given to honour her grandmother Susan Shoveller (nee Hann), first white child born in the Clarence River District. Corelli spent her former years growing up in the rough environment of the Rocks. She married Robert Archibald Rockwell at St. John's Church, Glebe on the 21st of September 1926, officiated by Rev. F. W. Tugwell.[15] At this time Bob Rockwell was working as a cab driver and living at 11

Charles St. in Forest Lodge with his parents. Corelli was listed as being a domestic, residing at 4 Upper Bayview St. North Sydney, with her twice widowed mother Lenore O'Sullivan.

The wedding was witnessed by Norman John Rockwell (brother) for Bob Rockwell and Lenore O'Sullivan (mother) for Corelli. Together they produced six children spanning the years from 1927 to 1946.

Robert Archibald Rockwell, was born in Forest Lodge on the 1st November 1904.[16] Bob Rockwell worked as a cabman, a carter, a wharf labourer and a postal worker. He died from a heart attack on 17th September 1966,[17] and Corelli outlived him by ten years before her passing on the 4th July 1976.[18] Together they produced six children *(see 10.2 Descendants of Octavia Corelli O'Sullivan & Robert Archibald Rockwell).*

4. Sylvia Veronica O'Sullivan

Sylvia Veronica O'Sullivan (1903-1914) was born in 1903,[19] but she tragically died in 1914 at the young age of 11.[20] The cause of her death is unknown and little else is known

▲ *(Standing from left): Ronie (14), Tracy (18mths), Rock (28), Betty (22), Bob (53), Lynette (18), Joy (30) & Janet Rockwell (11) crouching, in Market Lane at the rear of the Rockwell semi-detached cottage at 24 Market St, Naremburn, December 1957.*

10.2 Descendants of Octavia Corelli O'Sullivan & Robert Archibald Rockwell

Robert Archibald Rockwell (1904-1966), born at his home in Glebe. He married on the 21st Sep 1926 at St John's Church, Glebe to Octavia Corelli (1902-1976), dau of Humphrey & Lenore O'Sullivan, with issue:

1. Joy Corelli Rockwell (1927-2018), born 13th Apr 1927 at Naremburn. She married on the 9th Apr 1966 at St Cuthbert's Church, Naremburn to William HYDE (1925-2000), with issue:
1.1 Robert William HYDE (1967-2016) △

2. Robert Hunter ROCKWELL (1929-1984), born 25th Jun 1929 at Naremburn. He married on the 15th Jan 1954 at Sydney to Betty Jean (1935-1996), daughter of William W. Wardle & Mary A. Cummings, with issue:
2.1 Tracy Paul ROCKWELL (1955)
2.2 Robert Wayne ROCKWELL (1959–1963)*
2.3 Sandra Kay Rockwell (1964)

3. Elwood Lorraine ROCKWELL (1933-1987), born 9th Dec 1933 in Naremburn. He had partners, but never married, with no issue.

4. Lindsay Archibald ROCKWELL (1937), △ born 2nd Nov 1937 in Naremburn. He married on the 14th Sep 1957 at St

Cuthbert's Church, Naremburn to Lynette Ellen (1939-2006), daughter of Hugh & Alice Watson, with issue:
4.1 Rhonda Janine Rockwell (1960)
4.2 Glen Lindsay ROCKWELL (1962)

5. Ronie Malcolm ROCKWELL (1943-2000), born 26th Feb 1943 at Naremburn. He married firstly in 1961 to Coral Joy Stretton (1942-1981), with issue:
5.1 Brett Anthony ROCKWELL (1961)
5.2 Mark Malcolm ROCKWELL (1962)
5.3 Paul Steven ROCKWELL (1965)

Ronie married secondly in 1981 to Cheryl Joy Pooley (1945-2013), with issue:
5.4 Samuel Joshua ROCKWELL (1974)
5.5 Jessica Molly Rockwell (1977)

6. Janet Lenore Rockwell (1946), born 22nd Feb 1946 at Naremburn. She married firstly on the 19th Jun 1965 at St Cuthbert's Church, Naremburn to Roland Lawrence WHITING (c.1945-1982), with issue:
6.1 Michelle Lena Whiting (1965)
6.2 Stephen Hunter WHITING (1968)
6.3 Adam Roger WHITING (1971),

* Died before adulthood - d.s.p.

NB. The family of Robert and Octavia Corelli Rockwell are the subject of chapters 12 to 16.

Rockwell | *O'Sullivan*

The Mulroy Family

Bankrupt Gasman

Intermittency of work and sickness of his family were the reasons given by Patrick Joseph Mulroy, gasman, of Stockton, to the registrar in bankruptcy (Mr. Chiplin, C.P.S.) at Newcastle Bankruptcy Court to-day, for failure to pay his debts.

His liabilities amounted to £77 17s 3d, and his assets were nil. He said that during the past four years he had been working at the steel works. His income was about £250 a year, and his expenditure was that amount, plus bare living expenses.

Mr. Chiplin declared the public examination closed.

Drunken Wharf Labourer Fined

Mr. E. R. Harvey, S.M., in Central Police Court yesterday, fined Patrick Mulroy, 49, wharflabourer, £20 for being drunk on Darling Harbour wharf on Sunday.

Constable Robertson, of the Pillage Squad, said that at 4.30 p.m. on Sunday, Mulroy was drunk while working for Dalgety's Ltd.

In the past 12 months, Dalgety's Ltd. had lost labour and had been suspended for five and seven days for having had drunkenness on the company's wharves.

▲TOP (Left): Lesley and Lionel Mulroy with Elwood Rockwell at Naremburn, c.1950. (Right): Lionel Mulroy, his long-time partner Shirley, Lionel Mulroy Jr, and Lesley John Mulroy on the occasion of Lionel Sr's 66th birthday, 16th January 1994, at Woy Woy. ABOVE (Left): Photo of Patrick Joseph Mulroy (1903-1961). (Mid 1): Patrick Mulroy - Bankrupt (Newcastle Sun, 28th July 1928). (Mid 2): Patrick Mulroy - Fined for Drunkeness (SMH, 29th Jan 1952). (Right): Lionel Mulroy Sr. at Woy Woy just a few weeks before his death in 2010.

of dear Sylvia, except that she was buried at Rookwood Cemetery (*Portion-M2; Row-N; Plot-2314*).

5. Goldie Alathea O'Sullivan

Goldie Alathea O'Sullivan (1905-1982) was born on the 22nd February 1905 at Sydney, the baby of the family.[21] She celebrated her 21st birthday on the 22nd February 1926. There were rumours that during her earlier years, Goldie may have worked as a street girl, for which she could have suffered ostracism by the family. But she soon met a fellow by the name of Patrick Joseph (1903-1961), son of Patrick Joseph Mullery and Johanna Rooney, who was born in Uralla, NSW.[22] Just over a year later, Goldie married Patrick on the 9th July 1927 in Sydney.[23] For their initial years together, Goldie and her family resided at 7 Dawson St, Naremburn.

Patrick Mulroy initially worked as a gasman, but later joined the wharf labourers, whereas Goldie worked a number of odd jobs, including being a cleaner at Crows Nest Technical High School for many years. Goldie's and Patrick's first born became Lenore's fifth grandchild when they welcomed Lionel Raymond Mulroy (1928-2010) into the world on the 16th January 1928.[24]

Goldie and Patrick Mulroy delivered their second son Lesley John Mulroy, on the 14th July 1938.[25] Little is known of Lesley except that he married Judith Anne Clancey in 1958.[26] Les and Judith produced two sons in Lionel Raymond Mulroy Jr., obviously being named after his uncle, who was born in 1959, and Leslie Allan Mulroy in 1961. Both of Leslie's boys took wives with Lionel Mulroy Jr. marrying Anne and having two children, but have since separated. Allan also married and produced two children and resides somewhere on the North Coast. He worked for a while as a professional 'Beach Inspector/Lifeguard' with Waverley Council and patrolled the metropolitan beaches at Bondi, Tamarama and Bronte.

Allan Mulroy was even awarded a bravery medal for performing an outstanding rescue. The Bravery Medal (BM), created in February 1975, is a decoration awarded to Australians for acts of bravery in hazardous circumstances. The decorations recognise acts of bravery by members of the community who selflessly put themselves in jeopardy to protect the lives or property of others. It is ranked third of the Australian bravery decorations in the Australian Honours System. Recipients of the Bravery Medal are entitled to use the post-nominal letters "BM."[27] Al later joined the Fire Brigade.

The Mulroy family sadly lost their husband and father Patrick Joseph Mulroy at Chatswood on the 17th October 1961.[28] Goldie's son Lionel was very close to the Rockwell boys and paired up with both Robert and Elwood on many occasions and trips away. Lionel and Elwood became inseparable as first cousins and always socialised together, developing a mutual liking for plonk, mostly beer. Goldie was also slightly eccentric and would do things like stand in a tub of water in her second hand shoes to help stretch the leather.

Just as Elwood Rockwell remained with his mother Corelli, Lionel Mulroy resided with his mother Goldie at Naremburn. Then during the 1970's, Goldie and Lionel moved to the Central Coast where I can remember visiting them at their modest Woy Woy home about 1980. Goldie was very short and not very well groomed, but she had a happy disposition and was tremendously hospitable.

BRAVERY MEDAL
Mr Allan MULROY
O'Brien Street, Bondi NSW 2026

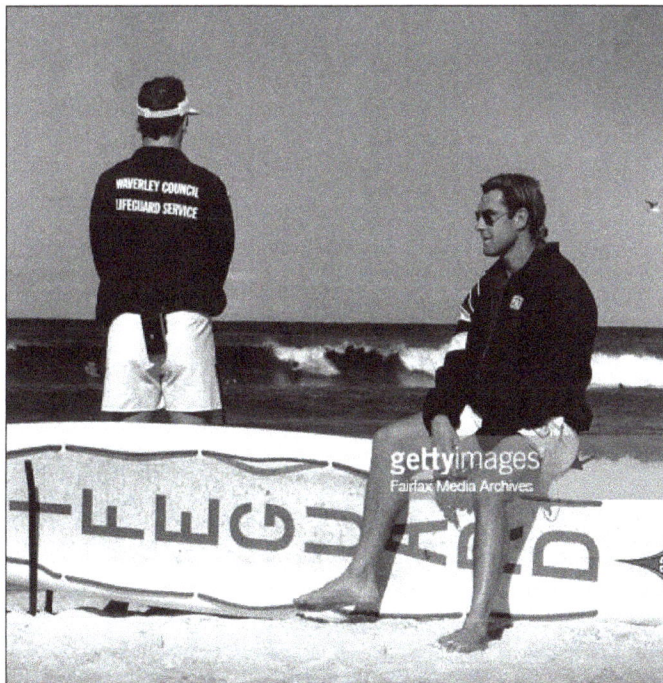

Seas remain treacherous

SYDNEY: Continued big seas and rips closed several Sydney beaches yesterday, while swimming conditions remained treacherous at other popular beaches.

Bronte and Tamarama near the city, southern beach Elouera and northern beaches North Narrabeen and beaches from Newport to Avalon were closed yesterday, the beach monitoring service, Beachwatch, said.

On Monday, six Bondi lifesavers performed 110 rescues at Bondi Beach — one of the largest number of rescues ever performed at the beach.

The surf was not as dangerous yesterday and there were fewer swimmers at the beach, but Bondi beach inspector Gavin Akers still expected a hectic day for lifesavers.

The big surfs of the past few days have been caused by the low pressure system off the South Coast, which created storms at sea and made for big swells on NSW beaches.

Beach inspector Allan Mulroy said there was little reward for lifesavers.

"About 50 per cent [of people rescued] don't say thanks and a lot of people just quickly say 'thanks mate' and walk off to avoid embarrassment," Mr Mulroy said.

▲LEFT: Bravery Medal and citation awarded to Allan Mulroy #865583 on the 1st November 1990 for 'Rescue from sea at Bondi Beach, NSW.' MID: Bondi Beach lifeguards Rob Csokas & Allan Mulroy on duty at Bondi Beach, c.1990. RIGHT: Allan Mulroy interviewed in 'Seas Remain Treacherous' (The Canberra Times, 8 January 1992, p.16)

Sadly, the last of Lenore's girls, Goldie Alathea Mulroy, passed away at Woy Woy on the 17th March 1982 aged 77, and was buried on the 22nd March 1982 with a memorial at Wamberal Cemetery (*Portion-Gen 1; Row-4; Plot-47*).[29] The descendants of Goldie Alathea and Patrick Mulroy are:

Lesley John Mulroy passed away around 1999, but the exact date of death and his burial location is unknown. His older brother Lionel was a lovable character, the kindest and most warm-hearted of his family and he always kept in contact through writing letters to his first cousin Joy Hyde (nee Rockwell), never complaining about his meagre existence at Woy Woy. He was a simple man who lived a simple life, an avid fan of documentaries, he would walk each day to the pub for a 'sherbet' (beer) or two. He was in relatively good shape, for all the alcohol he consumed, but in the end his cousins Joy Hyde, Lindsay Rockwell and the author visited Lionel in Woy Woy, with Shirley standing by him, as he succumbed to cancer on 14th June 2010.

In later years Valtie, who had married better became more aloof, while Corelli and

▲ABOVE (Left): Portrait of Goldie Alathea O'Sullivan, taken for her wedding on the 9th July 1927. (Right): Letter to her niece Joy Hyde (nee Rockwell), from Goldie Mulroy (nee O'Sullivan).

10.3 Descendants of Goldie Alathea O'Sullivan & Patrick Joseph Mulroy

Goldie Alathea O'Sullivan (1905-1982), was born in Glebe, and later married on the 9th July 1927 in Sydney to Patrick Joseph (1903-1961), son of Patrick Joseph MULROY & Johanna Rooney, with issue:

1. **Lionel Raymond MULROY (1928-2010),** was a companion to Shirley ?, no issue.

2. **Leslie John MULROY (1938-c.1999),** married in 1958 to Judith Anne Clancey in Sydney (#15130), with issue:
2.1 Lionel Raymond MULROY (1959) married to Anne ?, with issue:
a. Stella Mulroy (1995)
b. Unknown Mulroy?
2.2. Leslie Allan MULROY (c.1962), worked as a lifeguard

with Waverley Council, married to ?, with issue:
a. Unknown Mulroy?
b. Unknown Mulroy?

Mulroy

O'Sullivan

▲ TOP (Left): Tracy and Lindsay Rockwell with Lionel Mulroy at Woy Woy in 2008. (Right): Robert Hyde with Lionel Mulroy and Tracy at Woy Woy in 2008.
ABOVE: Lionel's humble rented cottage at Woy Woy.

Goldie struggled with husbands who lacked opportunity, and for whom life had passed turned its back. It is little wonder that the grandchildren of Corelli and Goldie O'Sullivan, all second cousins, have never met *(see 10.3 Descendants of Goldie Alathea O'Sullivan & Patrick Joseph Mulroy)*.

Where To From Here?

At this point, this genealogy digresses to explore the interesting lives of Valtie Minlena Chisholm, grandaughter of Lenore O'Sullivan, and her husband Frank Hammond. Thanks to Frank's business acumen, Valtie and Frank led a privileged and flambouyant life after the war, travelling often, and socialising in high circles. As the author listened to and interviewed Frank on a number of occasions, his tale of escape from the Nazi's in Europe just prior to World War II, is worth telling.

References

1. NSW Dept of BDM. (1891). Birth Certificate for Valteveredo Calceolaria Mackie #14676/1891.

2. NSW Dept of BDM. (1909). Marriage Certificate for Valtiveredo Calceolaria Mackie and Edmund W. Malins #10186/1909.

3. NSW Dept of BDM. (1910). Birth Certificate for Ronald Guildford Malins, #22382/1910.

4. NSW Dept of BDM. (1912). Birth Certificate for Alwyn Wooldridge Malins, #643/1912.

5. Wikipedia - RMS Titanic [https://en.wikipedia.org/wiki/Titanic].

6. NSW Dept of BDM. (1912). Death Certificate for Edmond W. Malins, #13979/1912.

7. NSW Dept of BDM. (1923). Marriage Certificate for Valtiveredo Calceolaria Malins (Mackie) and John William Chisholm, #4905/1923.

8. NSW Dept of BDM. (1926). Birth Certificate for Valtie Minlena Chisholm, #?????/1926.

9. NSW Dept of BDM. (1945). Death Certificate for Lenore O'Sullivan (Mackie, nee Shoveller) #13731/1945.

10. NSW Dept of BDM. (1963). Death Certificate for Jack Chisholm, #59195/1963.

11. NSW Dept of BDM. (1974). Death Certificate for Valtiveredo Calceolaria Chisholm (Malins, nee Mackie) #40229/1974.

12. Victorian Dept of BDM. (1975). Death Certificate for Ronald Guildford Malins, #14061/1975.

13. NSW Dept of BDM. (1901). Birth Certificate for Melecca O'Sullivan #7223/1901.

14. NSW Dept of BDM. (1902). Birth Certificate for Octavia Corelli Susan O'Sullivan #4112/1902.

15. NSW Dept of BDM. (1926). Marriage Certificate for Octavia Corelli O'Sullivan and Robert Archibald Rockwell, #15695/1926.

16. NSW Dept of BDM. (1904). Birth Certificate for Robert Archibald Rockwell, #32224/1904.

17. NSW Dept of BDM. (1966). Death Certificate for Robert Archibald Rockwell, #2720/1966.

18. NSW Dept of BDM. (1976). Death Certificate for Octavia Corelli Rockwell (nee O'Sullivan), #15733/1976.

19. NSW Dept of BDM. (1903). Birth Certificate for Sylvia Veronica O'Sullivan #11867/1903.

20. NSW Dept of BDM. (1914). Death Certificate for Sylvia Veronica O'Sullivan, #9782/1914.

21. NSW Dept of BDM. (1905). Birth Certificate for Goldie Alathea O'Sullivan #12992/1905.

22. NSW Dept of BDM. (1903). Birth Certificate for Patrick Joseph Mulroy, #7675/1903.

23. NSW Dept of BDM. (1927). Marriage Certificate for Goldie Alathea O'Sullivan and Patrick Joseph Mulroy, #10303/1927.

24. NSW Dept of BDM. (1928). Birth Certificate for Lionel Raymond Mulroy #?????/1928.

25. NSW Dept of BDM. (1939). Birth Certificate for Lesley John Mulroy #?????/1939.

26. NSW Dept of BDM. (1958). Marriage Certificate for Lesley John Mulroy and Judith Anne Clancey, #15130/1958.

27. Leslie Allan Mulroy - Bravery Medal (Commonwealth of Australia Gazette, 16 March, 1991 [Issue No S67], p.2).

28. NSW Dept of BDM. (1961). Death Certificate for Patrick Joseph Mulroy, #31235/1961.

29. NSW Dept of BDM. (1982). Death Certificate for Goldie Alathea Mulroy (nee O'Sullivan), #102136/1982.

Chapter Eleven

VALTIE CHISHOLM* & FRANK HAMMOND
(Half-cousin of Joy, Robert, Elwood, Lindsay, Ronie & Janet Rockwell)

Valtie Minlena Chisholm, half-cousin to the Rockwells, and her husband Frank Hammond lived a charmed existence, primarily due to Frank's business acumen, but also by virtue of Valtie's high-profile social connections. Although they had no children, some of their interesting life stories have been recorded and are worth summarising.

Frank Hammond [1]

Frank Hamburger (1911-2007) was the second child of Eric Wolfgang Hamburger (1877-1966) and Ida Blumberg (1889-1949) and was born into the Jewish faith in Prague, on the 24th of April 1911. Frank's older brother Walter Hamburger, was also born in

▲ Postcard of the Stadttheater at Gablonz, which was erected in 1906.

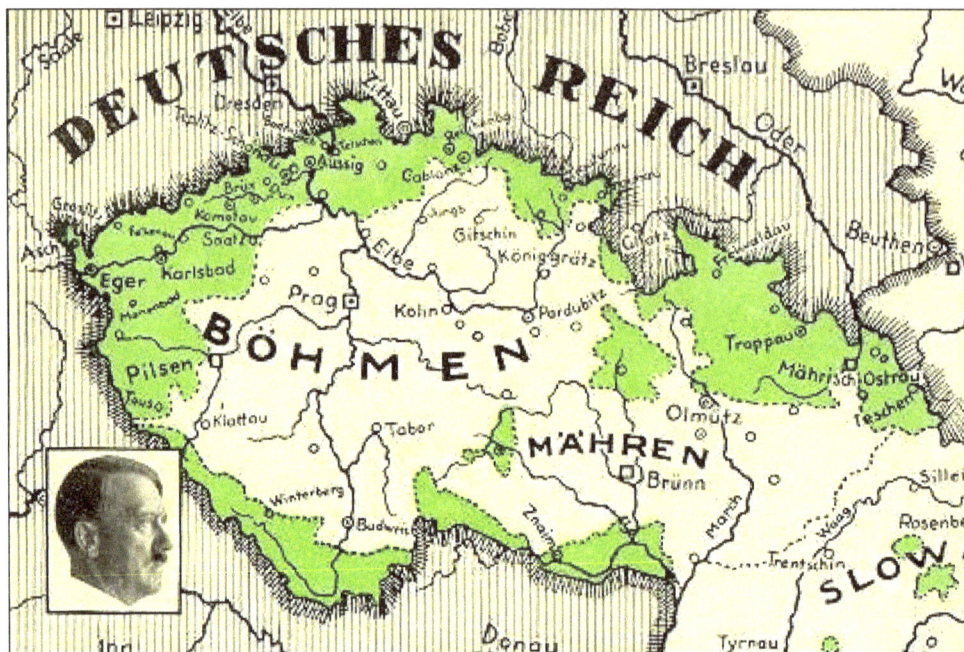

Frank Hamberger was born in Gablonz, situated in the German speaking province of Czechoslovakia, known as Sudetenland. ▲TOP (Left): Gablonz, Austria in 1914 with a German Zeppelin overhead. (Right): Kaiser Franz Josef in Gablonz. ABOVE: Map of Bohemia with German speaking regions highlighted in green.

Prague in 1908.

Frank can remember that his maternal grandmother, Therese Blumberg, also lived with his family in Prague. However, at around the age of five, possibly due to the deterioration of living conditions after World War I, the Hamburger family moved to Tannwald (sic) near Gablonz an Neisse, now Jablonec-nad-Nisou, Czech Republic, which was around 100km north east of Prague, but then in the Sudetenland province.

Frank started kindergarten at Bad Schlag Primary School, then at age 11 attended the Gymnasium in Gablonz until he turned 14. He remembers celebrating his 'bahmitzfah' at his house and receiving lots of presents. From age 14 to 17 he attended the Handel Academy in Gablonz. The family spoke German at home, but they were wealthy enough to have young Frank also tutored in English lessons.

After graduating from Handel Academy he enroled at the Ecole de Commerce, which was an all French speaking institution in Lausanne, Switzerland, where he continued his schooling until the age of 19. After returning to Gablonz, Frank gained his first job with the Landwirtschliche Bank in Prague as a clerk. A year later he was transferred to Karlsbad in Kalovy Vary, where he worked for a further 12 months with the bank.

These were happy times and Frank remembered the family always spent their summer holidays on an island in the Baltic Sea called Rügen, in north Germany, which he recalled often had a lot of jellyfish on the shores. In 1816 the first bathing resort had been founded at Putbus, on Rügen. Later more resorts were established, and Rügen remained the most famous holiday resort in Germany until World War II. On one particular trip he clearly remembers buying 10 boxes of German chocolates to take back to Gablonz. At other times

▲ TOP (Left): Gablonz swimming baths, c.1920. (Right): Postcard of Gablonz, Czechoslovakia pre WWII. MID: Postcards of Gablonz. ABOVE (Left): Gablonz street corners around 1910. (Right): Portrait of the wealthy industrialist Isidor Mautner (1852-1930).

▲TOP: Two pre WWII scenes of Gablonz, Czechoslovakia. MID: Germany marched into Czechoslovakia and annexed the Sudetenland, on the 1st October 1938. ABOVE (Left): Frank Hamburger and his dog 'Blitz' in Czechoslovakia, c.1922. (Right): The Hamburger house in Gablonz, Czechoslovakia.

they would journey to Reichenberg to visit Franks paternal grandmother, Paula Hamburger and his aunt Ellie.

Frank's father was apparently a successful businessman and the managing director of the Mautner Textile Works, which was developed by Frank's paternal grandfather, along with Mr. Isidor Mautner (1852-1930).[2] The business must have been immense as it reputedly had 48 different factories at one time and met the huge demand for textiles following WWI in what had by then become Czechoslovakia. However, the stock market crash in New York in 1929 dealt a heavy blow to many of their markets, as first suppliers and then the business itself deteriorated rapidly.

The crash must have been very bad as Frank was forced to start a wholesale costume jewellery business in Brunnengasse, Gablonz which he ran from 1932 until the events of 1938. He bought and sold his goods all over Europe. Then in 1935, his brother Walter married Ilse Stein (1911-?) the daughter of another wealthy Czech family. A year later Walter and Ilse delivered Rene (1936) in Gablonz.

By this time Frank was seeing a young lady by the name of Liese Hubner (1916-?) who was also a native of Gablonz, and after a brief engagement, they married on the 7th July 1937 in Gablonz. But political events were threatening Frank and his family as Gablonz was situated right in the middle of the German speaking province of Sudetenland. With three million ethnic Germans, the Sudetenland represented the largest German population outside the "Third Reich." Many residents supported reconciliation with Hitler's Nazi Germany and his hard line against the Jewish population. As anti-Czech and anti-semitic sentiments became more and more vocal and violent in the province, Frank's brother Walter was quick to see what was taking place and wasted no time in boarding a ship for Australia to investigate a possible safe haven, early in 1938. His wife Ilsa and their young daughter

▲TOP: Frank found sanctuary on the island of Rab on the Dalmation Coast, Yugoslavia. ABOVE (Left): The township of Dom Zdravlja on Rab, Yugoslavia, (Right): Pre WWII London was sympathetic to German nationalism and even flew Nazi flags (circled).

Rene followed later that same year. Unfortunately, Frank wasn't so lucky.

Following their wedding, Frank and his wife Liese lived on the first floor of his parents house in Gablonz for around 15 months and were residing there when the British Prime Minister Neville Chamberlain, flew to Germany and signed the Munich Pact with Hitler in late September, virtually wiping Czechoslovakia off the map by placing most of its territory in German hands.

Escape From Europe

In late October 1938, Frank and Liese decided to travel into the interior of Czechoslovakia for a brief holiday but, as events took their course, Frank was to never again return home. By this time, the anti-semitic situation throughout the country had become so dangerous that to avoid being arrested, Frank had to board a train for Prague and wait there for one day, which although very dangerous, allowed enough time for his wife to bring him a small suitcase of clothes and personal belongings. He then boarded another train, this time bound for Yugoslavia where he stayed for two weeks on the island of Rab, which is located around 100km south west of Trieste.

Feining illness, Frank telegraphed for Liese to join him, which she dutifully did. Somehow, he was able to arrange for a train journey for himself through to Brussels in Belgium as one of his customers from his jewellery business was willing to provide him with work. At this stage, he was very low on money and had to sell his wedding ring so that both he and Liese could survive.

Liese returned to Prague while Frank boarded another train, this time from Trieste and he travelled through the northern part of Italy, then Liechtenstein, Switzerland, France and possibly Luxembourg before finally entering Belgium, where he was temporarily safe. He had a bank account in Holland, but was unable to withdraw any money. Liese, virtually without any money, had to find her way back to Gablonz all by herself and although

▲ Frank Hammond emigrated to Australia aboard the "SS Strathnaver" in December 1938.

▲ Frank served in the AIF 12th Field Artillery Regiment in New Guinea.

she was a German by birth, being married to a Jew was enough to have her detained, interrogated and beaten by the Gestapo along the way. Frank and Liese were then forced to divorce while he was staying in Belgium, which at that time became compulsory for all German/Jewish marriages.

Frank stayed in Brussels for a few weeks and helped his Belgium friend manage the factory. But he was really waiting for his brother Walter to send him a permit to enter Australia, which would also give him entry to Britain and enough money to purchase his fare. Once that arrived, Frank boarded a cross-channel ferry to Britain in December 1938, which took him to Golders Green in London, where he was able to find temporary accommodation with two old spinsters for a few weeks. Golders Green was known for its large Jewish population as well as for being home to the largest Jewish kosher hub in the United Kingdom.

After four weeks in London, Frank embarked on board the "S.S. Strathnaver," which left from Tilbury in London just before Christmas 1938. The ship sailed through the Mediterranean Sea, Alexandria and the Suez Canal, then to Bombay, Calcutta, Fremantle and Adelaide, where Frank disembarked.

Once in Australia, his aim was to get to Sydney as soon as possible, as his brother had arranged a job for him. He boarded the train from Adelaide, which travelled through Melbourne and finally arrived in Sydney toward the end of February, where he then joined Hordern Bros. Clothing store in King St.

In the meantime, Franks parents were experiencing harassment back in Gablonz and encouraged by both their sons 'escapes,' they also decided to leave Czechoslovakia. Frank's mother Ida was working at the time as a housemaid for the British Consul in Prague, Sir Basil Cochrane Newton, KCMG (1889-1965), who apparently was able to help her gain the necessary entry permits into Britain. However, it was Walter who arranged for his parents permits into Australia, and Eric and Ida arrived safely in Sydney just three days before the start of World War II.

Frank lived with Walter and his wife Ilse at Manion Avenue, Rose Bay, until his parents arrived, then he moved into a rental house. Their rent was a mere £2/7s. and 6' per week.

MOTHER FOUND WIFE FOR SOLDIER SON

SYDNEY, Sat.: A chance meeting between a Sydney girl and a Czech woman started a pen friendship between the girl and the woman's soldier son which led to their marriage on Thursday last.

The girl, Valtie Chisholm, 18, of Naremburn, and the soldier, Private Frank Hammond, A.I.F., 32, of Rose Bay, corresponded for six months before they met.

"The whole affair has been very romantic from the beginning," said the girl.

"I was having lunch at a restaurant last September, and Frank's mother, whom I had never seen before, was sitting at the same table. I was interested in her because she was a foreigner, and we got into conversation.

"Mrs. Hammond told me her son, who was in New Guinea, was one of the few Czechs in the Australian Army. He wanted to correspond with some Australian girls, so I offered to write to him.

"I sent him my photograph after we had exchanged a few letters."

She added that she was visiting Mrs. Hammond one day when Frank walked in unexpectedly on leave.

Private Hammond's first words when he saw her were: "You're not a bit like the photograph."

Valtie said:

"I fell in love with him from the beginning.

"He had been corresponding with about 20 girls, but when he got to know me he said, 'You're the one. You've got me completely.' Two months later, in February, we became engaged."

Valtie Chisholm   Pte Hammond

I FRANK HAMMOND, of Czecho-Slovakian nationality, born at Prague, Czecho-Slovakia, and resident five years in Australia, now residing at 47 Chamberlain Avenue, Rose Bay, N.S.W., intend to apply for Naturalisation under the Nationality Act, 1920-1936.

HAMMOND—CHISHOLM.—The Engagement is announced of Miss Valtie Chisholm, only daughter of Mr. and Mrs. Chisholm, of Naremburn, to Gunner Frank Hammond, A.I.F. (returned), younger son of Mr. and Mrs. Hammond, of Rose Bay.

▲ LEFT: Valtie Minlena Chisholm and Frank Hammond Wedding (Sunday Times, 18th June 1944). RIGHT: 1-Frank Hammond in AIF uniform, and his mother Ida Blumberg in Sydney, 1944. 2-Frank Hammond - Naturalization notice (SMH, 21 Feb 1944, p1). 3-Frank Hammond and Valtie Minlena Chisholm - Engagement notice (SMH, 25th April 1944, p8).

Walter was working at Mark Foys Department Store in the jewellery department for £7/10s. per week. Frank then left Hordern Bros. and worked for a time at the ICI Glassworks factory on South Dowling Street. Later, with his father and brother, they began a textile business, which commenced at Petersham, but soon moved to St. Marys, and it was around this time that the Hamburger family anglicised their name to Hammond.

While the continent was reeling from the German juggernaut, which rolled across Europe from 1939 to 1941, Australia was still isolated and a world away from the conflict. All that changed however, when the Japanese bombed Pearl Harbour in Hawaii on the 7th of December 1941.

Many Australians had already answered the call to enlist and were fighting against Erwin Rommel and his panzer corps in North Africa however, a new and much closer threat had now emerged. Frank was among those who first tried to enlist in the RAAF ground crew, but he was rejected. Then he tried the AIF, but was rejected a second time on the grounds that his eyesight was poor. He was successful on his third attempt however, and went into six weeks of basic training for the AIF at Dubbo, which was, as Frank attested... "very hard work!"

Following the initial training, Frank was attached to the AIF 14th Field Regiment, which was stationed at Leppington, and he was appointed as a motor cycle despatch rider. A transfer eventually came through however, and Frank found himself in the 12th Field Regiment as a signaller for the artillery. The detachment left Sydney on a three day train trip to Townsville and was then transferred by ship to Port Moresby as reinforcements in late January 1942. At that stage, the Japanese had invaded New Guinea and the Australians were engaged in battle on the Kokoda trail. Frank performed many different duties including driving a 'half-track,' which carried cable for communications, and he recalled that the vehicle often got stuck in the thick mud. The regiment was engaged in a number of locations in the Pacific theatre over the next two years (e.g., Milne Bay, Lae and Red Beach) and Frank like many other soldiers was affected by both malaria, denghi fever and impetigo.

While in the army, Frank's mother Ida had her eyes open for a potential wife for her son, and she happened to make a casual contact over lunch one day with a very attractive young lady.

Valtie Minlena Chisholm

Valtie Minlena Chisholm (1927-2003) was the daughter of John William Chisholm, by his wife Valtie Calceolaria Malins (nee Mackie), and the younger sister to her two half-brothers Ronald and Alwyn Malins. Valtie grew up on the lower North Shore and attended Naremburn Public School, and then North Sydney Girls High School along with her half-cousin Joy Rockwell. Apparently Joy and Valtie, who didn't live far from one another, would often go off to a certain lollie shop in Naremburn and receive quite a sizeable pack of lollies for a single penny.[3]

At the outbreak of WWII, Valtie's older half-brother Ron, enlisted in the RAAF, while her other half-brother Alwyn was interred in Changi Prisoner of War Camp following the

▲LEFT: 1-Valtie Minlena Chisholm holding a bag sent from Singapore by brother Alwyn, 1945. 2-Valtie Minlena Chisholm on her wedding day, 15th June 1944. RIGHT: Frank and Valtie Hammond as newlyweds in Sydney, 1945.

Images from their trip scrapbook?

fall of Singapore. By 1944, with the war at arms length for most Australians, young Valtie Minlena Chisholm had developed into a beautiful young lady and was gradually introduced to the fashionable Sydney scene by her mother. Being an eligible batchelorette, her interest and exploration into fashion and culture expanded and became more profound, especially in late 1943 and early 1944.

Mother and daughter (aka 'the two Valties') would visit the Prince Albert Cafe and the Australia Hotel for afternoon tea, where apparently many of Sydney's more fashionable set gathered. It just so happened that one day just before Christmas in 1943, Frank Hammond's mother Ida, who was now also frequenting these places, had a chance meeting with the two Valties, while having lunch on the 6th floor of David Jones in Sydney.

Valtie was only 17 when she and her mother met Ida Hamburger that day, who by all accounts was quite taken by young Valtie, and she told them of her son Frank who was fighting in New Guinea. Apparently, Ida eventually encouraged Valtie to write to Frank, sight unseen! Unbeknowns to the Chisholm ladies however, was that Ida had apparently also asked a few other young ladies to do the same thing.

Frank received these letters, often with photographs attached and would write back where he could, but he must have been more than impressed at young Valtie's beauty when he received her letter in early January 1944.

Frank's reply to Valtie was a masterfully constructed letter and very descriptive, which greatly impressed her father Jack. Consequently, as Frank was returning to Sydney on leave in late January 1944, the two families arranged a meeting for the couple. Valtie's mother was by all accounts reluctant about the whole affair, but must have been encouraged by her husband Jack. The meeting took place at Ida's home in Rose Bay, and although Frank and young Valtie were instantly attracted to one another, Valtie's mother was all too conscious of the ethnic (as Europeans were treated suspiciously during the war years) and religious differences, not to mention the 15 year age discrepancy!

The Marriage Of Valtie Chisholm & Frank Hammond

Back then, and especially during a war, there was no stopping a young couple in love and a wedding was eventually arranged with Valtie's father Jack being very happy with the arrangement. Valtie's mother remained opposed and refused for a time to agree to the wedding. But she eventually came round and the happy event occurred on Valties's 18th birthday, the 15th of June 1944 at St. Michael's Church, Woollahra. A reception was held at Rose Bay with both sets of parents and Frank's brother Walter and family being present. Apparently, in somewhat of a snub, none of Valtie's extended family were invited. Walter Hammond was the best man, and Frank's niece Rene was the flowergirl.

The newlyweds had a very brief three day honeymoon to Toronto on Lake Macquarie, after which Frank eventually returned to his unit. With the surrender of Japan in August, Frank was finally demobilised from the AIF by Christmas of 1945.

After the war, the Hammonds moved in with Valtie's parents in Willoughby for their first six months. Then as rents were less costly in Sydney's eastern suburbs, due in part to the shelling of Bondi in 1942 by Japanese submarines, they moved through a series of flats at 33 Bulkara Rd. Bellevue Hill, 10 Billong Ave. and 22 Jenson Ave. Vaucluse, before settling into and later purchasing their home at 48 Chamberlain Avenue, Rose Bay. With little capital to make a start, Frank began another costume jewellery business and in time built it into a very successful means of income over the next 40 years.

(Clockwise from top left): Valtie in her 'small' car at Vaucluse, 1946; Valtie Hammond arrives by plane at Brisbane, Nov. 1946; The new Pontiac of Frank and Valtie Hammond, 1947; Valtie Minlena Hammond, c. 1948. Valtie Hammond in 1955; Valtie Hammond in 1960.

#NX150104 Frank Hammond (1911 - 2007)

After arriving in Australia, Frank Hammond apparently tried to enlist on three separate occasions in the AIF. He was successful on his third attempt in Port Moresby, and joined the 2/12th Field Regiment, an artillery regiment that was formed as part of the all volunteer Second Australian Imperial Force for overseas service during World War II. Recruited in the state of Victoria in early 1940, the 2/12th was initially formed as a medium artillery regiment, but was later converted to a field regiment due to a lack of medium guns. As a field regiment, the 2/12th deployed to the Middle East where they supported the 9th Division in several battles during the North African Campaign in 1941-42, and undertook garrison duty in Lebanon. After fighting in the Middle East, the 2/12th Field Regiment returned to Australia in mid 1942, aboard the transport "Ile de France" as part of the final transference of Australian ground troops from the Middle East to the Pacific.

In early 1943, the regiment returned to Australia, they prepared for deployment in New Guinea. After a period of leave, where Frank joined, 2/12th re-formed at Kairi, on the Atherton Tablelands in Queensland in April 1943. A period of reorganisation and training followed as the 2/12th was prepared for the rigours of jungle warfare. In late July, they embarked by detachments at Cairns upon several transports including "HMAS Manoora", "USS Van Heutz", "USS W Ellery Channing", "USS Henry T Allen" and the "USS Van Der Lijn", all bound for New Guinea where they were to join the fighting against the Japanese.

The 2/12th's next battleground was Milne Bay in Papua, where it arrived on 17 August 1942 and mounted a successful counter-attack against Japanese invasion forces between 31 August and 4 September. It occupied Goodenough Island between 22 October and 28 December and then returned to Papua for its most bitter and costly battles of the war - Buna and Sanananda. At Buna it delivered the coup de gras to the Japanese at Giropa Point on 1 January, but suffered 63 killed and 122 wounded in the process. The battalion's efforts, between 9 and 21 January to clear the Japanese from the torturous swamp country around Sanananda cost another 61 lives. The 2/12th returned home on 10 March 1943.

By early August 1943, the 2/12th Battalion was back in Papua. It trained around Port Moresby before deploying to the Finisterre Mountains in New Guinea on 31 December. The battalion's main effort there were its operations to capture the Prothero features on the northern end of Shaggy Ridge between 21 and 24 January. Patrolling at the head of the Ramu Valley subsequently kept the 2/12th occupied from February until April and marked the end of its service in New Guinea.

They subsequently took part in landings around Lae and then Finschhafen in September, and saw action during the Huon Peninsula campaign. Supporting the 20th Infantry Brigade during the initial landing around Scarlet Beach. Once Finschhafen was secured, the regiment's guns supported the attack on Sattelberg from the coastal plain, before supporting further advances north as part of the drive towards Sio. Arriving back in Australia on 17 May, the 2/12th spent a year training before undertaking its final operation of the war. After the year-long interlude training around Ravenshoe, Queensland, the regiment moved north to provide fire support during the Battle of North Borneo. Assigned to support the 24th Infantry Brigade, during the landing on Labuan two troops of the 2/12th came ashore alongside the assaulting infantry in LVTs, something the Australian Army had not done before. Later, during June, 14 guns from the regiment were moved by barge to support operations around Beaufort. At the end of the war, the regiment was disbanded with its last war diary entry being made on 1 March 1946. On 1 July 1945, it landed at Balikpapan in Borneo. Well supported by artillery and tanks it captured its objectives with relatively light casualties, and its active role was over by 5th July. Following the end of the war on 15 August, 2/12th personnel were progressively returned to Australia for discharge. The battalion formally disbanded at Balikpapan on the 1st January 1946.

World War Two Service

GUNNER
FRANK HAMMOND
NX150104

SERVICE	AUSTRALIAN ARMY
DATE OF BIRTH	24 APRIL 1911
PLACE OF BIRTH	PRAGUE, CZECHOSLOVAKIA
DATE OF ENLISTMENT	1 JANUARY 1943
LOCALITY ON ENLISTMENT	ROSE BAY, NSW
PLACE OF ENLISTMENT	PORT MORESBY, PAPUA
NEXT OF KIN	HAMMOND, ERIC
DATE OF DISCHARGE	17 MARCH 1945
POSTING AT DISCHARGE	2/110 Australian General Transport
ADDITIONAL SERVICE NUMBERS	N219500

Australian Government
Department of Veterans' Affairs

▲ LEFT: "HMAS Manoora" conveyed the 2/12th Field Regiment from Cairns to New Guinea. ◄ Personnel of the 2/12th Field Regiment artillery batteries in action at Milne Bay, 1943. ▼ The 2/12th Field Regiment Colour Patch.

▲ TOP (Left): Valtie Hammond in 1970. (Centre & Right): Frank & Valtie Hammond at Franks 90th birthday luncheon at Double Bay, 2001. ABOVE: Joy Hyde (1st cousin to Valtie), Valtie & Frank Hammond at Frank's 90th.

In 1949 Frank returned to Europe with Valtie for a three month vacation, primarily to check what was worth salvaging of his family's assets in Gablonz. To Frank's credit, their detailed holiday itinerary was certainly an incredible feat of organisation, with Valtie keeping a fascinating scrapbook of the concerts, matches and places they visited.

The Hammonds remained at Rose Bay all their lives, never producing children, and were seen to be socially aloof by other members of the family. Frank, who was not a practising Jew, retired from his business interests about 1990. He celebrated his 90th birthday at Double Bay on 24th April 2001, apologising to the many family and friends present for taking so long to reach 90... "I'll try to be a lot quicker over the next 90," he commented! They also attended the author's second wedding to Lamia Yammine at St. Andrew's Cathedral, as well as the reception at Oatlands House on the 2nd February, 2002. Indeed, the Hammond's and particularly Valtie seemed impressed by the rediscovered relationship with her second half-cousin once removed Tracy, and his fashionable and elegant new bride Lamia, who likely reminded Valtie of her own love for fashion in years goneby.

The Deaths of Valtie & Frank

However, quite tragically Valtie was stricken with colon cancer and underwent radical radio-therapy, but the dose was too high and she sadly passed away. Everyone was shocked, but perhaps most of all was Frank, who being 15 years older, never expected to outlive his much younger wife, and would now spend his remaining years alone. Living just five minutes away, I regularly checked in on Frank and took him to breakfast and the occasional dinner.

Valtie's relatives too, having expected her to outlive Frank and inherit his estate, were thrown into limbo as Frank's niece Rene, now became his closest living relative. Frank survived for another five years, but his keen mind, humerous and energetic spirit gradually left him and he passed away in 2007.

In the end, a deplorable event occurred in the administration of Frank's substantial will. His niece Rene received $1.5m, and Frank left $3.5m to the RSPCA as both he and Valtie were animal lovers. However, not long before he died, and unbeknowns to everyone, a shadowy Jewish organisation visited Frank in his home, a vulnerable 95 year old, and convinced him to bequeth the remainder of his assets to them. The remainder of his substantial estate, worth some $5 million plus was left to a so-called 'Israeli Fighting Fund,' and not a cent went to any of Valtie's relatives. Those most deserving were Valtie's half-niece Kaye Heaslip in Melbourne, and her half-cousins Joy Hyde and Lindsay Rockwell, who had always been supportive, but were all completely overlooked.

I was personally scathing of the organisation that twisted Frank on his death bed, a deplorable and criminal act, undertaken by members of a religion that always cry out about their persecution, never mind others! Some were cruelly heard to say about Frank to "dig the grave deeper!" It was a sad end to an otherwise fortunate and privileged life.

Where To From Here?

Having explored a tangential branch, the story re-focuses on the genealogy, and continues by exploring the life of Valtie's half-aunt Octavia Corelli O'Sullivan who became a Rockwell through her marriage to Robert Archibald Rockwell of Glebe, which effectively connected the Rockwell, Bantin, O'Sullivan and Shoveller family branches.

References

1. Hammond, Frank, 1911-2007 (Interviewee, 2003-2007). 'Frank Hammond interviewed by Tracy Rockwell on various occasions, at Rose Bay.'
2. Wikipedia - Isidor Mautner [https://en.wikipedia.org/wiki/Isidor_Mautner].
3. Hyde, Joy, 1927-2018 (Interviewee, 2001). 'Joy Hyde (nee Rockwell) interviewed by Tracy Rockwell on the 19th of August 2001, at Aspley, Brisbane.'

Chapter Twelve

Rockwell

ROBERT ARCHIBALD ROCKWELL

Robert Archibald Rockwell was the fourth child of William Henry Rockwell, a sailor and cabman who had emigrated sometime before the 1890s from England, and the eighth child of Elizabeth Carpenter (nee Bantin) a native of the Sydney suburb of Glebe, NSW. Born 1904 in Glebe, Robert was no different to his peers. Robert's mother Elizabeth, was herself born in Glebe from English parents who had arrived Sydney in 1857, but his father's ancestry is mysteriously vague. Both of Robert's parents were descendants of the mother country and despite Federation taking place in 1901, the links with Britain at that time remained steadfast. They had married at the Independent Presbyterian Church at 177 Liverpool St, Sydney on 16th December 1901, a second marriage for both with Elizabeth as a widow.[1]

Robert's birth occurred during a year in world history which saw United States Army engineers begin work on the Panama Canal, the continuance of the Russo-Japanese War, and the foundation of the International Alliance of Women. This year also brought about the third Modern Olympic Games and the opening of the Louisiana Purchase Exposition World's Fair, both held in St. Louis, Missouri. In England, a '3700 Class 3440 City of Truro' locomotive exceeded 100 miles per hour (160 km/h) on the Great Western Railway, while in Australia the Labor Party became the first political party to gain national government, under Chris Watson.

Notable people born in 1904 include the English actor Cary Grant (18 Jan), American

Rockwell & O'Sullivan Residences, 1900 - 1970

RESIDENCES
1. 83 Burfitt St, Leichhardt (O'Sullivan)
2. 11 Talfourd St, Glebe (Bantin)
3. 67 Hereford St, Glebe
4. 110 Cumberland St, The Rocks
5. 4 Upper Bayview St, Nth Sydney
6. 24 Market St, Naremburn.

▲ *1920 Map of Sydney showing locations of Rockwell & O'Sullivan residences from 1900 to 1970.*

children's author Dr. Seuss, (2 March), the English actor John Gielgud (14 April), American actress Joan Crawford (23 March), Spanish artist Salvador Dalí (11 May), American pianist and comedian Fats Waller (21 May), American swimmer and actor Johnny Weissmuller (aka Tarzan, 2 June), and English actress Greer Garson (29 Sep).

Robert was born at his home in 67 Hereford St, Forest Lodge and baptised at St. Johns Church, Glebe on the 30th November 1904.[2] His 45 year old father William Henry Rockwell, was an English emigrant, supposedly from London, who listed himself as a 'cabman' on the birth certificate, while his 38 year old mother Elizabeth, listed her birthplace as Glebe, in Sydney.

The Early Years

It is interesting to note that at the time of his birth, Robert was also welcomed into the world by his only surviving grandparent, his maternal grandmother Mary Bantin (nee Barrett), who was then 71 years of age. Mary was born in the village of Puttenham, Surrey, England in 1833.[3] She had arrived in Sydney in 1857 aboard the "Admiral Lyons" with her London born husband Robert Bantin, and they settled in Glebe.

Robert Archibald Rockwell was born into a ready made family as his mother had already produced four children from her first marriage to Arthur Carpenter.[4] Therefore, at the time of Robert's birth the Rockwell household consisted of Aileen (14), Arthur (13), Eric (11) and Leslie (9) Carpenter.[5,6,7,8] In addition, Elizabeth had also given birth to three Rockwell children ahead of Robert, who were William Henry Jr. (2½) and the twins Norman and Muriel, both just short of 18 months old.[9,10,11]

The Rockwell sons knew no paternal relatives, but were fortunate to have two maternal aunts in Mary Robertia Thuaux (1858-1936) and Jane Matilda Jones (1869-1935), as well as four maternal uncles in Auguste Thuaux (1844-1917), John William Jones (1865-1918), Richard John Bantin (1870-1956) and George Barrett Bantin (1874-1919).

Elizabeth's daughter Aileen Carpenter was a great support with the Rockwell babies, but one can just imagine the cramped and difficult living situation. A household of 12, with six children under the age of five was a lot of mouths to feed and must have been a great strain for both William and Elizabeth. Where she was able, Elizabeth's mother Mary Bantin, would no doubt have helped, although at 71 years of age her contributions would have been limited. In any case, Mary Bantin sadly passed away on the 20th October 1906,

▲ Robert Rockwell grew up on the inner city streets of Glebe and 'Surry Hills', Sydney, by Harold Cazneaux, 1911.

BIRTH REGISTERED IN NEW SOUTH WALES, AUSTRALIA.

CERTIFIED COPY FURNISHED UNDER PART V OF THE REGISTRATION OF BIRTHS, DEATHS AND MARRIAGES ACT, 1973.

No.	Date and place of birth of child	Name and whether present or not	Sex	Father's name, occupation, age and birthplace	Date and place of marriage - previous issue	Mother's name and maiden surname, age and birthplace	Informant	Witnesses	Particulars of registration	Name Reg

I, JOHN BRETTELL HOLLIDAY, HEREBY CERTIFY THAT THE ABOVE IS A TRUE COPY OF PARTICULARS RECORDED IN A REGISTER KEPT BY ME.

ISSUED AT SYDNEY. 1ST MAY. 1980.   PRINCIPAL REGISTRAR.

BAPTISMS Administered in the Parish of   in the

County of   in the Year 18 .

When Baptized.	When Born.	Child's Christian Name.	Parents' Names. Christian.	Surname.	Abode.	Quality or Profession.	By whom the Ceremony was performed.

▲ TOP: Birth Certificate for Robert Archibald Rockwell, 1st Nov, 1904 (NSW BDM #32224/1904). ABOVE (Left): The scene in Pitt St, Sydney at the time of Robert's birth in 1904. (Right): Railway Square, formerly known as Central Square, c.1913 .

when little Robert and his siblings, who were too young to remember, lost the connection to their last living grandparent.[12]

Six months later the last of William and Elizabeth Rockwell's family arrived with a surprise, in the form of a second set of twins. Alfred and Ernest Rockwell were born on the 2nd of January 1907, with Alf arriving first. By this stage the family had moved up the street to 99 Hereford St. Forest Lodge. Like the elder Rockwells, the twins were baptised at

St. Johns Church, Glebe on the 6th March 1907 by the minister Rev. S.S. Tovey.[13,14]

Sadly, the string of seemingly healthy children came to a tragic end, when Robert's older sister and the only Rockwell daughter Muriel, passed away on the 4th of February 1908, aged just four.[15] Muriel was buried on the 5th February 1908 at Rookwood Cemetery (*General Section, Anglican Zone C, Plot RRRR, Grave No. 218*).

Being so close in age, the five Rockwell brothers were very close growing up and were likely well-known in the Glebe neighbourhood. They were at the same time closely allied with St John's Church, as all five were at various times members of the church choir. Under the influence of the church, and in keeping with their Sunday School upbringing, it is probable that the Rockwell boys weren't of the troublemaking type. This attribute combined

'GLEBE IS A VERY DIRTY PLACE'

For some time there has been trouble between the teachers at the Forest Lodge Public School and the Glebe Council officers regarding the alleged littering by the boys of the streets adjacent to the school with papers and other rubbish.

PLAYGROUND FOR CHILDREN

The Mayor of Glebe (Alderman Cole) announced at last night's meeting that action had been taken in regard to providing special playgrounds for children. A letter had been sent to the Education Department stating that the council would set apart an area in Jubilee Park for this purpose. A tennis court, cricket pitch, and swings would be provided at an estimated cost of about £400 for the children of Forest Lodge School. As Jubilee Park was a bit far away for the children of the Glebe School an effort was being made to utilise University Park.

▲ TOP (Left): Robert Archibald Rockwell as a choirboy with St Johns Church, Glebe about 1914. (Right): 1-'Dirty Glebe' (The Sun, 7th Apr 1914, p.8); Playground For Glebe' (The Sun, 4th Jan 1916, p.7). ABOVE Glebe Point Road, Glebe c.1912, the inner Sydney suburb where the Rockwell family resided from 1901 until 1927.

with a stoicism likely passed down from their father, obviously played out throughout their lives, as there was never any legal or criminal proceedings against any of them.

Robert's father ran a Hansom cab business, so looking after the horses was a wonderful distraction for the young boys. The daily chores required attending to the horse and cleaning out the cab, which was a necessary part of their life at least until 1920, when more motor cars began to appear on Sydney's roads.

Forest Lodge Public School

The Rockwell residence in Hereford Street was just a stone's throw from Forest Lodge Public School where Robert and his brothers all attended. Robert first entered school in the kindergarten of 1909. Forest Lodge Public School was no different to any other school of its day, and as schools do nowadays, they celebrated on certain special occasions. One now forgotten celebration was Empire Day, which was always a huge event at the School with drums beating and flags waving.

▲TOP: Looking north along George Street with a tram, Model-T Ford and Hansom cab, from the Union Line Building, c.1920, by Sam Hood. ABOVE (Left): St. Johns Church, Glebe, c.1910. (Right): A photo of a trip to Bondi Beach reveals how much Sydney has developed since 1910.

▲TOP (Left): Glebe Terraces, c.1925. (Right): Empire Day celebrations at Forest Lodge School c.1910. ABOVE: Robert attended Forest Lodge Public School from Kindergarten in 1910 until at least Second Form (Year 8) in 1918.

Prior to 1901 it was celebrated as the Queen's Birthday, but Empire Day began in Canada and was promoted by the League of the Empire, first instituted in the United Kingdom in 1904 by Lord Meath, and was extended throughout the countries of the Commonwealth. This day was celebrated by lighting fireworks in back gardens or attending community bonfires. It gave the King's people a chance to show their pride in being a part of the British Empire.

Forest Lodge Public School, which began in 1883, was headed by Mr. William Bardsley, who guided the school for over 40 years. The school was very active in sport so it is possible that the Rockwell boys met Bardsley's son Warren, who was later selected in the 1909 Australian Cricket Team, which toured England.

When World War I broke out in 1914, the war effort completely dominated the period and ten year old Robert Rockwell and his brothers watched on as these momentous events impacted upon every facet of Australian life. Indeed, the Australian Imperial Force (AIF) departed by ship in a single convoy from Albany, Western Australia bound for Egypt on Roberts 10th birthday. Like many boys at the time, the Rockwell's would have been envious and closely followed news of their half-brothers Arthur (24) and Leslie (21) after they joined the AIF in 1915 and 1916 respectively. They watched one of their teachers go off

Glebe's Historic Legacy

- Edmund Barton was born in Glebe in 1849 and became the first Prime Minister of Australia in 1901.
- Glebe Rowing Club was the first suburban rowing club in Sydney in 1879.
- Sir Douglas Mawson, Antarctic Explorer, resided in Glebe from the 1893 to 1905.
- Frank Hurley, Antarctic photographer and adventurer, was raised in Glebe.
- Glebe Dirty Reds became one of the first Rugby League Clubs in Australia in 1908.
- Warren Bardsley, first test cricketer to score a century in each innings of a test match was a pupil at Forest Lodge Public School.
- Sir Robert Askin, NSW Premier, resided at 29 Talfourd St, Glebe, attended Forest Lodge School in same class as Alf and Ernie Rockwell.
- Lew Hoad, who grew up in Glebe, later won Wimbledon, the French and Australian Open tennis championships in 1956.

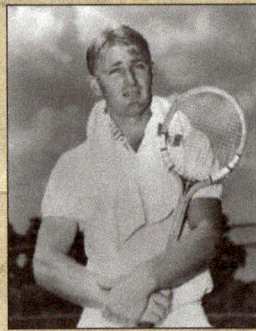

▲ TOP (From left): Edmund Barton, Australia's first Prime Minister; Warren Beardsley, Australian cricketer; Sir Douglas Mawson, Antarctic Explorer; Frank Hurley, Antarctic explorere and adventurer. MID (From left): Lew Hoad, international tennis champion; Sir Robert Askin, Premier of NSW (1965-1975); Glebe Rowing Club badge. ABOVE (Left): Perhaps an early flame, 'Love from Rene,' photo found in Bob Rockwell's lap desk. (Right): The opening of Grace Brothers Broadway in 1923 was a huge boost for the inner west of Sydney and would have been frequented by the Rockwell brothers.

to war when Mr Fred Darmody, then 30 years of age, went into the AIF camp in August 1915. He received a wristlet watch for the occasion, but a year later contracted meningitis and was sent home from the war. Sadly, he never recovered and passed away in 1924, aged just 38. Their first cousin Henry Ingleson Jones, also joined up but was killed in action at

Peronne in France, just two months before the end of the conflict.[16]

Back in Glebe, the estates were being rapidly developed throughout this period, so there were plenty of distractions for Robert and his brothers. Victoria Park and Sydney University were situated just across Parramatta Road, Blackwattle Bay was close by, Pyrmont Baths were a favourite place to swim, and the city was only a 40 minute walk, or a 15 minute tram ride away.

How close the Rockwell boys were to their nearest relatives is unclear, but they were sure to have had interactions with their first cousins. Aunt Mary Thuaux had Mary (b.1882), Robert (b.1884), Matthew (b.1887), and Richard (b.1889) and lived at Balmain. Aunt Jane Jones lived in Glebe and had Henry (b.1898) and Lillian (b.1906). Uncle Richard Bantin resided at Cleveland St, Chippendale and had Sarah (b.1893), Freda (b.1898), Mary (b.1904), Vera (b.1907) and Richard Jr. (b.1910). While uncle George Bantin lived at Marrickville and had George Jr. (b.1908), Linda (b.1908), Robert (b.1910), Frances

▲ Paintings by Bob Rockwell c.1918-1925. 'AIF soldier with the Empire flag', two paintings of Yellow Canaries, and the 'Superb Fairy Wren'.

(b.1913), John (b.1915), Dorothy (b.1919) and Frederick (b.1919).

Whether Robert, who was better known as Bob Rockwell remained at school after his 12th birthday isn't known, but if he did, it would probably have been at Forest Lodge Public School, which by then had become a 'Superior School.' The Rockwell's remained residents of Forest Lodge and Glebe right up until the boys were married and began establishing homes of their own.

By 1919 the Great War was over, but an influenza epidemic brought home by the returning soldiers caused thousands of deaths around the globe and Australia's shores, and thus claimed the lives of many including Bob's 45 year old maternal uncle George Bantin.[17] It forced the government into action, and a 'Relief Depot' was opened at Forest Lodge Public School for the provision of medical attention, nursing and other medical comforts provided for the sick.

Relatively little is known of Bob Rockwell's life as a young man, except that he was a diligent boy and grew into a responsible young man. Then, an event occurred in November of 1922 that captured the imagination of millions around the world including Bob. Howard Carter (1874–1939), an English archaeologist and Egyptologist, discovered the intact

▲TOP: Robert Rockwell's egyptian medallions. ABOVE: Robert Rockwell's drawings of... LEFT: 'Mohammad Ali, at the Citadel in Cairo'. RIGHT: 'Obelisk in the Desert, Egypt', c.1923.

▲ *Pyrmont Bridge at Dusk', by Harold Cazneaux, 1911. Young Robert Rockwell would have crossed the Pyrmont Bridge many times with his father.*

tomb of the 18th Dynasty Pharaoh, 'Tutankhamun', colloquially known as 'King Tut'.[18] The discovery sparked worldwide fascination, and obviously had a great affect on Robert Rockwell, who began collecting and painting all things Egyptian.

To get by at this time, Robert assisted his father as a driver of horse drawn transport, which was still widely used. He celebrated his 21st birthday on the 4th November 1925 with his parents and brothers around him at Glebe.

The post war period of the 1920's and 1930's were a time of great change. People forgot the old and embraced the new in an attempt to leave the hardship and the struggles of the war behind them. New appliances and technology were being created, with everything from toasters to motor cars becoming more accessible to the common people. The fashion world also witnessed great change, and it was about this time that Robert Archibald Rockwell met a young lady with a very distinctive name.

Where To From Here?

However, apart from snippets of information that have emerged during his time in Melbourne and Fremantle, questions are plentiful about William's earlier days as a sailor, with his first 40 years being much less well known and shrouded in mystery. This genealogy continues by researching the early life of Robert Archibald Rockwell's wife Octavia Corelli O'Sullivan, as it is by her that the Rockwell produced six children, and it is her story of survival that must next be told.

▲LEFT: Headlines from 'The Times' announcing the discovery of 'Tutankhamen's tomb' in January of 1923. CENTRE: Robert Rockwell was presented with a copy of 'The Young Ranchers' at Sunday School, December 1915. (RIGHT: Inscription inside 'The Young Ranchers,' awarded for 1st Prize in 7th Class at Sunday School, Dec. 1915.

References

1. NSW Dept of BDM. (1901). Marriage Certificate for William Henry Rockwell & Elizabeth Carpenter (nee Bantin), #8525/1901.
2. NSW Dept of BDM. (1904). Birth Certificate for Robert Archibald Rockwell, #32224/1904.
3. Parish Registers. (1833). Baptismal Registration for Mary Barrett, on the 9th June 1833, at St. John the Baptists Church, Puttenham, Surrey, ENG.
4. NSW Dept of BDM. (1889). Marriage Certificate for William Henry Rockwell and Elizabeth Carpenter (nee Bantin), #1321/1901.
5. NSW Dept of BDM. (1890). Birth Certificate for Aileen V. Carpenter, #13122/1890.
6. NSW Dept of BDM. (1891). Birth Certificate for Arthur C. Carpenter, #13638/1891.
7. NSW Dept of BDM. (1893). Birth Certificate for Eric D. Carpenter, #13871/1893.
8. NSW Dept of BDM. (1895). Birth Certificate for Leslie H. Carpenter, #19850/1895.
9. NSW Dept of BDM. (1902). Birth Certificate for William Henry Rockwell Jr., #21886/1902.
10. NSW Dept of BDM. (1903). Birth Certificate for Muriel Rockwell, #20948/1903.
11. NSW Dept of BDM. (1903). Birth Certificate for Norman John Rockwell, #20949/1903.
12. NSW Dept of BDM. (1906). Death Certificate for Mary Bantin (nee Barrett)., #848/1906.
13. St. John's Church Glebe (1907). Baptismal Record for Alfred Barrett Rockwell, 6th March 1907.
14. St. John's Church Glebe (1907). Baptismal Record for Ernest Barrett Rockwell, 6th March 1907.
15. NSW Dept of BDM. (1908). Death Certificate for Muriel Rockwell, #994/1908.
16. National Archives of Australia (1918). Item details for: B2455, Henry Ingelson Jones (#2928), Killed in Action at Peronne, France, 2nd September 1918. Buried at Peronne Communal Cemetery Extension.
17. NSW Dept of BDM. (1919). Death Certificate for George Barrett Bantin, #22265/1919.
18. Wikipedia - Howard Carter [https://en.wikipedia.org/wiki/Howard_Carter].

Chapter Thirteen

O'Sullivan

OCTAVIA CORELLI O'SULLIVAN

Octavia Corelli O'Sullivan was the second child of Humphrey Joseph O'Sullivan, a labourer and descendant of Irish stock, and the third child of Lenore Mackie (nee Shoveller), a native of the town of Grafton, on the north coast of NSW. Her parents had married at St Mary's Cathedral, Sydney on 11th July 1900, with Lenore declaring her status as a widow.[1]

Two years senior to her future husband Octavia Corelli O'Sullivan, who was known to most as 'Corelli,' was born to Australian born parents. Her father Humphrey O'Sullivan, was exclusively of Irish stock, one branch of which descended from ancient and royal origins, while Corelli's widowed mother Lenore Mackie (nee Shoveller), came from English forebears. Interestingly, Corelli's maternal blood flowed from convict great-grandparents passed down through her respective grandmothers. Each of these had been born from pioneers families, one of the northern and the other of the southern coastal districts of NSW.

Octavia was born on the 1st of February 1902,[2] a year in world history which saw the coronation of Edward VII at Westminster Abbey in London as King of the United Kingdom, the British Dominions and as the Emperor of India. In Australia the Commonwealth Public Service Act created Australia's Public Service, and the Parliament of the Commonwealth of Australia passed the uniform Commonwealth Franchise Act 1902, which enabled women to vote at elections for the Federal Parliament if they were 21 years of age or older. The

Pedigree for Octavia Corelli O'Sullivan

Ireland

Dukes of Normandy

This pedigree shows the descent of Octavia Corelli O'Sullivan (1902-1976) of Naremburn, New South Wales in Australia from Rollo, Chieftain of the Norse, who was buried in the year 930AD at Normandy. Through her ancestress Maria (c.1695-?), daughter of Denis MacCarthy of Springhouse, County Tipperary, Ireland, and wife of Daniel Mahony (1676-1747) of Dunloe Castle, Octavia Corelli O'Sullivan is shown to have been descended from William 'The Conqueror', King Henry I, King Henry II, King John, King Henry III, and King Edward I, through the families of De Bohun, Butler, FitzGerald, MacCarthy, Mahony and O'Sullivan. The pedigree further shows descendants of the said Octavia Corelli O'Sullivan, on both male and female lines, to the year 1950.

Rollo (846-930), Chieftain of the Norse = Poppa of Rennes
mc. 965 at (unknown)

William Longsword (893-942), Count of Rouen = Mistress Sprota
mc. 930 at Rouen, France

Richard I (930-996), Count of Rouen = Gunnora de Crepon (936-1031)
mc. 962 at Rouen, France

Richard II (963-1026), Duke of Normandy = Judith of Brittany (982-1017)
mc. 998 at Rennes, France

Plantagenet

Robert I (1000-1035), Duke of Normandy = Mistress Herleva of Falaise (1003-1050)
c. 1027 at Falaise, France

de Bohun

William I 'The Conqueror' (1028-1087), KING OF ENGLAND = Matilda of Flanders (1031-1083)
m. 1052 at Flanders, France

Henry I (1069-1135), KING OF ENGLAND = Matilda of Scotland (1080-1118)
m. 1100 at Westminster Abbey, London, England

Matilda (1102-1167), Empress of England = Geoffrey V (1113-1151), Count of Anjou
m. 1128 at Le Mans, Normandy, France

Henry II (1133-1189), KING OF ENGLAND = Eleanor (1122-1204), Duchess of Aquitane
m. 1152 at Poitiers, Normandy, France

John Lackland (1166-1216), KING OF ENGLAND = Isabella (1188-1246), Countess of Angoulême
m. 1200 at Westminster Abbey, London, England

Henry III (1207-1272), KING OF ENGLAND = Eleanor of Provence (1223-1291), Queen Consort
m. 1236 at Canterbury Cathedral, Kent, England

Edward I (1239-1307), KING OF ENGLAND = Eleanor of Castile I (1241-1290), Countess of Ponthieu
m. 1254 at Las Heulgas, Spain

Elizabeth of Rhuddlan (1282-1316) = Sir Humphrey de BOHUN (1275-1321), 4th Earl of Hereford
m. 1302 at Westminster Abbey, London, England

Butler

Eleanor de Bohun (1304-1363), Countess of Ormonde = James BUTLER (1304-1338), 1st Earl of Ormond
m. 1327 at Kilkenny Castle, County Kilkenny, Ireland

FitzGerald

James BUTLER (1331-1382), 2nd Earl of Ormond = Elizabeth Darcy (1332-1390), Countess of Ormond
m. 1346 at Ormond, Ireland

Eleanor Butler (1346-1404) = Gerald FitzMaurice FitzGERALD (1335-1398), 3rd Earl of Desmond
m. 1359 in Ireland

James FitzGERALD (c.1375-1462), 6th Earl of Desmond = Mary de Burgh (c.1400-?), Countess of Desmond
mc. 1418 in Ireland

Joan FitzGerald (c.1430-1462), Countess of Kildare = Thomas FitzGERALD (1421-1477), 7th Earl of Kildare
mc. 1450 in Ireland

Gerald FitzGERALD (1456-1513), 8th Earl of Kildare = Alison FitzEustace (1457-1495), Countess of Kildare
mc. 1480 in Ireland

Eleanor FitzGerald (1490-1530) = Donal MacCARTHY Reagh (1490-1531), 12th Prince of Carbery
mc. 1510 in Ireland

Sir Cormac Na Haoine MacCARTHY (1510-1567), 13th Prince of Carbery = Lady Julia MacCarthy (c.1515-?)
mc. 1535 in Ireland

Donal Na-Pipi MacCARTHY Reagh (c.1535-1612), 17th Prince of Carbery = Margaret FitzGerald (1540-1585)
mc. 1560 in Ireland

MacCarthy

Mahony

Owen MacCARTHY (c.1574-?) = Honoria MacCarthy (?-1665)
mc. 1620 at Dunmanway, Ireland

Donal MacCARTHY (1631-1666), of Knocknahinsy = Honoria O'Hea (1633-1666)
mc. 1650 at Corably, County Cork, Ireland

Denis MacCARTHY (c.1650-1713), of Spring House = Elizabeth Hackett (c.1650-?)
mc. 1670 at Ballyskillan, County Tipperary, Ireland

Maria McCarthy (c.1690-?) = Daniel MAHONY (1676-1747), of Dunloe
mc. 1714, at Springhouse, County Tipperary, Ireland

James MAHONY (c.1716-1794), of the Point = Jane Hennessy of Ballymacmoy (c.1720-?)
mc. 1745, at Killavullen, Co. Cork, Ireland

Lieut. John MAHONY (c.1750-1818), of the Point = Zenobia Anne Saunders (c.1773-1837)
mc. 1795, at Killarney, Co. Kerry, Ireland

Zenobia Anne Elizabeth Mahony (1800-1873) = Thadeus O'SULLIVAN Esq. (1800-1877), of Coomb
m. 1823 at Killarney, Co. Kerry, Ireland

James Mahony O'SULLIVAN (1837-1891). Emigrated & arrived Melbourne aboard the "Ocean Chief" 25th Feb 1859
1m. 1866 = Margaret Buckley (c.1845-1866): 2m. 1869 = Ellen Frawley (1842-1909), at Sydney, NSW, Australia

Humphrey Joseph O'Sullivan (1871-1905) = Lenore Mackie (nee Shoveller) (1866-1945)
m. 1900 at Sydney, NSW, Australia

O'Sullivan

Rockwell

Octavia Corelli Susan O'Sullivan (1902-1976) = Robert Archibald ROCKWELL (1904-1966)
m. 1926 at Glebe, NSW, Australia

| Joy Corelli Rockwell (1927-2018) | Robert Hunter ROCKWELL (1929-1984) | Elwood Lorraine ROCKWELL (1933-1987) | Lindsay Archibald ROCKWELL (1937) | Ronie Malcolm ROCKWELL (1943-2000) | Janet Lenore Rockwell (1946) |

Paternal Ancestry

O'Sullivan	Mahony of Dunloe	Frawley	McGarry
Originated from Rathmore, County Kerry, Ireland.	Originated from Killarney, County Kerry, Ireland.	Originated from Limerick, County Limerick, Ireland.	Originated from Limerick, County Limerick, Ireland.

Maternal Ancestry

Shoveller	Eastman	Hann	Thompson
Originated from Portsmouth, Hampshire, England.	Originated from Portsmouth, Hampshire, England.	Originated from East Stour, Dorset, England.	Originated from London, Middlesex, England.

▲ Birth certificate of Octavia Corelli O'Sullivan, born 1st February 1902 (NSW BDM #4112/1902).

States soon gave women over age 21 the vote, with New South Wales (1902), Tasmania (1903), Queensland (1905) and Victoria (1908) all following suit.

Notable people born in 1902 included the American actress Tallulah Bankhead (31 Jan), American aviator Charles Lindbergh (4 Feb), and the African-American writer Langston Hughes with American actor Clark Gable (1901), both sharing Octavia's birthday.

Octavia Corelli O'Sullivan Ancestry

Octavia inherited a unique mix of royal, aristocratic, pioneer and convict heritage, and yet the irony was that through no fault of her own, she had fallen to be amongst the lowest class of society. She arrived while her parents were residing at 83 Burfitt Street, Leichhardt, in Sydney NSW.[3] With a Protestant mother and a Catholic father Octavia's baptism is unclear, although being as her father was descended from the Irish, it is likely that their new baby girl was baptised into the Catholic faith.

Her father Humphrey O'Sullivan, had been born in the bush at Fish River Creek near Bathurst, was 31 years of age and was working as a general labourer. He descended from an Irish emigrant father of illustrious ancestry, and a mother who was noted for being the first white child born in the Monaro District of the far south coast of NSW. Octavia's mother Lenore Mackie (nee Shoveller), was 36 years old, and had been born in Grafton. She descended from an English emigrant father, with a mother who was equally notable for being the first white child born in the Clarence River District on the far north coast of NSW.

Life In The Rocks

By the 1900s the majority of residents living at 'The Rocks' were waterside workers. As men were only employed when a ship came in, wharf work was irregular, physically hard and often dangerous with low pay and poor conditions. At home, wives and mothers struggled to cope and families fell behind paying the rent, groceries were put on credit at the local shops and occasionally household items were pawned to make ends meet. Children were expected to finish school at age 14 and find a job. For some families the pressures of everyday life took their toll with households shattered by domestic violence. Yet the harbour also offered some relief through outings on ferries, cooling sea breezes, a place to swim and fish and tenants enjoyed the magnificent views of all the activity on and around the waterfront.

The streets and laneways of The Rocks were an extension of people's houses and their lives spilled out into them. They were places to talk to neighbours, to hang washing and for children to play. They were also places of business for the street hawkers who plied their wares, Chinese hawkers sold household linens and feather dusters, the clothes prop man, the rabbitoh who skinned rabbits while his customers waited, the carts selling freshly caught fish and the iceman. Ron Thompson, born at No 62 Cumberland St. in 1933, fondly remembered the clever cries of Jacko the fruit and vegetable seller, who would call... "peas young and green, and lettuces with hearts like heroes." For 90 years the corner shop at No 64 Cumberland St. was an integral part of the community, supplying a range of household groceries and extending credit to its customers.

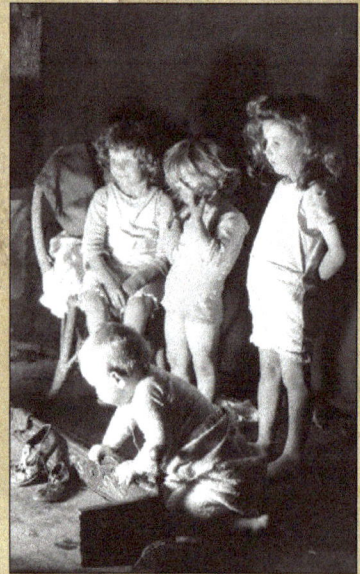

▲ TOP: The scene at Cumberland Place, at the Rocks, c.1910, where Corelli resided with her mother and sisters from 1908 to 1924. ABOVE: Three scenes of life in Sydney during the early 1900's by Harold Cazneaux (Left): Albion St, Surry Hills (1911). (Centre): A lane in Redfern (1910). (Right): Poignant photograph of four fatherless baby girls, entitled 'Getting ready for bed' (1914).

Octavia's pioneer forebears were certainly impressive, but it is her Irish ancestry that is most significant. From their father, the O'Sullivan girls inherited a noble ancestry, which can be traced back through the ancient Irish families of O'Sullivan, Mahony and MacCarthy; through the dynastic and aristocratic houses of FitzGerald and Butler to draw blood from not just one, but the five illustrious royal houses of England, Ireland, France, Scotland and Wales. For a detailed account of Octavia Corelli O'Sullivan's fascinating Irish ancestry see Volumes 3 and 4 of the Rockwell Genealogies - "The Mahonys of Dunloe,"[Ref] and "The Path That Few Tread: A Genealogy of James Mahony O'Sullivan."[Ref]

"If it be lawful to claim a share in the merits of by-gone generations, her name is adorned by the virtues and the greatness of a glorious array of ancestors..."

From 'Sermons of Abbe MacCarthy" by Nicolas Tuite de MacCarthy & C. Mahony [4]

I doubt also that she was randomly assigned her unusual name, it being more likely selected as a salute to Humphrey's paternal grandmother Zenobia Mahony, who was herself named for an ancient queen. If true, this would suggest that Humphrey Joseph O'Sullivan was indeed aware of his ancient Irish heritage.

Octavia was named after 'Octavia the Younger' (69BC–11BC), also known as 'Octavia Minor' or simply Octavia, who was the elder sister of the first Roman Emperor called

▲ TOP: *Looking south on Cumberland Street at the Rocks about 1895, which has since been completely replaced by the approaches to the Sydney Harbour Bridge. ABOVE (Left): The Argyle Cut, looking west by Harold Cazneaux (1912). (Right): The Australian Hotel on Cumberland St, at The Rocks.*

Busy Circular Quay was right on the doorstep for the O'Sullivan girls, who were residents of The Rocks from 1908 to 1924

Augustus, known also as Octavian. At some stage Octavia O'Sullivan adopted her middle name and from then on, people referred to her simply as 'Corelli.'

Octavia was an uncanny young lady, her blood was a rich broth of Anglo-Saxon, Irish and Australian strains.

Corelli was born into a family that already included a sibling, as her mother brought from her 1890 marriage to John Henry Mackie, her ten year old daughter Valtie.[5] As a result, at the time of Corelli's birth, the O'Sullivan household totalled four people, with Valtie being just a month short of her 11th birthday. Corelli's mother Lenore, had previously given birth to another daughter they named Melecca O'Sullivan, but she had sadly survived only four weeks and died on the 19th February 1901.[6]

It is interesting to note that at the time of her birth in February 1902, Corelli was fortunate to still have three of her four grandparents alive. Octavia became the fourth grandchild of Humphrey's mother Ellen O'Sullivan (nee Frawley) who then lived in Newcastle, and the sixth grandchild of Lenore's parents, Thomas and Susan Shoveller (nee Hann), who resided in Grafton.

Just over a year later the O'Sullivan's produced another daughter in Sylvia Veronica O'Sullivan, who arrived in 1903.[7] Then on the 22nd February 1905, while possibly striving for a son, yet another daughter arrived in Goldie Alathea, and in no time at all the O'Sullivan's had acquired a family of four growing daughters.[8] Young Valtie was a great

help to her mother, especially with the infant O'Sullivan girls.

By this stage the O'Sullivan's had moved to 99 Ferry Road in Glebe, but while all was seemingly going so well, just four months after Goldie's birth, their father was taken ill. He struggled at first with the flu, then bronchitis for two weeks before succumbing to pnuemonia on the 30th June 1905.[9] Corelli (3), Sylvia (2) and Goldie (four months) would sadly never remember their father, or be told of their illustrious Irish heritage. Lenore O'Sullivan at the age of 39, once again without a breadwinner, was left quite alone to care for a teenager and three infant girls under the age of five.

The Move to 'The Rocks'

Widowed and abandoned for a second time, where was Lenore to get the money she needed for rent, food, clothing and schooling? The tragic death of her husband placed her under a terrible strain. While Lenore moved into 27 Broughton St, Glebe for two years, she was soon forced to move on to where the rents weren't as high. With her baby girls clinging on, Lenore relocated to the much maligned area known as 'The Rocks', the oldest part of Sydney, where by 1908 they were residing at 108 Cumberland Street. In May of that same year, Lenore's father Thomas Eastman Shoveller, who was suffering from dimentia, passed away in Grafton aged 81.[10]

The very next year, Corelli's older half-sister Valtie, was married at a young 19 years

▲ TOP (Left): The flower sellers in Martin Place, Sydney by Harold Cazneaux (1910). (Right): The flannel flower store by Harold Cazneaux (1923).
ABOVE: Colour postcard of the flowers stalls in Martin Place (1907).

of age to Edmond W. Malins in 1909, in Sydney.[11] Despite a religious divide between protestant Valtie and the catholic O'Sullivan girls, it is likely that they played a part in Valtie's wedding, perhaps as flowergirls. For Lenore, Valtie's marriage and her departure from the home meant that she would now be the sole carer of Corelli (7), Sylvia (6) and Goldie (4). In 1909 aswell, Corelli's paternal grandmother Ellen O'Sullivan (nee Frawley) died and was buried in Newcastle.[12] Corelli and her sisters unfortunately grew up without the guiding hand of their father, but she and her sisters were fortunate to still have the attentions of their maternal grandmother Susan Shoveller, who had to journey to Sydney from Grafton by ship.

Fort Street Public School

Corelli may have commenced her schooling at Glebe Public School, but after moving to The Rocks, she and her sisters attended Fort Street Public School on Observatory Hill. By 1910 young Goldie joined Corelli and Sylvia at Fort Street and the three girls said they often heard the other children making jokes about their names as they walked into school together... "here comes Goldie, Sylvie and Bronzie!"[13]

On the 17th June 1910, Lenore's eldest daughter Valtie, delivered a son whom she named Ronald Guildford Malins, and he became Corelli's half-nephew.[14] Valtie soon followed up with another son, Alwyn Wooldridge Malins, who was also born in Sydney on the 12th March 1912.[15] Not long afterwards, Lenore moved her family around the corner into 197 Gloucester St. at The Rocks, and it was whilst there that two more family deaths occurred.

First, Valtie's young husband Edmond Malins, died of a brain tumour in 1912,[16] which was followed the next year by the death of their aunty Susan Meally (nee Shoveller) of Grafton, in August 1913.[17] Following the death of her eldest daughter, Susan Shoveller moved from Grafton to Sydney, to reside with her son George Shoveller and his wife Mary at 123 Mitchell St, Glebe. She was then able to contribute more to the support of her children and their families ie. Lenore (47), George (40), Mabel (35) and Clarence (33), who were all now residing in Sydney.

But much worse was to come when a year later Corelli's younger sister Sylvia, died suddenly on the 2nd September 1914 at the tender age of just 11.[18] We know little of Sylvia Veronica, and at this stage the cause of her death is also unknown, but she was buried in the Catholic section Rookwood Cemetery (*Portion M2; Row-N; Plot-2314*). The distressing loss was felt by the entire extended family and the calamity coincided with the outbreak of World War I.

With her father having descended from the Irish, the O'Sullivan girls had obviously been baptised into the catholic faith, but after his death Lenore, no longer subjected her

▲Scenes of life in Sydney during the early 1900's by Harold Cazneaux. TOP: The smoke belching Sydney ferries entitled 'Silver and grey' (1911). ABOVE: 'The Wharfies' at Circular Quay (1910).

daughters to popish influences and they presumably grew up adhering to the Church of England, or even perhaps without much religious influence at all? Sadly, Corelli's maternal grandmother Susan Shoveller, passed away in 1919 and was buried in an unmarked grave at Waverley Cemetery.[19] A few years later, Corelli's older half-sister Valtie married for a second time to Jack Chisholm in 1923, in Sydney.[20]

Lenore always had a piano in the home, so Corelli was of course taught to play. From all accounts Corelli was prim and proper, and she celebrated her 21st birthday on the 2nd February 1923. However, Corelli's sister Goldie became rebellious and began hanging around with the 'wrong crowd,' getting herself into trouble.

How close the O'Sullivan girls were to their near relatives is unclear, but they were sure to have had interactions with their first cousins. On the Shoveller side, aunt Susan Eva Meally had Edward (b.1879), Latona (b.1882) and Eva (b.1885), but they were in Grafton. Corelli's uncle George Shoveller was in Balmain, but was childless. Uncle Clarence Shoveller resided at The Rocks and had Thomas (b.1905), Susan (b.1907), John (b.1909) and Russell (b.1916), while aunt Mabel West was in Sussex St, Sydney in 1910 and had Reginald (b.1904), Sibyl (1905) and Sadie (1906). On the O'Sullivan side, Corelli's uncle James O'Sullivan lived a long way north in Ingham, Queensland, so contact with their first cousins Myrtle (b.1898) and Gladys (b.1901) was almost impossible. Aunty Ellen Therese O'Sullivan, who had been twice married, had no known children and was residing somewhere in the United States. Only uncle John Washington O'Sullivan and his two sons Victor (b.1908) and John (b.1913), in Willoughby, and aunt Blanche and son Claude

▲ TOP: Women's fashion changed considerably from 1910 to 1920. ABOVE (Left): 'Women in bathing suits on Collaroy Beach', photographed by Colin Caird (1908). (Right): Anzacs departing Sydney for the Suez on the troop ship "Malta" in 1915.

Fort Street Public School

Fort Street National School was established in 1849 at the old military hospital, which is now part of the National Trust Headquarters, a short walk south of the current school setting. It was one of the first public schools in Australia and known to locals in Sydney as "the school on the hill."

The school was proposed by the Board of National Education, which itself was established in 1848 to fund and run the first government schools in Australia. Under the leadership of William Watkins in the 1850s, the school set the standard for public education in NSW for other schools to follow. Fort Street Training School also adjoined and trained all the school teachers for NSW.

From the 1850s, Fort Street Model School offered its older pupils a secondary education. In 1881, Fort Street Model School was raised in status to become Fort Street Superior Public School. This meant the provision of better secondary education for older pupils.

By 1911, three schools were formed from Fort Street Superior Public School, which was split into Fort Street Boys High School, Fort Street Girls High School and Fort Street Public School. All three schools existed on the one campus, in what is now the National Trust Headquarters.

▲ TOP (Left): Empire Day at Fort Street School, c.1908. (Right): Fort Street School, at the Rocks about 1915. ABOVE: A class photograph of female students at Fort Street School, c.1913.

(b.1901), would have been nearby.

Just three months prior to their wedding, Corelli's half-sister Valtie, delivered a daughter on the 15th June 1926, whom she named Valtie Minlena Chisholm, becoming Corelli's half-niece.[21] The fact that members of the Shoveller family were residing in and around Glebe might account for how Corelli eventually came into contact with a young Glebe gentleman... her husband to be, Robert Archibald Rockwell.

Where To From Here?

Octavia likely met her future husband sometime in 1925 or early 1926, and while they married soonafter, it may have been for love or as an honourable gesture to prevent Octavia's unborn child from being born into illegitimacy. Whatever the reason, their early lives together and the formation of a family are the subject of the next chapter.

▲ *This rare photo portrait is one of just a handful of images of Octavia Corelli O'Sullivan, taken in Sydney when she was about age of 12 (c.1914).*

References

1. NSW Dept of BDM. (1901). Marriage Certificate for William Henry Rockwell & Elizabeth Carpenter (nee Bantin), #8525/1901.

2. NSW Dept of BDM. (1902). Birth Certificate for Octavia Corelli Susan O'Sullivan, #4112/1902.

3. NSW Dept of BDM. (1902). Birth Certificate for Octavia Corelli Susan O'Sullivan, #4112/1902.

4. MacCarthy, Nicolas Tuite de [1769-1833] & Mahony, C. (1848). 'Sermons of Abbe MacCarthy,' James Duffy, Dublin, p.xiii.

5. NSW Dept of BDM. (1890). Marriage Certificate for John Henry Mackie & Lenore Shoveller, #3797/1890.

6. NSW Dept of BDM. (1901). Birth Certificate for Melecca O'Sullivan #7223/1901.

7. NSW Dept of BDM. (1903). Birth Certificate for Sylvia Veronica O'Sullivan #11867/1903.

8. NSW Dept of BDM. (1905). Birth Certificate for Goldie Alathea O'Sullivan #12992/1905.

9. NSW Dept of BDM. (1905). Death Certificate for Humphrey Joseph O'Sullivan, #9853/1905.

10. NSW Dept of BDM. (1908). Death Certificate for Thomas Eastman Shoveller, #5484/1908.

11. NSW Dept of BDM. (1909). Marriage Certificate for Valtiveredo Calceolaria Mackie and Edmond W. Malins #10186/1909.

12. NSW Dept of BDM. (1909). Death Certificate for Ellen O'Sullivan #10250/1909.

13. Hyde, Joy, 1927-2018 (Interviewee, 2001). 'Joy Hyde (nee Rockwell). interviewed by Tracy Rockwell on the 19th of August 2001, at Aspley, Brisbane'.

14. NSW Dept of BDM. (1910). Birth Certificate for Ronald Guildford Malins, #22382/1910.

15. NSW Dept of BDM. (1912). Birth Certificate for Alwyn Wooldridge Malins, #643/1912.

16. NSW Dept of BDM. (1912). Death Certificate for Edmond W. Malins, #13979/1912.

17. NSW Dept of BDM. (1913). Death Certificate for Susan Eva Meally, #12979/1913.

18. NSW Dept of BDM. (1914). Death Certificate for Sylvia Veronica O'Sullivan, #9782/1914.

19. NSW Dept of BDM. (1919). Death Certificate for Susan Shoveller, #1344/1919.

20. NSW Dept of BDM. (1923). Marriage Certificate for Valtiveredo Calceolaria Malins (Mackie) and John William Chisholm, #4905/1923.

21. NSW Dept of BDM. (1926). Birth Certificate for Valtie Minlena Chisholm, #?/1926.

Chapter Fourteen

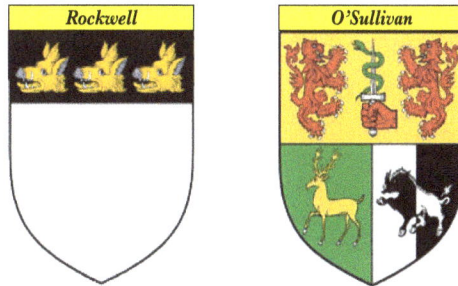

ROBERT ARCHIBALD ROCKWELL & OCTAVIA CORELLI O'SULLIVAN

The year 1926 was a pivotal one with the League of Nations Slavery Convention abolishing all types of slavery, Lebanon received its first constitution under the French Mandate and became a republic with Charles Debbas as its first president, and in sport Gene Tunney defeated Jack Dempsey to become heavyweight boxing champion of the world, while Gertrude Ederle became the first woman to swim the English Channel, from France to England. This year also brought the deaths of Italian actor Rudolph Valentino (23 August), Hungarian-born American escapologist Harry Houdini (31 Oct), and French painter Claude Monet (5 Dec).

Notable people born in 1926 include the American comedian, humanitarian and philanthropist Jerry Lewis (16 March), Northern Irish politician Ian Paisley (6 April), American magazine editor of Playboy Hugh Hefner (9 April), British broadcaster, naturalist, and producer Sir David Attenborough (8 May), American actress Marilyn Monroe (1 June), Cuban revolutionary and politician Fidel Castro (13 August), American singer-songwriter and guitarist Chuck Berry (18 Oct), and Queen Elizabeth II of the United Kingdom (21 April).

The Marriage of Bob Rockwell & Corelli O'Sullivan

How and when Bob and Corelli met, or for how long their courtship lasted is unknown. However, on the 21st of September 1926, Robert Archibald Rockwell and Octavia Corelli O'Sullivan were married by the Rev. F.W. Tugwell (minister) according to Anglican rights at St. Johns Church, Glebe.[1] The marriage was witnessed by Bob's brother Norman Rockwell, and Corelli's mother Lenore O'Sullivan, the event formally joining the Rockwell, Bantin

▲TOP: Robert Archibald Rockwell and Octavia Corelli O'Sullivan on their wedding day, 21st September 1926, held at St. Johns Church, Glebe. Marriage Certificate for Robert and Corelli Rockwell, 21st September 1926 (NSW BDM #15695/1926).

and Barrett families with the O'Sullivan, Frawley, Shoveller and Hann families.

At this time Bob was working as a driver and residing with his parents at 11 Charles St. Forest Lodge. Corelli was listed on the marriage certificate as a domestic, residing at 4 Upper Bayview St. North Sydney, with her twice widowed mother.

Both Corelli and Bob were almost certainly unaware of the ancient aristocratic and royal heritage that had been passed down through Corelli's paternal O'Sullivan lineage. Their descendants too, would remain oblivious to their unique origins until the rediscovery and re-awakening of their long lost ancestry in 2018.

Bob Rockwell had beaten all his brothers to the alter, but shortly afterwards followed a series of family weddings with Ernie Rockwell marrying Alice Greenup on the 16th July 1927.[2] This was followed by Norman (Jack) Rockwell who also married in 1927 to Stella Edgerton,[3] ahead of William Henry Rockwell Jr. who married Rose Menier in 1928.[4] Bob's younger brother Alfred (Ernie's twin) married much later to Olive Ruth Loader in 1939.[5]

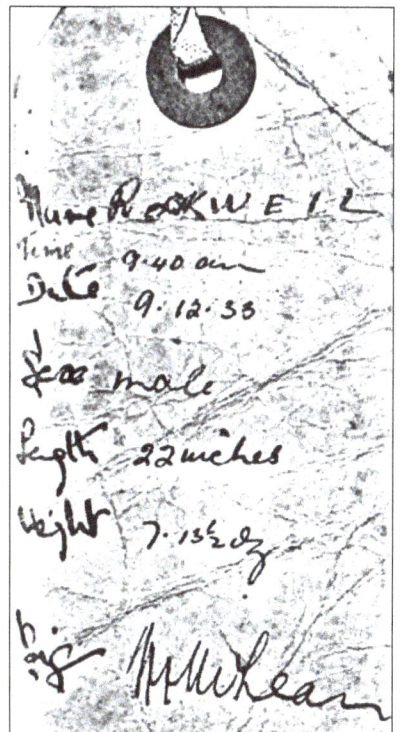

▲TOP (Left): The first residence of Bob and Corelli Rockwell at 48 Slade St, Naremburn. (Right): 1-A gold bar engraved for Joy. 2-A tiny engraved gold plate 'R.R. 1/11/28' for Bob's 24th birthday. 3-Baby tag for Elwood Rockwell (1933). ◀LEFT: Joy Corelli Rockwell, born 13th April 1927. RIGHT: Robert Hunter Rockwell, born 25th June 1929.

Likewise, Corelli was first of the O'Sullivan girls to marry, beating her younger sister Goldie Alathea to the alter by 10 months, when she married Patrick Joseph Mulroy on the 9th July 1927.[6] During those conservative Edwardian years, it turned out that there was a motive for Bob and Corelli's hasty nuptials, as Corelli was actually nine weeks pregnant

Parliament House, Canberra

A competition was announced on 30th June 1914 to design a Parliament House in Canberra, with prize money of £7,000. However, due to the start of World War I the next month, the competition was cancelled. It was re-announced in August 1916, but again postponed indefinitely on 24 November 1916. In the meantime, John Smith Murdoch, the Commonwealth's Chief Architect, worked on the design as part of his official duties. He had little personal enthusiasm for the project, as he felt the waste of money and expenditure on it could not be justified at the time. Nevertheless, he designed the building by default. The construction of Old Parliament House was commenced on 28th August 1923 and completed in early 1927. It was built by the Commonwealth Department of Works, using tradesmen and materials from all over Australia. The final cost was about £600,000, which was more than three times the original estimate. It was designed to last for a maximum of 50 years until a permanent facility could be built.

In 1923, Canberra was a small, dispersed town with few facilities and no administrative or parliamentary functions. The building of Old Parliament House effectively doubled the town's (very small) population. The workers required for the project and their families were housed in camps and settlements who had to endure Canberra's harsh weather conditions. Once Parliament commenced sitting in Canberra the transfer of Commonwealth public servants from Melbourne required the construction of suitable housing in the areas of Ainslie, Civic, Forrest (formerly called Blandfordia), Griffith and Kingston.

The building was opened on 9th May 1927 by the Duke and Duchess of York, later King George VI and Queen Elizabeth 'The Queen Mother.' The opening ceremonies were both splendid and incongruous, given the sparsely built nature of Canberra and its small population, at the time. The building was extensively decorated with British Empire and Australian flags and bunting. Similar schemes were used at later events, most notably in 1954 when Queen Elizabeth II visited Canberra for the first time and opened Parliament. Temporary stands were erected bordering the lawns in front of the Parliament and these were filled with crowds. A Wiradjuri elder, Jimmy Clements, was one of only two aboriginal Australians present, having walked for about a week from Brungle Station (near Tumut) to be at the event. Dame Nellie Melba sang the National Anthem, which was at that time 'God Save the King.' The Duke of York unlocked the front doors with a golden key, and led the official party into King's Hall where he unveiled the statue of his father, King George V. The Duke then opened the first parliamentary session in the new Senate Chamber.

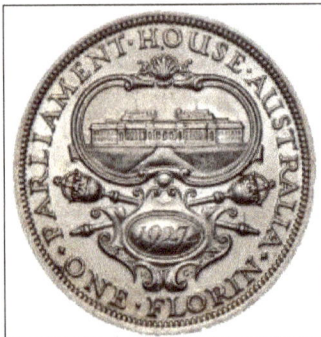

▲TOP: Australia's brand new Parliament House in Canberra was opened on 9th May 1927 by the Duke and Duchess of York. ABOVE (Left): Reverse of the 1927 commemorative florin. (Right): Stamps for the opening of the new parliament building in Canberra, 1927.

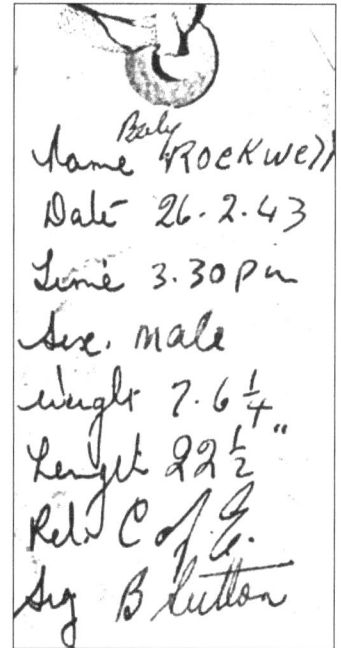

Name Baby ROCKWELL
Date 26.2.43
Time 3.30 p.m.
Sex. male
weight 7.6¼
Length 22½"
Rel C of E.
Sig B lutton

▲▶ABOVE: The Rockwell residence at 24 Market St, Naremburn, was actually entered from the rear at Adolphus St. MID (Left):(Right): Baby tag for Ronie Rockwell (1943).▼ Elizabeth Rockwell, with her grandaughter Shirley, daughter Aileen Sampson, and son Bob Rockwell, at their home in Hurstville, c.1940.

when the marriage took place.

Of course, Corelli's mother Lenore was present at both of her daughter's weddings, just as William Henry Rockwell and Elizabeth were also present at the various weddings of their sons. Unfortunately, sometime in 1926, Bob's father experienced a severe stroke, which left him paralysed on one side of his body and he apparently became quite difficult to care for.

Naremburn

Following their wedding, Bob and Corelli Rockwell moved north across the Harbour, as during the early 1920s, Glebe had become the haunt of criminals. Thugs fought for control of illegal activities such as off-course betting and the sly grog trade. Vying for supremacy were mobs named for their local areas like... 'The Rocks', 'The Loo', 'The Railway', 'Surry

◄ *A stern looking big sister Joy Rockwell, keeps a firm watch on Elwood, Lindsay and Robert on a visit to Aunty Aileen's, the boys all sporting shoes with home-spun haircuts, c.1940.* ▲ *Bicentennial Reserve near Small Street, Willoughby is where the upper valley of Flat Rock Creek began. Early last century, the creek passed under Willoughby Road at Flat Rock Creek Bridge before cascading over Naremburn Falls, the highest waterfall in the Sydney region, into what was known as 'The Devil's Hole' to the east of Willoughby Road. It then flowed down to Long Bay after passing under the Suspension Bridge at Cammeray.*

Hills', 'Redfern' and 'Newtown'.

The Glebe mob hung out at the 'Australian Youth Hotel' run by Mick McGrath, who conducted an SP bookmaking operation there and lived around the corner. Other popular watering holes were the 'Ancient Briton Hotel' and the 'Toxteth Hotel.'

Juvenile mobsters were mostly engaged in shoplifting, thieving and fighting. Some became career criminals, like Glebe 'heavies' Harry 'Boo' Stanton, 'Tinker' Wilson, 'Googer' Morgan, Charles 'Kicker' Kelly, 'housebreaker' Roy Shirley (alias Arthur Roy Shirley, alias Augustine Arthur Roy Shirley, alias John Williams), 'Chow' Hayes and 'Paddy' Roache.

The Glebe roughians were all the incentive Bob and Corelli needed to relocate, and they set up home at 48 Slade Street in Naremburn, with the added incentive of being closer to Corelli's mother, and her half-sister Valtie in Willoughby.

The other benefit that came with setting up residence in Sydney's northern suburbs, was that the rents weren't as savage as the inner city. Corelli's mother may have also had something to do with the move as she was a resident at Blue's Point at the time. But, such a move in the late 1920's was more difficult than today as without a bridge, it entailed crossing the harbour by ferry for work, social and family occasions.

Not long after his marriage in 1926, Bob Rockwell began working on the Sydney waterside as a 'stevedore.' These workers were also known as dockworkers, dockers, dock laborers, wharfies, wharf rats, lumpers, longshoreman or waterfront manual labourers who were involved in loading and unloading ships. Bob had to take a tram to Blues Point, then make a double trip across Sydney Harbour each day to get to and from his work.

Babies were quick to arrive in all of the new Rockwell families with Joy Corelli Rockwell being the first born to Bob and Corelli on the 13th April 1927, becoming a new grandchild for Lenore O'Sullivan, William Henry and Elizabeth Rockwell.[7] Joy was born at Royal North Shore Hospital and baptised at St. Cuthbert's Church in Naremburn, which became the family church for many years. After Joy, Bob and Corelli produced quite a family with five more children spanning the years from 1929 to 1946.

Six months later, Ronald Ernest Rockwell was born to Bob's brother Ernie and Alice Rockwell, on the 25th of November 1927.[8] Then Lionel Raymond arrived to Corelli's sister Goldie and Patrick Mulroy on 16th January 1928.[9] The children kept coming with

▲ TOP (Left): Bob Rockwell was employed as a wharf labourer until well after WWII, which was at times back-breaking work. RIGHT: The Waterside Workers Federation of Australia became an immensely powerful trade union. ABOVE: A photograph looking west at the Suspension Bridge, Northbridge, which had the concrete supporting arch added in 1938, with the developing suburb of Naremburn in the background.

Sydney Harbour Bridge

SYDNEY HARBOUR BRIDGE - JULY, 1930.

There had been plans to build a bridge as early as 1815, when convict and noted architect Francis Greenway reputedly proposed to Governor Lachlan Macquarie that a bridge be built from the northern to the southern shore of the harbour. In 1825, Greenway wrote a letter to the then "The Australian" newspaper stating that such a bridge would "give an idea of strength and magnificence that would reflect credit and glory on the colony and the Mother Country." Although nothing came of Greenway's suggestions, the idea remained alive.

In 1900, the Lyne government committed to building a new Central Railway Station and organised a worldwide competition for the design and construction of a harbour bridge. Local engineer Norman Selfe submitted a design for a suspension bridge and won the subsequent competition outright. However, due to an economic downturn and a change of government at the 1904 NSW State election, construction never began. A unique three-span bridge was proposed in 1922 by Ernest Stowe with connections at Balls Head, Millers Point and Balmain with a memorial tower and hub on Goat Island.

In 1914 John Bradfield was appointed "Chief Engineer of Sydney Harbour Bridge and Metropolitan Railway Construction", and his work on the project over many years earned him the legacy as the "father" of the bridge. Bradfield's preference at the time was for a cantilever bridge without piers, and in 1916 the NSW Legislative Assembly passed a bill for such a structure, however it did not proceed as the Legislative Council rejected the legislation on the basis that the money would be better spent on the war effort.

Following World War I, plans to build the bridge regained momentum. Bradfield persevered with the project, fleshing out the details of the specifications and financing for his cantilever bridge proposal, and in 1921 he travelled overseas to investigate tenders. On return from his travels Bradfield decided that an arch design would also be suitable and he and officers of the NSW Department of Public Works prepared a general design for a single-arch bridge based upon New York City's Hell Gate Bridge. In 1922 the government passed the Sydney Harbour Bridge Act No. 28, specifying the construction of a high-level cantilever or arch bridge across the harbour between Dawes Point and Milsons Point, along with construction of necessary approaches and electric railway lines, and worldwide tenders were invited for the project.

As a result of the tendering process, the government received twenty proposals from six companies and on 24th March 1924 the contract was awarded to English firm Dorman Long and Co Ltd, of Middlesbrough, who were well known as the contractors who built the similar Tyne Bridge of Newcastle Upon Tyne, for an arch bridge at a quoted price of AU£4,217,721 11s 10d. The arch design was cheaper than alternative cantilever and suspension bridge proposals, and also provided greater rigidity making it better suited for the heavy loads expected. Bradfield and his staff were ultimately to oversee the entire bridge design and building process, while Dorman Long and Co's Consulting Engineer, Sir Ralph Freeman of Sir Douglas Fox and Partners, and his associate Mr. G.C. Imbault, carried out the detailed design and erection process of the bridge. Architects for the contractors were from the British firm John Burnet & Partners of Glasgow, Scotland.

The building of the bridge coincided with the construction of a system of underground railways in Sydney's CBD, known today as the City Circle, and the bridge was designed with this in mind. The bridge was designed to carry six lanes of road traffic, flanked on each side by two railway tracks and a footpath. Both sets of rail tracks were linked into the underground Wynyard railway station on the south (city) side of the bridge by symmetrical ramps and tunnels. The eastern-side railway tracks were intended for use by a planned rail link to the Northern Beaches. In the interim they were used to carry trams from the North Shore into a terminal within Wynyard Station, and when tram services were discontinued in 1958, they were converted into extra traffic lanes. The Bradfield Highway, which is the main roadway section of the bridge and its approaches, is named in honour of Bradfield's contribution to the bridge.

The official ceremony to mark the "turning of the first sod" occurred on 28th July 1923, on the spot at Milsons Point on the north shore where two workshops to assist in building the bridge were to be constructed. An estimated 469 buildings on the north shore, both private homes and commercial operations, were demolished to allow construction to proceed, with little or no compensation being paid. Work on the bridge itself commenced with the construction of approaches and approach spans, and by September 1926 concrete piers to support the approach spans were in place on each side of the harbour. As construction of the approaches took place, work was also started on preparing the foundations required to support the enormous weight of the arch and loadings. Concrete and granite faced abutment towers were constructed, with the angled foundations built into their sides.

Once work had progressed sufficiently on the support structures, a giant "creeper crane" was erected on each side of the harbour. These cranes were fitted with a cradle, and then used to hoist men and materials into position to allow for erection of the steelwork. To stabilise works while building the arches, tunnels were excavated on each shore with steel cables passed through them and then fixed to the upper sections of each half-arch to stop them collapsing as they extended outwards.

Arch construction itself began on 26th October 1928. The southern end of the bridge was worked on ahead of the northern end, to detect any errors and to help with alignment. The cranes would "creep" along the arches as they were constructed, eventually meeting up in the middle. In less than two years, on Tuesday, 19 August 1930, the two halves of the arch touched for the first time. Workers riveted both top and bottom sections of the arch together, and the arch became self-supporting, allowing the support cables to be removed. On 20 August 1930 the joining of the arches was celebrated by flying the flags of Australia and the United Kingdom from the jibs of the creeper cranes.

Once the arch was completed, the creeper cranes were then worked back down the arches, allowing the roadway and other parts of the bridge to be constructed from the centre out. The vertical hangers were attached to the arch, and these were then joined with horizontal crossbeams. The deck for the roadway and railway were built on top of the crossbeams, with the deck itself being completed by June 1931. Rails for trains and trams were laid, and the road was surfaced using concrete topped with asphalt. Power and telephone lines, water, gas and drainage pipes were also all added to the bridge in 1931.

The pylons were built atop the abutment towers, with construction advancing rapidly from July 1931. Carpenters built wooden scaffolding, with concreters and masons then setting the masonry and pouring the concrete behind it. Gangers built the steelwork in the towers, while day labourers manually cleaned the granite with wire brushes. The last stone of the north-west pylon was set in place on 15th January 1932, and the timber towers used to support the cranes were removed. On 19th January 1932, the first test train, a steam locomotive, safely crossed the bridge. Load testing of the bridge took place in February 1932, with the four rail tracks being loaded with as many as 96 steam locomotives positioned end-to-end. The bridge underwent testing for three weeks, after which it was declared safe and ready to be opened. The construction worksheds were demolished after the bridge was completed, and the land that they were on was occupied by Luna Park.

The standards of industrial safety during construction were poor by today's standards. Sixteen workers died during construction, but surprisingly only two from falling off the bridge. Several more were injured from unsafe work practices undertaken whilst heating and inserting its rivets, and the deafness experienced by many of the workers in later years was blamed on the project. The total financial cost of the bridge was £6.25 million, which was not paid off in full until 1988.

The bridge was formally opened on Saturday, 19th March 1932. Amongst those who attended and gave speeches were the state Governor, Sir Philip Game, and the Minister for Public Works, Lawrence Ennis. The Labor Premier of New South Wales, Jack Lang, was to open the bridge by cutting a ribbon at its southern end. However, just as Lang was about to cut the ribbon, a man in military uniform rode up on a horse, slashing the ribbon with his sword and opening the Sydney Harbour Bridge in the name of the people of New South Wales before the official ceremony began and was promptly arrested. The ribbon was hurriedly retied and Lang performed the official opening ceremony. After he did so, there was a 21-gun salute and an RAAF flypast. The intruder was identified as Francis de Groot. He was convicted of offensive behaviour and fined £5 after a psychiatric test proved he was sane, but this verdict was reversed on appeal. De Groot then successfully sued the Commissioner of Police for wrongful arrest, and was awarded an undisclosed out of court settlement. De Groot was a member of a right-wing paramilitary group called the New Guard, opposed to Lang's leftist policies and resentful of the fact that a member of the Royal Family had not been asked to open the bridge. De Groot was not a member of the regular army, but his uniform allowed him to blend in with the real cavalry. This incident was one of several involving Lang and the New Guard during that year.

A similar ribbon-cutting ceremony on the bridge's northern side by North Sydney's mayor, Alderman Hubert Leslie Primrose, was carried out without incident. It was later discovered that Primrose was also a New Guard member, but his role in and knowledge of the de Groot incident, if any, are unclear. The pair of golden scissors used in the ribbon cutting ceremonies on both sides of the bridge was also used to cut the ribbon at the dedication of the Bayonne Bridge, which had opened in Bayonne, New Jersey, close to New York City, the year before.

Despite the bridge opening in the midst of the Great Depression, opening celebrations were organised by the Citizens of Sydney Organising Committee, an influential body of prominent men and politicians that formed in 1931 under the chairmanship of the Lord Mayor to oversee the festivities. The celebrations included an array of decorated floats, a procession of passenger ships sailing below the bridge, and a Venetian Carnival. A message from a primary school in Tottenham, 515 km (320 mi) away in rural New South Wales, arrived at the bridge on the day and was presented at the opening ceremony. It had been carried all the way from Tottenham to the bridge by relays of school children, with the final relay being run by two children from the nearby Fort Street Boys' and Girls' schools. After the official ceremonies, the public was allowed to walk across the bridge on the deck, something that would not be repeated until the 50th anniversary celebrations. Estimates suggest that between 300,000 and one million people took part in the opening festivities, a phenomenal number given that the entire population of Sydney at the time was estimated to be 1,256,000.

The bridge itself was regarded as a triumph over the Depression years, earning the nickname "the Iron Lung", as it kept many Depression-era workers employed. The Sydney Harbour Bridge was nicknamed "The Coathanger" because of its arch-based design. The arch has a span of 504 m (1,654 ft) and its summit is 134 m (440 ft) above mean sea level. However, expansion of the steel structure on hot days can increase the height of the arch by as much as 18 cm (7.1 in). The total weight of the steelwork of the bridge is 52,800 tonnes and about 79% of the steel was imported from England, with the rest being sourced from Newcastle. The bridge is held together by six million Australian-made hand-driven rivets supplied by the McPherson company of Melbourne, the last being driven through the deck on 21st January 1932. It is still the sixth longest spanning-arch bridge in the world and the tallest steel arch bridge, measuring 134 m (440 ft) from top to water level. It was also the world's widest long-span bridge, at 48.8 m (160 ft) wide, until 2012.

OPPOSITE: 1-Eastern Main Bearing, Dawes Point and officers of the Sydney Harbour Bridge Branch of the Public Works Department, c. 1927; 2-View of the Sydney Harbour Bridge under construction from the Church of England Grammar School, 6th January 1930; 3-Sydney Harbour Bridge under construction; 4-Joining Harbour Bridge arch on the 19th August 1930; 5-1932 Sydney Harbour Bridge Opening - looking into the superstructure. ▲1-The busy Blues Pt Wharf in 1931; 2-Sydney Harbour Bridge Celebrations in March 1932; 3-Load-testing of the Harbour Bridge when fifty steam locos were run on the western side, February 1932, by Ted Hood.

▲Living on the north side of Sydney meant for many that they daily needed to cross the harbour for work, with these pre-World War II ferries being well known at the time. TOP (Left): "Karingal"; (Right): "Kirrule"; "MID (Left): Kulgoa" passes under the partially constructed Sydney harbour Bridge; (Right): "Kuttabul"; ABOVE (Left): Ferries at Circular Quay; (Right): The Manly ferry "South Steyne."

Norman Alfred Rockwell being born to Ernie and Alice Rockwell on the 16th December 1928.[10] Then Bob and Corelli Rockwell welcomed their second child in Robert Hunter Rockwell, on the 25th June 1929 at Royal North Shore Hospital, who was baptised at St. Cuthbert's Church in Naremburn.[11] Elaine Faye Rockwell was born to Ernie and Alice Rockwell the year after on the 31st May 1930.[12]

Unfortunately, with the coming of the Great Depression the economic environment collapsed in October of 1929 and all of these families had to surmount great difficulties for many years thereafter. January of 1932 saw Joy begin kindergarten at Naremburn Public School in what was the beginning of a 25 year relationship between that school and the Rockwell family.

Crossing The Harbour

Throughout these years a monumental project had been underway in Sydney. The ceremony to turn the sod and commence construction on the Sydney Harbour Bridge was initially held in July 1923, but the bridge took nine years to complete, before being officially opened on the 19th March 1932.[13] Both Joy and Robert were toddlers at this time, but its not inconceivable that Bob and Corelli Rockwell joined thousands of other Sydney-siders who witnessed the celebrations, and they may have even walked across the bridge that special day?

Sadly, just three months later and despite surviving seven years beyond the debilitating consequences of his severe stroke, Bob's father William Henry Rockwell, passed away on the 1st July 1932.[14] He died from the combined effects of hardening of the arteries (arteriosclerosis) and inflammation of the heart muscle (myocarditis), both of which he had been battling for years.

Eighteen months later, Elwood Lorraine Rockwell arrived on the 10th of December 1933.[15] Elwood's middle name honoured the relationship with Corelli's uncle George Lorraine Shoveller, and he was baptised at St. Cuthbert's Church, Naremburn in 1934. The next year, Richard Adrian Rockwell was born to Bill Jr. and Rose May Rockwell in 1935.[16]

At this time, the Depression was still affecting the economy and both jobs and money were scarce. Bob Rockwell grew what little vegetables he could and planted tomatoes, a choko vine, some rhubarb, mint and a few fruit trees, but making ends meet remained difficult:

> I remember the 'Howard' piano being taken away from the house in Slade St. by the bailiff. It was heartbreaking for mum (Corelli Rockwell) and Nanna (Lenore O'Sullivan) as they always declared… "it wasn't a home without a baby in the cradle and a piano in the house!"
>
> Joy Hyde (nee Rockwell), 2000 [17]

Lenore 'Nanna' O'Sullivan was a frequent visitor to the Rockwell household and even lived with Bob and Corelli for different periods that coincided with the birth of Corelli's children, and she often gave advice:

> "I remember Nanna (viz. Lenore) saying… "never interfere in a domestic fight, or you'll be the one turned on"."
>
> Joy Hyde (nee Rockwell), 2000 [18]

Then on the 2nd of November 1937 Lindsay Archibald Rockwell arrived, his name honouring the middle name of his father.[19] Lindsay was baptised at St. Cuthbert's Church, Naremburn in early 1938. Corelli's sister Goldie and her family lived close by and 1938 saw the birth of Goldie's second child in Lesley John Mulroy.[20]

Joy left Naremburn Primary School in 1939 and commenced her high school years at Willoughby Girls Domestic Science School. That same year saw Bob Rockwell's younger brother Alfred, the older twin of Ernie, marry Ruth Olga Loader at Hurstville.[21] Corelli dressed all her children up for the occasion and photographs of the wedding show Robert (11), Elwood (7) and Lindsay (3) being kept in check by their stern big sister Joy (13).

Where To From Here?

By 1939 the Rockwells had endured the difficult period known as the depression and already had four children under the age of 12. But along with families the world over few could see the coming prospect of another world war that lay just over the horizon.

References

1. NSW Dept of BDM. (1926). Marriage Certificate for Octavia Corelli O'Sullivan and Robert Archibald Rockwell, #15695/1926.

2. NSW Dept of BDM. (1927). Marriage Cert. for Ernest Barrett Rockwell and Alice Maud Greenup, #10459/1927.

3. NSW Dept of BDM. (1927). Marriage Cert. for Norman John Rockwell and Stella R. Edgerton, #17407/1927.

4. NSW Dept of BDM. (1928). Marriage Certificate for William Henry Rockwell Jr. and Rose M. Menier, #16318/1928.

5. NSW Dept of BDM. (1939). Marriage Certificate for Alfred Barrett Rockwell and Olive Ruth Loader, #21737/1939.

6. NSW Dept of BDM. (1927). Marriage Certificate for Goldie Alathea O'Sullivan and Patrick Joseph Mulroy, #10303/1927.

7. NSW Dept of BDM. (1927). Birth Certificate for Joy Corelli Rockwell, #?/1927.

8. NSW Dept of BDM. (1927). Birth Certificate for Ronald Ernest Rockwell, #?/1927.

9. NSW Dept of BDM. (1928). Birth Certificate for Lionel Raymond Mulroy, #?/1928.

10. NSW Dept of BDM. (1928). Birth Certificate for Norman Alfred Rockwell, #?/1928.

11. NSW Dept of BDM. (1929). Birth Certificate for Robert Hunter Rockwell, #?/1929.

12. NSW Dept of BDM. (1930). Birth Certificate for Elaine Faye Rockwell, #?/1930.

13. Wikipedia - Sydney Harbour Bridge [https://en.wikipedia.org/wiki/Sydney_Harbour_Bridge].

14. NSW Dept of BDM. (1932). Death Certificate for William Henry Rockwell, #13545/1932.

15. NSW Dept of BDM. (1933). Birth Certificate for Elwood Lorraine Rockwell, #?/1933.

16. NSW Dept of BDM. (1935). Birth Certificate for Richard Adrian Rockwell, #?/1935.

17. Hyde, Joy, 1927-2018 (Interviewee, 2001). 'Joy Hyde (nee Rockwell). interviewed by Tracy Rockwell on the 19th of August 2001, at Aspley, Brisbane.'

18. Ibid.

19. NSW Dept of BDM. (1937). Birth Certificate for Lindsay Archibald Rockwell, #?/1937.

20. NSW Dept of BDM. (1939). Birth Certificate for Lesley John Mulroy #?/1939.

21. NSW Dept of BDM. (1939). Marriage Certificate for Alfred Barrett Rockwell and Olive Ruth Loader, #21737/1939.

Chapter Fifteen

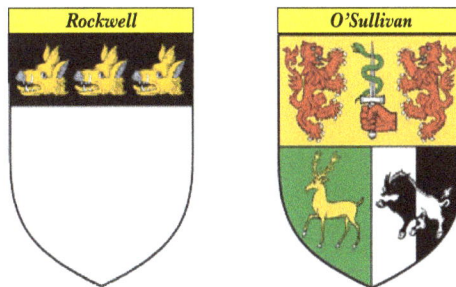

THE WAR YEARS

For 150 years Australia had relied on the British Empire for its external defence. But Britain's military and strategic focus on Europe in the early 20th century caused many Australians concern about a Japanese invasion of our resource-rich continent. By the 1920s Britain, with support from Australia, had formulated its Singapore Strategy whereby it would build a huge naval base on the island as a means of protecting its interests in the region. But the fall of Singapore in 1942 led the Australian Government to reconsider its alliance with Britain.

Back home in Sydney, Bob Rockwell ran a 'tight ship' at home and controlled his household with an iron glove, which was likely due to his stern upbringing as a boy. But as Bob's sons matured, the firm discipline began to wear thin with the boys growing restless, and they soon began to wander. As youths they created a gang, which ruled the bush below Northbridge, known as Flat Rock Gully, and they invented special whistles and bird calls

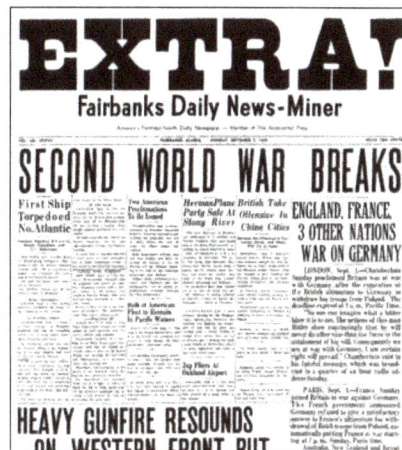

▲ News of the outbreak of the Second World War reverberated around the globe in early September 1939.

War Coupons & Ration Books

In Australia, many things had to change for those who remained at home during the war. New industries had to be created to supply the troops with weapons, uniforms and ammunition. The government had to control the buying and selling of scarce goods, to ensure that everyone received a fair share.

Australians began to experience shortages of almost everything they needed in daily life. At the time of World War II, most people drank tea, not coffee. When the Japanese captured many of the countries that grew the tea supplied to Australia, this caused severe shortages. Enemy action in the Pacific also disrupted the normal supply of goods by ship to Australia. Australian troops abroad had to be supplied with food produced in Australia, and when thousands of American troops arrived in Australia to fight the war in the Pacific, they also had to be fed.

To ensure that everyone received a basic amount of essential supplies such as meat, butter, sugar and tea, the government introduced a system of rationing. Everyone had to apply for ration books, which contained a number of coupons. Each coupon gave the holder permission to buy a certain amount of something, usually over a weekly period. Despite the hardship, rationing was well received by the public because it applied to everyone equally. Nevertheless, when the government announced in May 1942 that they would impose rationing on clothing, there was a rush to buy as much as possible before rationing began.

People were encouraged to be as self-sufficient as possible, to keep hens for eggs, and to grow their own vegetables at home. Even some public parks were dug up for vegetable gardens. Shortages and rationing also led to hoarding where people who had access to some rare commodity, such as petrol, would store up as much as they could, for their own use in the future. This only made shortages worse. It also led to a black market where items that were in demand were sold privately, at very high prices, outside the rationing system.

But rationing was not enough. The government also needed large amounts of money to pay for weapons, aeroplanes, ships, tanks, ammunition and soldier's wages. One source of this money was the savings of individual citizens, who were encouraged to lend money to the Government by purchasing bonds called 'Victory Loans.' In order for people to have more money to spend on bonds, the government tried to discourage them from spending it on themselves, for things like cigarettes, beer, movies and gambling.

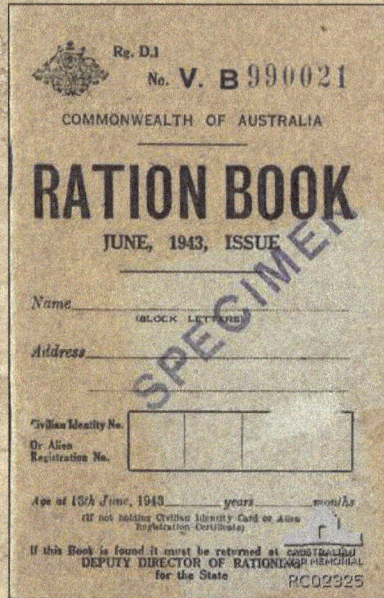

Relatives of Robert & Corelli Rockwell in WWII

OF ROBERT ARCHIBALD ROCKWELL:

Mary Bantin & Auguste THUAUX Descendants:

Jack Harding	1st C, 1 R	POW Died
Albert August Thuaux	1st C, 1 R	Returned
John Ernest Thuaux	1st C, 1 R	Returned
Robert Selwyn Thuaux	1st C, 1 R	Returned
Robert E. Thuaux	1st C, 1 R	Returned
Norman K. Thuaux	1st C, 1 R	Returned

Arthur & Lillian CARPENTER Descendants:

Arthur Fred Carpenter	Half-Nephew	Returned

Eric & Mabel CARPENTER Descendants:

Arthur Eric Carpenter	Half-Nephew	Returned

Richard & Clarissa BANTIN Descendants:

Richard William Bantin	1st Cousin	Returned
Arthur S. Fairbairn	1st C, 1 R	Returned
Reginald H. Fairbairn	1st C, 1 R	Returned

George & Florence BANTIN Descendants:

Robert John Bantin	1st Cousin	Died
John Henry Bantin	1st Cousin	Returned
Frederick Kevin Bantin	1st Cousin	Returned

OF OCTAVIA CORELLI O'SULLIVAN:

John & Sarah O'SULLIVAN Descendants:

Victor James O'Sullivan	1st Cousin	Returned
John William O'Sullivan	1st Cousin	Returned

Susan Shoveller & Edward MEALLY Descendants:

Lloyd Meally Carr	1st C 1 R	Returned

Valtie Mackie & Edmond MALINS Descendants:

Ronald G. Malins	Half-Nephew	Returned
Alwyn W. Malins	Half-Nephew	POW Ret

Clarence & Mary SHOVELLER Descendants:

Russell L. Shoveller	1st Cousin	Returned
Thomas J. Shoveller	1st C 1 R	At Home

NB: C = cousin, R = generations removed

▲TOP (Left): 'Change over to a victory job' wartime recruitment poster, 1942. (Centre): A specimen Ration Book for Australian civilians during World War II. (Right): War poster promoting 'Australia For Ever!.' ABOVE (Left): List of Bob and Corelli Rockwell's cousins that enlisted in World War II. (Right): While Darwin received constant bombardment, Australian skies were relatively quiet throughout the war, which contrasted markedly with the dogfights over London during the Battle of Britain.

to alert each other to the appearance of any rivals.

Although they lived in a regular suburb, the gully became their backyard and they created tracks, hideouts and lairs, and swam in the water holes in summer, which were natural and unpolluted back then. They explored the caves and aboriginal carvings, they also fished and collected birds, lizards, turtles and frogs, which they turned into pets. Robert Jr. once confessed to performing an experiment by attaching a handkerchief parachute to a stray cat, which they ceremonially launched off the 70m high suspension bridge. Unfortunately for the poor cat, the experiment was unsuccessful.

The magnificent bridge was originally opened to span Northbridge gully in January of 1892, but by 1936 considerable corrosion was found in the suspension bridge steelwork and cables, and it was immediately closed to trams and all vehicular traffic. Northbridge residents were forced to walk over the bridge to catch trams on the Cammeray side while a technologically advanced concrete support arch was constructed.[1] The Tudor towers were retained to maintain the heritage elements of the old bridge. The new bridge was

▲ TOP: The loss of HMAS Sydney (II) is Australia's greatest naval tragedy. Its disappearance in 1941 without a trace left a legacy of uncertainty for decades. In March 2008, renewed efforts to find the Sydney came to fruition, confirming her fate and bringing closure to the mystery. ABOVE (Left): "HMS Hood" the largest ship in the British Empire, at anchor in Sydney Harbour in 1924. (Right): The immense guns of "HMS Hood" were thought ot be an effective deterrant to aggression by potential enemies.

formally opened at a well-attended ceremony on the 9th September 1939, with the young Rockwell boys perhaps even being spectators on the day. However, in that very same week, the world had been plunged once again into another more devastating world war.

The War Years

The world had witnessed Hitler's aggression for years, but the war began in earnest when Germany invaded Poland on the 1st September 1939. Britain and France retaliated by declaring war on Germany, which brought all of

▲ TOP: The finest harbour in the world provided refuge for shipping, but brought Japanese subs to our doorstep. Panorama of Darling Harbour from Railway House, 27 October 1944. ABOVE: Three scenes of the tranquil waters of Sydney Harbour by David Moore. ◄ Map of the considerable number of ships attacked and sunk by Japanese submarines along the New South Wales coast during WW2, which was strictly censored to prevent fear and panic amongst the population.

Britain's allies and former colonies into the conflict, including Australia.

At the start of World War II all unmarried men aged 21 were called up for three month's military training. These men could only serve in Australia or its territories. However, conscription was effectively introduced in mid-1942, when all men aged 18 to 35, and single men aged 35 to 45, were required to join the Citizens Military Force (CMF). Volunteers with the Australian Imperial Force (AIF) scorned the CMF conscripts as 'chocolate soldiers', or 'chockos', because it was believed

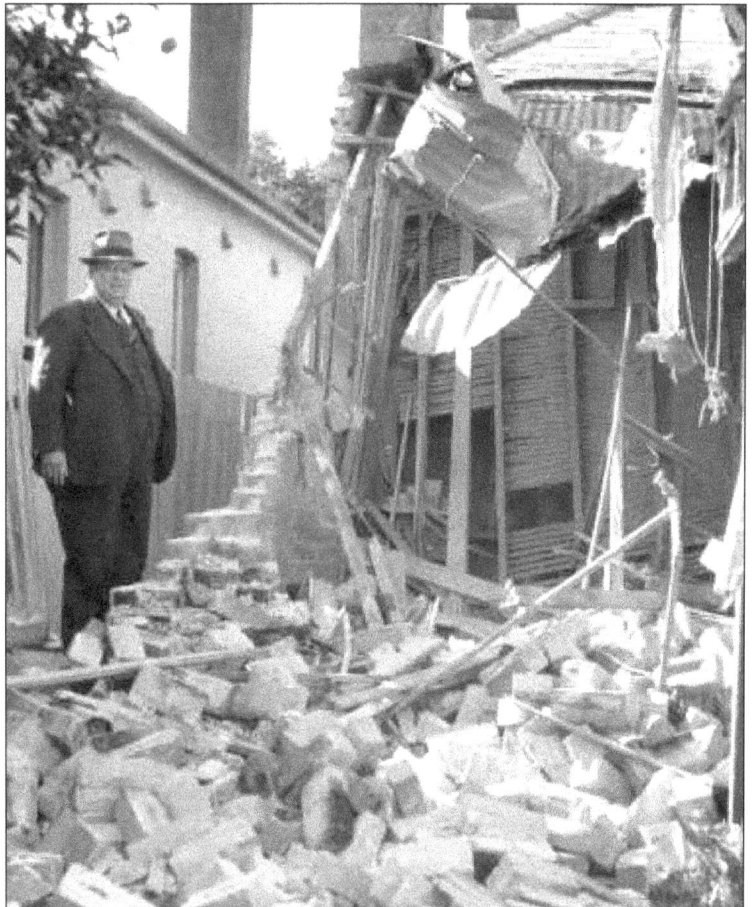

▲ MID (Left): Sunken RAN accommodation ship "HMAS Kuttabul" was destroyed during the Japanese midget submarine attack. (Right): The midget Japanese submarine that attacked Sydney Harbour on the 1st June 1942. ▶ Property prices crashed in Sydney's eastern suburbs as a result of the Japanese shelling of Bondi in June 1942.

they would melt under the hazardous conditions of battle.

Therefore, most fit Australian men of military age were conscripted into the armed forces, although exceptions were given to those who performed vital jobs for the country and the war effort, which could not be abandoned or performed by others. Not only were such people exempt from being conscripted, they were often prohibited from enlisting on their own initiative, and were required to remain in their posts, under what was known as reserved occupations (also known as essential services). Examples of such reserved occupations included medical practitioners and police officers, but what was or was not a reserved occupation depended on war needs and the particular circumstances.

Being 38 and married, Bob Rockwell was exempt from the call-up as were all his brothers. Additionally, as a 'wharfie' his work was classified as a 'reserved occupation', and therefore he was prohibited from enlisting in military service. Bob's sons as well, were all way too young, with the eldest Robert Jr., being only ten years of age when war was declared. However, at least 14 of Bob's cousins did enlist, while a further seven of Corelli's relatives were also involved.

July of 1940 sadly brought about the death of Corelli's uncle Clarence Shoveller, who passed aged 60.[2] Bob's first cousin Robert John Bantin, son of their deceased uncle George Bantin had enlisted, but was tragically killed aboard the "SS Chakdina," while being evacuated from Tobruk on the 5th December 1941.[3] He had been a member of the 2/13th Battalion, the famed 'Rats of Tobruk.'

The Japanese attack on Pearl Harbour occurred just two days later on the 7th December 1941, which brought the Japanese a lot closer to Australia, but also heralded the entry of the United States into the war.

Attacks on Sydney & Shipping

In late May 1942, submarines belonging to the Imperial Japanese Navy made a series of attacks on the cities of Sydney and Newcastle in New South Wales. From the 31st May to 1st June, three Ko-hyoteki class midget submarines, each with a two-member crew, entered Sydney Harbour. They skillfully avoided the partially constructed Sydney Harbour anti-submarine boom net, and attempted to sink a number of Allied warships. Two of the midget submarines were detected and attacked before they could successfully engage any Allied vessels, with the crews scutting their disabled boats and killing themselves. These submarines were later recovered by the Allies. The third submarine attempted to torpedo the heavy cruiser "USS Chicago", but instead sank the converted ferry "HMAS Kuttabul," killing some 21 sailors, with Bob Rockwell, being at work on the wharves during the actual attack. This particular midget submarine's fate was unknown until 2006, when amateur scuba divers discovered the wreck off Sydney's northern beaches.

Immediately following the raid, the five Japanese fleet submarines that carried the midget submarines to Australia embarked on a campaign to disrupt merchant shipping in eastern Australian waters. Over the next month, the submarines attacked at least seven merchant vessels, sinking three ships and killing 50 sailors. During this period, between midnight and 02:30am on the 8th June, two of the submarines surfaced off the coast and shelled the ports of Sydney and Newcastle with explosions in Rose Bay, Bellevue Hill, Woollahra and Bondi.[4]

But life went on and in the midst of the conflict, Corelli delivered her fifth child when Ronie Malcolm Rockwell arrived on the 26th of February 1943.[5] He was baptised at St.

Cuthbert's Church in Naremburn on the 2nd May 1943. Another bright moment occurred on the 15th June 1944 with the wedding of Corelli's half-niece, young Valtie Chisholm to Frank Hammond, although neither the Rockwells or Mulroys were invited to the wedding.[6] Together and without children, Valtie and Frank led an interesting and charmed life (*see Chapter 12*).

Victory and Post War Events

The war in Europe concluded with the unconditional surrender of the Germans on the 7th May 1945, to great celebrations around the world including Australia. Life started to take a turn for the better with the harsh restrictions of the war gradually being lifted. Bob Rockwell was still working as a wharf labourer, while Corelli toiled at home to bring up her large family, now ably assisted by Joy, who turned 18 in April of 1945.

However, the celebrations surrounding the end of the war were tarnished somewhat, first by the loss of Lenore's younger sister, and Corelli's aunt Mabel on the 5th July.[7] Then just three weeks later, when Corelli lost her mother Lenore O'Sullivan to inflammation of the heart muscle (myocarditis) and senility on the 21st of July 1945, at 78 years of age.[8]

Lenore's funeral was conducted at Northern Suburbs Crematorium and was attended by her only surviving sibling George Shoveller, her daughter's Valtie Chisholm, Corelli Rockwell, Goldie Mulroy, sons in law, and her grandchildren Valtie Hammond (19), Joy (18), Robert Jr. (16), Elwood (12), Lindsay (8) and Ronie (2), Rockwell, as well as Lionel

▲ TOP (Left): The cruiser "HMAS Sydney" glides into Circular Quay in 1940. (Right): "HMS King George V" was one of the many ships of the South Pacific Fleet to undergo maintenance at Garden Island. ABOVE (Left): "HMS Illustrious" entering the Captain Cook Graving Dock, Sydney on the 11th February 1945. (Right): Ships of the British Pacific Fleet berthed at Woolloomooloo in 1945 with the destroyer "HMS Wessex" in the foreground, while "HMS Kiing George V" can be seen berthed at the finger wharf in the background (State Library of Victoria).

▲LEFT: Despite its strength, the British Empire was on its knees by the end of the war. RIGHT: Victory in Europe was declared on the 9th May 1945.

(17) and Lesley (6) Mulroy. Both Ron (35) and Alwyn (33) Malins, were likely not yet returned from war service.

The war against the Japanese in the Pacific dragged on for a while longer, but concluded on the 15th August when Japan was forced into unconditional surrender by the dropping of the atomic bomb on Nagasaki (August 6th), and the hydrogen bomb on Hiroshima (August 9th). On the 2nd September, a formal surrender ceremony was conducted in Tokyo Bay, aboard the battleship "USS Missouri."[9]

Where To From Here?

With World War II passing into history, the Rockwells knuckled down to provide a better future for their family as they greeted two more children, attended weddings and were bouyed by the arrival of grandchildren before they themselves, like all their ancestors before them, had to face the prospect of eternity.

References

1. Wikipedia - Long Gully Bridge [https://en.wikipedia.org/wiki/Long_Gully_Bridge].
2. NSW Dept of BDM. (1940). Death Certificate for Clarence John Hann Shoveller, #18255/1940.
3. Victoria University of Wellington - Sinking Of "SS Chakdina" [https://nzetc.victoria.ac.nz/tm/scholarly/tei-WH2MMed-c8-19.html].
4. Wikipedia - Attack On Sydney Harbour [https://en.wikipedia.org/wiki/Attack_on_Sydney_Harbour.
5. NSW Dept of BDM. (1943). Birth Certificate for Ronie Malcolm Rockwell, #?/1943.
6. NSW Dept of BDM. (1944). Marriage Certificate for Valtie Minlena Chisholm and Frank Hammond, #13629/1944.
7. NSW Dept of BDM. (1945). Death Certificate for Mabel Susan West (Hayes, nee Shoveller). #20451/1945.
8. NSW Dept of BDM. (1945). Death Certificate for Lenore O'Sullivan (Mackie, nee Shoveller). #13731/1945.
9. Wikipedia - Surrender Of Japan [https://en.wikipedia.org/wiki/Surrender_of_Japan].

Chapter Sixteen

ROCKWELL RECOLLECTIONS

World War II officially ended on 2nd September 1945, with the surrender of Japan aboard the USS Missouri. Before that, the United States had dropped two atomic bombs on Japan, and the Soviet Union declared war on Japan, causing Emperor Hirohito to announce the acceptance of the Potsdam Declaration on the 15th August 1945, which would eventually lead to the surrender ceremony in Tokyo Bay. The Americans occupied Japan after the end of the war until the 28th April 1952, when the Treaty of San Francisco came into effect.

Six months after the end of hostilities in Naremburn NSW, Corelli delivered their last child in Janet Lenore Rockwell, who arrived on the 22nd of February 1946.[1] Her middle name was given in honour of her recently deceased maternal grandmother, whom she would sadly never meet. Janet was baptised at St. Cuthbert's Church, Naremburn in 1946. Sadly, Corelli's uncle George Shoveller passed away in August of 1946, which brought an end to all connections with the close Shoveller relatives.[2]

Bob and Corelli Rockwell, who lived at 24 Market St, Naremburn, resided in close proximity to both of Corelli's sisters Valtie and Goldie, as they were situated at Union St. North Sydney, and 7 Dawson St. Naremburn respectively. A favourite family pastime at this time was listening to the radio of an evening. Bob, Corelli and the children would find themselves something small to work on, or a game to play and gather in the loungeroom around the radio, listening to programs like 'The Adventures of Biggles,' 'Superman,' 'The Green Hornet,' 'The Bob Dyer Show' or 'Australia's Amateur Hour.'

Bob sometimes visited his mother Elizabeth Rockwell at Aunty Aileen's home with his family, but without a car they had to spend a considerable amount of time travelling by public transport to and from Naremburn to Hurstville. Apparently Aileen and Elizabeth were very strict with Bob's children whenever they visited. Joy remembers there was always a beautiful smell throughout their house, and never a speck of dirt.

> "Whenever we visited, we were greeted with a beautifully set table, tablecloth with serviettes etc. We also had to sit in complete silence and listen to Aileen's daughter Shirley play the piano, and you dare not even sneeze! Grandma (Elizabeth) Rockwell would often keep herself busy with jobs such as polishing the brass and silver as well as shelling peas." [3]

Bob and Corelli Rockwell had a difficult time coping financially with such a large family and at times couldn't make ends meet. Later on, perhaps during the early 1950's Bob Rockwell left the waterside and gained another job with the Post Office. His new position was at the 'Parcels and Bulk Postage Counter' at the General Post Office (GPO) in Martin Place, Sydney.

The Masonic Lodge

After the war, Bob Rockwell joined the brotherhood of masonry, which over time became a very important part of his life, as he and his brothers became intricately associated with the Masonic movement. At one stage there were eight Rockwell's up on the dais of Lodge Fidelity Lewis consisting of Bob's brothers and their sons. The Grand Master in attendance commenting that he had... "never seen such a phenomenon in all the years of his masonry." [4]

Masonic Record for Robert Archibald Rockwell

> On 7 April 1946 was initiated into Lodge Langlea in the United Grand Lodge of Masons. He subsequently resigned from that Lodge and joined the Sydney Lodge of Research, which basically conducted workshops and discussions on various codes of morals, ethics and philosophies. Later he joined at the Lodge Northshore No. 440. By working his way up through the various Chairs and Offices, he became the Grand Worshipful Master of the Lodge in September 1964 and held that chair for a period of 12 months.

Lodge Records, Mr McBurney, 26th May 1980

Although none of Bob Rockwell's four sons ever joined the Masons, he himself became a staunch member and was in both the Red and Blue Lodges, and also in the Cryptic Lodge. He was apparently a very good ritualist and possessed a lot of regalia in the form of Masonic collars and jewels.

Joy was always one for being proper keeping the best manners, but with four younger brothers to watch over, she often had her hands full. Bob's eldest son and namesake, Robert Hunter was by now a young man and he left home seeking work about 1947. Elwood was still only 14, but in tandem with his cousin Lionel, they were always looking for adventure.

One night, they apparently broke into Naremburn School and ransacked the office. During the fun, Elwood allegedly became fascinated with the office typewriter and did what most people would do when having access to such a fun thing... he typed his name and address! Of course the police found the damning evidence the next morning amidst the vandalised office and were very soon around at the Rockwell residence, although apparently the boys were only given a wrap over the knuckles.

The Rockwell's always paid rent for their house and never owned property, but both Joy and Elwood began contributing to the household expenses as they matured. Bob and Corelli continued tending to their dependents, but by 1954 Joy had reached 27, Elwood was 21, Lindsay was 17, Ronie was 11 and Janet was eight years of age, and surprisingly all five were still living in the home at Naremburn.

They resided in that same small, rented, two bedroom, semi-detached bungalow for almost 30 years from around 1935. Situated on a very steep block, the house had a long

The Masonry Movement [41]

Masonic historians have variously dated the origins of Masonry from about 1425 to the beginning of the 18th century, with the 15th century seeing the first evidence of ceremonial regalia. The minutes of the Lodge of Edinburgh (Mary's Chapel) No. 1 in Scotland show a continuity from an operative lodge in 1598 to a modern speculative Lodge, and is reputed to be the oldest Masonic Lodge in the world. The first Grand Lodge, the Grand Lodge of London and Westminster, later called the Grand Lodge of England (GLE), was founded on 24 June 1717, when four existing London Lodges met for a joint dinner.

Freemasonry or Masonry consists of fraternal organisations that trace their origins to the local fraternities of stonemasons, which from the end of the 14th century regulated the qualifications of stonemasons and their interaction with authorities and clients. The degrees of freemasonry retain the three grades of medieval craft guilds, those of Apprentice, Journeyman or Fellow (now called Fellowcraft), and Master Mason. These are the degrees offered by Craft (or Blue Lodge) Freemasonry. Members of these organisations are known as Freemasons or Masons. There are additional degrees, which vary with locality and jurisdiction, and are usually administered by different bodies than the craft degrees.

The basic, local organisational unit of Freemasonry is the Lodge. The Lodges are usually supervised and governed at the regional level, usually coterminous with either a state, province, or national border, by a Grand Lodge or Grand Orient. There is no international, worldwide Grand Lodge that supervises all of Freemasonry as each Grand Lodge is independent, and they do not necessarily recognise each other as being legitimate.

Freemasonry describes itself as a "beautiful system of morality, veiled in allegory and illustrated by symbols." The symbolism is mainly, but not exclusively, drawn from the manual tools of stonemasons such as the square and compass, the level and plumb rule and the trowel, among others. A moral lesson is attached to each of these tools, although the assignment is by no means consistent. The meaning of the symbolism is taught and explored through ritual.

The idea of Masonic brotherhood probably descends from a 16th century legal definition of a brother as one who has taken an oath of mutual support to another. Accordingly, Masons swear at each degree to keep the contents of that degree secret, and to support and protect their brethren unless they have broken the law. In most Lodges the oath or obligation is taken on a Volume of Sacred Law, whichever book of divine revelation is appropriate to the religious beliefs of the individual brother (usually the Bible in the Anglo-American tradition). In Progressive continental Freemasonry, books other than scripture are permissible, a cause of rupture between some Grand Lodges.

▲ Robert Archibald Rockwell in the Masonic Lodge (circled), c. 1946.

balcony at the front overlooking Market St, with a very steep 10m drop below the house. However, everyone came and went through the kitchen at the rear of the property via Adolphus Street, which despite being a dirt laneway gave much easier access to the home.

The first of Bob and Corelli's children to wed was Robert Hunter Rockwell (aka Rock) and his young bride Betty Jean Wardle (1935-1996), who were married at the Registrar Generals Office in Sydney on the 15th January 1954.[5]

Bob Rockwell doesn't seem to have been very close to his brothers Bill Jr., Norman (aka Jack), Ernie or Alfred (aka Mick), and his relationship with his half-sister Aileen, and half-brothers Arthur, Eric and Les Carpenter was even less existent. On the other hand, Corelli kept quite close links with her older half-sister Valtie and younger sister Goldie, as they lived close by. Bob Rockwell normally had a gruff personality, but he could loosen up as Lindsay Rockwell recalled on one occasion when his father had a few too many drinks and met the boys at the top of Adolphus St. He decided to jump on Ronie's bicycle and ride

▲ TOP (Left): 'Pansies' painted by Robert Archibald Rockwell on glass, c.1923, found in his lap desk. (Right): Badges and ephemera found in William Henry Rockwell's lap desk - most probably belongong to Robert Archibald Rockwell. TOP LINE: Badge for "HMAS Adelaide" (sterling silver); Badge from the Royal Life Saving Society awarded to P. Rockwell (16th Dec, 1943); Egyptian medallions; Faded 150th Anniversary of Settlement medallion. 2ND LINE: Triangular Egyptian medal; 150th Anniversary of Settlement with Governor Arthur Phillip on the obverse & motto "Youth Carries On'; The Scots badge (sterling silver); Fifty Years Commonwealth of Austalia Medallion 1901-1951; Crows Nest Hotel, North Sydney - You Pay Token. 3RD LINE: The St John Ambulance Association Badge (engraved Robert Rockwell A246519) - registered at St Johns gate, London (1958, 1959); Waterside Workers Federation of Australia Badge, Sydney Branch #3047 (1948); Stevedoring Industry Commission Badge, Reg'd Waterside Worker #3047; Volunteer Observer, Air Observers Corps (This badge is the property of the Dept of Air, #4006 (Stokes); Masonic Badge 'Advanced' - 'Son of Man - Mark Well' (7th Apr, 1948). BOTTOM LINE: Badge with 'MN' initials; 7mm bullet. ABOVE: Photograph showing tram services along Willoughby Road at Naremburn, c.1953.

home, but amused all by crashing into the fence.[6]

Over time, Joy and young Valtie became very close as half-cousins and continued that relationship right throughout their lives. Goldie's boys Lionel and Lesley, were also very close to the Rockwell boys, and Lionel teamed up with Rock and Elwood on many occasions.

By the mid 1950's Bob Rockwell's mother Elizabeth Rockwell, had achieved the very respectable age of 88 years, but she sadly passed away from cardiovascular degeneration and senility on the 4th June 1955, while residing with her daughter Aileen at 892 King Georges Rd. Hurstville.[7] Bob and his brothers wanted their mother to be buried alongside their father William Henry Rockwell at Rookwood Cemetery, but Aileen wouldn't allow it! Aileen reasoned that as her mother had lived with her for the past 23 years, she could take matters into her own hands and bury Elizabeth as she saw fit![8] Accordingly Elizabeth Rockwell was cremated and now rests alone with a memorial at Woronora Crematorium, in Sutherland. This might explain why William Henry Rockwell's grave remained unmarked, as the brothers were perhaps waiting for their mother to die and never got around to erecting a monument for their father.

On the brighter side, Bob and Corelli were soon after rewarded with the birth of their first grandchild, Tracy Paul Rockwell, first son of Rock and Betty Rockwell, who arrived on the 15th July 1955.[9] Two years later on the 14th September 1957, their third son Lindsay

▲ TOP: Photograph showing tram services at Crows Nest, c.1959. ABOVE (Left): A baby Ronie and big brother Lindsay Rockwell, c.1944. (Centre): Lindsay Archibald Rockwell aged 12, keeps a watch over his three year old sister Janet, and his six year old brother Ronie Rockwell, c.1949. (Right): LEFT: Photograph of Robert Archibald Rockwell, c.1960.

Rockwell married Lynette Ellen Watson (1939-2006) at Naremburn.[10] Lindsay's older brother Rock, was best man and photographs bear witness to the happy occasion.

Two years later again saw Rock and Betty Rockwell's second son Robert Wayne Rockwell, arrive with thanks to the staff of the Crown St. Womens Hospital on the 12th of August 1959.[11] More grandchildren followed, with Lindsay and Lynette's daughter Rhonda Janine Rockwell being born on the13th October 1960.[12]

Throughout this time, Bob Rockwell continued working at the GPO in Market Street, Sydney. Then in 1961, Bob's 18 year old son Ronie Rockwell married Coral Joy Stretton (c.1943-1981).[13] From all accounts, many of the family advised Ronie not to enter into the marriage at such a young age, but not heeding their advice, the event went ahead. Already pregnant at the wedding, Ronie and Coral produced three boys in quick succession through the births of Brett Anthony Rockwell in 1961, Mark Malcolm Rockwell in 1962 and Paul Steven Rockwell in 1965.[14,15,16] Another grandson had also arrived during this period, with the birth of Lindsay and Lynette Rockwell's son Glen Lindsay Rockwell, on the 13th of December 1962.[17]

However, all were devastated on the 14th July 1963 by the sudden and dreadful death

▲TOP: The 1957 wedding of Lindsay Rockwell and Lynette Watson with (from left) Betty, Bob, Corelli, Lynette and Lindsay Rockwell. ABOVE (Left): Photo of the Rockwell's at Adolphus St , Naremburn featuring Ronie, Tracy, Rock and Bob Rockwell, c.1957. (Centre): Bob Rockwell dressed for a family wedding, possibly Ronie, Janet or Joy? (Right): Photo of the Rockwell's looking east along Adolphus St, their house being to the immediate right, and features Ronie, Tracy, Rock and Betty Rockwell with Janet (kneeling), Bob Rockwell, Lynette and Joy... all Rockwell's, c.1957.

▲ *LEFT: Bob Rockwell at work in the Parcels and Bulk Postage Counter at the GPO, c.1964. RIGHT: Ronie, Lindsay, Bob, Janet & Elwood Rockwell holding Ronie's first son Brett Anthony Rockwell, 1961.*

of Wayne Rockwell, aged just three years and 11 months, from pnuemonia.[18] Rock, Betty and eight year old Tracy suffered bitterly along with all members of both families, and his loss took many years to resolve. To help overcome their grief, Rock and Betty decided soon after to have another child, and Sandra Kay Rockwell arrived on the 6th of October 1964, with gladness from the whole family.[19]

Unfortunately, Ronie couldn't cope with the pressures of being a father at such a young age and left his wife and young family, escaping to Germany before his third son was even born, and sadly becoming estranged for many years from his three sons in the process.

While working as a postman at the GPO in Martin Place, Bob Rockwell occasionally caught up with his younger brother Ernie, who was then working as an elevator driver at G. J. Coles in King St, Sydney. Around mid 1965, Bob apparently asked Ernie to lend him some money to help bring his son Ronie back from Germany. On this occasion, Ernie recalled Bob speaking of a 'Janet' who he had never heard of. Bob of course declared that Janet was his daughter! Ernie was even more shocked to find that she was 19 years old, as Ernie had no idea Bob had a younger daughter at all! In the end, it was Jack (aka Norman) who apparently loaned the funds to Bob, to pay for Ronie's return.

Next of Bob and Corelli's children to marry was their youngest child Janet, who had begun a relationship with Roland Lawrence Whiting (c.1945-1982). Tragically, Roley was later involved in a severe motor vehicle accident and became permanently disabled as a paraplegic. However, Janet honoured her marital commitment until they split in the mid-1970s.[20] Relatively quickly out of this marriage came grandchild number nine in Michele Lena Whiting, being born on the 10th December 1965.[21]

Throughout this time, Elwood remained with his parents at Naremburn and was happy to simply plug along. While Bob Rockwell's four sons adapted to the changing times and threw off their stern upbringing, Joy was always more graceful, reserved and conservative and personified the Rockwell dignity. She was restrained and well mannered, a legacy perhaps of her grandmother Elizabeth. However, despite having moved into a flat of her own, as she rapidly approached 40, most of the family had doubts that Joy would ever find a partner. But she surprised everyone in starting up a relationship with an Englishman by the name of William Hyde (1925-2000). Joy soon after became the last of Bob and Corelli's

Recollections of Naremburn [42]

Unfortunately, not many of their descendants would remember Bob and Corelli Rockwell. Despite being much less frequent visitors to Naremburn than to my mother's family, as the eldest grandchild, I do however retain a very clear memory of our grandparents, and their house at Naremburn.

A trip to my Rockwell grandparents always began with driving across the Sydney Harbour Bridge, which was always a fascinating experience. There were no freeways back then, and the bridge toll collectors were a feature of the trip. The route from Darlington, where we lived at the time, via Pyrmont, Kent Street and onto the Harbour Bridge, then via the Pacific Highway to Crows Nest, then down Willoughby Road with a right turn into Naremburn. The Rockwell address was at 24 Market Street, but the house was built high up on the block, and everyone entered from the rear of the property, in fact there was no front door into the house. Adolphus Street was more of a dead end dirt laneway, than a street. We would enter the house via a small gate in the rear yard, walk past the outside brick toilet overgrown by a choko vine, and through the back porch door directly into the kitchen. The home seemingly always had a fresh fragrance that consisted of a mixture of cloves and green apples.

The floors throughout the home were either timber or linoleum with rugs placed here and there. The kitchen consisted of a large vinyl covered table and chairs surrounded by benches with a terrazo sink and a separate brick pantry. The china was elegant and looked old, as was the cutlery. The gas oven looked ancient and perhaps there was a refrigerator, but it might have been an ice-box. Turning left into the lounge room revealed another large table with a green velvet tablecloth and chairs, a lounge and cane rocking chair, a set of dark wooden bookshelves, a dark wooden sideboard, and a dark wooden piano in the corner. On special occasions such as Christmas, the family would stand around the piano and sing while Janet played carols and then other popular songs from the 40's and 50's. My favourite job was to turn the song book pages.

The interior of the house had a darkish tone, which was due to the dark wood stained skirting boards, doors and architraves. The walls were decorated here and there with a few paintings. From what I can remember there was one of a still life consisting of fruit falling out of a large bowl, and another of a fierce looking American Indian chief complete in his impressive headress. The bookshelves were crammed with the spines of old, but what I always found to be fascinating books, and the sideboard displayed decorative vases and bowls. Coming off that room to the right, was a hallway that led to the back porch, but had bedroom doors to the right (grandparents), and to the left (Joy and Janet), with all the beds being of the brass knobed variety. The timber verandah opened up at the end of the hall, which was divided into another curtained off, but enclosed bedroom to the right (for Elwood, Lindsay and Ronie), and a bathroom to the far left. The central part of the verandah was open to the elements, but had a large striped canvas blind that rolled out to protect the verandah.

I can't ever recall staying with my Rockwell grandparents overnight, as it was probably too crowded to do so, or perhaps too far, but I was definitely bathed there by Nana. The bathroom on the verandah consisted of a footed cast iron bath with a gas fired heater that seemingly exploded into life, but the water was always hot and memories of the soapy fragrance will stay with me forever.

I would amuse myself by thumbing through the wonderful books in the library, or playing with things out of the games cupboard like 'pick up sticks', dominoes and building card houses. But what interested me most was the set of wooden blocks that were covered on every side by picture pieces. I would spend hours making the six different scenes from the set of 24 blocks, or building and breaking down towers. I was never allowed into any of the bedrooms, and was firmly made aware that possessions in those rooms belonged solely to my aunts and uncles.

My grandparents garden was an endless source of fun, especially as I lived in a yard-less flat in Darlington. The rear garden grew vegetables and a choko vine, which covered the outside pull-chain toilet. There were tall 'Kentia' palms, which grew long strands of nuts, and loquat trees with delicious yellow fruit. Grandad also grew passionfruit and I always scoured the vines in search of the delicious black fruit. The front yard was quite steep, and rolling on your side down the slope was also a lot of fun. I remember watching Grandad mow the grass with his rusty old push mower, which I didn't have the strength to move. But probably the highlight, was watching the antics of the birds in the aviary, especially when Grandad went into the aviary to clean or feed his much loved canaries and finches.

I would have been nine or ten years of age when my father first took me down the narrow bush track to the gully, and showed me where he once played with his friends as a child. He took me to all his old haunts including the large trees, rocks and caves that they hid behind, the creek and water pools they swam in, and where turtles could be found. He made the bird-like signals the gang would make to warn one another, whenever intruders were spotted. The whole experience was just so much fun that from then on, upon every future visit to Naremburn, I couldn't wait to descend into the gully and explore.

FROM TOP: The green velvet tablecloth in the loungeroom was matched by green velvet curtains; Framed picture in the loungeroom featured an impressive American Indian Chief in full headress, and a very detailed and colourful still life painting of 'fruit spilling out of a bowl'; The entry to 24 Market St, Naremburn was through the back gate via Adolphus St; All the beds throughout the house were brass knobed. OPPOSITE: A sketch plan of the home at 24 Market St, Naremburn; Loquat trees were grown in the front sloping yard; the hand powered push mower; Nuts fell from the Kentia palms; the set of picture blocks kept kids occupied for hours; Grandad's christmas pudding would be hung from a doorway; the gas water heater worked efficiently, but was a scary relic; the bookshelves were packed with an interesting and varied library; and there were always sweet peas in the garden.

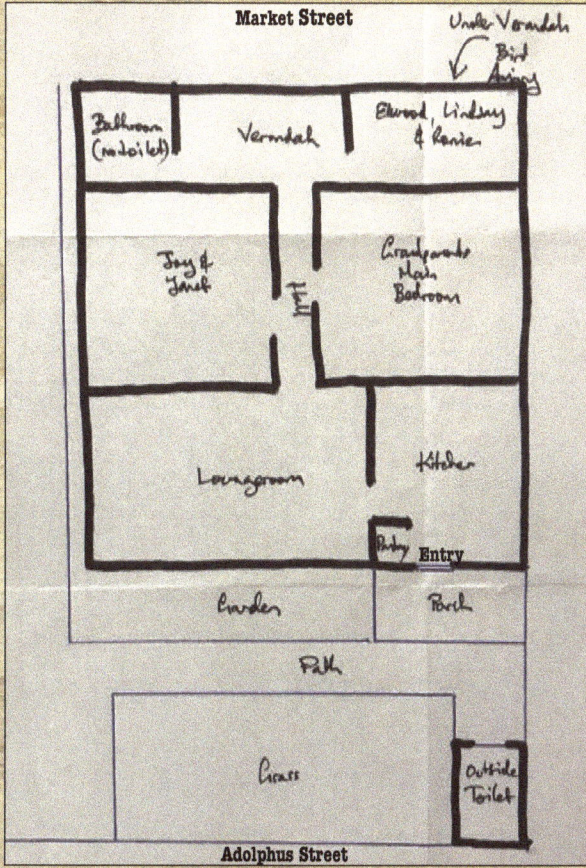

Market Street

Adolphus Street

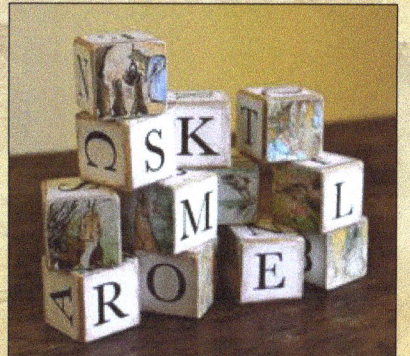

St Cuthbert's Church

Cuthbert (c.634–20 March 687) was a saint of the early Northumbrian church in the Celtic tradition. He was a monk, bishop and hermit, associated with the monasteries of Melrose and Lindisfarne in what might loosely be termed the Kingdom of Northumbria in the North East of England and South East of Scotland. After his death he became one of the most important medieval saints of Northern England, with a cult centred on his tomb at Durham Cathedral. Cuthbert is regarded as the patron saint of Northern England. His feast days are 20th March and 4th September.

In post-World War I Sydney, there was an upsurge in church construction, among which erected was St Cuthbert's Church at Naremburn. Throughout the 1950s, '60s and '70s the Parish of St Cuthbert's Naremburn and the Parish of All Saints' Cammeray were quite busy. In those days, the Sunday Schools had over 350 children attending each week and St Cuthbert's won three cricket premierships in the local competition. At that time, there were four churches, three halls, and two rectories. But by 1997, two of the churches had been disposed of, the three halls had been demolished, and two rectories had been sold. In recent years however, the decline in attendance and congregation size has been slightly reversed.

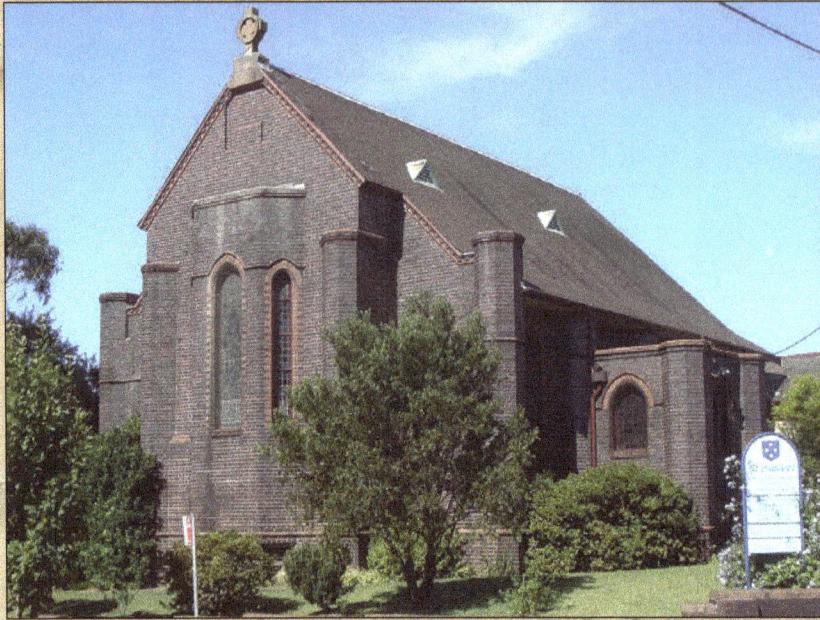

▲ LEFT: St Cuthbert's Church on the corner of Willoughby Rd and Merrenburn Ave, Naremburn, was the hub for many Rockwell baptisms, marriages and funerals from 1927 to 1970. RIGHT: A one year old Kay Rockwell, photographed on the front lawn at 24 Market St, Naremburn, with Grandad's under-deck canary aviary in the background.

children to marry on the 9th April 1966 at the family church, St Cuthbert's, Naremburn.[22]

Sport, Stamps, Gardening and Birds

Outside of the time he spent at work, Bob Rockwell was somehat of a hobbyist, and with six children he relished time to himself. He was quite a decent artist and produced a number of drawings and paintings, which are with various members of the family. Apparently even his brother Ernie and family hold artworks that were painted by Bob Rockwell.

He enjoyed following the horse racing and family didn't ever dare disturb him on a Saturday afternoon. Those were pre-TAB days, when punters placed their bets with 'starting price' (SP) bookmakers, which although illegal, provided access to gambling on horse racing for thousands. It had been the introduction of radio and telephones in Australia that opened the door for starting price bookies. Back then Aussies were only permitted to bet with an on course bookmaker, but 1931 saw the rise of the SP bookie throughout Australia.

SP bookies would often hang around pubs and clubs, conducting their business. Punters wouldn't be able to get a fixed price on their bet until after the race was run, at which point the bookie would be told, via an intermediary or runner, the average odds of each horse from a range of on course bookies. Starting price bookies were technically illegal in Australia, but they flourished none the less thanks to society's needs at the time and everyone feigned ignorance with police.

Possibly due to the moral compass of his masonry, Bob Rockwell was quite prepared to give of his own free time to help others and often donated his weekends to volunteering for the St John Ambulance Brigade, spending his time on the sidelines at various football matches and community events.

Perhaps after taking on the job at the GPO, Bob Rockwell began his stamp collecting, as at work he had access to thousands of cancelled stamps that were usually just thrown away, but were from all around the world. Bob's stamp collection was small by today's standards, but immensely varied and showcased stamps from well over 100 nations, albeit all of them having been cut from cancelled envelopes. The remnants of his collection have today been merged with that of the author.

Another interest, which tangibly helped the household was Bob's love for gardening. He grew peas and beans, tomatoes, rhubarb, choko's, passionfruit and locusts, and his flower garden was also something to be admired with dahlia's, roses and the most amazing and fragrant bouquets of sweet peas.

But his real passion was his birds. Bob managed to erect a substantial aviary under the front porch, enclosed in chicken wire and fitted out with perching rods, sticks and nesting boxes. He stocked the enclosure with budgerigar's, finches and yellow canarie's, which sang the most beautiful of songs of a morning. Tending to his birds, protecting their eggs and helping to rear the nestlings provided him with an ideal interest and delivered a great deal of pleasure.

Personality of Grandad and Nana Rockwell

Grandad was a stern man, who rarely smiled, and who I found a little scary at times. He didn't often reveal his emotions from behind his glasses, but was dignified and often well dressed. He was a firm man, ruled his home and demanded respect from his wife and children. But he was softer with me, and would mutter the phrase... "guda, guda, guda", while he bounced me on his knee, which much warmed me to him. He would show off his garden and the birds, but I was never allowed near anything of value.

On the other hand, although shy and unassuming, Nana Rockwell was the kindest,

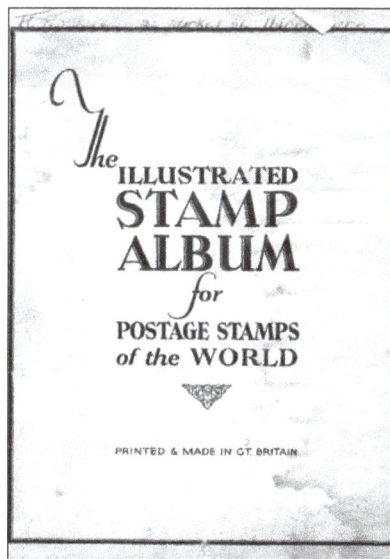

▲TOP: Bob Rockwell's address on the visit of the "Queen Mary." ABOVE (Left): Bob Rockwell's stamp collection consisted of cancelled stamps taken off used envelopes, probably obtained through his work at the GPO. (Right): ABOVE: Bob's main interest was keeping his beloved birds, especially the beautifully voiced songs of the Canary's.

Rockwell Family Recipes

Nana Rockwell's 'Puffdaloons'

INGREDIENTS
2 cups   plain flour
⅓ cup   full-cream milk powder
1 tbsp   baking powder
100g   dripping, suet or clarified butter
      (see Notes)

METHOD
Sift flour, milk powder and baking powder into a bowl and combine. Make a well in the centre and pour in 250 ml (1 cup) water. Using a fork, draw in flour until combined. Turn out dough onto a lightly floured work surface and knead lightly until smooth. Shape into a 2 cm-thick disc. Using a 5 cm biscuit cutter, cut out 14 rounds. Place on a lightly floured tray.

Melt 50g dripping in a heavy-based frying pan over medium heat. Reduce heat to low and carefully add half the dough rounds and cook, turning, for 10 minutes or until cooked through and golden. Drain on paper towel and repeat with remaining dripping and dough. Serve warm with butter and jam.

NOTES
• Dripping is fat that comes away from beef or lamb during cooking and is available clarified from supermarkets and selected butchers.
• Suet is fat that surrounds the kidneys of beef or lamb and is available from butchers.
• Oven temperatures are for conventional; if using fan-forced (convection), reduce the temperature by 20˚C. Use Australian tablespoons and cups (1 teaspoon equals 5 ml; 1 tablespoon equals 20 ml; 1 cup equals 250 ml).
• Serve with butter and 'Rosella jam'

Bob Rockwell's 'Christmas Pudding'

INGREDIENTS
150g   sultanas
150g   currants
1⅔ cup   raisins, halved
150g   pitted dates or prunes, chopped
125g   candied peel
⅓ cup   brandy or sherry
250g   butter
¼ cup   brown sugar
¼ cup   white sugar
3   eggs
85g   slivered almonds
1 cup   plain (all-purpose) flour
1 tsp   ground cinnamon
1 tsp   mixed spice
250g   breadcrumbs
150ml   milk
10   silver threepence's

METHOD
Place the sultanas, currants, raisins, dates, peel and brandy in a large bowl and allow to soak for at least 4 hours or overnight.

Beat the butter, with the brown and white sugar in an electric mixer until light and creamy. Add eggs and beat well. Place the butter mixture in a large bowl along with the sultana mixture, almonds, flour, cinnamon, mixed spice, breadcrumbs and milk. Mix until well combined.

Place pudding mixture in the middle of your prepared piece of calico* and gather up the ends. Tie tightly with string as close to the pudding as possible, making a loop at the end for hanging. Immerse pudding in a large saucepan of boiling water and boil for 4½ hours. Remove pudding from pan (wear rubber gloves to protect your hands) and hang over a sink or bucket on a broomstick so it hangs freely. Allow to dry and cool. Store in the fridge for up to 2 months.**

To reheat, immerse pudding in a saucepan of boiling water and boil for 45 minutes. Allow to drain for 5 minutes before unwrapping.

Insert the silver threepences randomly into the pudding and serve with warm brandy custard. Serves 6–8.

NOTES
*You will need an 80cm-square piece of calico. Rinse it under hot water to remove the starch. Wearing rubber gloves, dip it into boiling water, then wring out. Place ½ cup (125g) plain (all-purpose) flour in the centre of the cloth. Rub in a circular motion to spread in a thin layer about 50cm diameter.
**To prevent the cloth-wrapped pudding from going mouldy due to humidity, wrap it loosely in a tea towel and keep it in the vegetable crisper of the fridge.
***You will know the pudding is hot enough, if the cloth comes away easily.

▲ LEFT: Nana Rockwell's 'Puffdaloons.' RIGHT: The Rockwell 'Christmas Pudding.'

softest and most loving of grandmothers. She always had a smile on her face and often sputted out a little laugh, finding amusement in everything and anything. Nana had the softest skin. She would wear knee high stockings, sometimes with a slip that was longer than her dress, often exuding a pleasant fragrance. She always wore glasses as she had a pronounced condition called 'amblyopia', more commonly known as lazy eye, noted by reduced vision not correctable by glasses, but it was not due to any disease. This affected only one eye, but manifested a reduction of vision in both eyes.

Although Grandad disdained the habit, Nana was an occasional smoker, but she did it most elegantly and prevented staining her fingers with nicotene by holding her cigarettes between a bobby pin. This was in stark contrast to my mother and her family, who all smoked like chimneys. Corelli also loved her glass of sherry when Bob wasn't home.

My most vivid memories are of Nana 'Corelli' Rockwell preparing 'apple and orange', which was simply a mixture of grated green apples combined with the juice of an orange... delicious and so refreshing. My other favourite was a slice of fresh tank loaf bread with butter and golden syrup. Memories of the entire Rockwell family sitting around to enjoy a Sunday baked dinner are also vivid. Grandad would first stand to sharpen the carving knife for a minute of so before using the large knife and fork, to slice the roast and dish out the spoils. Roast potatoes and peas with mint taken directly from the garden usually accompanied the meal, with plenty of bread and butter to go around. At Christmas time, we would be given a helping of Grandad's traditional christmas pudding with custard, which had been hung over a doorway for weeks. Grandad drizzled it with brandy before lighting it up, and a special wish awaited anyone that found one of the hidden silver threepences that had been baked into the pudding. The adults then sat back to play cards and talk over cups of tea, which was usually my cue to play outside and explore the garden.

The Deaths of Robert Archibald & Corelli Rockwell

By his early 60's, Bob Rockwell was gradually losing his strength, and after doing the shopping he had to walk up the Slade Street hill at Naremburn. While never admitting to Corelli, he told his brother Ernie that..."I have trouble getting up that hill unless I put an angenine tablet under my tongue."[23]

Bob's end came one night while he was sleeping, with a cough that forced him to get out of bed for some water. Evidently the coughing became so severe that he collapsed on the floor. Elwood and Corelli tried to hold Bob up and they called Joy and Bill for help, who eventually got him into bed before calling the ambulance. Sadly, Robert Archibald Rockwell died in the early hours of the following morning, the 17th September 1966 of acute pulmonary oedema and myocardial infarction at Royal North Shore Hospital, at just 62 years of age.[24] He was cremated at Northern Suburbs Crematorium three days later and has a memorial plaque there (25VV).

At the time of Bob Rockwell's death, Rock and Betty Rockwell were residing at flat 1 of No.2 Darlington Rd, Darlington and I can still remember my father bursting into tears at the news of his father's sudden death. It was the first time I ever saw my father cry.

Bob Rockwell was first amongst his siblings to die, and was followed by his half-brother, Arthur Clazebrook Carpenter in 1967, and then Alf Rockwell in 1969.[25,26] Bill Rockwell Jr., passed away next in 1970 and was followed in 1971 by Les Carpenter and Jack (Norman) Rockwell in 1972.[27,28,29] Bob's youngest brother Ernie died in 1978, followed by his half-brother Eric Carpenter in 1980 and half-sister Aileen Sampson in 1985, who reached the celebrated age of 95.[30,31,32]

More grandchildren arrived following Bob Rockwell's death with Robert William Hyde being born to Joy and Bill Hyde on the 21st February 1967.[33] Robert was closely followed by two sons for Janet and Roley Whiting with Stephen Hunter Whiting arriving on the 20th August 1968, and then Adam Roger Whiting being born on the 18th September 1971.[34,35]

After Bob's death, Corelli continued to reside in the house at 24 Market Street, Naremburn with Elwood, who was quite happy to remain at home, and this also gave Corelli a purpose and some company. But Elwood often rolled into the house drunk, so Corelli occasionally stayed with her other married children Joy, Rock and Lindsay for extended periods. Corelli's older half-sister Valtie Chisholm, also occasionally popped in, and despite losing her own husband Jack Chisholm in 1963, Valtie lived for another 11 years before she too passed away in 1974 at the respectable age of 83.[36]

Not long after Ronie returned from Germany in 1966-67, he met and established a defacto relationship with Cheryl Joy Pooley (1945-2013). After much difficulty for Cheryl in falling pregnant, their first child Samuel Joshua Rockwell, was eventually conceived and

Death Notice

ROCKWELL, Robert Archibald, September 17, 1966 (suddenly) at hospital. Of Naremburn, beloved husband of Octavio Corelli and loved father of Joy (Mrs Hyde), Robert, Elwood, Lindsay, Ronie, and Janet (Mrs Whiting).

Funeral Notices

ROCKWELL. The funeral of the late Mr Robert Archibald Rockwell, of Naremburn, will leave St. Cuthbert's Church of England, Willoughby Road and Merrenburn Avenue, Naremburn tomorrow (Tuesday) after service commencing at 3:00pm for the Northern Suburbs Crematorium.

ROCKWELL. Lodge North Shore 440 U.G.L. of New South Wales. The officers and brethren of the above lodge are requested to attend the funeral of their late Wor. Bro., Robert Archibald Rockwell. For particulars see family notice.
G.L. Roberts W.M.
G.C. Hardwick, Secretary

ROCKWELL. Lodge Northern Chapter No.284 Rose Croix of Heredom. The officers and brethren of the above lodge kindly invited to attend the funeral of the late esteemed member, Brother Robert Archibald Rockwell M.W.S. For funeral arrangements see family notice.
J.W. Bull, Recorder
SMH, 19th September, 1966

Column		
DEATHS registered in the District of Sydney, at St. Leonards. in the State of New South Wales by Neville Solomon Lazarus. Assistant District Registrar.		
1. No. in Register		2720.
2. Christian name and surname of deceased; Occupation		Robert Archibald ROCKWELL. Postal Clerk.
3. Sex and age		Male. 62 years.
4. When and where died; Usual residence		17th September, 1966. The Royal North Shore Hospital of Sydney, St. Leonards. 24 Market Street, Naremburn.
5. Where born; Length of residence in Australia		Sydney, N.S.W. -
6. Christian name and surname of father; Occupation; Christian name and maiden surname of mother		William Henry Rockwell Horse and Cab Owner. Elizabeth Barton.
If deceased was married— 7. Where; At what age; To whom; Conjugal condition of deceased at time of death		Glebe, N.S.W. 22 years. Octavia Corelli O'Sullivan. Married.
8. Issue in order of birth (living and deceased)		Joy C. 38 years, Robert H. 36, Elwood L. 33. Lindsay A. 29, Ronie M. 23. Janet L. 20. None deceased.
9. Name, description and residence of informant		O. C. Rockwell, Widow. 6 Quist Avenue, Hillview.
10. Cause of death; Duration of last illness; By whom certified		1. (a) Acute pulmonary oedema. hours. (b) Myocardial infarct. days. I. R. Fielding. Registered.
11. When and where buried or cremated; Undertaker or Superintendent by whom certified		20th September, 1966. Northern Suburbs Crematorium. R. McLeod. Superintendent.
12. Name and religion of Minister; Names of witnesses to burial or cremation		A. W. Hayman. Church of England. E. W. Warburton.
13. Signature of Assistant District Registrar; Date of registration		Lazarus 26th September, 1966.

Mourners at Robert Archibald Rockwell's Funeral, 20 Sept 1966

Immediate family not recorded...

Shirley & Philip	Aunty	H. Irving & family	?
Judy & Les Mulroy	Nephew	Kitty & George Austin	?
Freda Hine [Bantin]	Cousin	Margaret Jackson	?
Sister Valtie [Chisholm]	Sister-in-law	Mrs Laws (Topsy)	Grocers
Ernie & Alice Rockwell	Brother	Mr & Mrs Williams & family	?
Mrs Cashel	Betty's mother	Mr & Mrs Gooding	?
George & Bell Bantin	Cousin	Bill & Sylvia Byrne	?
W. Stretton & family	Coral's father	Harriette & Boys	?
Lil Edwards [Jones]	Cousin	Mrs Stone & family	?
Francis [Bantin] & Les Carroll	Cousin	J.M. & John Bull	?
Florrie, Linda [Bantin] & family	Cousin	Les [Carpenter]	Half-brother
Mr & Mrs E.P. Haylen? & family	?	Lilly [Edwards, nee Bantin]	Cousin
Ivy & A. D. Faunce	?	T.H. Skelton, Director - Post & Telegraphs	
Spencer Whitehead	?	The Parcels & Bulk Postage Counter G.P.O.	
Errol	?	The Most Excellent First Grand Principal, Officers	
Wendy & Bruce Smith	?	and Companions of the Supreme Grand Chapter	
Clive Gilder	?	of Royal Arch Masons of NSW.	

▲TOP (Left): Death & Funeral Notices for Robert Archibald Rockwell. (Right): Death Certificate for Robert Archibald Rockwell, 17th September 1966 (NSW BDM #27190/1966), just four days short of his 40th wedding anniversary. ABOVE: List of mourners at the funeral.

IN MEMORY OF
ROBERT ARCHIBALD ROCKWELL
A LOVED HUSBAND AND FATHER
DIED 17TH SEPTEMBER 1966
AGED 62 YEARS

IN MEMORY OF
OCTAVIA CORELLI ROCKWELL
LOVED WIFE AND MOTHER
DIED 4TH JULY 1976
AGED 74 YEARS

REGISTRATION NUMBER
15733/1976

NEW SOUTH WALES
REGISTER OF DEATHS

Surname of deceased	ROCKWELL
Other names	Octavia Corelli
Occupation	-
Sex and Age	Female 75 years
Marital status	Widow
Date of death	4th July, 1976
Place of death	Meadowbank (Laurels Nursing Home)
Usual residence	34 See Street, Meadowbank
Place of birth	Sydney, N.S.W.
Father - Surname	O'SULLIVAN
Other names	Humphrey
Mother - Maiden surname	SHOVELLOR
Other names	Lenore
Place of marriage	Sydney, N.S.W.
Age at marriage	24 years
To whom married	Robert Rockwell
Children of marriage	Joy 49 years, Robert 47, Elwood 43, Lindsey 38, Rowie 33, Janet 30
Informant	J.C. Hyde, daughter 1 Pearl Parade, Pearl Beach
Cause of death	(a) Bilateral bronchopneumonia 3 days (b) Cerebral atherosclerosis 3 years
By whom certified	M.J. Sevier, Medical Practitioner
Particulars of burial or cremation	6th July, 1976 Northern Suburbs Crematorium
Particulars of registration	*J.B. Holliday* Principal Registrar	Date 14th July, 1976 Number 15733

Before accepting copies, sight unaltered original. The original has a coloured background.

REGISTRY OF BIRTHS
DEATHS AND MARRIAGES

SYDNEY   20 March 2020

I hereby certify that this is a true copy of particulars recorded in a Register in the State of New South Wales, in the Commonwealth of Australia

Registrar

▲ *TOP (Left): Memorial for Robert Archibald Rockwell at Northern Suburbs Crematorium, Sydney. (Right): Memorial for Octavia Corelli Rockwell (nee O'Sullivan) at Northern Suburbs Crematorium, Sydney. ABOVE: Death Certificate for Octavia Corelli Rockwell (NSW BDM #15733/1976).*

arrived on the 11th of September 1974.[37]

Although Corelli continued to live at Naremburn for most of her declining years, towards the end of her life she had to be cared for as a resident of the Laurels Nursing Home, Meadowbank. She suffered from thyroid complications and dementia, and was going blind from glaucoma, possibly because she wasn't given the appropriate medication.

Despite surviving her husband Bob Rockwell by a good ten years, Octavia Corelli Rockwell sadly passed away on the 4th July 1976.[38] She was cremated and has a memorial alongside her husband at Northern Suburbs Crematorium (*25VV*). Corelli's younger sister

Goldie Mulroy was the last to die, but being as the O'Sullivans were descended from ancient Irish heritage, it was fitting that she passed away on St Patrick's Day, the 17th March 1982, aged 77.[39] Remarkably, Bob and Corelli's 14th and last grandchild was born to Ronie and Cheryl Rockwell on the exact anniversary of Corelli's death, when Jessica Molly Rockwell arrived on the 4th July 1977.[40]

Where To From Here?

The union between Robert and Corelli Rockwell delivered six children and all survived into adulthood. Five went on to marry and they collectively produced 14 grandchildren, with numerous great grandchildren resulting. The final chapter of this book reveals all that is known of Robert and Corelli's children and their descendants.

References

1. NSW Dept of BDM. (1946). Birth Certificate for Janet Lenore Rockwell, #?/1946.
2. NSW Dept of BDM. (1946). Death Certificate for George Lorraine Shoveller, #20194/1946.
3. Hyde, Joy, 1927-2018 (Interviewee, 2001). 'Joy Hyde (nee Rockwell). interviewed by Tracy Rockwell on the 19th of August 2001, at Aspley, Brisbane.'
4. Rockwell, Alice, 1911-1997 (Interviewee, 1980). 'Alice Rockwell (nee Greenup) interviewed by Tracy Rockwell on the 12th of June 1980, at Kyeemagh, Sydney.'
5. NSW Dept of BDM. (1954). Marriage Certificate for Robert Hunter Rockwell and Betty Jean Wardle, #198/1954.
6. Rockwell, Lindsay, 1937- (Interviewee, 2014). 'Lindsay A. Rockwell interviewed by Tracy Rockwell on the 22nd of November 2014, at Chain Valley Bay'.
7. NSW Dept of BDM. (1955). Death Certificate for Elizabeth Rockwell (Carpenter, nee Bantin), #9914/1955.
8. Rockwell, Alice, 1911-1997 (Interviewee, 1980). op.cit.
9. NSW Dept of BDM. (1955). Birth Certificate for Tracy Paul Rockwell, #?/1955.
10. NSW Dept of BDM. (1957). Marriage Certificate for Lindsay Archibald Rockwell and Lynette Ellen Watson, #18138/1957.
11. NSW Dept of BDM. (1959). Birth Certificate for Robert Wayne Rockwell, #?/1959.
12. NSW Dept of BDM. (1960). Birth Certificate for Rhonda Janine Rockwell, #?/1960.
13. NSW Dept of BDM. (1961). Marriage Certificate for Ronie Malcolm Rockwell and Coral Joy Stretton, #1212/1961.
14. NSW Dept of BDM. (1961). Birth Certificate for Brett Anthony Rockwell, #?/1961.
15. NSW Dept of BDM. (1962). Birth Certificate for Mark Malcolm Rockwell, #?/1962.
16. NSW Dept of BDM. (1965). Birth Certificate for Paul Steven Rockwell, #?/1965.
17. NSW Dept of BDM. (1962). Birth Certificate for Glen Lindsay Rockwell, #?/1962.
18. NSW Dept of BDM. (1963). Death Certificate for Robert Wayne Rockwell, #24088/1963.
19. NSW Dept of BDM. (1964). Birth Certificate for Sandra Kay Rockwell, #?/1964.
20. NSW Dept of BDM. (1965). Marriage Certificate for Janet Lenore Rockwell and Roland Lawrence Whiting, #19723/1965.
21. NSW Dept of BDM. (1965). Birth Certificate for Michele Lenore Whiting #?/1965.
22. NSW Dept of BDM. (1966). Marriage Certificate for Joy Corelli Rockwell and William Hyde, #194051965.
23. Hyde, Joy, 1927-2018 (Interviewee, 2001). op. cit.
24. NSW Dept of BDM. (1966). Death Certificate for Robert Archibald Rockwell, #27190/1966.
25. NSW Dept of BDM. (1967). Death Certificate for Arthur Clazebrook Carpenter, #24421/1967.
26. NSW Dept of BDM. (1969). Death Certificate for Alfred Barrett Rockwell, #30108/1969.
27. NSW Dept of BDM. (1970). Death Certificate for William Henry Rockwell Jr., #42096/1970.
28. Victorian Dept of BDM. (1966). Death Certificate for Leslie Harold Carpenter, #?/1966.
29. NSW Dept of BDM. (1973). Death Certificate for Norman JohnRockwell, #65959/1973.
30. NSW Dept of BDM. (1978). Death Certificate for Ernest Barrett Rockwell, #13359/1978.
31. NSW Dept of BDM. (1980). Death Certificate for Eric D'Arcy Carpenter, #8408/1980.
32. NSW Dept of BDM. (1985). Death Certificate for Aileen Vera Sampson, #173431985.
33. NSW Dept of BDM. (1967). Birth Certificate for Robert William Hyde #?/1967.
34. NSW Dept of BDM. (1968). Birth Certificate for Steven Hunter Whiting #?/1968.
35. NSW Dept of BDM. (1971). Birth Certificate for Adam Roger Whiting #?/1971.
36. NSW Dept of BDM. (1974). Death Certificate for Valtiveredo Calceolaria Chisholm (Malins, nee Mackie). #40229/1974.
37. NSW Dept of BDM. (1974). Birth Certificate for Samuel Joshua Rockwell, #?/1974.
38. NSW Dept of BDM. (1976). Death Certificate for Octavia Corelli Rockwell (nee O'Sullivan), #15733/1976.
39. NSW Dept of BDM. (1982). Death Certificate for Goldie Alathea Mulroy (nee O'Sullivan), #102136/1982
40. NSW Dept of BDM. (1977). Birth Certificate for Jessica Molly Rockwell, #?/1977.
41. Wikipedia - Masonry [https://en.wikipedia.org/wiki/Masonry.
42. Recollections of Tracy Rockwell, eldest grandchild of Robert & Corelli Rockwell (Recorded 2021).

Chapter Seventeen

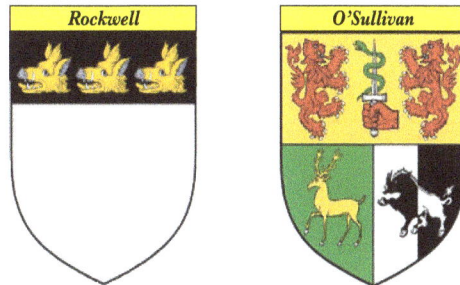

THE DESCENDANTS OF ROBERT & CORELLI ROCKWELL

Robert Archibald and Octavia Corelli Rockwell (nee O'Sullivan) left a legacy of six children, 14 grandchildren and at the time of publication, there were some 24 great grandchildren, who have become the most numerous branch of the Rockwell family in Australia. The following information is all that is currently known about these descendants and their respective families.

1. Joy Corelli Rockwell (1927-2018)

Joy Corelli Rockwell was born on the 13th April 1927, whilst her family and grandfather William Henry Rockwell, were residing at 48 Slade Street. She was the first child born to Bob and Corelli Rockwell, and was baptised at St. Cuthbert's Church, Naremburn. Joy wouldn't have remembered her grandfather William Henry Rockwell, who passed away when she was just four years of age, but both grandmothers, Lenore O'Sullivan and Elizabeth Rockwell were well known to her. She attended Naremburn Public School and Willoughby Girls High School. Being the eldest, piano was an essential skill for Joy and she became a second mother to her younger siblings and was a permanent part of the Rockwell

 Bignell
 Clarke
 Eastman
 Grey
 Hann
 Hazard
 Hewitt
 Lamborn

Chart 17.0
Ancestors & Descendants of
Robert Archibald & Octavia Corelli
Rockwell of Naremburn, NSW
▲ = Served in Australian Military Forces

Rockwell

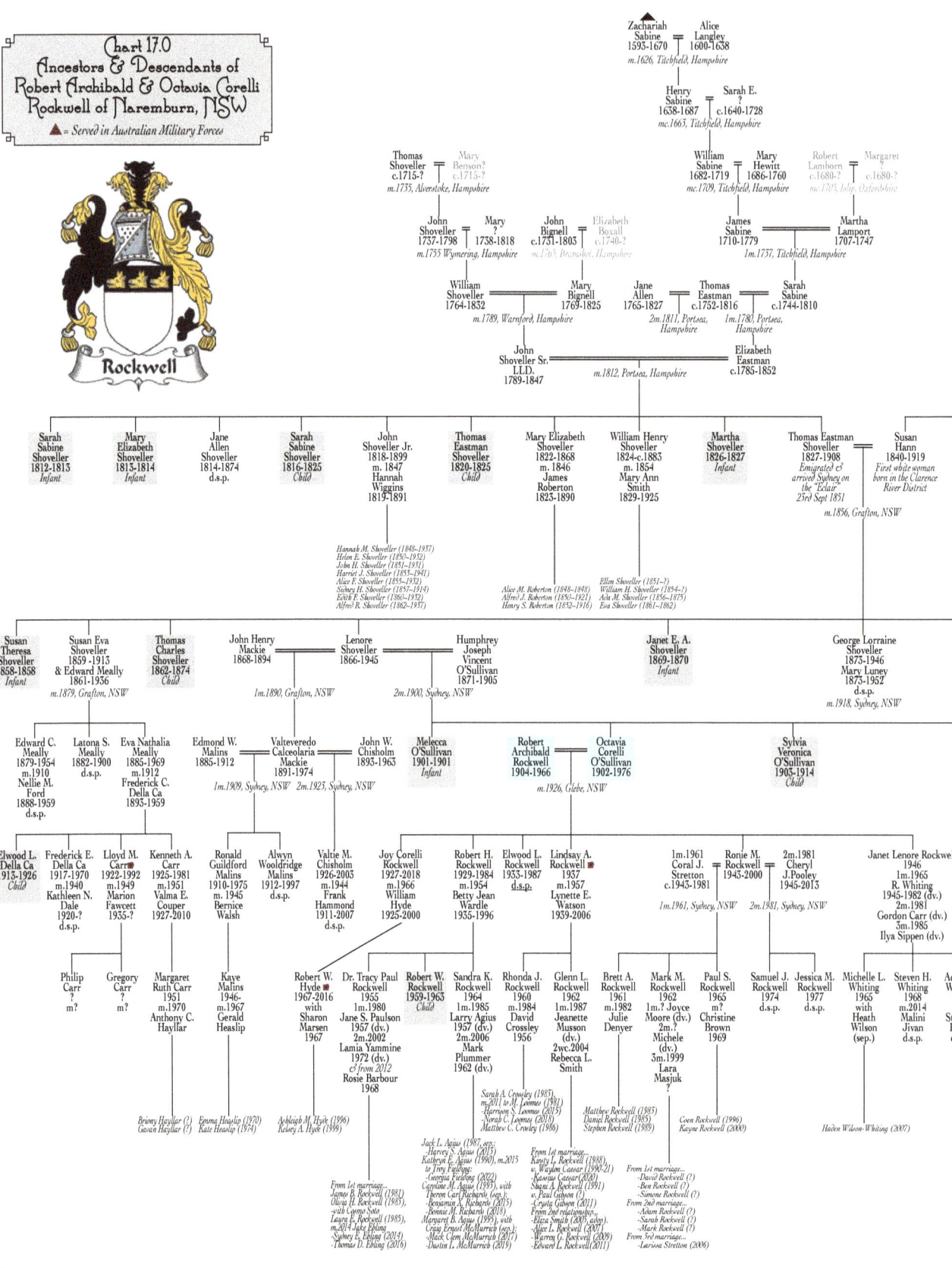

Zachariah Sabine 1593-1670 = Alice Langley 1600-1638
m.1626, Titchfield, Hampshire

Henry Sabine 1638-1687 = Sarah E. ? c.1640-1728
mc.1663, Titchfield, Hampshire

William Sabine 1682-1719 = Mary Hewitt 1686-1760
mc.1709, Titchfield, Hampshire

Robert Lamborn c.1680-? = Margaret ? c.1680-?
mc.1705, Islip, Oxfordshire

Thomas Shoveller c.1715-? = Mary Benson? c.1715-?
m.1755, Alverstoke, Hampshire

James Sabine 1710-1779 = Martha Lamport 1707-1747
1m.1737, Titchfield, Hampshire

John Shoveller 1737-1798 = Mary ? 1738-1818
m.1755 Wymering, Hampshire

John Bignell c.1751-1803 = Elizabeth Boxall c.1740-?
m.1765, Broxnshot, Hampshire

Jane Allen 1765-1827 = Thomas Eastman c.1752-1816 = Sarah Sabine c.1744-1810
2m.1811, Portsea, Hampshire 1m.1780, Portsea, Hampshire

William Shoveller 1764-1832 = Mary Bignell 1769-1825
m.1789, Warnford, Hampshire

John Shoveller Sr. LLD. 1789-1847 = Elizabeth Eastman c.1785-1852
m.1812, Portsea, Hampshire

Sarah Sabine Shoveller 1812-1813 Infant
Mary Elizabeth Shoveller 1813-1814 Infant
Jane Allen Shoveller 1814-1874 d.s.p.
Sarah Sabine Shoveller 1816-1825 Child
John Shoveller Jr. 1818-1899 m. 1847 Hannah Wiggins 1819-1891
Thomas Eastman Shoveller 1820-1825 Child
Mary Elizabeth Shoveller 1822-1868 m. 1846 James Roberton 1823-1890
William Henry Shoveller 1824-c.1883 m. 1854 Mary Ann Smith 1829-1925
Martha Shoveller 1826-1827 Infant
Thomas Eastman Shoveller 1827-1908 Emigrated & arrived Sydney on the "Eclair" 23rd Sept 1851 = Susan Hann 1840-1919 First white woman born in the Clarence River District
m.1856, Grafton, NSW

Hannah M. Shoveller (1848-1937)
Helen E. Shoveller (1850-1932)
John H. Shoveller (1851-1951)
Harriet J. Shoveller (1853-1941)
Alice F. Shoveller (1855-1932)
Sidney H. Shoveller (1857-1914)
Edith F. Shoveller (1860-1952)
Alfred R. Shoveller (1862-1937)

Alice M. Roberton (1848-1848)
Alfred J. Roberton (1850-1921)
Henry S. Roberton (1852-1916)

Ellen Shoveller (1851-?)
William H. Shoveller (1854-?)
Ada M. Shoveller (1856-1875)
Eva Shoveller (1861-1862)

Susan Theresa Shoveller 1858-1858 Infant
Susan Eva Shoveller 1859 -1913 & Edward Mealy 1861-1936 m.1879, Grafton, NSW
Thomas Charles Shoveller 1862-1874 Child
John Henry Mackie 1868-1894 = Lenore Shoveller 1866-1945 = Humphrey Joseph Vincent O'Sullivan 1871-1905
1m.1890, Grafton, NSW   2m.1900, Sydney, NSW
Janet E. A. Shoveller 1869-1870 Infant
George Lorraine Shoveller 1873-1952 = Mary Luney 1873-1952 d.s.p. m.1918, Sydney, NSW

Edward C. Meally 1879-1954 m.1910 Nellie M. Ford 1888-1959 d.s.p.
Latona S. Meally 1882-1900 d.s.p.
Eva Nathalia Meally 1885-1969 m.1912 Frederick C. Della Ca 1893-1959
Edmond W. Malins 1885-1912
Valteveredo Calceolaria Mackie 1891-1974 1m.1909, Sydney, NSW 2m.1923, Sydney, NSW
John W. Chisholm 1893-1963
Melecca O'Sullivan 1901-1901 Infant
Robert Archibald Rockwell 1904-1966 = Octavia Corelli O'Sullivan 1902-1976 m.1926, Glebe, NSW
Sylvia Veronica O'Sullivan 1903-1914 Child

Elwood L. Della Ca 1913-1926 Child
Frederick E. Della Ca 1917-1970 m.1940 Kathleen N. Dale 1920-? d.s.p.
Lloyd M. Carr 1922-1992 m.1949 Marion Fawcett 1935-?
Kenneth A. Carr 1925-1981 m.1951 Valma E. Couper 1927-2010
Ronald Guildford Malins 1910-1975 m. 1945 Bernice Walsh
Alwyn Wooldridge Malins 1912-1997 d.s.p.
Valtie M. Chisholm 1926-2003 m.1944 Frank Hammond 1911-2007 d.s.p.
Joy Corelli Rockwell 1927-2018 m.1966 William Hyde 1925-2000
Robert H. Rockwell 1929-1984 m.1954 Betty Jean Wardle 1935-1996
Elwood L. Rockwell 1933-1987 d.s.p.
Lindsay A. Rockwell 1937 m.1957 Lynette E. Watson 1939-2006
1m.1961 Coral J. Stretton c.1943-1981 = Ronie M. Rockwell 1943-2000 = 2m.1981 Cheryl J.Pooley 1945-2013
1m.1961, Sydney, NSW 2m.1981, Sydney, NSW
Janet Lenore Rockwell 1946 1m.1965 R. Whiting 1945-1982 (dv.) 2m.1981 Gordon Carr (dv.) 3m.1985 Ilya Sippen (dv.)

Philip Carr ? m?
Gregory Carr ? m?
Margaret Ruth Carr 1951 m.1970 Anthony C. Hayllar
Kaye Malins 1946- m.1967 Gerald Heaslip
Robert W. Hyde 1967-2016 with Sharon Marsen 1967
Dr. Tracy Paul Rockwell 1955 1m.1980 Jane S. Paulson 1957 (dv.) 2m.2002 Lamia Yammine 1972 (dv.) & from 2012 Rosie Barbour 1968
Robert W. Rockwell 1959-1963 Child
Sandra K. Rockwell 1964 1m.1985 Larry Agius 1957 (dv.) 2m.2006 Mark Plummer 1962 (dv.)
Rhonda J. Rockwell 1960 m.1984 David Crossley 1956
Glenn L. Rockwell 1962 1m.1987 Jeanette Musson (dv.) 2wc.2004 Rebecca L. Smith
Brett A. Rockwell 1961 m.1982 Julie Denyer
Mark M. Rockwell 1962 1m.? Joyce Moore (dv.) 2m.? Michele (dv.) 3m.1999 Lara Masjuk ?
Paul S. Rockwell 1965 m? Christine Brown 1969
Samuel J. Rockwell 1974 d.s.p.
Jessica M. Rockwell 1977 d.s.p.
Michelle L. Whiting 1965 with Heath Wilson (sep.)
Steven H. Whiting 1968 m.2014 Malini Jivan d.s.p.
Adam Whiting 1971 with Stephen Burns d.s.p.

Briony Hayllar (?)
Gavin Hayllar (?)
Emma Heaslip (1970)
Kate Heaslip (1974)
Ayhleigh M. Hyde (1996)
Kelsey A. Hyde (1999)

Sarah A. Crossley (1985)
Harrison S. Loomes (1981)
Norah C. Loomes (2018)
Matthew C. Crossley (1986)

Matthew Rockwell (1983)
Daniel Rockwell (1985)
Stephen Rockwell (1989)

Coen Rockwell (1996)
Kayne Rockwell (2000)

Haiden Wilson-Whiting (2007)

Jack L. Agius (1987, sep.):
-Harvey S. Agius (2015)
Kathryn E. Agius (1990), m.2015 to Troy Fielding:
-Georgia Fielding (2022)
Caroline M. Agius (1993), with Theron Carl Richards (sep.):
-Benjamin X. Richards (2015)
-Bonnie M. Richards (2018)
Margaret B. Agius (1995), with Craig Ernest McMurrich (sep.):
-Mack Cleim McMurrich (2017)
-Dustin L. McMurrich (2019)

From 1st marriage...
-James B. Rockwell (1981)
Olivia H. Rockwell (1983), with Cosmo Soto
Laura E. Rockwell (1985), m.2014 Jake Ebling
-Sydney E. Ebling (2014)
-Thomas D. Ebling (2016)

From 1st marriage...
Kasity L. Rockwell (1988), w. Waylon Caesar (1990-21)
-Kassius Caesar (2020)
Sami A. Rockwell (1991), w. Paul Gibson (?)
-Crysta Gibson (2011)
From 2nd relationship...
-Eliza Smith (2005, adpt.)
Alice L. Rockwell (2007)
-Warren G. Rockwell (2009)
Edward L. Rockwell (2011)

From 1st marriage...
-David Rockwell (?)
-Ben Rockwell (?)
-Simone Rockwell (?)
From 2nd marriage...
-Adam Rockwell (?)
-Sarah Rockwell (?)
-Mark Rockwell (?)
From 3rd marriage...
-Larissa Stretton (2006)

Coats of arms: Lane · Martin · Plowman · Sabine · Samways · Seymour · Shoveller · Thompson

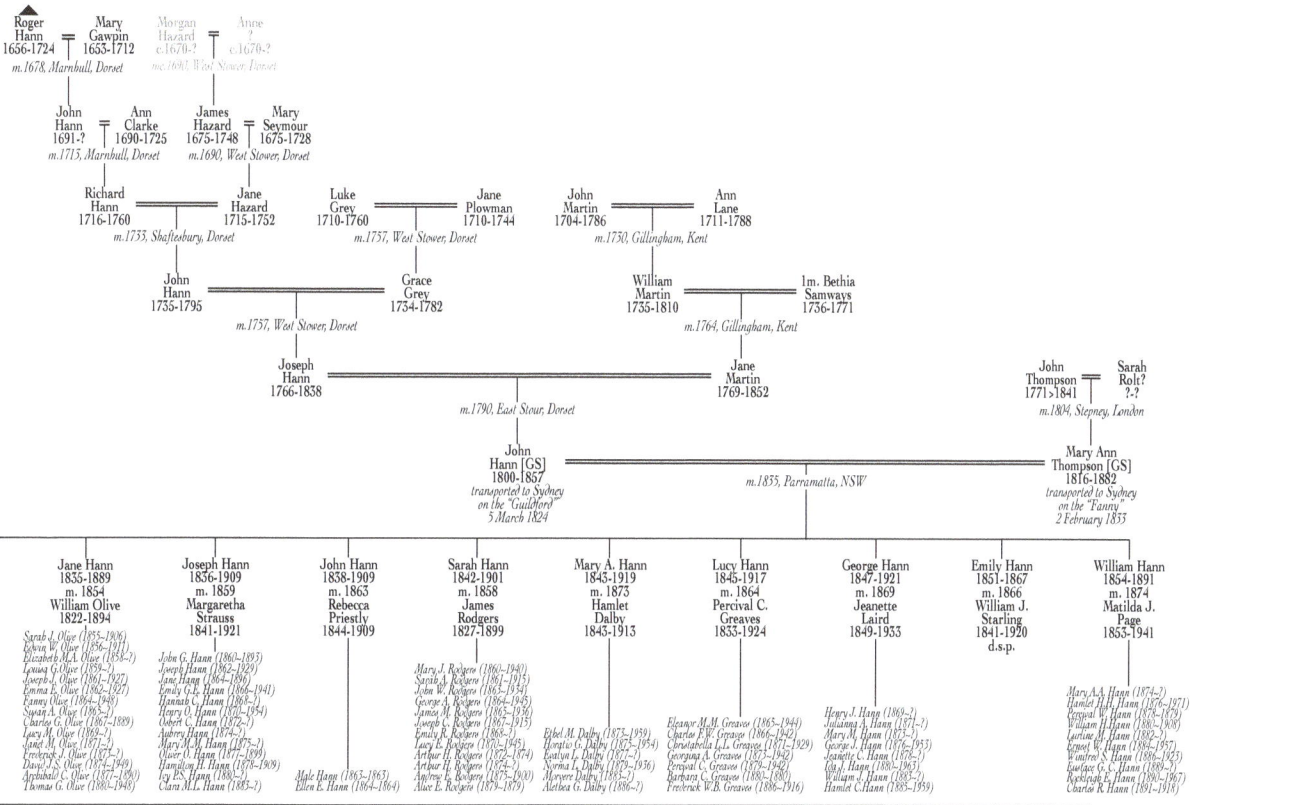

Roger Hann 1656-1724 = Mary Gawpin 1653-1712 — m.1678, Marnhull, Dorset

Morgan Hazard c.1670-? = Anne ? c.1670-? — m.1690, West Stower, Dorset

John Hann 1691-? = Ann Clarke 1690-1725 — m.1713, Marnhull, Dorset
James Hazard 1675-1748 = Mary Seymour 1675-1728 — m.1690, West Stower, Dorset

Richard Hann 1716-1760 = Jane Hazard 1715-1752 — m.1733, Shaftesbury, Dorset
Luke Grey 1710-1760 = Jane Plowman 1710-1744 — m.1757, West Stower, Dorset
John Martin 1704-1786 = Ann Lane 1711-1788 — m.1750, Gillingham, Kent

John Hann 1735-1795 = Grace Grey 1734-1782 — m.1757, West Stower, Dorset
William Martin 1735-1810 = 1m. Bethia Samways 1736-1771 — m.1764, Gillingham, Kent

Joseph Hann 1766-1838 = Jane Martin 1769-1852 — m.1790, East Stour, Dorset
John Thompson 1771>1841 = Sarah Rolt? ?-? — m.1804, Stepney, London

John Hann [GS] 1800-1857, transported to Sydney on the "Guildford" 5 March 1824 = Mary Ann Thompson [GS] 1816-1882, transported to Sydney on the "Fanny" 2 February 1833 — m.1855, Parramatta, NSW

Children of John Hann & Mary Ann Thompson:

Jane Hann 1835-1889, m.1854, William Olive 1822-1894
Sarah J. Olive (1855-1906); Edwin W. Olive (1856-1911); Elizabeth M.A Olive (1858-?); Louisa G. Olive (1859-?); Joseph J. Olive (1861-1927); Emma E. Olive (1862-1927); Fanny Olive (1864-1948); Susan A. Olive (1865-?); Charles G. Olive (1867-1889); Lucy M. Olive (1869-?); Janet M. Olive (1871-?); Oliver C. Olive (1872-1899); David J.S. Olive (1874-1949); Archibald C. Olive (1877-1890); Thomas G. Olive (1880-1948)

Joseph Hann 1836-1909, m.1859, Margaretha Strauss 1841-1921
John G. Hann (1860-1893); Joseph Hann (1862-1929); Jane Hann (1864-1896); Emily G.E. Hann (1866-1941); Hannah C. Hann (1868-?); Henry O. Hann (1870-1954); Robert C. Hann (1872-?); Aubrey Hann (1874-?); Mary M.M. Hann (1875-?); Oliver O. Hann (1877-1899); Hamilton H. Hann (1878-1909); Ivy P.S. Hann (1880-?); Clara M.L. Hann (1885-?)

John Hann 1838-1909, m.1863, Rebecca Priestly 1844-1909
Male Hann (1863-1863); Ellen E. Hann (1864-1864)

Sarah Hann 1842-1901, m.1858, James Rodgers 1827-1899
Mary J. Rodgers (1860-1940); Sarah A. Rodgers (1861-1915); John W. Rodgers (1863-1934); George A. Rodgers (1864-1945); James M. Rodgers (1865-1936); Joseph G. Rodgers (1867-1915); Emily R. Rodgers (1868-?); Lucy E. Rodgers (1870-1945); Arthur H. Rodgers (1872-1874); Evelyn L. Rodgers (1873-?); Arthur P. Rodgers (1874-?); Norma L. Rodgers (1877-?); Andrew E. Rodgers (1875-1900); Alice E. Rodgers (1879-1879)

Mary A. Hann 1843-1919, m.1873, Hamlet Dalby 1843-1913
Ethel M. Dalby (1873-1959); Horatio G. Dalby (1875-1954); Evelyn L. Dalby (1877-?); Norma L. Dalby (1879-1936); Maryere Dalby (1883-?); Aletheas G. Dalby (1886-?)

Lucy Hann 1845-1917, m.1864, Percival C. Greaves 1833-1924
Eleanor M.M. Greaves (1865-1944); Charles F.W. Greaves (1866-1942); Christabella L.L. Greaves (1871-1929); Georgina A. Greaves (1873-1942); Percival C. Greaves (1879-1942); Barbara C. Greaves (1880-1880); Frederick W.B. Greaves (1886-1916)

George Hann 1847-1921, m.1869, Jeanette Laird 1849-1933
Henry J. Hann (1869-?); Julianna A. Hann (1871-?); Mary M. Hann (1873-?); Olive M. Hann (1876-1953); Jeanette C. Hann (1878-?); Ida J. Hann (1880-1965); William J. Hann (1883-?); Hamlet C. Hann (1885-1959)

Emily Hann 1851-1867, m.1866, William J. Starling 1841-1920, d.s.p.

William Hann 1854-1891, m.1874, Matilda J. Page 1853-1941
Mary A.A. Hann (1874-?); Hamlet H.H. Hann (1876-1971); William H. Hann (1880-1900); Lurline M. Hann (1882-?); Ernest W. Hann (1886-1957); Winifred S. Hann (1886-1925); Ruelace G.S. Hann (1888-?); Rockleah E. Hann (1890-1967); Charles R. Hann (1891-1918)

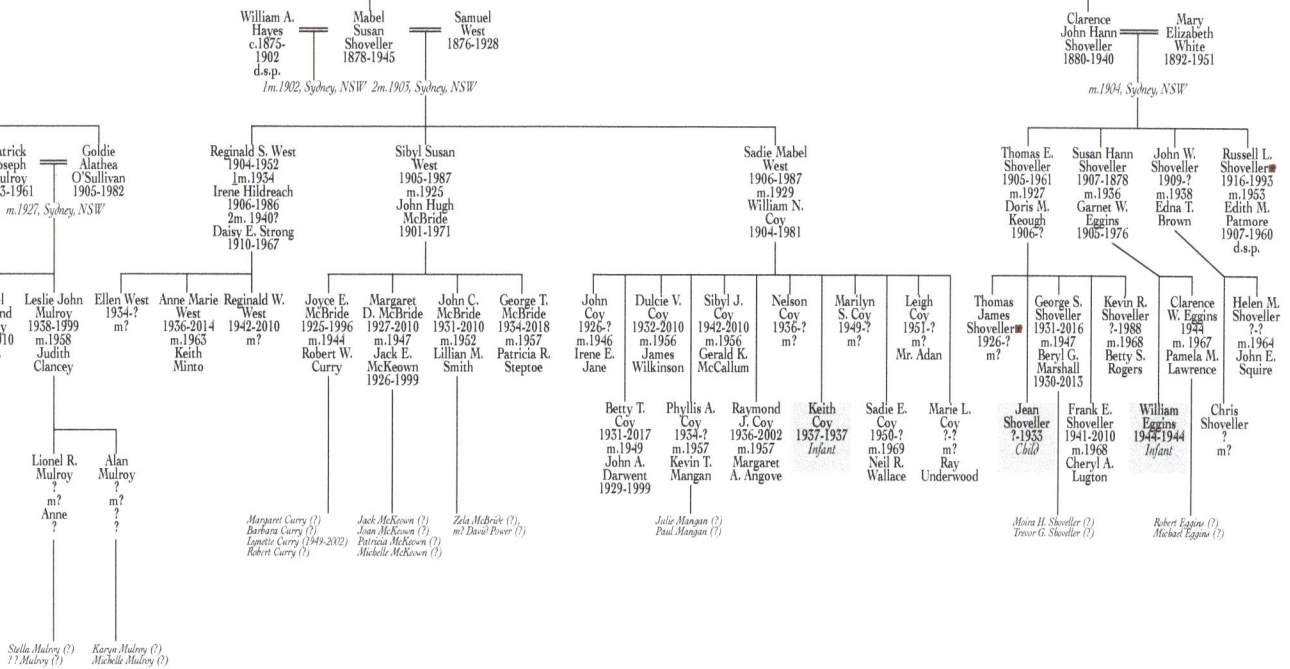

William A. Hayes c.1875-1902 d.s.p. = Mabel Susan Shoveller 1878-1945 = Samuel West 1876-1928 — 1m.1902, Sydney, NSW 2m.1903, Sydney, NSW

Clarence John Hann Shoveller 1880-1940 = Mary Elizabeth White 1892-1951 — m.1904, Sydney, NSW

Patrick Joseph Mulroy [1]903-1961 = Goldie Alathea O'Sullivan 1905-1982 — m.1927, Sydney, NSW

Reginald S. West 1904-1952, 1m.1934 Irene Hildreach 1906-1986, 2m. 1940? Daisy E. Strong 1910-1967
Sibyl Susan West 1905-1987, m.1925, John Hugh McBride 1901-1971
Sadie Mabel West 1906-1987, m.1929, William N. Coy 1904-1981
Thomas E. Shoveller 1905-1961, m.1927, Doris M. Keough 1906-?
Susan Hann Shoveller 1907-1878, m.1936, Garnet W. Eggins 1905-1976
John W. Shoveller 1909-?, m.1938, Edna T. Brown
Russell L. Shoveller 1916-1993, m.1953, Edith M. Patmore 1907-1960 d.s.p.

...el ...ond ...roy ...2010 p.
Leslie John Mulroy 1938-1999, m.1958, Judith Clancey
Ellen West 1934-?, m?
Anne Marie West 1936-2014, m.1963, Keith Minto
Reginald W. West 1942-2010, m?
Joyce E. McBride 1925-1996, m.1944, Robert W. Curry
Margaret D. McBride 1927-2010, m.1947, Jack E. McKeown 1926-1999
John C. McBride 1931-2010, m.1952, Lillian M. Smith
George T. McBride 1934-2018, m.1957, Patricia R. Steptoe
John Coy 1926-?, m.1946, Irene E. Jane
Dulcie V. Coy 1932-2010, m.1956, James Wilkinson
Sibyl J. Coy 1942-2010, m.1956, Gerald K. McCallum
Nelson Coy 1936-?, m?
Marilyn S. Coy 1949-?, m?
Leigh Coy 1951-?, m? Mr. Adan
Thomas James Shoveller 1926-?, m?
George S. Shoveller 1931-2016, m.1947, Beryl G. Marshall 1930-2013
Kevin R. Shoveller ?-1988, m.1968, Betty S. Rogers
Clarence W. Eggins 1944, m. 1967, Pamela M. Lawrence
Helen M. Shoveller ?-?, m.1964, John E. Squire

Lionel R. Mulroy ?, m? Anne ?
Alan Mulroy ?, m? ?
Betty T. Coy 1931-2017, m.1949, John A. Darwent 1929-1999
Phyllis A. Coy 1934-?, m.1957, Kevin T. Mangan
Raymond J. Coy 1936-2002, m.1957, Margaret A. Angove
Keith Coy 1937-1937 Infant
Sadie E. Coy 1950-?, m.1969, Neil R. Wallace
Marie L. Coy ?-?, m? Ray Underwood
Jean Shoveller ?-1933 Child
Frank E. Shoveller 1941-2010, m.1968, Cheryl A. Lugton
William Eggins 1944-1944 Infant
Chris Shoveller ?, m?

Margaret Curry (?); Barbara Curry (?); Lynette Curry (1949-2002); Robert Curry (?)
Jack McKeown (?); Joan McKeown (?); Patricia McKeown (?); Michelle McKeown (?)
Zela McBride (?), m? David Power (?)
Julie Mangan (?); Paul Mangan (?)
Moira H. Shoveller (?); Trevor G. Shoveller (?)
Robert Eggins (?); Michael Eggins (?)

Lionel R. Mulroy ?, m? Anne ?
Alan Mulroy ?, m? ?
Stella Mulroy (?); ? ? Mulroy (?)
Karen Mulroy (?); Michelle Mulroy (?)

household until well into her late 30's, when she eventually took a small flat in Crows Nest.

She married at the age of 39 to William Hyde (1925-2000), who had emigrated from England, the ceremony being conducted at St Cuthbert's Church at Naremburn on the 9th April 1966. Joy and Bill took up an extended career with Australia Post and managed post offices at Pearl Beach, Bellata and Wallabadah, NSW.

Bill Hyde was a member of the Masonic Lodge and passed this tradition onto his son Robert, before he died in 2000.[1] After her husbands death, Joy moved in with her son Robert and his partner Sharon Marson (1965) at Aspley in Brisbane, where she resided for many years. She saw the birth of two grandchildren, but witnessed the premature and tragic death of her son Robert in 2016,[2] after which she lost her motivation and died on the 14th January 2018.[3] Upon reaching the age of 90, Joy became the longest living member of the Rockwell/O'Sullivan family, and was only eclipsed by her half-Aunty Aileen Sampson, who had reached 95. Joy's demeanour always reminded me of Queen Elizabeth. The sole descendants of Joy and Bill Hyde was Robert William Hyde (1967-2016), who was born on the 21st February 1967, but died suddenly on the 4th April 2016 aged just 49. Robert maintained a de facto relationship with Sharon Marsen (1965), and produced two daughters in Ashleigh Maree Hyde (b.1996) and Kelsey Ann Hyde (b.1999).

▲ TOP: Photograph of Pearl Beach, where Joy and Bill Hyde took on their very first Licensed Post Office... an idyllic location, now populated by millionaires. ABOVE: Photo portraits of William (Bill) Hyde, Joy Corelli Rockwell and their son WIlliam Hyde.

The Art of Joy Hyde (nee Rockwell)

▲Joy was a very talented artist, a trait she probably inherited from her father.

Descendants of Joy & Bill Hyde

Celebrating the Life of

Robert William Hyde

21-02-1967 ~ 04-04-2016

Age 49

As a Family we would like to thank you for attending this morning to celebrate Robs life. There will be refreshments following the service in the Bridgeman Lounge.

Please also join us back at our family home at 6 Cara Street, Aspley for Robs signature 'Sausage Sizzle' and to continue the memories and celebration of Robs life.

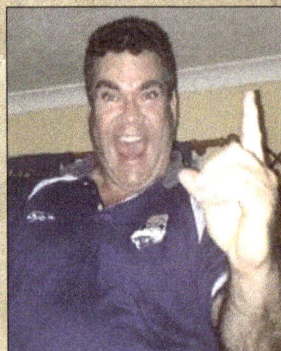

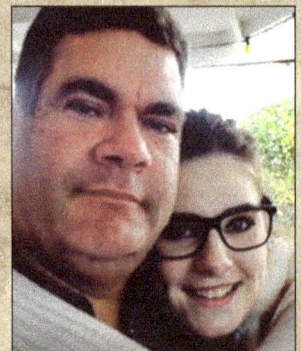

▲TOP ROW (Left): 1-Photo of Ashleigh Hyde in Primary School uniform; 2-An early photo of Joy's granddaughters Ashleigh Maree and Kelsey Anne Hyde. (Right): Robert spent many years in the regular Army, and his untimely death came as a shock to all, but his funeral was a most respectful affair with the Army providing full military honours, as seen by the flag draped casket and Australian Army slouch hat. 2ND ROW (Left): Memorial card for Joy's son Robert William Hyde (1967-2016). (Right): 1-Photograph of Ashleigh Hyde, with her mother Sharon Marson. 2-Tracy and Ashleigh at the wake for her father Robert, in 2016. ABOVE (From left): 1-Portrait of Ashleigh Hyde sporting her glasses; 2-Robert Hyde celebrating a win; 3-Portrait of Joy Hyde (nee Rockwell); 4-Photo of Robert and Ashleigh Hyde, c.2014.

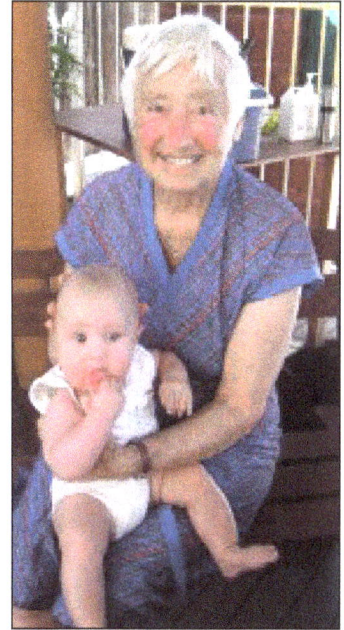

▲*LEFT: More artwork by Joy. RIGHT: Joy Hyde holding her grand-nephew, Haden Wilson-Whiting, c.2007.*

2. Robert Hunter Rockwell (1929-1984)

Robert Hunter Rockwell was born on the 25th June 1929, while his family were living at 36 Slade Street, Naremburn. He attended Naremburn Public School and Crows Nest Technical High School, often in bare feet. Robert was adventurous in his outlook on life and left 'Crowie Tech' at the age of just 15. He gained employment in a string of different vocations including as a refrigerator salesman, bulldozer driver, commercial cleaner, postal van driver, caravan park proprietor, property developer, entrepreneur, equities investor, stock trader and handyman. Rock was remarkably resourceful and could literally turn his hand to anything.

Rock married Betty Jean (1935-1996), the daughter of William Wallace Wardle and Mary Agnes Cummings, at the Registrar Generals Office in Sydney on the 15th January 1954. Rock and Betty resided at Darlington, Coogee, Noosa Heads and Maroubra, but separated in 1976 and again in late 1983. But just like his father, Rock died tragically and suddenly of a heart attack at Tweed Heads, on the 7th April 1984, aged just 54.[4] He was far too young, and his grandchildren were sadly never know of their affable grandfather. Betty too, sorrowfully contracted Leukemia and passed away under treatment some 12 years later on the 9th February 1996 at St George Hospital, Kogarah.[5] Rock and Betty both left this world well before their time, but not without producing a son in Tracy Paul (the author, b.1955) and adding a second son in Robert Wayne (1959-1963), who tragically passed away in 1963 of pnuemonia. They then tried again and delivered a daughter in Sandra Kay (b.1964), and two offspring have been responsible for adding seven grandchildren and eight great-grandchildren as their legacy to date *(see 17.1 Descendants of Robert Hunter Rockwell & Betty Jean Wardle).*

3. Elwood Lorraine Rockwell (1933-1987)

Elwood Lorraine Rockwell was born on the 9th December 1933. His middle name honoured his relationship with his great uncle George Lorraine Shoveller. Elwood was baptised at St. Cuthbert's Church in Naremburn in 1934.

17.1 Descendants of Robert Hunter Rockwell & Betty Jean Wardle

Robert Hunter Rockwell (1929-1984), born at Naremburn, later married on the 15th Jan 1954 in Sydney to Betty Jean (1936-1996), dau. of William Wallace Wardle & Mary Agnes Cummings, with issue:

1. Tracy Paul ROCKWELL (1955), born at Crown St. Womens Hospital, Surry Hills, NSW. Married firstly on the 5th January 1980 to Jane Sule (1957), daughter of Dr Dwayne Richard Paulson & Corinne Sule, in Portland, Oregon, USA (Div. 1998), with issue:

1.1 James Barrett ROCKWELL (13th Mar 1981)

1.2 Olivia Hansen Rockwell (17th July 1983)

1.3 Laura Eastman Rockwell (19th Dec 1985), married in 2014 to Jacob Ebling in Portland, Oregon, with issue:
a. Sydney Elizabeth Ebling (2014)
b. Thomas Daniel EBLING (2016)

Tracy married secondly on 2nd Feb 2002 to Lamia Lily (1972), daughter of Joseph Yammine & Berta Maroun of Belfield, NSW, at St Andrew's Cathedral, Sydney (Div. 2014), no issue.
Tracy with Marie Rose Barbour from May 2012.

2. Robert Wayne ROCKWELL (1959–1963)*, born on the 10th Aug 1959 at Crown St. Womens Hospital, Surry Hills, NSW, but tragically died of pnuemonia on the 14th July 1963 at Royal Alexandra Hospital for Children, Camperdown, NSW, d.s.p.

3. Sandra Kay Rockwell (1964), born on the 6th October 1964 at Crown St. Womens Hospital, Surry Hills, NSW. Married firstly on the 15th March 1986 to Lawrence AGIUS (13th July 1957) at St. Mary's Cathedral, Sydney (Div. 2007?), with issue:

3.1 Jack Lawrence AGIUS (20th Nov 1987), with issue:
a. Harvey Scott AGIUS (2013)

3.2 Kathryn Elizabeth Agius (10th Mar 1990) married to Troy FIELDING in 2015 at Coogee.
a. Georgia Fielding (2022)

3.3 Caroline Mary Agius (11th Oct 1993), with Theron Carl RICHARDS, with issue:
a. Benjamin Xavier RICHARDS (2015)
b. Bonnie Michelle Richards (2018)

3.4 Margaret Bernadette Agius (8th Apr 1995), with Craig Ernest McMURRICH, with issue:
a. Mack Clem McMURRICH (2017)
b.Dustin Laurence McMURRICH (2019)

Kay Agius (nee Rockwell) married secondly in 2006 to Mark PLUMMER at Grey's Point (Div. 2012), no issue.

* Died before adulthood - d.s.p.

▲CLOCKWISE (from top left): Robert Hunter Rockwell, c.1946; With friend at Manly, c.1945; Betty singing in Sydney; Betty with second son Robert Wayne Rockwell, who died of pnuemonia in 1963; Wedding photograph of Rock and Betty at the Sydney Registry, 15th January 1954.

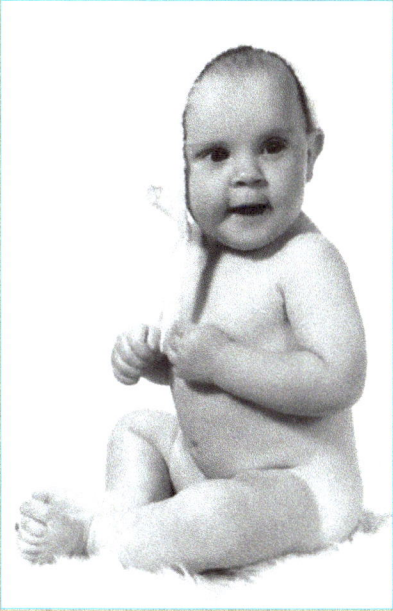

▲ TOP ROW (Left): Sandra Kay Rockwell was born on the 6th October 1964. (Right): Rock and Betty went into a partnership with Caesar & Joan Cristini (Betty's sister) re Sunrise Caravan Park at Noosa Heads (1973-1976). 2ND ROW (Left): Rock, Cheryl, Sam and Ronie aboard "MY Martindale," c.1977. (Right): Rock and Betty in Hong Kong, c.1976. ABOVE (Left): Tracy and Rock with the Australian Water Polo team aboard the magnificent 66 foot long "MY Martindale", during a cruise on Sydney Harbour, c.1978. (Right): Photo of Rock and Betty in their later years, c.1980.

Robert & Betty Rockwell & Descendants

▲TOP ROW (From Left): 1-James Barrett Rockwell, a QANTAS steward; 2-Tracy & Olivia Hansen Rockwell; 3-Jane Harold (nee Paulson) & Olivia Rockwell; 4-Thomas Ebling. 2ND ROW: 1-Laura Eastman Ebling (nee Rockwell) & Sydney Elizabeth Ebling; 2-Olivia Rockwell & Cosmo; 3-Olivia, James & Tracy at James' 40th Birthday celebrations; 4-James, Olivia & Laura (Rockwell) with Thomas & Sydney Ebling at Portland Airport. 3RD ROW: 1- Kay Rockwell with her daughters Caroline, Kathryn & Margaret at Kay's 50th Birthday celebrations; 2a-Jake, Thomas and Sydney Ebling; 2b-Sandra Kay Rockwell. ABOVE: 1-Jack Lawrence Agius; 2-Kathryn & Troy Fielding; 3-Kay & Caroline Agius; 4-Margaret Agius.

Elwood looked up to his older brother and often worked for, and assisted Rock with his various enterprises. But later in life, he joined up with North Sydney Council as a 'garbologist'... running behind and driving the Council garbage trucks that emptied the resident's bins. 'El' as he was affectionately known, was mostly content with a simple life that allowed him to finish his work early and get to the club for a drink.

Despite his soft mumbled voice and penchant for alcohol, Elwood was a favourite uncle.

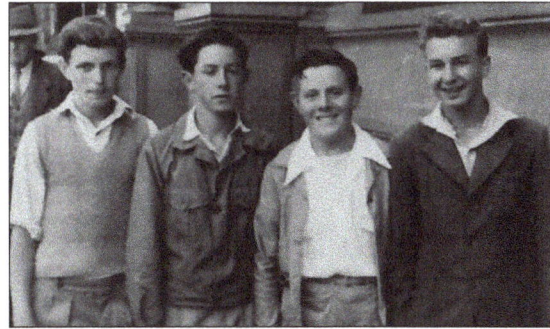

▲TOP: Elwood with BSA motor cycle at Bobbin Head, about 1949. 2ND ROW (Left): Elwood between friends Goog and Les in Sydney (c.1948). (Right): Elwood at about 14 years of age in Sydney with his mates (c.1947). ABOVE: Photo of class 2A at Naremburn Public School c.1940, with Elwood (circled).

Elwood Lorraine Rockwell - Family & Friends

▲CLOCKWISE (from top left): Elwood Lorraine Rockwell, whom everyone simply called 'El', and an FJ Holden about 1950; Elwood with friend and 'Crippo', at the Kiewa Hydro-Electric Scheme (Victoria), the second-largest in mainland Australia after the Snowy Mountains Scheme; Elwood was close to his two first cousins Les and Lionel Mulroy, c.1953; Photo of workers on the Clover Dam section of the Kiewa Valley Hydro-Electric Scheme in the Mount Bogong–Feathertop–Hotham area of Victoria's highlands (Elwood circled); Elwood handling a python at Lone Pine Animal Park, Brisbane c.1948. With his mates... Sid, Les, Elwood and Goog in Sydney, c.1951.

He was always generous with birthday and christmas gifts, which usually consisted of detailed and fascinating books. I was always personally excited to receive gifts from Uncle El, as before the internet, books were the main window into life. As I immersed myself deeply into swimming and sport, Elwood would often turn up to watch me win my school swimming races or compete at water polo and rugby matches.

Following the death of Corelli in 1976, El was at something of a loss, but moved in with his partner Mary. He sadly passed away on the 7th April 1987, the exact third anniversary of the death of his older brother and mentor, Rock.[6]

Death & Funeral Notice

ROCKWELL, Elwood - April 7, 1987, husband of Mary, a brother of Joy, Robert (deceased), Lindsay, Ron and Janet, aged 52 years. Sadly missed by family and friends. His funeral service will be held at Northern Suburbs Crematorium at 9;30am on Monday (April 13th, 1987).[7]

4. Lindsay Archibald Rockwell (1937)

Lindsay Archibald Rockwell was the third son of Robert Archibald Rockwell and Octavia Corelli O'Sullivan. Lindsay was the only one of the four brothers to join the army. He married Lynette Ellen (9th Sept 1939 - 10th March 2006) daughter of Hugh Airlie Watson and Alice, at St Cuthbert's Church, Naremburn in 1957.[8]

Lindsay and Lynette initially resided at Mosman and then Liverpool, where Lindsay worked in sales for Amco Jeans. But as their children grew, they took on a very successful career as hotel managers. They notably managed the wonderful old 'Carrington Hotel' under flamboyant owner Theo Morris in Katoomba from about 1980. Following this lengthy stint, they moved to the O'Connell Hotel, Mana Island Resort in Fiji, the Alice Motel at Tamarama and then Cremorne Point Manor, before Lynette sadly passed away on the 10th March 2006.[9] After Lynette's death, Lindsay met Judy Sherman and now resides at Chain Valley Bay on beautiful Lake Macquarie. Of all the Rockwell siblings, perhaps the most artistically talented was Lindsay, who whenever asked if he was related... always replied jokingly that he was "influenced by his Uncle Norm" (viz. the famous American artistNorman Rockwell). For many years, Lindsay and Lynette Rockwell managed the impressive old world hotel in Katoomba, built in 1882 and known as 'The Carrington.' Lindsay and Lynette produced a daughter in Rhonda Janine (b.1960) and a son in Glen

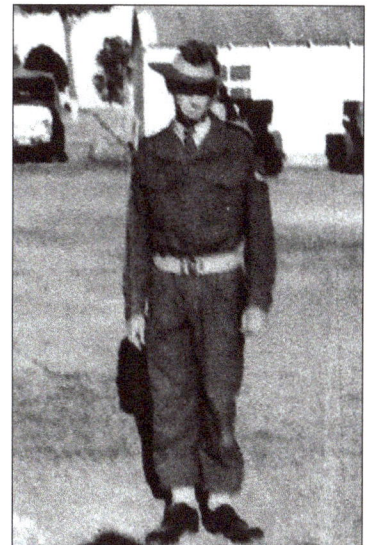

▲LEFT: Photograph of class 1C at Naremburn Public School, with Lindsay Rockwell (circled), c.1944. RIGHT: Lindsay Archibald Rockwell entered the Citizens Military Force (CMF) for a short time... seen here at Holsworthy Army Base, c.1955.

Lindsay (b.1962), who have been responsible for adding seven grandchildren and four great-grandchildren to date *(see 17.2 Descendants of Lindsay Archibald Rockwell & Lynette Ellen Watson).*

▲ *TOP: Post wedding portrait of (from left): Betty Rockwell, Bob & Corelli Rockwell, Lynette & Lindsay Rockwell, Elwood Rockwell, Joy Rockwell and Lynette's parents with Tracy, 2 and Janet, 11 below (other children were from the Watson side). ABOVE (Left): Lindsay and Lynette cutting the cake at their 1957 wedding reception. (Right): Lindsay and Lynette Rockwell's 1957 wedding with Rock the best man at left, aged 28, Ronie aged 14 at right, with Bob and Joy Rockwell behind, 1957.*

17.2 Descendants of Lindsay Archibald Rockwell & Lynette Ellen Watson

Lindsay Archibald Rockwell (1937), was born in Naremburn, and later married in November of 1957 at St Cuthberts Church, Naremburn to Lynette Watson (1911-1997), dau. of Hugh & Alice Watson, with issue:

1. Rhonda Janine Rockwell (1960), married 20th July 1984 at the Carrington Hotel, Katoomba to David Edward CROSSLEY (1956), with issue:

1.1 Sarah Alice Crossley (1983) married 3rd Sept 2011 at St. Aloysius College, Kirribilli to Marcus LOOMES (1981), with issue:
a. Harrison Stephen LOOMES (2015)
b. Norah Catherine Loomes (2018)

1.2 Matthew Charles CROSSLEY (1986) with Catherine Heenan.

2. Glen Lindsay ROCKWELL (1962), born on the 13th December 1962. Married firstly in 1987 to Jennette

May Musson (1956), Separated 2003, with issue:

2.1 Kirsty Lee Rockwell (24/12/1988), with Waylon CAESAR (1990- 2021) with issue:
a. Kassius Leon CAESAR (2020)

2.2 Shani Ann Rockwell (12/7/1991), with Paul GIBSON (?), with issue:
a. Crysta Kirsty Gibson (11/3/2011)

Following his divorce, Glen met Rebecca Louise Smith (1977) from about 2004, Separated 2018, with issue:

2.3 Alice Lynette Rockwell (30/10/2007)

2.4 Warren Glen ROCKWELL (13/9/2009)

2.5 Edward Louis ROCKWELL (19/12/2011).

Rockwell

Watson

The Art of Lindsay Archibald Rockwell

▲TOP: Painting of Bondi Beach' by Lindsay Rockwell. ABOVE (Left): Painting of 'Balmoral Beach' by Lindsay Rockwell; (Right): 1-The Carrington Hotel, Katoomba; 2-Lindsay Rockwell (manager) stands under the famous dome at the Carrington Hotel, Katoomba. Photo by Gary McLean (SMH, 28th Nov 1986).

Lindsay & Lynette Rockwell & Descendants

O'CONNELL PUB

N S DORMAN 75

▲ TOP ROW (From Left): 1-Portrait of Lindsay Rockwell, when employed as a Sales Rep with Amco Jeans Co; 2-Portrait of Lindsay Archbald Rockwell, c.1984; 3-JPortrait of Lynette Ellen Rockwell (nee Watson); 4-Lynette and Lindsay manning the bar at the Carrington Hotel. 2ND ROW: 1-Rhonda Rockwell; 2-Dave Crossley; 3-Rhonda Crossley (nee Rockwell) trail riding; 4-Rhonda hands on at the helm. 3RD ROW: 1- Postcard of the historic O'Connell Hotel [built 1865] at Oberon, another property managed by Lindsay and Lynette Rockwell; 2a-Lindsay with older sister Joy and companion Judy Sherman at their home in Chain Valley Bay at Lake Macquarie; 2b-Alice Lynette Rockwell, c.2008. ABOVE (From left): 1-Sarah Crossley; 2-Mathew Crossley; 3-Glen Rockwell with his daughter Alice, c.2007; 4-Glen Rockwell aboard his impressive wheels.

5. Ronie Malcolm Rockwell (1943-2000)

Ronie Malcolm Rockwell was born on the 26th February 1943 at Royal North Shore Hospital, the fourth son of Bob and Corelli Rockwell. He married firstly in 1961 to Coral Joy (1942-1981),[10] the daughter of George Stretton and Winifred Brooker, producing three boys in quick succession. However, the marriage didn't last with Ronie leaving the relationship and travelling to Germany in 1964, where he spent two years. There is some doubt as to whether Coral's third son Paul, was actually fathered by Ronie, as he was possibly in Germany at the time of conception?

Ronny eventually returned to Australia two years later, then soonafter met and resided with Cheryl Joy (12th May 1945-2013), the daughter of Arthur William Pooley and Molly Jeanne Graham, in a de facto relationship for a number of years, which produced both Samuel Joshua (1974) and Jessica Molly (1977). After Ronie's first wife Coral Rockwell (nee Stretton) died in 1981,[11] Ronie and Cheryl married later that same year on the 28th August.[12] They established a successful travel agency at St. Ives, known as 'Rockwell Travel', which later took on a Harvey World Travel franchise. Tragically, Ronie died from a freak motor cycle accident on the 11th May 2000.[13] Cheryl Rockwell (nee Pooley) died from complications of diabetes in 2013.[14] Ronie produced five children in total, three sons in Brett (b.1961), Mark (b.1962) and Stephen (b.1965) to his first wife Coral; and a fourth

▲ LEFT: Portrait of Ronie Rockwell c.1990. RIGHT: Photograph at the wedding celebrations for Glen Rockwell and Jeanette Musson, held at the Carrington in 1987, with Lindsay, Tracy and Ronie Rockwell.

17.3 Descendants of Ronie M. Rockwell, Coral Stretton & Cheryl Pooley

Ronie Malcolm Rockwell (1943-2000), born at Naremburn, married in 1961 at Sydney to Coral Joy (1942-1981), dau. of George & Winifred Stretton, with issue:

1. Brett Anthony ROCKWELL (1961), born on the 30th Sep 1961, he married in 1982 to Julie Denyer, with issue:

1.1 Matthew ROCKWELL (1983)

1.2 Daniel ROCKWELL (1985)

1.3 Stephen ROCKWELL (1989)

2. Mark Malcolm ROCKWELL (1962), born on the 20th Sep 1962, he married firstly c.1980 to Joyce Moore, with issue:

2.1 Adam ROCKWELL (c.1977)

2.2 Sarah Rockwell (c.1978)

2.3 David ROCKWELL (c.1980)

Mark married secondly c.1982 to Michele Thomas, with issue:

2.4 Mark ROCKWELL (c.1982)

2.5 Simone Rockwell (c.1983)

2.6 Ben ROCKWELL (c.1984)

Mark married thirdly in 1999 to Lara Musjuk, and reverted to his mother's maiden name of STRETTON, with issue:

2.7 Larissa Valentina Stretton (2006)

3. Paul Steven ROCKWELL (1965), born on the 9th Sep 1965, and with Christine Brown (1969), with issue:

3.1 Coen ROCKWELL (1996)

3.2 Kayne ROCKWELL (2000)

The descendants of Ronie and Cheryl Rockwell are:

4. Samuel Joshua ROCKWELL (1974), born on the 11th Sept.1974.

5. Jessica Molly Rockwell (1977), born on the 4th July 1977.

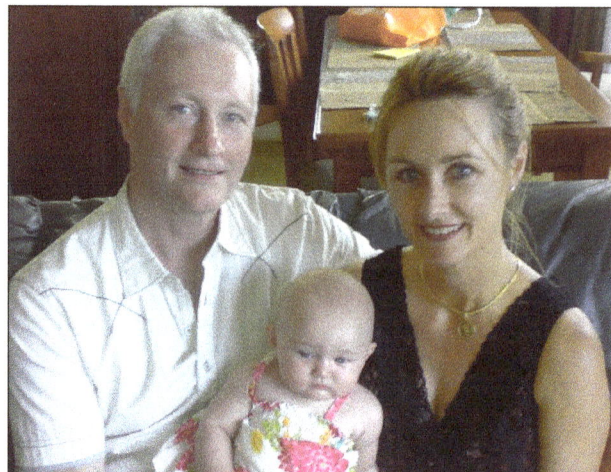

▲LEFT: ???? RIGHT: Ronie's second son Mark Malcolm Rockwell (b.1962), with his wife Lara and daughter Larissa Stretton, c.2006.

Eulogy for Ronie Malcolm Rockwell (1943-2000)

The Early Years

Now, I'd like to reminisce about Ronie and his life. It was the middle of World War II, Erwin Rommel and the German Africa Corps were being squeezed out of North Africa by Montgomery & General George S. Patton (US Army), who was 57 at the time. Half a world away, Ronie Malcolm Rockwell, arrived on 26th February 1943, a son to Robert Archibald Rockwell, and Octavia Corelli O'Sullivan, in Naremburn, and he was the fifth child born to the family, following Joy, my father Robert, Elwood, and Lindsay. Janet, the baby of the family was still a twinkle in her parents eyes!

The Rockwells endured difficult times and the tiny two bedroom semi they occupied was overcrowded with children, where they were even forced to sleep on the exposed verandah. The verandah would become soaked in heavy rain, Ronie had to use army blankets to keep him warm and it wasn't unknown for the occasional huntsman or red back spider to drop in unannounced. After Janet arrived, being closer in age to Ronie, they used to play marbles together, run through the house and scream at the sound of hailstones hitting the tin roof, and peel off the fruit labels on jam to play shop.

But despite the hardships and the large gaps between the other siblings, the family always came together to celebrate the special occasions. At christmas time they made their own decorations and with few presents to go around, what the kids did receive were usually spruced up hand-me-downs from the older siblings. In fact Ronie's clothes were even passed on to Janet at one stage. At these times, Ronie would watch his father scrub the old copper out to make the christmas pudding, and his mother making puff daloons, (dough fried in beef dripping, and covering in golden syrup), or potato chips placed in a funnel made of newspaper. One christmas tradition was that Ronie's father had each member of the family have a stir of the christmas pudding and place the threepences into the batter for christmas wishes. Grandad always wore his mother's white apron during the preparations.

It was a simple life, not hurried, and very much different to the way we live today. It was in this environment that Ronie learnt not to be wasteful, and one year during the boiling of the christmas pudding, the gas went off due to water in the pipe under the house. Wanting to save the cost of a plumber, Ronies dad decided to unblock the pipe himself, so he had the boys hold a candle each while he unscrewed the gas pipe to let the water out. Well, apparently not only water came out of the pipe, and in an instant the whole yard was alight, the Fire Dept arrived to put out the blaze, destroying the garden in the process, but their father never let them forget that the pudding was saved!

Growing Up

As he grew up, Ronie attended Naremburn Public School, and I'll bet the teachers wondered when this string of Rockwell children would ever end. In his spare time he continued the local club that his older brothers had started...the 'Naremburn Bush Patrol,' which is now covered by Flat Rock Drive at Naremburn. Apparently the whole gully was off limits to anyone who wasn't a member of the NBP, and Ronie's mum often mentioned that she could glimpse the white skin of the boys naked bodies through the bush, but she would summon them home for dinner with a whistle blast from the back verandah.

Ronie looked up to his older brothers, who always seemed to find something to keep them occupied, in fact the exploits of the Rockwell boys gained notoriety around the north shore. While my father Robert and his friends dropped cats from the suspension bridge at Northbridge to see if the hankies they'd attached as parachutes had any effect, Elwood once broke into the local public school. After vandalising the school office however, Elwood inadvertently left a clue, when he saw the school typewriter and started to type out a few letters, eventually typing out his name. Apparently the police were waiting for him when he got home. Lindsay wasn't to be outdone either and together with his cousin Les Mulroy, they used to climb underneath the roadway on northbridge and try to catch the pidgeons, but Lindsay tells me it never worked. So Ronie didn't have the best of examples to follow, and they weren't too high on the intelligence scores either, but his older brothers must have had a big influence on Ronie.

Some of these examples obviuosly rubbed off, and Ronie at times could be a little wreckless. He had a wild streak that more often than not needed to be released, somehow, somewhere, in fact this wreckless behaviour left its mark on many people, and in my case it still remains. When just 12 years old, while Ronie was cutting grass at home in Naremburn with a pair of hedging shears, he accidentally collected the tip of my little finger, the scar of which remains today. But to his credit he did try to rectify the mistake and after fishing around in the grass for the stump proceeded to stick it back together with a band-aid! I was 1 at the time!

The Teen Years

As he developed Ronie liked playing sport, was a talented athlete, playing rugby union for NSW schoolboys against a NZ Schoolboys team, and was invloved in a number of premiership teams. By now, Ronie had grown into a pretty handsome kid, and every girl in the neighbourhood wanted to be Janet's best friend so they could get to meet her brother. He went on to attend Crows Nest Technical High School, and gained a respectable pass in his intermediate exams, but left school at age 15. Around this time Ronie developed a number of very close friendships, some of whom are here today... Bernie Brennan, Phil Langford, Trevor Simmons, Keith Wilcox, Noel Taylor and Didgi Gerber, and apparently Janet had to do most of the errands to the shop as Ronie and his mates were always on their bikes (push bikes at that stage).

On the job front, his father wanted him to be a fitter and turner, but it didn't suit Ronie, and he worked in a string of jobs including bread carting for Gartrell White, and laying tiles for Graham Tiles. He also visited his big brother Rock who was driving bulldozers in the Kiewa Hydro-Electric Scheme, in Victoria, and picked up a taste for the adventurous and wild side of life, we still have photographs of the mohican haircuts they gave each other at the workers camp, and it was still the earlt 1950's...they were 40 years ahead of the rest!

Marriage, and Early Family

At a very early age and without too much guidance, Ronie showed he was both courageous and loyal by getting married at the age of 17 to Coral Joy Stretton after she fell pregnant, and they had Brett, Mark, and Paul in very quick succession. But the burden of supporting such a large family at that young age became too much for him to cope with, and he left his family, a decision which I know he deeply regretted, to spend the next two years in Germany. By the time he returned to Sydney in 1965, he could speak fluent German.

▲LEFT: Sam, Jessica and Cheryl Rockwell, c.1979. RIGHT: Ronie and Cheryl Rockwell at their home on Ayers Road in St. Ives, c.1985.

Meeting Cheryl

Not long after his return, Ronie applied for a job with Cussons as a soap deliveryman where he was given his start by Jack Ball who has remained a life long friend. It was around this time that Ron and Cheryl met at the Concordia Club at Stanmore, and it didn't take Ronie long to realise that Cheryl was the woman for him, in fact it only took one day, as they met on the Saturday night, and Cheryl moved in to Ronie's on the Sunday. Such is the appeal of the Rockwell man! Their first flat was at McMahon's Point, and for a time they took on the shop in Blues Point tower, where Cheryl's parents took up residence. Then they moved to the unit at Mosman, which I can remember, had a terrific view. Then in 1970 they moved again, this time into the house in Ayers Rd. St. Ives, which became their home for the next 29 years. But everywhere they went, I can still remember being amazed by the box loads of Cussons Imperial Leather soap, which seemed to follow them around, and lasted for literally decades.

Ron & Cheryl's house became a focus for the family as not only were they terrific hosts, but the house had a pool, and they hosted many luncheons and bar-b-q's that ended up in water polo or swimming contests on those hot summer days. Samuel Joshua came along in 1974, and he was closely followed by Jessica Molly in 1977, and two more beautiful kids you'd never find. By the time Jessica was four, I was working with Qantas and when Cheryl would say to Jess "Where is Tracy?" Jess would reply "Pwacey's on the Pwane".

But having been bitten by the travel bug, probably on his early trip to Germany, I think Ronie was always enticed by the prospect of travel and around this time he embarked on an evening tech course in the travel field. Then in 1980 Ronie was given a chance to work for Waltons who were just starting off their retail travel centre at Bankstown. After a number of years with Waltons Travel, Ronie was astute enough to see the opportunities in travel, and launched into the field on his own when he and Cheryl formed Rockwell Travel at St. Ives, with which most of you would be familiar. They worked hard and put in countless hours to build up their business, and were able to send Sam off to Newington College, and Jessica to Pymble Ladies College, and I know both Sam and Jess now appreciate the devoted efforts their parents must have gone to, in order to provide a flying start for them.

The Sailor

While their business was growing, Ronie felt the urge for adventure, and he got the sailing bug in the early eighties. He owned a series of small yachts and at the same time crewed on a number of other boats, forming some of his closest friendships in the process. With his own boat he was of course very careful, and I can remember one day trip when Ronie didn't want to pull his boat up to the wharf to offload Cheryl and the kids because of a small swell, so as not to risk any damage to the boat, so he asked me to row them to the beach in the dinghy. Now as you know Cheryl is not the most nimble of mothers, and as the swell was still running & I approached the beach in the dinghy, I told Cheryl to jump out when I gave her the signal. Well, as she tried to clamber over the side the swell lifted the boat and Cheryl dropped into the water, her terry towel tracksuit being emerged in a perfect diagonal pattern across her body. I can still see Cheryl walking up the beach, stopping every two or three steps to shake her one soaked leg, and cursing Ronie in a way that only Cheryl knew how.

Sailing became a regular weekend activity for Ronie and the family, although he did confess to getting a lttle worried from time to time about the effect of this elitist lifestyle on Sam & Jess. He once made mention of the time he was sailing with Sam, and a much larger boat came alongside. Apparently Sam ducked for cover, because the boat belonged to his friend from school, and he was concerned to be seen aboard such a wallowing little tub! Ronie corrected that attitude quicksmart!

Medical Problems

In terms of his health, Ronie had more than his share of medical problems and around 1989 he was diagnosed with cancer which was luckily removed, but then in 1995 he developed heart problems and underwent a quadruple coronary artery heart bypass. Fortunately he made a full recovery from both of these potentially fatal conditions and those of us who knew him well regarded him as somewhat of a medical marvel. By this time their Travel Agency had grown into a successful business, and they converted Rockwell Travel to a Harvey World Travel franchise in 1995. Then unexpectedly, in 1998 after roughly 20 years of work in a retail environment, most of which was alongside Cheryl, Ronie finally realised that he wasn't very good at being nice to people.

Ronie was a spiritual person, you could see his reflective moods take over when he was sailing, he was proud aswell, but always always available to help. In fact, I've only recently completed renovations to my house which Ronie helped me with, and I can still remember his reply when I called him for help with some painting, only 6 months ago. He said 'what's in it for me?' But of course he was joking, in his own way, and he was always willing to help out whenever he was asked.

I know he coveted a connection with his three sons Brett, Mark and Paul, and was very proud of both Sam and Jessica, who have all turned out to be a credit to Ronie, but not without difficulty. A few years ago, Jessica, who was unlicensed at the time, took Ronie's motor bike out for a spin and had a small accident (a few dents and scratches), so she called Sam to come and get her and the bike. Sam had to take the blame for his sister, as she was unlicensed, and for the last few years Ronie blamed Sam for the damage, but Jessica couldn't live with the white lie, and recently came out with the true story, and I know Ronie was very proud of both of them for coming clean.

Over the last couple of years, having thrown off the stresses of their business which they sold in 1998, Ronie was in very good health, and his sense of adventure resurfaced. He took on a job with the post office, got into motor cycling in a big way, and thoroughly enjoyed the freedom of riding, and the new friends it brought him in contact with. In 1998 also, Ron and Cheryl took six months off, bought a four wheel drive, a caravan ,and headed off on a 6 month tour around Australia, and had a terrific trip, with many memories and photographs to prove it. In April last year Ron and Cheryl moved into their new apartment at Killara, and by the time of the accident had racked up over 35 years together. Cheryl added the other day...'and never a cross word', sarcastic as ever, but we who are here know that they shared a very close and special bond. Ronie is now in charge of watching over Cheryl, Sam, Jess, Brett, Mark, Paul and his grandchildren, and I know he'll do his best job.

By Tracy Rockwell (Nephew), 18th May 2000

Ronie Malcolm Rockwell & Descendants

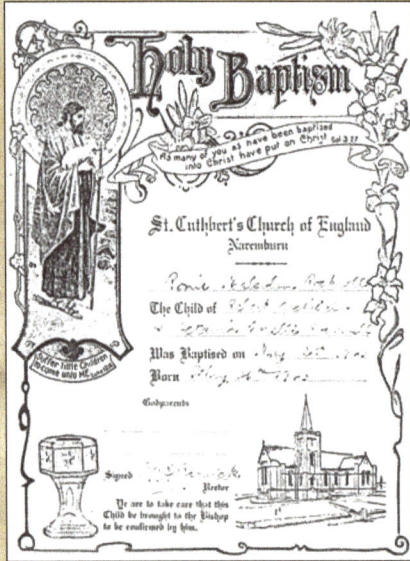

New Waltons Travel branch at Bankstown

Waltons Travel has opened its second N.S.W. office at Bankstown department store. Mr. Ron Rockwell, previously area travel supervisor for Bankstown/West Ryde, is the branch travel manager.

Until now the sole N.S.W. branch has been at Park Street department store, attached to Waltons Travel Head Office. In Victoria and Queensland there are branches at Bourke Street department store and Valley department store.

Waltons Travel Manager Mr. Doug Rowlison said that Bankstown was a logical choice for a branch as it was well situated to serve the populous western and southern suburbs of Sydney. Also, Mr Rockwell had outstanding qualifications as the new branch travel manager.

Ron Rockwell joined the Company as a home service representative at West Ryde in 1974, was promo-
ted to sales supervisor and has a good record in the field in both capacities. Right from the start he showed particular interest in travel prospects and an enthusiasm for finalising sales.

Early in 1978 he was appointed to Waltons Travel as its second travel sales supervisor. In this role he followed up prospects submitted by the field force, provided personalised service in the home and was responsible for the travel sales results of the credit branches in his area.

MR. RON ROCKWELL, with tourist poster in background.

(Mr. Dennis Thompson, now Liverpool/Burwood area, was the first travel sales supervisor. Others are Mr. Jack Thompson, Blacktown/Burwood, and Mr. Frank Gibbons, Melbourne.)

Diploma course

Mr. Rockwell has completed the Qantas/AFTA course on fares, ticketing, etc. He has also been successful in the first two years of a four-year associate diploma course at the Australian Institute of Travel and Tourism (this embraces all facets of the travel industry — marketing, promotions, sales, administration and so on).

In his new appointment, Ron has several main aims. He would like to see a build-up of staff members using Waltons Travel and intends also to engender a competitive spirit between Bankstown and Park Street that

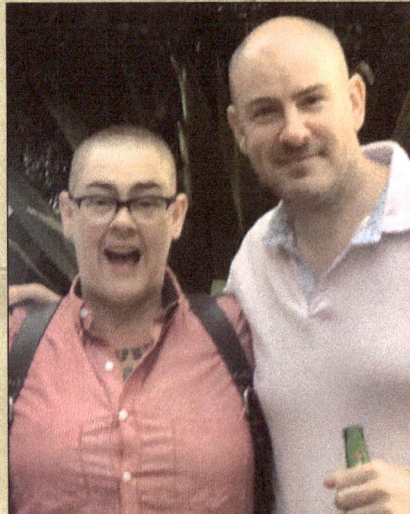

A CELEBRATION FOR

Ronie Malcolm Rockwell (Ron)

Born: 26 February 1943

Died: 11 May 2000

'He will live forever in our hearts'

▲ TOP ROW (Left): Baptismal Certificate for Ronie Malcolm Rockwell, St Cuthbert's Church, Naremburn, 1943. (Centre): Ronie and nephew Tracy Rockwell, at St. Ives, c.1998. (Right): Feature article on Ronie Rockwell, from 'Walton's On The Move' Newsletter, Nov-Dec, 1980. 2ND ROW (Left): Photo of Jessica Molly Rockwell, and brother Sam Rockwell, 2019. (Right): Memorial Card for Ronie Malcolm Rockwell. ABOVE (Left): Ronie's family gathered to release his ashes into Sydney Harbour, c.2004. (From left: Jessica, Lindsay, Sam, Cheryl, Olivia and Tracy... all Rockwells). (Right): Portrait of Ronie's fourth son Sam Rockwell, c.2000.

ROCKWELL (nee Pooley). — September 11, at Royal North Shore. Cheryl and Ron proudly announce the birth of their son (Samuel Joshua). Our thanks to the doctors and nurses for all their wonderful care.

Ron and Cheryl are happy to announce their marriage was celebrated at the Sydney Registry Office on Friday 28th August, 1981 at 7.20pm.

ROCKWELL Ronie Malcolm. — 26/2/1943 — 11/5/2000. Result of an accident. Beloved husband and soulmate of Cheryl, adored Dad "Fully" of Sam and Jessica, father of Brett, Mark and Paul, cherished by Shauna, Emma and Lara, much loved son-in-law of Molly Pooley, brother of Joy, Robert (deceased), Elwood (deceased), Lindsay and Janet, loved uncle of Tracy, Glen and all his nieces and nephews. Treasured friend of David and Erica Bailey, Peter and Anna Press, David and Caroline Turner, Albert and Margaret Lacey, Ashara Branson and Denis Weedon. Proud member of the Ulysses Club.

"Onya Bike"

Ron's family and friends are warmly invited to attend his funeral service, to be held this Thursday (May 18, 2000) at St. Ives Uniting Church, corner of Mona Vale Road and Douglas Street, St. Ives, commencing at 1.30 p.m.
Following the service the cortege will leave the church for the Northern Suburbs Crematorium.
No flowers by request.
If prefered, a donation in Ron's memory to the Hunter Westpac Rescue Helicopter Service, PO Box 230, New Lambton 2305 would be appreciated.

WHITE LADY FUNERALS
66 Pacific Highway Roseville

▲ TOP (Left): 1-Birth notice for Sam Rockwell (SMH, 11th Sep 1974). 2-Wedding announcement for Ronie Rockwell and Cheryl Pooley in 1981. (Right): Death and funeral notices for Ronie Malcolm Rockwell (SMH, 13th May 2000). ABOVE: Ronie and Lindsay Rockwell at the wake held their older brother Robert Rockwell at Ron & Cheryl Rockwell's home at St. Ives, mid-April, 1984.

son Sam (b.1974) as well as a daughter Jessica (b.1977) to his second wife Cheryl, who together have been responsible for producing 12 grandchildren to date *(see 17.3 Descendants of Ronie Malcolm Rockwell, Coral Joy Stretton & Cheryl Joy Pooley).*

6. Janet Lenore Rockwell (1946) [15]

Janet Lenore Rockwell was born at Royal North Shore Hospital in Sydney, the sixth and final child of Bob and Corelli Rockwell. She was baptised at St. Cuthbert's Church, Naremburn as had the rest of her four brothers and sister in what had beceome a Rockwell tradition. She was very involved in music, having learnt piano from the age of seven. Janet also studied piano at Palings in George Street. She recalled one time when she had entered an under 12 piano competition at the Sydney Conservatorium of Music. Her father Bob came to watch and seemed happy that she finished second, which warranted a pat on the head.

Janet remembers playing in the local gully on many occasions when she was young, as her older brothers had built a hideout at Flat Rock. They would echo coo-ee's through the bush and could hear their mother blowing the whistle to come home for dinner, which could be heard right across the gully. Janet also remembers the lovely dresses she had as a young girl. Her mum would say "go and show your dad, but he was too involved with his horses."

She recalls how proud Corelli was with simple tasks like doing the laundry and would call Janet to the window to watch through the lace curtains, the sheets blowing in the wind on the propped up washing lines. Corelli also played the piano and they would often spend time playing a duet together, but had to keep an eye out for Joy, who didn't like them playing her piano. After Joy moved out, they had a piano put in the lounge room.

Janet loved going to Crows Nest with her mum, as they'd both have a banana split at the milk bar, although sometimes Corelli chose a cream bun and Janet, an eclair. She sometimes travelled to the city with her mum where they'd visit David Jones, ordering tea and sponge cake with toffee topping. She always looked forward to riding over the Harbour Bridge on the tram. The seats were wooden and there were canvas blinds outside, while regardless of the weather, the conductor would balance himself outside to collect your ticket.

Janet recalled life at Naremburn and remembers the spider in the TV at home, as Elwood would try to put her hand on it. He would also scare her by turning the hall lights off, then shine the torch upwards on his grizzly face. She remembers doing things with Ronie, like running and screaming through the house as the hail pelted on the tin roof, and poking sticks down the bull ants nest while sitting on the back steps.

She remembers well how her dad carryied boiling water from the downstairs 'copper' upstairs to fill the bath, via a steep path. The family later bought a water heater for the upstairs bath, but it was a frightening experience to light up the gas.

Janet attended Naremburn Public School and then Willoughby Girls High School, and later in life played keyboard and piano accordion, but also sang and belonged to the Queensland Accordion Orchestra.

She married firstly to Roland Laurence Whiting (c.1945-1982) at St Cuthbert's Church,

▲*TOP (Left): Janet at Christmas 1946. (Right): Janet & Elwood at Naremburn, c.1947. ABOVE (Left): Ronie & Janet Rockwell at Naremburn in 1949. (Right): Joy, Janet, Lindsay & Ronie at Whale Beach in 1952.*

17.4 Descendants of Janet Lenore Rockwell & Roland Lawrence Whiting

Janet Lenore Rockwell (1946), was born at Naremburn, and later married on the 19th June 1965 at St Cuthbert's Church, Naremburn to Roland Laurence WHITING (c.1945-1982), with issue:

1. Michelle Lena Whiting (1965), born on the 10th Dec 1965, and with Heath Wilson (sep.) had issue:

1.1 Haden Wilson-Whiting (2007).

2. Stephen Hunter WHITING (1968), born on the 20th Aug 1968, and married to Malini Jivan in 2014.

3. Adam Roger WHITING (1971), born on the 18th Sep 1971, and is with Steven Burns.

The marriage failed in the late 1970s and they separated. Janet married secondly in 1981 at Burra Station to Gordon CHALLIS, no issue.

Janet then moved to New Zealand and married thirdly in 1987 at Wellington to Ilya SIPPEN (?), but this came to en end in 2011, no issue.

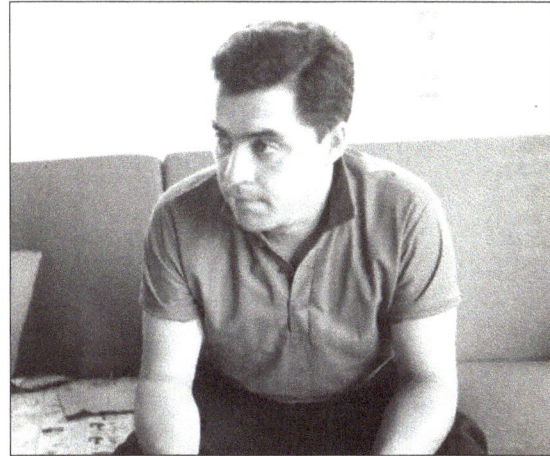

▲ TOP (Left): Janet & Roland's wedding in June 1965. (Right): Roland Laurence Whiting about 1967. ABOVE (Left): Adam on Flute, Janet - piano, Michele - clarinet, and Stephen on violin in Wellington, NZ, c.1988. (Right): Ilya & Janet Sippen, with Lindsay & Ronie Rockwell in Wellington, June 1991.

Naremburn on 19th June 1965,[16] from which relationship they produced their three children. Michele Lena Whiting was born on the 10th December of that year and they afterwards moved from Roly's mother's house at North Ryde to Artarmon. Michele was later confirmed at St Andrews Church, Braidwood in 1976.

Roland had been involved in a shocking car accident prior to their wedding, which left him paralysed and incapable of work. After the legal case was completed, the payout they received was enough to purchase a house at Artarmon. Three years later they moved to St Ives, where Stephen Hunter Whiting was born on 20th August 1868 and christened at St Stevens Church, Artarmon.

They next moved to Turramurra where Adam Roger Whiting was born on 18th September 1971. Adam was christened at St Columb's Church, West Ryde. After four years

Janet Lenore Rockwell, Family & Descendants

▲TOP ROW (From left): 1-Janet about 1949; 2-Tracy & Janet at Lindsay & Lynette's 1957 wedding; 3-Ronie Rockwell in the limousine that Janet organised in Wellington, NZ, about 1990; 4-Janet and Ronie at the wake for their older brother Robert in April 1984, held at Ronie's home in St. Ives. 2ND ROW: 1-Maria Sippen & Adam Whiting celebrating Christmas about 1990; Portrait of Janet at Wellington Real Estate, NZ about 1990; 3-Janet's third husband... Ilya Sippen, c.2000. 3RD ROW: 1-Stephen Whiting, Ilya Sippen, Jessica Rockwell, Janet Sippen, Steven Burns & Adam Whiting with Ronie Rockwell in December 1995; 2-Janet playing accordion for the Phillipine Dance Night. ABOVE: 1-Janet and Ilya Sippen at Capalaba in Brisbane; 2-Janet playing accordion and singing at the Brisbane Town Hall.

▲ TOP ROW (From left): 1-Rockwell siblings... Janet Sippen at the piano, Joy Hyde and Lindsay Rockwell, are joined by their great nephew, Jack Agius at the 2001 engagement function for Tracy to his second wife Lamia, at Kay's home at Carss Park. (Right): Janet, Lindsay and Joy in 2001. 2ND ROW: Rallying round to support Cheryl at the wake for Ronie Rockwell was (from left): Lynette Rockwell, Joy Hyde, Janet Sippen, Mark Malcolm Rockwell, Cheryl Rockwell and Lindsay Rockwell. ABOVE (Left): A six month old Haden Wilson-Whiting with his mum Michele Lena Whiting in 2007. (Right): Cousins and spouses at the wake for Robert William Hyde in Brisbane, 2016. At Rear - Heath Wilson and Tracy Rockwell; Middle row - Adam and Steven Whiting; In Front - Kay Rockwell, Michelle Lena Whiting and Malini Whiting.

they left Turramurra and moved to Braidwood, where they bought a country cottage. It was both a lovely, but very difficult time. Janet learned to chop wood for the fuel stove, look after their pet sheep, wrapped the pipes when the cold winter came. In the end it proved too much, with an old cottage, a sick and disabled husband and three children. Money was also getting scarce and the marriage failed, so Janet left with the children for Canberra. She worked at the Canberra School of Music for seven years, then started as a receptionist, before working up to the purchasing office and then to Assistant Concert Manager. Rolly sadly passed away in 1982.[17]

Janet then met and married secondly to Gordon Challis, as his daughter Erica happened to be studying french horn at the school. Janet and Gordon married on the 17th May 1981 at Burra Station, Burra, but later moved to Wellington in New Zealand, where Gordon, a published poet, worked as a psychologist. However, the children were not happy with the move or the new husband, as Gordon himself was having problems, so they parted in 1986. Janet bought a house in Kilbirnie, where her and the children lived for four more years. During this time she worked for the Vice Chancellor of Victoria University in Wellington.

Janet remembers the time her brother Ronie flew to New Zealand to visit her and the family. She organised a limousine to meet him at the airport, and he was thrilled when the chauffeur opened the car door. They drove like royalty around Oriental Bay with a glass of champagne in hand.

Eventually a strange Ukranian with his daughter Maria, moved in next door and that was the beginning of another relationship. Ilya Sippen, who was originally from Kiev, was quite naive to anglo-saxon ways, and his English and grammar was poor, but they clicked and a serious relationship soon blossomed. They became involved in the Russian community, both joining the Russian choir with Janet singing and playing keyboards. Janet married thirdly to Ilya at Orsini's Restaurant in Wellington, New Zealand on 16th May 1987. They later returned to Brisbane and bought a home at Capalaba. In their years together, they travelled to 11 countries and developed many friends, but the relationship came to an end in 2011, without further issue.

Janet remained in Brisbane for a while, before relocating to Hobart in Tasmania for a

▲ TOP (Left): Photograph of siblings Lindsay Rockwell, Joy Hyde and Janet Sippen at the wake for Joy's son Robert William Hyde in Brisbane, 2016. (Right): Janet's 70th Birthday celebrations in Brisbane (From left: Malini Whiting, Adam Whiting, Janet Sippen, Michele Whiting, Stephen Whiting with Haden Wilson-Whiting and Heath Wilson in front).

▲ Photograph of the Rockwell family at the wake for Robert Hunter Rockwell on 21st April 1984. Back row (from left): Bill Hyde, Robert Hyde, Ronie Rockwell, Lindsay Rockwell, Cheryl Rockwell, Glen Rockwell, Tracy Rockwell. Front row: James and Jessica Rockwell, Kay Rockwell, Joy Hyde, Betty Rockwell (the widow), Lynette Rockwell, Joan Cristini (Betty's half-sister), and Samuel Joshua Rockwell.

'tree change', where she spent a number of years, but as of 2020 she returned to Chermside in Brisbane to be closer to family. Janet and her first husband Roly Whiting produced a daughter in Michele Lena (b.1965), who has produced the only grandchild to date, as well as two sons in Steven Hunter (b.1968), and Adam Roger (b.1971) *(see 17.4 Descendants of Janet Lenore Rockwell & Roland Laurence Whiting)*.

Summary

While this genealogy is dedicated to the memory of Robert Archibald Rockwell and his wife Octavia Corelli O'Sullivan, the material honours all the ancestors that went before them. The research was undertaken to preserve family memories and old stories, verses, photographs, traditions, pedigrees and such flotsam and jetsam that might be otherwise hopelessly lost. My sincere hope in recording and publishing these details is to have done some justice to the memory, labours and hardships of our beloved ancestors from whom we descend. And it doesn't end there as the lineage of Rockwell, Bantin, O'Sullivan, Shoveller and their associated families continues today, with the blood of these forebears flowing at this very moment through the bodies of their descendants, all immensely proud and thankful for their foresight and courage.

They evolved out of the early post-Federation years, overcoming four of the greatest challenges of human history, which were the Spanish Influenza of 1919, the Great Depression and the two World Wars. Against these greatest of difficulties they accomplished the tasks necessary for survival, and succeeded in rearing their six children. Their struggles have delivered a legacy of 14 grandchildren, and 16 great-grandchildren to date, of whom all share a unique ancestry. This genealogy extends further in following the path of one son in Robert Hunter Rockwell, through his life, marriage and descendants, which is available in

Volume 12 of the Rockwell Genealogies entitled... 'Robbers, Rascals & Royals: The Life & Ancestry of Dr Tracy Rockwell.'

While much of the detailed history of the ancestors in these pages shall remain buried forever in the sands of time, I hope to have shone a light upon the fascinating lives of a few, for its the past that tells us who we are. It is my sincere hope to have rescued from the waters of oblivion the lovingly collected material contained in these pages, and desire it to be of benefit to those who are passionate about these families, the people, the historic events they experienced and their many captivating stories and anecdotes.

References

1. NSW Dept of BDM. (2000). Death Certificate for William Hyde, #?/2000.
2. Queensland Dept of BDM. (2016). Death Certificate for Robert William Hyde, #?/2016.
3. Queensland Dept of BDM. (2018). Death Certificate for Joy Corelli Hyde (nee Rockwell)., #?/2018.
4. NSW Dept of BDM. (1984). Death Certificate for Robert Hunter Rockwell, #102772/1984.
5. NSW Dept of BDM. (1996). Death Certificate for Betty Jean Rockwell (nee Wardle), #?/1996.
6. NSW Dept of BDM. (1987). Death Certificate for Elwood Lorraine Rockwell, #9171/1987.
7. Elwood Lorraine Rockwell - Death & Funeral notice (Sydney Morning Herald, 9th April 1987).
8. NSW Dept of BDM. (1957). Marriage Certificate for Lindsay Archibald Rockwell and Lynette Ellen Watson, #18138/1957.
9. NSW Dept of BDM. (2006). Death Certificate for Lynette Ellen Rockwell, (nee Watson), #?/2006.
10. NSW Dept of BDM. (1961). Marriage Certificate for Ronie Malcolm Rockwell and Coral Joy Stretton, #1212/1961.
11. NSW Dept of BDM. (1981). Death Certificate for Coral Joy Rockwell (nee Stretton), #15477/1981.
12. NSW Dept of BDM. (1981). Marriage Certificate for Ronie Malcolm Rockwell and Cheryl Joy Pooley, #?/1981.
13. NSW Dept of BDM. (2000). Death Certificate for Ronie Malcolm Rockwell, #?/2000.
14. NSW Dept of BDM. (2013). Death Certificate for Cheryl Joy Rockwell (nee Pooley), #?/2013.
15. Recollections of Janet Lenore (Sippen, Carr, Whiting nee Rockwell), youngest daughter of Robert & Corelli Rockwell (Letter, April 2021).
16. NSW Dept of BDM. (1965). Marriage Certificate for Janet Lenore Rockwell and Roland Laurence Whiting, #19723/1965.
17. NSW Dept of BDM. (1982). Death Certificate for Rowland Whiting, #14742/1982.

Appendices

Roll of Arms
for

ROBERT ARCHIBALD ROCKWELL

Bantin · Bignell · Eastman · Hewitt · Lamborn

Langley · Sabine · Shoveller · Wood

OCTAVIA CORELLI O'SULLIVAN

Benson · Bignell · Eastman · Hewitt · Lamborn

Langley · Sabine · Shoveller · Wood

APPENDIX A

The Parents of William Henry Rockwell
by Dr Tracy Rockwrell

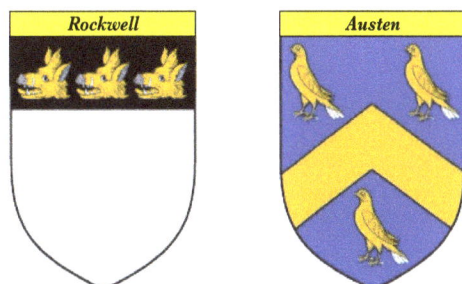

AUGUSTUS ROCKWELL & FRANCES AUSTEN

(Possible paternal grandparents of Robert Archibald Rockwell)

AUGUSTUS ROCKWELL

Augustus Rockwell was recorded by William Henry Rockwell as being the name of his father, which was listed as such on a number of official documents. It was also stated that Augustus worked as a missionary or evangelist, although where and how he espoused his doctrine is unknown.

William Henry Rockwell recorded his birth to have occurred about 1861 in Kent, England on the registration of his first marriage (1894).[1] He later recorded his birth to have been about 1862 in London on the registration of his second marriage (1901).[2] He was listed as being born in 1862 and 1859 respectively in London, on the registrations of his son's births in 1902 and 1904.[3,4] But he was listed as being born about 1858 in London, by his son Robert, on the registration of his death (1932).[5] Therefore, the possible range for William Henry Rockwell's year of birth could span anywhere from 1858 to 1862, with the location of his birth varying between Kent and London.

Unfortunately, according to the 'FreeBMD Database'[6], 'Family Search'[7], and the 'National Register of Scotland'[8], no birth registration has been found for William Henry Rockwell during the years from 1855 to 1865, anywhere in either England or Wales. But, the registration of births was compulsory, so how could it be that no birth registration has been found for William Henry Rockwell in London, Kent or elsewhere in England or Wales?

Before 1837 only churches recorded birth, marriage and death information in England and Wales. During the early 1800s, Parliament recognized the need for accurate records for voting, planning, taxation and defense purposes. Legislation was passed to create a civil registration of births, marriages and deaths for England and Wales, and for registering the same for British subjects abroad. England and Wales registration began on the 1st July 1837 and covered births, marriages, divorces and deaths. However, coverage was not

Table C1.1-1 Birth's, Residences

NAME	INDEX/REFERENCE	BIRTH	PLACE	DEATH
Lewis Augustus Rockwell	Find A Grave Index	26 Jan 1807	?	9 Jan 1880
Augustus Rockwell	Connecticut Births and Christenings, 1649-1906	14 Mar 1809	Middletown, Conn	?
Augustus Rockwell	Find A Grave Index	7 Apr 1822	?	14 Apr 1882
Augustus Rockwell	New York State Census, 1855	1822	?	Res: 1855
Augustus Rockwell	New York State Census, 1865	1824	?	Res: 1865
Augustus Rockwell	United States Census, 1860	1826	New York	Res: 1860
Augustus Rockwell	United States Census, 1860	1824	Tennessee	Res: 1860
Augustus Rockwell	United States Census, 1860	1828	New York	Res: 1860
Augustus Rockwell	United States Census, 1830	?	?	Res: 1830
Augustus A. Rockwell	Find A Grave Index	30 May 1832	?	23 July 1867
Frederick Augustus Rockwell	Rhode Island Deaths and Burials, 1802-1950	27 Dec 1834	?	7 Sep 1909
Augustus P. Rockwell	New York, State Death Index, 1880-1956	1840	?	1 June 1903
Augustus P. Rockwell	Find A Grave Index	4 Mar 1840	?	1 June 1903
A. P. Rockwell	Morning Post (Eng.), 18th June 1869 , p.5	?	?	Res: 1869
Augustus Rockwell	United States Census, 1880	1840	?	Res: 1870
Augustus Rockwell	United States Census, 1880 (fur dealer)	1840	?	Res: 1880
Augustus Rockwell	United States Census, 1900	April 1840	New York	Res: 1900
Augustus P. Rockwell	New York Passenger Lists, 1820-1891 (merchant)	1840	New York	Immig: 1879
A. Rockwell	New York Passenger Lists, 1820-1891	1839	New York	Immig: 1881
Augustus Rockwell	New York Passenger Lists, 1820-1891 (merchant)	1840	New York	Immig: 1888
Augustus Rockwell	United States Census, 1860	1842	Vermont	Res: 1860
Augustus Rockwell	United States Civil War Soldiers Index, 1861-1865	?	From 1861 to 1865	?
Augustus Rockwell	United States Civil War Soldiers Index, 1861-1865	?	From 1861 to 1865	?
Augustus H. Rockwell	United States Census, 1850	1837'	New Jersey	Res: 1850
Augustus H. Rockwell	Genealogy Bank, Newspaper Obituaries, 1815-2011	?	?	24 July 1867
Augustus Rockwell (father)...	Illinois Births and Christenings, 1824-1940	?	?	
Augustus Rockwell (father)...	New Jersey Births and Christenings, 1660-1980	?	?	

▲LEFT: 'Self-portrait' by an Augustus Rockwell (1822-1882), portrait painter from Manlius, Onondaga, New York, but he is not the father of William Henry Rockwell. RIGHT: Table listing birth, residence and death events for persons named Augustus Rockwell from 1800-1910.

universal, especially in the earlier years before tougher laws were introduced in 1874.[9]

Although there exist a number of possible lines of research, the lack of basic evidence makes further research into the Rockwell ancestry problematic. Indeed, the lack of a birth registration for William Henry Rockwell creates doubt as to whether his parents were actually married, or indeed if they even existed?

It could be that William Henry Rockwell's birth registration was accidentally lost or recorded under another name? Finding a mis-filed or mis-spelt record can be almost impossible, although a few attempts have been made to search for his birth registration under other names eg. Rockell, Rodwell or Rockhill etc. But as the name Rockwell is easy enough to pronounce and spell, such an explanation would seem unlikely. More feasible is the possibility that the lack of official registration was intentional, but if so, why?

One obvious reason might be that the birth was illegitimate, with the mother perhaps protecting, unwilling or even ignorant of divulging the fathers name. It could be that the father of William Henry Rockwell was intentionally omitted and the birth was registered under the mother's maiden name *(see Frances Austin)*?

If the father was unknown, it could have been that William was told by his mother, that Augustus Rockwell was his father? Or it could be that William Henry Rockwell was an orphan and fabricated his father's name and occupation? There are numerous possibilities.

What is known is that documents consistently list Augustus Rockwell as William's father, whom he also recorded as being a missionary or evangelist. But it should be noted that the surname 'Rockwell' is in itself an uncommon name, and when combined with 'Augustus' becomes even more unusual, making the merger of the two quite rare. Consequently, it seems odd, that if William Henry Rockwell did fabricate a name for a father he never knew, why would he make it as distinctive as 'Augustus Rockwell?'

Needless to say, researching William Henry Rockwell's parents has been extraordinarily difficult. However, investigations have been conducted into individuals that might conceivably have been William Henry Rockwell's father.

Although a number of people with the name 'Augustus Rockwell' have been found in the United States, unfortunately no Augustus Rockwells have so far been identified to have

or Augustus Rockwell, 1800-1910

PLACE	OTHER FAMILY
Buried - Fort Atkinson, Jefferson, Wisconsin, USA	?
?	Noadiah Rockwell (F), Esther (M)
Buried - Buffalo, Erie, New York, USA	?
E.D. 2, Ward 2, Buffalo City, Erie, New York, USA	Jane M Rockwell (spouse), Florence Rockwell (dau.)
District 03, Ward 2, Buffalo, Erie, New York, USA	Jane Rockwell (spouse), Florrena Rockwell, Harriet Rockwell & Harriet Mernot, Minerva Mernot
4th Ward Buffalo City, Erie, New York, USA	Jane Rockwell, Florence A Rockwell, Harriett Rockwell, Maria Merritt & Julia Buhner
Subdivision 66, Shelby, Illinois, USA	w/Littan Smith, Elizabeth Smith, Richard B Smith, Caroline Smith, Cyrus Smith, Frances...
Williamsburgh, Hampshire, Mass, USA	w/Alfred Root, Hrraretta Root, Ann Root, Ansel Root, Henry Ives, Lewis Ring, Henry...
East Windsor, Hartford, Connecticut, USA	?
Buried - Newark, Essex, New Jersey, USA	?
Buried - Providence, Rhode Island, USA	Jabez Rockwell (F), Eunice Rockwell (M)
Bronxville, Westchester, New York, USA	?
Buried - Menands, Albany, New York, USA	?
Mauricy's Hotel, Regent Street, London	Hotel Arrivals: Mr & Mrs A. P. Rockwell & Mr. & Mrs. J. A. Rockwell
New York, USA	Harriett Rockwell (spouse, 34), Fannie (6), Hattie (4) & Josephine Jacobinson (Sweden, 36)
Brooklyn, Kings, New York, USA	Hattie R Rockwell (spouse), Fannie W. (15), Bessie P. (6) & Anna Hanson (other)
Bromville, Westchester New York, USA	Lodger
into New York City, New York, USA	"Gallia" from Liverpool
into New York City, New York, USA	"B M Moore" from England
into New York City, New York, USA	"Brittanic" from ?
Brandon, Rutland, Vermont, USA	w/Benj W Johnson, Mary Johnson, Robert Johnson, Sally Preston, Betsey Durgey, Huldah...
Veteran Reserve Corps	
63rd Regt. Georgia Infantry	
Newark, Essex, New Jersey, USA	Ann Rockwell (M), George Rockwell (7), Augusta Rockwell (5)
Newark, New Jersey, USA (Buried - Cleveland, Ohio)	?
	Effie Reece (spouse) & Ruby M. Rockwell
	Margaret Mc Donnell (spouse) & Mary Augusta Rockwell

▲ RIGHT: 'Self-portrait' by an Augustus Rockwell (1822-1882), portrait painter from Manlius, Onondaga, New York, but he is not be the father of William Henry Rockwell. u: Table listing birth, residence and death events for persons named Augustus Rockwell (1800-1910).

been born or married in England, during the years necessary to have been the father of William Henry Rockwell.

To this end, a wider search was made of the death indexes at the National Archives (England & Wales), for an 'Augustus Rockwell' or similar between the years 1855 and 1915, with only one 'remote' result being identified:

1899, Augustus Rockall, born c.1810, Oxfordshire.

However, the census consistently revealed that this Augustus Rockall was a cabinet maker, who married a woman by the name of Lucy, and was therefore proabably not Williams father.

A worldwide search was then conducted using the Family Search (IGI) database, with a number of results being identified for 'Augustus Rockwell,' except that all of these were found in North America *(see Table C1.1-1)*.

Therefore, if William Henry Rockwell's father was indeed Augustus Rockwell, it seems more than likely that his Rockwell ancestors came from North America. However, the evidence has been unable to confirm any links whatsover between these American Rockwells, and whether any could have fathered William Henry Rockwell.

Of the 'Augustus Rockwells' listed in Table C1.1-1, perhaps one stands out in Augustus P. Rockwell, who was born on the 4th March 1840 in Albany, New York. Whether he had any interest in evangelism seems unlikely as his occupation is listed as a fur dealer and merchant. However, he made a number of trans-Atlantic crossings between the USA and England, and even stayed at Mauricy's Hotel in Regent St, London in 1869, on at least one of those trips, which would have put him in close enough proximity to William's mother.

"There is only one Augustus Rockwell who I found to have any connection with England, (there were a few in the USA), an Augustus P. Rockwell, who travelled to England a few times in the 1870s and 1890s as a merchant. He was born around 1840, so was old enough to be William's father. However, I was really hoping to find him visiting England around 1860, but alas no trace."

Mathew Homewood, Genealogist, 3rd May 2018

But making a link from such a tenuous connection could be erroneous. Another possible link was found to an Augustus Rockwell, who was born on the 7th April 1822 at a place

▲LEFT: Augustus Rockwell was recorded as being a missionary/evangelist, converting and encouraging followers of the gospel. RIGHT: Dr David Livingstone, 'Preaching from a Wagon', printed by the London Missionary Society, c.1840's.

called Manlius, Onondaga, New York. Although this is the only other matching Augustus Rockwell in any database with dates that seem to align, this Augustus Rockwell proved to be a portrait painter, and had a family in Buffalo, New York at the time of the 1860 US Census, so this link also remains just another unlikely clue.

Unfortunately, without William's birth or baptismal certificate (and one may not exist) all explanations concerning the origins of William Henry Rockwell, his father or his mother, are just guess work at this stage. Progress can't be made without either a birth certificate for William Henry Rockwell that names his father, or a death certificate for Augustus Rockwell, that names his son William, either of which might solve the puzzle.

Missionary/Evangelist

As for explanations as to what may have happened to Augustus Rockwell, he may have worked as a missionary or evangelist in some far off land? The 19th century Christian revivalist movement gained much support and many unordained lay people joined the cause, often manning missions in very dangerous places. The possibility of researching missionary societies or church archives for 19th century evangelists is a possible avenue that remains to be investigated.

One random piece of information that came to light was a list of passengers aboard the British & African Steam Navigation Company's ship "SS Matadi", which departed from Liverpool, England on the 11th May 1892, enroute to the Congo, Central Africa. On the list of passengers was a Rev. & Mrs. Rockwell, which seemed a promising lead. Our Augustus Rockwell may very well have been a missionary in dangerous new territories such as the Congo, and could be buried out there somewhere?

"Augustus Rockwell, a missionary, is a rather elaborate name and occupation to fabricate, and I have little doubt that this man existed."

Mathew Homewood, Genealogist, 3rd May 2018

DNA Research

During 2020, both the author Tracy Rockwell, and his uncle Lindsay Archibald Rockwell underwent a paternal 'Y' DNA analysis through 'Family Tree DNA.' The result was a revelation, in that expecting English ancestry, we were very surprised to find that our Rockwell ancestry was connected to the parent haplogroup identified as 'N-M231', which were people who descended from Northern Eurasia, Siberia and Mongolia, but with a high frequency from Finland. How far back this connection extends or when the jump to England occurred is still to be determined.

As the technology for DNA analysis, and researching genealogy in general becomes more sophisticated, it is possible that the origin of William Henry Rockwell, his ancestors and connections might eventually be unveiled. Sadly, not being able to move beyond Augustus Rockwell prevents any further research into uncovering the Rockwell paternal ancestry at this stage.

Where To From Here?

This genealogy continues by searching for evidence of William Henry Rockwell's recorded mother on his 1894 marriage certificate i.e, Frances Austin.

▲ LEFT: List of passengers showing a Reverend Rockwell (Pax on "SS Matadi" from Liverpool to the Congo on the 11th May 1892 (Passenger Lists Leaving UK 1890-1960). RIGHT (Top): An Augustus P. Rockwell stayed at Mauricy's Hotel, London in 1869 (Morning Post, 18th June 1869). (Mid): Certificate listing Augustus Rockwell as a Missionary. (Below): Massacre in the Congo (The Telegraph, 18 Nov 1892, p.5).

🔲 A? Rockwell	
New York Passenger Lists	
Name	A? Rockwell
Event Type	Immigration
Event Date	1881
Event Place	New York City, New York, United States
Gender	Male
Age	42
Birth Year (Estimated)	1839
Birthplace	England
Ship Name	B M Moore

▲ *TOP (Left) & Right: A person by the name of A. Rockwell passed through New York Immigration in 1881 (New York Passenger Lists). ABOVE: Map of Northern Europe & Finland. A paternal 'Y' DNA trail was discovered in 2020, which established that our Rockwell ancestry descends from the country known today as Finland, albeit probably more than 400-600 years ago.*

THE AUSTEN ANCESTORS

The Surname of Austen

This famous surname recorded in the spellings of Austen, Austin and Auston, derives originally from the Roman (latin) 'Augustine,' and is the medieval vernacular form, being first recorded as a surname in the 13th century, and is associated chiefly with southeastern England, especially Kent, from a reduced German form of the personal name Augustin.

The first Archbishop of Canterbury was St. Augustine, who died in 605 A.D., however, the name totally lost popularity until the 12th century, when during the Christian revival period, also associated with the Crusades, the religious order known as "the Austin Canons" was established. The present name is probably habitational in origin, as the order was celibate, and referred to people who worked at the various properties owned by the order.

As the popularity of the 'Austin' order spread, the name became baptismal in its own right. A coat of arms was granted to the 'Austins of Surrey' in 1611, being silver with three black chevrons, the centre being charged with three gold crosses. The name was introduced into America early with Edward Austin aged 26 yrs, being a passenger on the "Speedwell" from London in May of 1625.

Less happy circumstances attended Thomas Austin of Somerset, who on 12th October 1685, was ordered by "Bloody" Judge Jeffreys to be transported to Barbados or any other of His Majesty's plantations for the conviction of being a "Monmouth Rebel." The first recorded spelling of this surname is shown to be that of Henry Austin, which dated to 1275, in the 'County Pipe Rolls of Worcestershire,' during the reign of King Edward 1, otherwise known as 'The Hammer of the Scots.'

Famous & Notable 'Austins'

Jane Austen

Perhaps the most famous bearer of the surname 'Austen' was Jane Austen (16 December 1775–18 July 1817), who was an English novelist known primarily for her six major novels, which interpreted, critiqued and commented upon the British landed gentry at the end of the 18th century. Austen's plots often explored the dependence of women on marriage in the pursuit of favourable social standing and economic security. Her works critiqued the novels of sensibility of the second half of the 18th century and are part of the transition to 19th-century literary realism (no known relation).

Sir Francis Austen

Admiral of the Fleet Sir Francis William Austen, GCB (23 April 1774–10 August 1865) was a Royal Navy officer, and older brother to Jane Austen.[1] As commanding officer of the sloop "HMS Peterel," he captured some 40 ships, a French squadron and led the operation where the French brig "Ligurienne" was captured off Marseille. In "HMS Canopus" he took part in the pursuit of the French fleet, under command of Admiral Pierre-Charles Villeneuve, to the West Indies and back in 1805, but was detached from the fleet for convoy duty in the Mediterranean and missed the 'Battle of Trafalgar.' He was promoted to Rear Admiral on 22nd July 1830. Austen was advanced to Knight Commander of the Order of the Bath on 28th February 1837 and promoted to Vice Admiral on 28th June 1838, then served as Commander-in-Chief, North America and the West Indies Station (no known relation).

But now to an examination of our ancestors, who may also bear the surname of Austin.

Frances Austin

William Henry Rockwell recorded his mother's name as 'Frances Austin' on the registration of his first marriage (1894).[2] He later recorded his mother to have been 'Frances Unknown' on the registration of his second marriage (1901),[3] and his son Robert Archibald Rockwell recorded his paternal grandmother to have been 'Frances Thruyac' on the registration of his fathers death in 1932, the latter surname being most obscure.[4]

It has been known for many years that the christian name of William Henry Rockwell's mother, was Frances. However, after almost 40 years of research, her maiden surname was only revealed in 2017 as being 'Austin,' when a first marriage was discovered for William Henry Rockwell, which occurred in Melbourne on the 24th February 1894.

While this leap forward was initially seen as a breakthrough, it very quickly became evident, that the revelation would be useless without further research. Confirmation of William Henry Rockwell's parents requires the discovery of a registered marriage between Augustus Rockwell and Frances Austin, and following that, a birth certificate for William Henry Rockwell himself that identifies Augustus Rockwell and Frances Austin as being his bona fide parents.

To that end, the following indexes were checked for the marriage of Augustus Rockwell

1861 Census for England and Wales	HOUSES In-habit-ed	Un-inhabited (U.), or Building (B.)	NAME and Surname of each Person	RELATION to Head of Family	CON-DITION	AGE of Male|Female	Rank, Profession, or OCCUPATION		WHERE BORN
9 Ivy Lane?	1		M Frances Austen	Head	Widow	31	Charwoman.		Kent, Berwick
			Selina Austen	Daur		8	Scholar		D° Ealing
			Thomas T°	Son		3			D° D°
			William T°	Son		1			D° D°

▲1861 England and Wales Census for Frances Austen and family.

and Frances Austin:

* The National Archives, birth, marriage and death indexes for England and Wales through the FreeBMD Index.[5]
* The Church of Jesus Christ of Latter-day Saints - 'Family Seach Register' (IGI).[6]
* The National Register of Scotland.[7]

Unfortunately, no such marriage has been found during the years from 1835 to 1865 in England. This meant that a birth registration needed to be found for their son William Henry Rockwell, listing preferably both, but at least one of the declared parents.

William listed his birthplace as being in Kent, England on his first marriage certificate in 1894, when aged about 35. However, he recorded his birthplace as being London, England on his second marriage certificate in 1901, when aged 42, and that information was repeated on the birth certificates of his first and third sons (William Henry Rockwell Jr. & Robert Archibald Rockwell), as well as on his death certificate in 1932, aged 74, although the latter was completed by his son Robert, as informant. To that end, the following indexes were thoroughly, but unsuccessfully checked for the birth of a William Henry Rockwell:

* The National Archives, birth, marriage and death indexes for England and Wales through the FreeBMD Index.[5]
* The Church of Jesus Christ of Latter-day Saints - 'Family Seach Register' (IGI).[6]

Unfortunately, although a number of 'William Rockwells' were born in the United States at that time, no William or William Henry Rockwells were found to have been born anywhere in England between 1855 and 1865. This lack of evidence left no other option than to investigate a number of different theories, each hypothesis being researched and rejected in turn, with the following results:

Theory 1. That William Henry Rockwell was born out of wedlock, from a relationship between Augustus Rockwell and Frances Austin, but the birth was not officially registered?

England and Wales mandated the compulsory registration of all births, marriages and deaths from the 1st July 1837, and an act of omission was an offence. However, an intentional non-registration of a birth, perhaps due to scandal if the birth was illegitimate, which would be impossible to prove, would effectively end this avenue of investigation. If that was not the case however, the next best theory was:

Theory 2. That William Henry Rockwell was born out of wedlock, from a relationship between Augustus Rockwell and Frances Austin, but was given his mother's surname of Austin (or Austen)?

An investigation of the registration of births in the National Archives (England & Wales) bearing the name of either William or William Henry Austin (or Austen), was conducted. The target area was in Kent, Sussex and London from 1857 to 1862, the date range being calculated from William Henry Rockwell's two marriages and death certificate. Being a more common surname, some 43 boys were identified as having been born and registered with the surname of Austin (or Austen), for this period.

Austin Births at Family Search (IGI)

1858	Austen, William	Birling, Kent	1861 Census
1858	Austen, William	Birling, Kent	1871 Census
1858	Austin, William	Sevenoaks, Kent	1871 Census
1858	Austen, William	Sevenoaks, Kent	1881 Census

Investigating the above births for mothers by the name of Frances Austin (or Austen) would mean applying for many individual birth certificates, an exhaustive and expensive exercise, which has not been undertaken to date.

However, this question was also researched using the Family Search (IGI) database, with some results. Two possible marriages were revealed where the mother was identified by the name of Frances Austen, oddly with both having exactly the same marriage date! The first result showed that a Frances 'Bourner' was married on the 12th April 1851 to a John Austen in Tenterden, Kent. The second result revealed that a Frances West was married on the 12th April 1851 to James Austen in Birling, Kent.

The Austins of Birling/Ryarsh, Kent

Further investigation checked whether either of these marriages produced children. The former marriage revealed nothing, while the James Austen and Frances West marriage brought forth the following issue:

Selina Austen (bp. 6 Feb 1853 at Birling, Kent)
George Austen (bp. 12 Oct 1855 at Birling, Kent)
William 'flodge' Austen (bp. 28 Sep 1857 at Birling, Kent)
Thomas Austen (bp. 1 Nov 1857 at Birling, Kent)

Table C1.3-1 Austin/Austen Births in the National Archives 1857-1862

1857	1-Mar	Austen	William	Holborn	1859	1-Mar	Austin	William	Lambeth	1861	2-Jun	Austin	William	St James
1857	1-Mar	Austin	William	Petworth	1859	1-Mar	Austin	William	Mile End	1861	4-Dec	Austin	William Henry	Clerkenwell
1857	1-Mar	Austin	William	Steyning	1859	2-Jun	Austin	William	**Malling**	1861	4-Dec	Austin	William	Cranbrook
1857	2-Jun	Austin	William	Hendon	1859	2-Jun	Austen	Florence	**Malling**	1861	4-Dec	Austen	William	Cranbrook
1857	2-Jun	Austin	William	Marylebone	1859	4-Dec	Austin	William	Canterbury	1861	4-Dec	Austin	William	Royston
1857	2-Jun	Austin	William	Pancras	1859	4-Dec	Austin	William	Canterbury	1861	4-Dec	Austin	William Henry	Stoke Damerel
1857	2-Jun	Austen	William Henry	Thanet	1859	4-Dec	Austin	William	Dover	1862	1-Mar	Austin	William	Clerkenwell
1858	1-Mar	Austin	William	Blean	1859	4-Dec	Austin	William	Dover	1862	1-Mar	Austin	William	Sheppey
1858	1-Mar	Austin	William	Faversham	1859	4-Dec	Austin	William	Hastings	1862	1-Mar	Austin	William	Tenterden
1858	1-Mar	Austin	William	Horsham	1859	4-Dec	Austin	William	St Olave	1862	2-Jun	Austin	William Henry	Kensington
1858	1-Mar	Austin	William Henry	Islington	1860	1-Mar	Austin	William	Dover	1862	2-Jun	Austin	William Henry	Poplar
1858	2-Jun	Austin	William Henry	East London	1860	2-Jun	Austen	William Henry	Nth. Aylesford	1862	3-Sep	Austin	William	Milton
1858	2-Jun	Austin	William	St Martin in Field	1860	3-Sep	Austin	William	Lambeth	1862	4-Dec	Austin	William	Islington
1858	2-Jun	Austen	William Henry	Romney Marsh	1861	1-Mar	Austin	William	Dover			Investigated without success.		
1858	4-Dec	Austen	William Henry	Blean	1861	1-Mar	Austin	William	Tenterden					

▲TOP: 1871 England & Wales Census for a Frances Austen and family residing in Birling. ABOVE: List of Austin/Austen births in the National Archives from 1857 to 1862.

However, by the time of the 1861 Census of England and Wales, Frances' husband James had died, along with their first born son George.

George Austen (d. 1857 at Malling, Kent)

At this time Frances Austen was a widow, looking after Selina (aged 8) and her two seemingly twin brothers William and Thomas (aged 3) in 'Leg Lane', Birling, Kent. Ten years later, despite Frances Austen being a widow, the 1871 Census of England and Wales revealed that she had brought forth yet another daughter at Birling, Kent, apparently sometime in 1864.

Edith M. Austen (b.1864 at Gravesend, Kent) [IGI]

To prove a relationship between William Austin and his mother Frances Austin on the evidence put forward so far, is tenuous at best and is confounded by the conflicting middle name of 'Hodge.'

However, some of the stories and anecdotes passed down through the Rockwell family were validated by information in this Frances Austen's 1861 Census return. Firstly, Frances West had twin boys, and was joined by a 50 year old lady by the name of 'Elizabeth Sprigs.'

On the face it, these occurrences substantiated Rockwell family statements that William Henry Rockwell had a twin brother. More significantly however, was the fact that by the 1871 Census, the young Austen family had been joined by an elderly late, who according to Rockwell family anecdotes was a rather harsh and cruel aunt. This circumstance could have been the cause of William Henry Rockwell's early departure from the family home.

Without performing a totally thorough investigation of 'Theory 2,' there seemed to be some coincidences between the circumstances of William (Hodge) Austen and his mother Frances, that compared closely with William Henry Rockwell's upbringing, so the situation in Birling, Kent is certainly seemed worthy of further investigation.

▲ Civil registration districts in Kent, England as of 1837.

▲ Civil registration districts in London, England as of 1881.

To that end, it may be worthwhile investigating whether the 'William Hodge Austen' christened at Birling, Kent on the 28th Sept 1857 was actually the son of James Austen, or illegitimate.

However, until indisputable evidence is produced to confirm the parentage of who we know to be 'William Henry Rockwell' has been demonstrated, no further links to possible ancestors can be reported, and the theories listed above shall remain unanswered.

Unfortunately, moving forward without proof opens up a number of 'what if' scenario's that generate far too many hunches to investigate at this stage.

But in order to move forward, professional help was engaged in May of 2018 to try and solve the origins of William Henry Rockwell (see report at the end of this chapter).

Accordingly, this promising line of enquiry was brought to an abrupt halt after Mathew Homewood reported the following:

> "I notice you wrote quite a bit on William Hodge Austen of Birling, Kent, and his parents Frances and James as possible parents to your William. I must admit, with the twin brother and the aunt, it did seem very plausible. However, a quick search of the death registers revealed that William Hodge Austen died in 1909, aged 52. So it definitely could not be him.

Mathew Homewood, Genealogist, 3rd May 2018

Non-Paternity Events & Causes

It could be that William Henry Rockwell or one of his ancestors was the subject of a non-paternity event (NPE), whereby they had a different father. Some causes of NPE's are:

- Allegiance to the Lord/Chief.
- Adoption/Fostering or Guardianship.
- Widows remarrying with children.
- Legal condition of marriage/inheritance.
- Taking the mothers name upon marriage.
- Coupling with powerful people.
- Infidelity (different under Brehon law).
- Illegitimacy (different under Brehon law).
- Anglicisation of the surname.
- Orphans fabricating a surname.
- Criminals fabricating ancestry as an alias.
- Other causes

Where To From Here?

This convoluted and confusing set of possibilities is problematic, and even if proven, would only lead to further questions as to how and why William Henry 'Austen' might have changed his name to 'William Henry Rockwell', or why he may have fabricated 'Augustus Rockwell' as his father?

The key to the puzzle will be to place an Augustus Rockwell (evangelist) in the proximity of London or Kent sometime in the late 1850's, or early 1860's. What seems convincing is that William's father was indeed Augustus Rockwell, a missionary or evangelist, as this information was recorded by William personally on both of his marriage certificates, as well as on his death certificate by his son Robert Archibald Rockwell.

However, without verified evidence of the existence of Augustus Rockwell and his wife Frances (Austin or Thruyac), research into this branch of the family can only commence from William Henry Rockwell himself.

FRANCES REFERENCES

1. Wikipedia - Sir Francis William Austen [https://en.wikipedia.org/wiki/Francis_Austen].
2. Victorian Dept of BDM, (1894). Marriage Cert. for William Henry Rockwell & Mary Bates (nee Brook) - #63/1894.
3. NSW Dept of BDM, (1901). Marriage Certificate for William Henry Rockwell & Elizabeth Carpenter (nee Bantin), #8525/1901.
4. NSW Dept of BDM. (1932) Death Certificate for William Henry Rockwell, #13545/1932.
5. Free BMD, "Basic Search," database, FreeREG (http://www.freereg.org.uk/cgi/Search.pl: accessed 1 April 2021), birth entry for William Henry Rockwell for the years 1858

▲ *Civil registration districts in Kent, England as of 1837.*

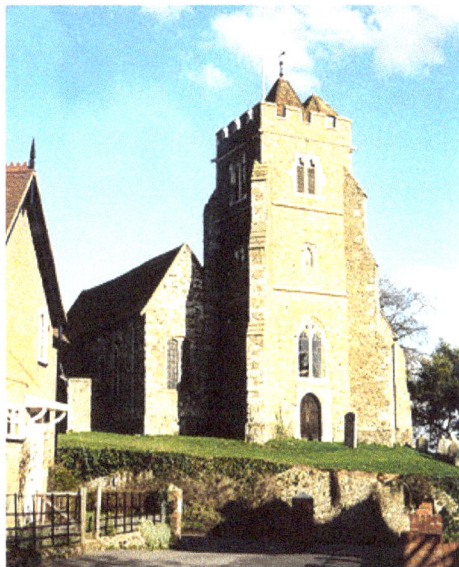

▲ Civil registration districts in Kent, England as of 1837.

to 1863.

6. "England & Wales Birth Registrations, 1858-1863," index and images, in 'FamilySearch' (IGI, accessed 1 April 2021).

7. The National Register of Scotland. Search for the marriage of Augustus Rockwell and Frances Austin from 1835 to 1865.

FURTHER RESEARCH

Other possible connections to Augustus Rockwell from the IGI Records:

AUGUSTUS R. ROCKWELL (IGI)
  March 04, 1842 Guilford, Chnng., New York

AUGUSTUS P. ROCKWELL mentioned in 'Germans To America 1875-1888'.

APPLY FOR CERTIFICATES
William Austen ?
b. 1859 June, Malling, Kent
Vol. 2a, p.333
Vol. 2a, p.365

APPLY FOR CERTIFICATE
James Austen
d. 1859 Sep, Malling, Kent
Vol 2a, p.247

Birth of William Henry filed under RODWELL?

1857 Sep	Rodwell	William Henry	St Saviour S	1D8
1858 Jun	Rodwell	William Henry	W Ham	4a46
1859 Sep	Rodwell	William Henry	Leicester	7a18

Avenell	Barrett	Shoveller
Bantin	Barry	Benson
Barrett	Bastable	Bignell
Bushell	Boulton	Eastman
Colles	Butler	Hewitt
Crasten	Darcy	Lamborn
Crouch	de Bohun	Langley
Drewe	de Burgh	Sabine
Giles	FitzEustace	Wood
Gillingham	FitzGerald	
Gould	Frawley	Clarke
Heath	Hackett	Durant
Hooper	Heffernan	Eccles?
Inwood	Hennessy	Gawpin
Jenkins	Herbert	Gould
Leighton	Jones	Grey
Luffe	Kenney	Hann
March	Lewis	Hazard
Morgan	McCarthy	Humphrey
Owen	McGarry	Lane
Page	Mahony	Martin
Quicke	Merriell	Plowman
Rundle	O'Brien	Thompson
Seller	O'Donovan	Rolt
Stedman	O'Hea	Rossiter?
Vaughn	O'Sullivan	Samways
Worden	Plantagenet	Seamer
	Price	Seymour
	Ryan	Williams
	Saunders	

References

1. Victorian Dept of BDM, (1894). Marriage Cert. for William Henry Rockwell & Mary Bates (nee Brook) - #63/1894.

2. NSW Dept of BDM, (1901). Marriage Certificate for William Henry Rockwell & Elizabeth Carpenter (nee Bantin), #8525/1901.

3. NSW Dept of BDM. (1902) Birth Certificate for William Henry Rockwell Jr., #21886/1902.

4. NSW Dept of BDM. (1904) Birth Certificate for Robert Archibald Rockwell, #32224/1904.

5. NSW Dept of BDM. (1932) Death Certificate for William Henry Rockwell, #13545/1932.

6. Free BMD, "Basic Search," database, FreeREG (http://www.freereg.org.uk/cgi/Search.pl: accessed 1 April 2021), birth entry for William Henry Rockwell for the years 1858 to 1863.

7. "England & Wales Birth Registrations, 1858-1863," index and images, in 'FamilySearch' (accessed 1 April 2021).

8. The National Register of Scotland. Search for the marriage of Augustus Rockwell and Frances Austin from 1835 to 1865.

9. Family Search [https://www.familysearch.org/wiki/en/England_Civil_Registration].

Roll of Honour
Rockwell & O'Sullivan

Descendants That Served In

Australian Military Forces

Name	Lifespan	Conflict	Reg. No.	Rank	Unit	Page
Carpenter, Arthur Clazebrook	1891-1967	WWI	#2804	Private	25th Howitzer Brigade	?
Carpenter, Arthur Frederick	1923-2000	WWII	#N467215	Lance Corporal	17th Battalion Volunteers	?
Carpenter, Leslie Harold	1895-1971	WWI	#5662	Lance Corporal	3rd Battalion	?
Hammond, Frank	1911-2007	WWII	#NX150104	Gunner	2/110 Aust Gen. Transport	?
Hyde, Robert William	1967-2016	Post WWII	?	?	Australian Regular Army	?
Malins, Alwyn Wooldridge *(POW)*	1912-1997	WWII	#N235394	Sub-Lieutenant	Admiralty Naval Police	?
Malins, Ronald Guildford	1910-1975	WWII	#60834	Corporal	Air Force - RD & TU	?
Rockwell, Elwood Lorraine	1933-1987	Post WWII	?	Private	Civilian Military Forces	?
Rockwell, Ernest Barrett	1907-1978	Interwar	#155459	Corporal	55th Bn/2 Div. Sig.	?
Rockwell, Lindsay Archibald	1937	Post WWII	?	Private	Civilian Military Forces	?

KIA - Killed In Action
POW - Prisoner of War

APPENDIX C

Research Report on the Origins of William Henry Rockwell

by Mathew Homewood of 'traditionalfamilytrees.co.uk', May 2018

In May 2018, a professional genealogist Mr. Mathew Homewood, of 'Traditional Families' in London was engaged to investigate the origins of William Henry Rockwell, with the aim of identifying his parents, either Augustus Rockwell and Frances Austin, or perhaps someone else. The investigation was by no means extensive, but produced some results and recommendations for future research. His final report is presented below:

THE FACTS AS PRESENTED
As recorded by William Henry Rockwell (himself):
On his 1st Marriage Certificate to Mary Brook in Melbourne in Feb. 1894.
WHR Age: 33, born Kent, England (Sailor).
Father: Augustus Rockwell, evangelist.
Mother: Frances Rockwell (nee Austin).
On his 2nd Marriage Certificate to Elizabeth Carpenter (nee Bantin) in Dec. 1901.
WHR Age: 39, London, England (Coach Driver).
Father: Augustus Rockwell, missionary.
Mother: Frances (unknown).

As recorded by Elizabeth Rockwell (wife & mother):
On the Birth Certificate of their son William Henry Rockwell Jr. in July 1902.
WHR Age: 40, born London, England.
On the Birth Certificate of their son Robert Archibald Rockwell in Nov 1904.
WHR Age: 45, born London, England.

As recorded by Robert Archibald Rockwell (son):
On the Death Certificate for William Henry Rockwell in July 1932.
WHR Age: 74, born London, England.

If the above statements made by William Henry Rockwell himself were true, it would appear that he was born in Kent in 1861, or a few months either side. William Henry consistently states his father as being Augustus Rockwell. His mother's name was recorded on his first marriage in 1894 as being Frances Austin (maiden name).

The 1901 marriage certificate does hint that Frances may not have been Frances Rockwell at the time of William's birth, as he stated her surname as 'unknown.'

In 1889 the parishes in modern-day South London changed from 'Kent' and 'Surrey' parishes to 'London' parishes. This may explain William's inconsistency with his place of birth. He may have been born in a 'Kent' parish, which became a 'London' parish in 1889.

A. SEARCH FOR WILLIAM HENRY ROCKWELL
a. Search for the Birth of William Henry Rockwell
A search was made of the birth registers for the surname 'Rockwell' in England and Wales, 1850-1870. Rockwell is not a common surname at all, so a wide search, both by date and location, was not too time-consuming, with 12 results being identified:

All these results were checked against the General Register Office lists in order to note the mother's maiden names, listed below and linked to the district of birth:
Mitchell (Wycombe, Buckinghamshire)
Pearce (Wycombe, Buckinghamshire)
Shreeve (Caistor, Lincolnshire)
Roberts (Salford, Lancashire)
Adey (Reading, Berkshire)
Band (Stourbridge, Worcestershire)

No results were found in or around London and Kent, and no mother's maiden names were remotely related to Austin. None of these children were recorded as illegitimate either.

A search was made for marriages of these six couples, to check if any of these mothers were called Frances. All marriages were traced, apart from the 'Roberts/Rockwell' marriage. None of the mothers had the christian name of Frances.

A search was made for all births for a 'Rockwell' or similar spelling in England and Wales within 5 years of 1861 with 24 results being identified:

Similar spellings were investigated for Rockwill, Rockell, Rockall, Rochell, Rotchell, but no results were found for a 'William Henry.'

A search was made of all births for a 'William Henry Austin/Austen' in London or Kent, 1858-1862 with 9 results being identified:

These have already been found and listed by Tracy Rockwell. However, a search was made for the maiden name of the mothers of each of these nine children with Buyss, Rawley, Smith, Phillips, Smetzer, Bassett, Swike, Harrison, Hulph resulting, with none of the children being recorded as illegitimate.

B. SEARCH FOR AUGUSTUS ROCKWELL & FRANCES AUSTIN
If William Henry Rockwell was born around 1860, one would expect his parents to have been born somewhere between 1810 and 1844.
1. Searches in England & Wales
a. Search for Death of Augustus Rockwell

A search was made of the death registers for an 'Augustus Rockwell' or similar between 1859 and 1915 with 1 result was identified:
1899, Augustus Rockall, born c.1810, Oxfordshire.

However, the census returns consistently show this Augustus to have been a cabinet maker, and married to Lucy.

A search was made of the death registers for a 'Frances Rockwell' or similar between 1859 and 1915 with 4 results being identified:

Only one reached adulthood and was old enough to be William's mother, which occurred in:
1871, Frances Rockwell, bc.1814, St George in the East, London

However, there was no trace of this person on the census returns.
b. Search for Marriage of Augustus Rockwell

A search of the birth and marriage registers for an 'Augustus Rockwell' or similar produced no results.

A search was made of the marriage register for a 'Frances Rockwell' or similar between 1859 and 1915 (in case William's mother had re-married after William was born), but produced no results.

c. Search for Marriage of Frances Austin

A search was made of the marriage register for a 'Frances Austin' in England and Wales, 1837-1865, which produced 20 results for 'Austin,' although none married an 'Augustus' or a 'Rockwell', or any similar names. For the other variation, 10 results were found for 'Austen':

There was one partial match in 1849, for Frances Emma Austen, who married an Augustus Falck, a tailor from Lambeth, London. And there is one Frances Austen who married in Kent in 1860, whose husband is yet to be traced?

2. Searches in Ireland

A search was made for the surname 'Rockwell' within the available civil records of Ireland.

Births: 1864-1900 – no results
Marriages: 1845-1900 – no results
Deaths: 1864 onwards – no results

There was only one mention of a 'Rockwell', which was the maiden name of a Rosanna Meehan (wife of George Meehan) on the death certificate of their daughter, dated 1914.

3. Searches in Scotland

A search was made for the surname 'Rockwell' within the parish and civil records of Scotland. No results were found in the birth, marriage, or burial records 1800-1940. A few 'Rockwell' surnames were listed, but the earliest was in 1942.

4. Searches of Census Returns

A search was made of the census returns for England and Wales for any Augustus Rockwell, or similar with 1 result being identified:

This was not a match, but was the cabinet maker previously found, who was married to Lucy (nee Harris).

A search was made of the census returns for England and Wales 1861, 1871 and 1881, for any Frances Rockwell, or similar, of the right age with 3 results being identified, but none matched:

1881: Frances Rockwell, born c.1839, wife of Arthur, cork sock maker, Lambeth.
1861: Frances Rockell, born c.1820, wife of Charles, Ostler, Surrey.
1871: Frances B. Rockell, born c.1841, wife of Thomas, sea captain, Lancashire.

A search was made of the 1851 census returns for England and Wales for any Frances Austin/Austen born between 1810 and 1845, and living in Kent or London, with 5 results each being identified for both 'Austen' and 'Austin':

Results for 'AUSTEN'
Frances Austen, born c.1815, wife of Edmund, Sevenoaks, Kent
Frances Austen, born c.1817, wife of George, Brenchley, Kent
Frances Austen, born c.1831, daughter of Frances, Tonbridge, Kent
Frances Eliza Austen, born c.1838, daughter of John & Charlotte, West Wickham, Kent
Frances Austen, born c.1842, daughter of William & Alice, Hackington, Canterbury, Kent

Results for 'AUSTIN'
Frances Austin, born c.1812, wife of James, Chart Sutton, Kent
Frances Austin, born c.1824, wife of Edward, Goudhurst, Kent
Frances Austin, born c.1829, wife of Georg, Canterbury, Kent
Frances Austin, born c.1839, daughter of William & Sarah, Sheldwich, Kent
Frances Austin, born c.1840, sister of Elizabeth Mills, Greenwich, Kent

These may be worthy of further investigation.

5. Searches Outside the UK

A search was conducted outside the UK for Augustus Rockwell and Frances Rockwell (nee Austin).

A search was made of all other records on Ancestry.com for an 'Augustus Rockwell' of the right age. All results were found to be in the United States:

US census 1860 and 1870 revealed four Augustus Rockwell's, but none of these are matches for William's father.

Voters Lists:
1861: Augustus H. Rockwell, age 23, sailmaker, Savannah, born c.1838.

Burials:
1867: Augustus A. Rockwell, Fairmont Cemetery, New Jersey, born c.1832
1903: Augustus P. Rockwell, New York, born c.1840

Military:
1863: Augustus Rockwell of New York, age 23, hatter, born c.1840
1863: Augustus Rockwell of New York, age 20, artist, born c.1843

Immigration:
1879, 1889 & 1889, Augustus P. Rockwell born c.1840, merchant, travelling between New York and Liverpool.

The latter find was promising, as here we had an Augustus Rockwell frequently visiting England. However, the earliest finding of him travelling to England was in 1869 and long after William's birth.

CONCLUSION

William Henry Rockwell was fairly consistent with his year of birth, and his father's name. However, the fact he stated on his 1901 marriage certificate that he was unsure of his mother's maiden name/surname is a concern, especially as he claimed to know it seven years earlier.

The surname 'Rockwell' is not common at all, and 'Augustus Rockwell' is a very unusual name. So much so, that this name has only been found in the United States. Illegitimate children often 'invented' a father for their marriage certificates, simply to save embarrassment. However, 'Augustus Rockwell', a missionary, is a rather elaborate name and occupation to fabricate, and I have little doubt that this man existed.

If Augustus was indeed a missionary, this would probably have meant that he spent a considerable amount of his adult life abroad, and most likely in poverty-stricken countries. Having said that, there were also many missionaries who worked within English shores.

Some research had already been carried out on the possibility William Henry might have been the William Hodge Austen, son of Frances and James Austen. However, this surely is the same William Hodges Austen listed on the burial register in Kent in 1909, aged 52. So despite stated dates and circumstances seemingly in agreement with family versions of events, William Hodge Austen has no connection with the William Henry under investigation.

The set of research above is not an exhaustive one, and there is some more that could be done on this; in particular looking into the 12 Frances Austens/Austins found on the 1851 census.

It may also be worth searching through anyone with the name 'Frances' who married an 'Austin/Austen', in case Austen was a married name of William's mother, and not a maiden name.

However, we must accept the possibility that we may be on a 'wild goose chase' with the 'Austin' connection, or that Augustus Rockwell never married Frances, and perhaps died abroad.

There are also many 'Frances Rockwells' listed on documents around the world, which might be worth looking into at some point.

Matthew Homewood, 2018

THE AUTHOR

Dr Tracy Rockwell originally taught in both primary and high schools and was later appointed as a lecturer in Human Movement at the Faculty of Education at Sydney University, where he spent 25 years, ahead of launching out on his own as a sports writer, photographer, artist, author and scholar. As a sportman he was a swimmer, surf life saver, rugby player, a NSW representative water polo player and in 2021 was Oceanic Indoor Rowing champion for his age group. With a penchant for history he published 'Water Warriors: Chronicle of Australian Water Polo' in 2009, and received the 'Harry Quittner Medal' for his contribution to Australian Water Polo. He is also an avid genealogist and adds his 2nd volume in the 'Rockwell Genealogies' with this publication. Other books and illustrated journals by Dr. Rockwell are available through Pegasus Publishing:

TITLE	ISBN	GENRE	FORMAT	PUB.	PAGES
Water Warriors: Chronicle of Australian Water Polo	978-0-646488-61-5	Sports History	Hardback	2009	597
The Complete Guide to Rugby World Cup (2015)	978-0-994201-42-3	Sports History	Ebook	2015	161
Play Water Polo: An Interactive Instructional Sports Guide	978-0-994201-40-9	Sports Development	Ebook [interactive]	2016	94
The Unknown Journey (Editor)	978-0-994201-48-5	Autobiography	Ebook	2016	136
The Unknown Journey: Surviving Hodgkin's Lymphoma (Editor)	978-0-994201-49-2	Autobiography	Paperback	2016	136
How to Play Water Polo: The Complete Guide to Mastering the Game	978-0-994201-41-6	Sports Development	Paperback	2018	215
Juega Polo Acuático: Guía Interactiva de Deportes de Instrucción	978-0-994201-43-0	Sports Development	Ebook	2018	96
Love Never Lets You Go: Aphorisms about Love Journal [Illust.]	978-0-994201-46-1	Sociology	Paperback	2018	216
One Day at a Time: Aphorisms about Life Journal [Illust.]	978-0-994201-47-8	Sociology	Paperback	2018	218
Journal of Life's Lessons: With Vintage Images and Aphorisms [Illust.]	978-0-994201-44-7	Sociology	Hardback	2019	218
Who's There? Worlds Funniest A-Z Book of 737 Knock Knock Jokes	978-0-994201-45-4	Childrens-Fiction	Paperback	2019	107
Who's There? Worlds Funniest A-Z Book of 737 Knock Knock Jokes	978-1-925909-28-9	Childrens-Fiction	Ebook	2019	107
Australian Seascapes Journal [Illust.]	978-1-925909-05-0	Sociology	Paperback	2019	128
Australian Landscapes Journal [Illust.]	978-1-925909-06-7	Sociology	Paperback	2019	128
The Complete Guide to Rugby World Cup (2019)	978-1-925909-07-4	Sports History	Paperback	2019	198
My Handy Cruise Journal [Illust.]	978-1-925909-10-4	Sociology	Paperback	2019	130
My Handy Travel Journal [Illust.]	978-1-925909-11-1	Sociology	Paperback	2019	130
A History of the Ancestors of James Mahoney O'Sullivan and Ellen Frawley	978-1-925909-00-5	Genealogy	Paperback	2020	584
Australian Animals: Through the Looking Glass	978-1-925909-01-2	Childrens-Animals	Paperback	2020	68
Bush Dreaming and Other Plays (Editor)	978-1-925909-02-9	Literature-Drama	Paperback	2020	212
The Spirit of Bronte: A History of Bronte Amateur Water Polo Club 1943-1975	978-1-925909-03-6	Sports History	Paperback	2020	329
Tracy Rockwell: Catalogue Raisonné 2000-2020	978-1-925909-12-8	Visual Art	Paperback	2021	342
Mystery at Melon Flats (Editor)	978-1-925909-04-3	Literature-Novel	Paperback	2022	192
Mystery at Melon Flats (Editor)	978-1-925909-09-8	Literature-Novel	Ebook	2022	192
The Long Road To Grafton: A Genealogy of Thomas Eastman Shoveller	978-1-925909-08-1	Genealogy	Paperback	2022	340
The Complete Guide to Rugby World Cup (2023, 2nd Edition)	978-0-994201-42-3	Sports History	Paperback	2023	218
Nostalgia for Naremburn: The Ancestors of Robert A.Rockwell & Octavia C.O'Sullivan	978-1-925909-13-5	Genealogy	Paperback	2023	2902

www.ingramcontent.com/pod-product-compliance
Lightning Source LLC
Chambersburg PA
CBHW042338030426
42335CB00030B/3384